REMEMBERING
LUDLOW
BUT FORGETTING
THE COLUMBINE

MINING THE AMERICAN WEST

SERIES EDITORS: DUANE A. SMITH | ROBERT A. TRENNERT | LIPING ZHU

REMEMBERING
LUDLOW
BUT FORGETTING
THE COLUMBINE

The 1927–1928 Colorado Coal Strike

LEIGH CAMPBELL-HALE

UNIVERSITY PRESS OF COLORADO
Denver

© 2023 by University Press of Colorado

Published by University Press of Colorado
1624 Market Street, Suite 226
PMB 39883
Denver, Colorado 80202-1559

 The University Press of Colorado is a proud member of
the Association of University Presses.

The University Press of Colorado is a cooperative publishing enterprise supported, in part,
by Adams State University, Colorado State University, Fort Lewis College, Metropolitan State
University of Denver, University of Alaska Fairbanks, University of Colorado, University of
Denver, University of Northern Colorado, University of Wyoming, Utah State University, and
Western Colorado University.

∞ This paper meets the requirements of the ANSI/NISO Z39.48-1992 (Permanence of Paper).

ISBN: 978-1-64642-301-9 (hardcover)
ISBN: 978-1-64642-302-6 (ebook)
https://doi.org/10.5876/9781646423026

Cataloging-in-Publication data for this title is available online at the Library of Congress.

Cover photograph: unknown speaker and location photographed during the 1927–1928 Colorado
Coal Strike, courtesy of Steelworks Museum.

Contents

REMEMBERING
LUDLOW
BUT FORGETTING
THE COLUMBINE

Introduction

At dawn on November 21, 1927, at least five hundred marchers approached Serene, the company town Rocky Mountain Fuel Company (RMFC) built twenty miles northwest of Denver. Serene housed coalminers and their families at the RMFC's newest and most valuable property, the Columbine coalmine. On October 18, 1927, the majority of Colorado's 12,500 coalminers had voted to go on strike, and the following day, most of the state's coalmines closed. The RMFC management, however, decided to keep the Columbine open, which turned the town into an anything-but-serene target. Almost daily, as strikebreakers readied for work, strike supporters marched through town, behind an American flagbearer, boisterously singing "Solidarity," the anthem of the union leading the strike, the Industrial Workers of the World (IWW).

On November 21, for the first time, Serene's gates were locked. Inside, a handful of Weld County sheriffs, RMFC officials, and reporters nervously mingled outside the camp's office, and a phalanx of twenty newly commissioned state strike police lined the fence. Marchers demanded entrance for their morning "parade," but Louis Scherf, the strike police leader, refused.

https://doi.org/10.5876/9781646423026.c000

When Scherf insisted upon speaking to their leader, the crowd replied, "We are all leaders!" After that, eyewitness accounts diverge, but this much is certain: Police shot and killed six striking coalminers and wounded perhaps sixty more. That violence soon became known as the Columbine Massacre, and it was the turning point of the 1927–1928 Colorado Coal Strike. This book is about that strike and its historical legacies, which, ironically perhaps, includes its omission from the dominant United States historical narrative.

Several elements of this walkout make it worth knowing more about. For example, from generalized textbooks to specialized IWW monographs, historians have declared that the IWW died out after its intense World War I–era persecution. Yet, if the IWW was truly dead, how did it lead a successful, statewide strike in 1927 and 1928? To appropriate Mark Twain's sardonic quote, perhaps reports of the IWW's death have been greatly exaggerated, especially when compared with the relative strength of the United Mine Workers (UMW) during that same era.

Josephine Roche could also use additional historical examination. Biographies of Roche and accounts of the 1927–1928 strike have, until now, repeated the following narrative: Roche did not legally or financially control the RMFC when the Columbine Massacre occurred, so she could not have prevented it. Only after gaining control of the company in March of 1928 was Roche able to implement her vision of industrial democracy, which led to the September 1, 1928, contract between the RMFC and the UMW. Since, as I will explore, this contract wielded an outsized influence on national labor policies, it is worth knowing more about, and my research began with this question: Since the only role the UMW played in the IWW-led strike was denouncing it, why did the UMW get that contract?

Little research has gone into answering that question, probably because most historians looking at Roche have viewed her through the lens of women's history, not labor history. It is hardly surprising that Roche is celebrated as a significant figure in women's history, even before that field got subsumed by gender studies. Roche was probably the only woman to run a coal company in United States history. Then, she leveraged that position to achieve even more remarkable accomplishments in politics and at the UMW. In 1935, she ran for governor of Colorado. Although she lost, it was a first in state history. From 1935 through 1937, Roche served as assistant secretary of the

Treasury, which made her the second-highest-ranking cabinet member in President Franklin D. Roosevelt's New Deal. (The highest-ranking was her friend, Secretary of Labor Frances Perkins.) Until 1940, Roche chaired FDR's interdepartmental health committee, charged with exploring and proposing policies to expand national health care. Beyond Roche's significant government service, because of her influence within the UMW, she also played key roles in influencing the nation's coal policies. As a direct consequence of the 1928 RMFC–UMW contract, Roche and John L. Lewis, president of the UMW, forged a decades-long personal and professional relationship, and throughout the 1930s, they helped shape federal labor policies. In 1945, Lewis hired Roche to design and administer the UMW Retirement and Pension Fund. Even after her forced resignation from the fund in 1972, four years before her death, Roche continued to influence the United States labor movement as she had for over half a century. In spite of Roche's significant impact on labor policies, however, Roche's biographers have primarily written about her through the admiring lens of women's history. For example, Roche biographer Elinor McGinn calls Roche an "angel of the coalmines."[1] Another Roche biographer, University of Maryland professor Robyn Muncy, argues that Roche was a "relentless reformer."[2] I will argue that Roche was neither. My aim is not to demonize Roche, but I do intend to tarnish her halo. Roche was not a saint, but a complex human being whose influence upon American labor has largely gone unexamined. Especially unexamined has been her role in the 1927–1928 Colorado Coal Strike, and specifically, the Columbine Massacre, events that not only changed the trajectory of Roche's life but also influenced the trajectories of the UMW, John L. Lewis, and the United States labor movement.

Also deserving closer examination are historical accounts that portray 1920s' and early 1930s' workers as quiescent. They were not. Even a cursory look through the online *New York Times* using the word *strike* as a search term pulls up the following number of articles: In 1925, 2,514; in 1926, 4,025; in 1927, 2,579; in 1929, 1,841; and in 1929, 2,358, and the overwhelming majority of these hits are about labor strikes. For example, in 1926, New York City fur makers, baggage handlers, plasterers, bricklayers, Pennsylvania anthracite coalminers, Chicago gravediggers, and Connecticut musicians went out on strike. In 1927, along with Colorado coalminers, New York City box makers, plumbers, teamsters, and taxi drivers also struck. In the taxi-driver strike, at least one person was shot to death and three others were badly beaten. In 1928, carpenters, textile workers (3,500 in Paterson, New Jersey, and 15,000 in Rhode Island), dental mechanics, laundry workers, dry cleaners, and even New Jersey doctors went on strike. In 1929, Texas railroad workers, oil truck drivers, and cafeteria workers, among others, walked off their jobs. The New York City truck drivers' strike led to street fights, and the cafeteria workers' strike resulted in at least 455 pickets, most extremely militant women, getting arrested. In the Elizabethtown, Tennessee, textile strike that year, again with mostly women strikers, state troopers had to be stationed at the mill for it to reopen.

Even though its articles reflected, as they do today, a distinctly regional focus, by the late 1920s, the *Times* increasingly promoted itself as the nation's news source.[3] In this capacity, the newspaper and its reporters helped write, as the saying aptly goes, the first draft of history. The *Times*'s dominance today, and its easily searchable online archives, award it continued power over historical narratives. So, while the strike article examples above prove that the newspaper did report on events throughout the country, including the 1927–1928 Colorado Coal Strike, it also reflects important biases. For example, the Colorado strike—a statewide, seven-month conflict led by the IWW—warranted just thirty-four total articles. That coverage suggests that, if anything, the *Times* under-reported strikes nationwide, and ignored other regions of the country entirely, probably because it did not employ stringers in non-urban areas.[4]

United States' coalfields were especially volatile, yet this is not how they are portrayed in dominant historical narratives, exemplified by textbooks. These narratives mostly go like this: In June of 1933, President Franklin D. Roosevelt signed the National Industrial Relations Act (NIRA) with its 7(a) clause that endorsed labor unions into law and, combined with the bold leadership of John L. Lewis, who flooded the coalfields with UMW organizers, a wave of UMW memberships jumpstarted the nation's organized labor movement. That "great men, great deeds" interpretation of labor history still dominates 1930s' historical narratives, even though there is little evidence it is true. In fact, I will argue that narrative has it backwards. Militant workers, especially coalminers, inspired so much fear among policymakers, their militancy proved the proximate cause that led to New Deal labor reforms. Contrary to textbook accounts, evidence shows that coalminers neither awaited FDR's blessing nor obediently followed Lewis's directives when they joined the UMW. Furthermore, the 1927–1928 Colorado Coal Strike is one of many examples demonstrating that coalminer militancy arose *before* the summer of 1933.

Another reason to learn more about the 1927–1928 Colorado Coal Strike is because what little we know about it stands in stark contrast to the abundance of popular and scholarly histories generated about the 1913–1914 phase of the coal strike in Colorado, which includes the April 20, 1914, Ludlow Massacre.⁵ This documentary discrepancy between the two strikes raises important questions about how and why certain historical events get incorporated into our national historical narrative and others do not. For example, although the Ludlow Massacre briefly appears in many secondary and college United States history textbooks, the 1927–1928 Colorado Coal Strike and the Columbine Massacre go unmentioned. Why do historians remember Ludlow but forget the Columbine? Exploring answers to that question requires examining historiography itself, an exploration I will pursue in the pages that follow.

Chapters 1 through 3 focus on the lives of Josephine Roche, Powers Hapgood, and A. S. Embree, respectively, three historical actors closely associated with the 1927–1928 Colorado Coal Strike. Roche led the RMFC where the Columbine Massacre took place, Hapgood was a ubiquitous labor figure who went to work for Roche four months after the 1928 RMFC–UMW contract went into effect, and Embree was the primary IWW strike leader of the 1927–1928 walkout.

These chapters also introduce the theme of industrial democracy, which threads throughout the book. From the progressive era through the end of World War II, the concept of industrial democracy drove public discourse and policy debates, although its definitions varied as much as its advocates, which included Roche, Hapgood, and Embree. As a helpful baseline, Joseph McCartin offers three visions of industrial democracy that inspired policy decisions during World War I. He writes, "One vision was advanced by a group of farsighted employers, influenced by renegades from the scientific management movement who had begun to recognize that workers' participation could influence the efficiency of production. Another vision, championed by the leadership of the AFL [American Federation of Labor], posited the trade union collective bargaining agreement as the sine qua non of democratic industrial relations. A third vision, less fully articulated than the other two, emerged from the ranks of trade union militants and their allies. It linked industrial democracy to a radical restructuring of workplace and social relations."[6]

These definitions generally align with the visions of industrial democracy Roche, Hapgood, and Embree acted upon in the late 1920s. Roche represents the enlightened employer, although she also pushed for the UMW contract at the RMFC. Hapgood pushed for AFL contracts, but he also worked alongside organizers like Embree, whose militancy made such contracts possible. Embree absolutely hoped workers would change the world, yet he was also a pragmatic labor leader. Therefore, none of these historical actors was an ideologue, and their actions demonstrate that, over time, they all modified their beliefs in response to changing circumstances. Even so, their fundamental visions of industrial democracy remained remarkably consistent, which allows us to follow them, their ideas, and their influence over a large swath of time, from the late 1800s through the 1980s. My aim is not to write three biographies, however, because both Roche and Hapgood, although not Embree, already have biographers. Instead, I examine evidence associated with all three that has not been included in previous sources or that relates to the 1927–1928 strike. That approach allows the inclusion of additional historical actors (such as George Creel, John Brophy, or John L. Lewis) and themes (such as worker militancy and gender) that help place the strike's significance within the larger arc of a fairly consistent United States labor history narrative.

Chapter 1 follows Roche's life as a progressive reformer through her 1927 inheritance of half of the RMFC, and it ends when the 1927–1928 Colorado Coal Strike begins. It demonstrates that, contrary to Robyn Muncy's claims, Roche had not been living her life to "right the wrongs of Ludlow."[7] Chapter 2 examines Hapgood's unsuccessful efforts to democratize the UMW from within during the 1920s, a movement that contextualizes why the 1928 RMFC–UMW contract proved so significant to Lewis. Chapter 3 follows Embree through the rise and purported fall of the IWW up until the union sends him to Colorado in 1926.

Chapters 4 through 6 trace the 1927–1928 Colorado Coal strike from its unofficial beginning August 8, 1927, through its official end on February 18, 1928. These chapters follow the chronological development of the strike and contextualize the various local, state, and national social and political pressures that influenced the strike's trajectory.

Chapters 7 through 10 examine the legacies of the strike, including how and why it has been included, but mostly forgotten, in history. Chapter 7 looks at the strike's short-term consequences, especially for Roche and the RMFC. Negative reactions to the Columbine Massacre prompted Roche to finally assert control over the RMFC, and one of her first tasks was to create "spin control" in response to that violence. Her narrative soon evolved into the "elevator pitch" she made to potential investors; a pitch that, unsurprisingly, painted both Roche and the RMFC in a favorable light. What is remarkable is that the narrative she spun has gone unexamined for so long. In chapter 8, I examine how the disastrous impacts of the Great Depression pushed Roche, Hapgood, and Embree deep into the orbit of John L. Lewis and the CIO.[8]

Chapter 9 follows two of the divergent paths organized labor took during the early Cold War. Although the concept of industrial democracy no longer drove public debates and policies, the roots these divergent paths followed can be traced to earlier WWI-era visions of industrial democracy. The path Mine Mill organizers Maurice Travis and Clinton Jencks pursued was built upon Embree's egalitarian vision of industrial democracy. The path Roche forged at the UMW Retirement and Pension Fund combined the industrial democracy visions of enlightened employers and the AFL's emphasis on contracts, a combination that seemed to represent the best hopes and worst fears that bread-and-butter unionism had to offer. Anti-Communist fears and deindustrialization, however, brought both paths to ignoble ends in the 1960s.

There are many historiographical reasons why postwar historians continue to remember Ludlow but forget the Columbine, and chapter 10 explores two of these. One relates to Fred Thompson, who has dominated historical constructions of the IWW, especially regarding the 1927–1928 Colorado Coal Strike. The second relates to the oral history "boom" of the 1970s, when, at last, participants were asked to recall the 1927–1928 Colorado Coal Strike. Even though informants tried to remember the Columbine, however, they continued remembering Ludlow instead.

1

Josephine Roche

Becoming a Maternalist Reformer, 1886–1927

If not for the November 21, 1927, Columbine Massacre, Josephine Roche probably would be an unknown, instead of a little-known, historical figure. Most Roche biographers and historians of the 1927–1928 Colorado Coal Strike have painted Roche in an impossibly positive light. Even Roche's most recent and best biographer, Robyn Muncy, makes clear that Roche was no saint,[1] but she also claims that Roche lived her life to "right the wrongs of Ludlow."[2] Before the Columbine Massacre, however, there is little evidence to support that claim.

Until the Columbine Massacre, Roche lived her life as a "maternalist" reformer.[3] This maternalist cohort of women, comprised mostly of middle class, highly educated, progressive-era activists, helped create the modern welfare state. Like the paternalists who inspired their moniker, they also exhibited the twin impulses of progressivism: social reform *and* social control. Because Roche self-identified as a lifelong progressive, it is important to understand Roche's progressive, pre-Columbine life because it provides important context on how Roche shaped her vision of industrial democracy, a vision that aimed to civilize capitalism. Often mentioned as a remarkable

https://doi.org/10.5876/9781646423026.c001

first, but until now, unexamined in depth, Roche's extremely brief stint as Denver's first female police officer illustrates well the twin, entwined impulses of progressivism, social reform, and social control. Briefly following her trajectory through 1927 also helps illuminate Roche's progressive worldview that she exhibited her entire life.

Josephine's father, John Roche, was born on a Wisconsin farm and graduated from Wisconsin State Normal College. He briefly taught school before becoming a lawyer, then later, a businessman. Josephine's mother, Ella, was born in Maine but graduated from Wisconsin's teacher college and, like her husband, also taught school. After their marriage, they moved to Neligh, Nebraska, where John established the First National Bank and dabbled in politics, even serving in Nebraska's state legislature. Neligh was where Josephine, their only child, was born, in 1886. In 1893, the Roches moved to Omaha, where John first presided over the London and Sioux City Finance Company and by 1898, he worked for the Omaha Cattle Loan Company.[4]

The Roches possessed enough wealth and social ambition to send Josephine to excellent private schools, and in 1904, she graduated from Brownell Hall, an Episcopalian girls' school in Omaha.[5] The following fall Roche entered Vassar, where she "debated with Qui Vive, visited slum settlements in Poughkeepsie, joined the basketball and track clubs and double majored in Economics and Classics."[6] During her summer breaks, she lived with her parents, and after they moved to Denver, Roche worked in Judge Ben Lindsey's juvenile court. After graduation, Roche enrolled at Columbia University in New York City, earning her masters' degree in 1910.

Except for her masters' thesis, Roche left almost no records of her university days, but Frances Perkins, her friend and Colombia cohort, did.[7] Perkins served as secretary of labor between 1933 and 1945, so, understandably, she has garnered more historical attention than Roche. Since Perkins and Roche lived, worked, studied, and shared the same network of political and social reformer friends and allies in New York City for two years, they surely shared similar experiences, an assumption borne out by several nostalgic letters Roche and Perkins exchanged in 1959 and 1960.[8] Therefore, I will speculate what Roche's personal life might have been like through Perkins's experiences, an imperfect exercise to be sure, but one as close as I can get to describe Roche's life before she moved full-time to Denver in December of 1912.

Between 1890 and 1920, Greenwich Village developed into a bohemian magnet that attracted a fascinating variety of newcomers who forged a new sense of identity and modernity in American culture. As Perkins and Roche received excellent educations, they lived and worked among new immigrants in a Greenwich Village settlement house while rubbing elbows with labor organizers, journalists, publishers, socialites, and artists who planned strikes, wrote, ate, drank, smoked, but mostly talked, talked, and talked some more in a wide-open cultural exchange the United States would not experience again until the 1960s.[9] Perkins's biographers have described the exciting life she led, filled with agitating and organizing on behalf of women, children, and immigrants, alongside art show openings, poetry, and novel readings.[10]

In spite of their flirtations with bohemian life, neither Perkins nor Roche ever wore bobbed hair or short skirts, but instead cultivated lifelong matronly images.[11] Both used the title "miss" and retained their maiden names, even though Perkins was married to a man who cycled in and out of psychiatric hospitals until his 1952 death, and Roche married writer Edward Hale Bierstadt in 1920, divorcing in 1922. Although Roche left no records, we know that Bierstadt worked for Roche in George Creel's World War I Committee on Public Information (CPI), which is probably where they met, his great uncle was the famous landscape painter Albert Bierstadt, and in the 1930s, he wrote scripts for the popular radio show *The Shadow*.[12] Bierstadt would be the only man with whom Roche was ever publicly, romantically, linked.

Both women forged influential friendships that served their futures well. Perkins allied with important New York politicians, including state governor and 1928 Democratic presidential nominee Al Smith; United States senator, Robert Wagner; and future president, Franklin D. Roosevelt. Roche shared those same influential friends, and in Denver, she allied with progressives Lindsey, Edward Keating, Edward Costigan, Merle Vincent, and George Creel. Although both women valued personal loyalty, Roche deserted Lindsey in 1927 and Perkins abandoned Smith in 1928, demonstrating that loyalties had limits, especially if they stood in the way of professional advancement.

Although definitions for maternalists vary, they usually describe progressive-era women who graduated from prestigious colleges and worked on reforms that concerned traditional, female concerns, including women's working conditions, education, health care, mothers' pensions, and child labor. In helping create the modern welfare state, maternalists also expanded their own political power.[13] Paradoxically, while valorizing traditional women's values of purity and piety, maternalists limited socially acceptable definitions of womanhood.[14]

Often excluded from inner political circles where important decisions got made, maternalists, including Roche and Perkins, created their own inner circle, which included close friendships with the wives of influential men with whom they worked. As their mutual friend Eleanor Roosevelt demonstrates, a politician's wife sometimes exerted more political power than elected politicians. As prominent women in the public eye, they were judged harshly, which probably led them, by the mid-1930s, to shun the press and guard their private lives. Unlike their male counterparts, everything they did was open to public scrutiny. Occasionally, Perkins drank enough hard liquor to raise eyebrows within FDR's inner circle, just as Roche's chain smoking and divorcée status damaged her politically when she ran in the 1934 Democratic primary for Colorado governor.[15] While we can never really understand Roche and Perkins's interior lives, from the progressive era that shaped their identities until their deaths, their public personas represented remarkable continuity across time.

Historians generally agree that progressives, middle class and newly urban, sought to regulate the excesses of big business and ameliorate shameful conditions for the poor by increasing the scope of government. In short, they wanted to civilize capitalism. They excelled at creating public pressure campaigns that produced new laws, agencies, commissions, and remarkably, four Constitutional amendments. Usually periodized from the early 1900s through the beginning of World War I, progressivism exhibited dual impulses: social reform and social control. Exploring this duality is important because Roche consistently exercised both impulses throughout her life. Progressives promoted top-down moral uplift, supported by mounds of data supplied by experts, including maternalists, but they did not necessarily welcome, or even encourage, democratic participation.

Maternalists generated much of their political pressure through private organizations, and probably the most important was the National Consumers' League (NCL). Both Perkins and Roche worked extensively in the NCL, and both revered the NCL's Florence Kelly as their role model.[16] The organization, whose membership peaked in 1916, exemplifies the social reform side of the progressive era.[17] It promoted minimum wage laws and safe working conditions (especially for women), the abolition of child labor, and ethical consumption.[18] The NCL's motto—"investigate, agitate, legislate"— summarized the methods and goals a generation of maternalists, including Josephine Roche, used to advance their goals.[19]

Just as the NCL exemplified the social reform half of the progressive reform agenda, the white slavery campaign exemplified its evil twin, social control. Both Perkins and Roche cut their political teeth within that movement, and its goals often overlapped the NCL's. It would be difficult to find a more fascinating historical topic than white slavery because it intermingles histories of sex, gender, race, and racism, as well as local, state, and federal politics. Furthermore, all these categories intersect around fears of urbanization, immigration, crime, independent women wage earners, and a new social culture that former agrarian Victorians struggled to understand.

White slavery hysteria lasted from around 1908 to 1913, not coincidentally, when progressives dominated politics. It peaked in 1910 with the passage of the federal Mann Act, which outlawed transporting women across state lines for immoral purposes. Although social reformers such as Jane Addams, Perkins, and Roche preferred the term *the social evil* to white slavery, their preference proved too polite for a controversy that blazed across the pages of popular muckraking magazines like *McClure's*, the *Outlook*, and *Collier's*, as well as widely circulated popular pamphlets like Doctor C. C. Quale's *Thrilling Stories of White Slavery*.[20]

White slavery is a loaded enough term to provide a lifetime of analysis, although most historians agree that the movement played a "critical role in creating racial hierarchy and demarcating racial and ethnic boundaries" during the progressive era.[21] That argument is supported by one of the rare Mann Act prosecutions, brought against heavyweight boxer Jack Johnson. Documentary filmmaker Ken Burns argues that Johnson was convicted for his crime of "unforgiveable blackness." Johnson was no pimp, but he openly lived with a white woman, behavior that defied miscegenation norms during the Jim Crow era.[22] That race-mixing fear helps explain why Southern politicians overrode their almost sacred Southern principle of states' rights when they voted in favor of the Mann Act.[23]

Today, the word *segregation* usually refers to racial segregation, but during the white slavery era, segregation referred exclusively to red-light districts, which, according to progressives, could be found in almost every major American city. In segregated districts, prostitution was an open secret, local police arrested neither prostitutes nor their customers, and visiting businessmen knew where to go to have a good time, since local boosters purportedly touted red-light districts as tourist attractions. Progressives' white slavery campaigns emphasized the symbiotic relationships between vice and boss-dominated urban political machines, fueled by graft and favors, and such corruption cried out for political intervention. Cleaning up the streets would clean up politics.

Progressives built a strong national movement to advance their causes, and Chicago reformers—including Jane Addams, her Hull House associates, juvenile court workers, and various Chicago politicians, especially Representative James R. Mann—often led the way. Mann, and others, inventively employed the Constitution's commerce clause to expand the federal government's power over what had previously been strictly local issues. The clause underpinned the Mann Act as well as the Mann-Elkins Act, which regulated railroad rates, and the Pure Food and Drug Act. For progressive reformers, it was a small legislative and philosophical step "from pure food to pure women."[24]

The newly created juvenile courts also played an active role in trying to eliminate the root causes of white slavery with the data it collected. Jane Addams dedicated her 1911 book, *A New Conscience and an Ancient Evil*, a collection of previously serialized magazine articles, to "the Juvenile Protective Association of Chicago, whose superintendent and field officers have collected much of the material for this book."[25] Chicago gets most of the historical credit for spearheading the anti-white slavery movement, although parallel movements developed in other parts of the country, including Denver, and in both cities, the juvenile court and its employees were key to those reforms. Jane Addams was Chicago's best-known progressive reformer, and Judge Ben Lindsey was Denver's. He built a national reputation by touring the Midwest as a featured speaker on the Redpath Chautauqua circuit, offering advice as an expert on children in ghostwritten articles published in progressive-era periodicals, and serving as a highly visible member of the National Child Labor Committee, whose publicity campaign contributed to the passage of the 1916 Owens-Keating Act, which outlawed child labor. The bill's co-sponsor, Edward Keating, a progressive ally of Roche's, served in the federal

House of Representatives from 1913 to 1919. (In 1918, the Supreme Court declared the Owens-Keating Act unconstitutional, and not until 1938 would the Fair Labor Standards Act finally forbid it.)

Although Chicago's reformers mightily disagreed, Lindsey boasted that *he* had founded the nation's first juvenile court in Denver.[26] Lindsey—a little man (standing barely five feet tall and weighing close to one hundred pounds) with an enormous ego—did not limit his reform efforts to the juvenile court, since he was in the forefront of almost every progressive reform effort from the early 1900s through his 1943 death. In December of 1912, the twenty-six-year-old Roche moved from New York City to Denver to begin full-time employment for Lindsey. Her parents had moved to Denver when John Roche bought a half share of what in 1911 would be re-named the Rocky Mountain Fuel Company (RMFC). John was a civic-minded joiner who belonged to the Chamber of Commerce and "various Masonic bodies,"[27] and Roche's mother, Ella, was also active in the Denver community, especially the Denver Woman's Club, the city's leading philanthropic group and political backer of Lindsey's juvenile court, because Colorado women had been casting their ballots since 1893.[28] Whenever Josephine was in Denver, she lived with her parents, and during the summers, she had worked for Lindsey. It is interesting to imagine the relationship among the Roches, especially in light of the 1910–1914 Colorado Coal Strike and Roche's willingness, by the early 1930s, to invoke her recently deceased father as an anti-union narrative foil to promote her own biographical narrative.

Edward Keating resigned as Denver's *Rocky Mountain News* editor to pursue politics, and George Creel arrived from Kansas City in 1911 to take his place.[29] Creel, a lower-case progressive (the movement), allied himself with Denver's capital "P" Progressives (the party), which included Roche, Lindsey, Vincent, and Costigan. Between 1911 and 1913, upper- and lower-case progressives took political control of Denver and made huge inroads throughout the state, too. Colorado's 1912 ballot included a staggering number of initiatives (another recent progressive victory)—thirty-two—most written by Progressives, including Costigan and Lindsey.[30] Some of the initiatives voters approved that year included workman's compensation, mothers' pensions, and an eight-hour workday for women and coalminers. As the long strike proved, many of those laws, including the eight-hour workday for coalminers, proved easier to pass than to enforce.

Progressives even briefly convinced Denver voters to convert their mayoral form of city government to a commission model, and those commissioners appointed Creel the new police chief. Creel continued editing the *Rocky Mountain News*, and he used both positions to crack down on laws that, although on the books, had largely gone unenforced, especially those regarding prostitution. If Creel's following description is accurate, Denver's red-light district really was a cesspool that needed to be abolished: "Under [former mayor] Speer the infamous 'crib system' had been tolerated and even encouraged. This was an artificial street lined both sides with cubicles in which half-naked women sat for sale beside a soiled bed and a dirty washbowl. When a customer mounted the short flight of steps, a corrugated shutter was pulled down. Every night the street was packed and jammed with milling crowds, men for the most part, but with a high percentage of veiled women, and even more distressingly, many teen-age boys and girls."[31]

As Creel made clear, cleaning up the red-light district would save both prostitutes and juveniles. Since controlling public and private behaviors required controlling public and private spaces, most progressives advocated closing saloons, where working-class men drank, socialized, and politicked, which, progressives argued, corrupted men and politics alike. Since saloons also promoted drunkenness, and drunkenness led to crime, in 1916, Colorado progressives led the successful fight to pass statewide prohibition, three years before prohibition was ratified as a federal Constitutional amendment.

Prohibition was aimed at men, but young, working-class women's "pursuit of pleasure did not lead them to the traditional domain of workingmen, but to emergent forms of commercialized recreation, such as dance halls, amusement parks, and movie theatres."[32] Therefore, "Believing that commercialized amusement had a very definite connection with commercialized vice, I [Creel] appointed Josephine Roche as a special officer to ride herd on dance halls and skating rinks."[33] In January of 1913, Roche officially became Denver's first policewoman, with the newly created title of inspector of amusements. She worked for both the police department and Lindsey's juvenile court, a typical arrangement for the nation's first lady cops.[34] A month before taking office, Creel's *Rocky Mountain News* introduced Roche to the city with a lengthy, laudatory, colorfully illustrated feature story that included sensationalistic descriptions of her recent experiences in New York City, especially her

FIGURE 1.1. *This is one of several full-color illustrations from "Denver's Petticoated Copper," a feature story in the Sunday* Rocky Mountain News *on December 1, 1912, that introduced Josephine Roche to Denver readers just before she was appointed Denver's first "lady cop" in January of 1913.*

efforts to clean up "hell's kitchen."[35] Roche's "beat" required her to monitor "cheap amusements," including movie theaters, dance halls, amusement parks, skating rinks, and "wine parlors." Although her career was short—appointed in January, officially fired in March, reinstated in May, unpaid, only through August 1—albeit temporarily, she certainly shook up Denver.[36] Working closely with other progressive reformers, her job consisted of trying to prevent underage drinking and other behaviors that could lead to juvenile delinquency, which for girls (but not boys) was almost always associated with moral laxity, the first step on a slippery slope leading to white slavery.

Roche had been concerned with moral laxity for a while. She began her 1910 Columbia University masters' thesis declaring that "Delinquency is not synonymous with prostitution" but spent the remainder of her investigative study disproving that assertation.[37] Her entire thesis—its structure, arguments,

and even writing style—is remarkably similar to Jane Addams's 1911 white slavery book, which itself had been serialized as magazine articles in 1910, the same year of Roche's thesis. Women's low pay outraged them both, but they emphasized that low pay alone did not necessarily lead to vice. Sometimes the nature of the workplace was the problem, and both reformers focused on the moral dangers factory and department store work posed for women. Factory work led to boredom, and boredom led to trouble. Although department store work was not as boring, girls faced constant temptation because they were surrounded by beautiful consumer goods they could not afford with their paltry salaries. Furthermore, unlike factory work, practically any man could approach a department store employee as often as he wished, filling her naïve head with enticing ways to make easy money. So, whether from factory work's boredom or department stores' temptations, both workplaces encouraged girls to socialize, which could lead to prostitution. Roche wrote, "We can safely say that at first an immoral life is seldom in the minds of these girls" who only want "the natural craving for a good time and attention, and accept invitations to dinner or the theatre with no thought of any more serious outcome."[38] However, accepting these invitations was dangerous, because "one by one the things at which she draws the line vanish, leaving in their place increasing tolerance toward overstepping the final, all-important line between honor and dishonor. Once the first step is taken, continuance is not hard."[39]

Roche's job as Denver's first policewoman was to prevent that first step toward immorality, an extension of Lindsey's juvenile court model. Also emulating Denver's juvenile court, which sent delinquents to a reformatory school in the countryside, away from the evil cities (without a trial or a lawyer to represent them, something unchanged until the 1967 Supreme Court decision *In re Gault*), Denver hoped to establish a rural institution that would rehabilitate prostitutes. As recent books have shown, such reha-bilitation might also have included forced sterilizations.[40] The progressive plan in Denver, again in Creel's words, was to "take over a 266-acre farm owned by the city and equip it with hospitals and dormitories where Denver's human wreckage could be collected, treated, and sorted. Here treatment would be provided not only for disease, but for the rehabilitation of the drug fiends and the drunkards . . . handling all with regard for nothing but purely social considerations."[41] However, the farm never came to pass, because the public pushed back when it came to the hospital and all it entailed.[42]

WOMAN AS POLICEMAN WILL FORCE REFORMS IN CITY DANCE HALLS

Will Miss Josephine Roche, Denver's first policewoman, who was appointed by the fire and police board, look like this when she reports for duty?

FIGURE 1.2. *As the pre-photoshopped but comically altered English Bobby portrayal of Roche demonstrates, Denver newspapers less sympathetic to Roche and her progressive allies openly mocked Roche and her new job.*

Although some Denver citizens, including health organizations and members of the city's women's clubs, welcomed the hygienic and medical implications of progressives' anti-prostitution efforts, Denver's less well-heeled citizens, not to mention the politicians they had recently defeated, loathed the progressives and their self-righteous campaigns.[43]

As the fire and police departments attacked Creel over these new red-light policies,[44] another newspaper article documents why their policies proved so unpopular. Roche had sworn out a vagrancy warrant on a young woman

who was taken to the county hospital then sent to the county jail where her sister was also being held. Their seventy-year-old mother then filed a writ of habeas corpus, trying to get both daughters released.[45] Although no further articles inform us whether the mother's lawsuit was successful or not, we are left to wonder if these sisters were actually prostitutes or if they just happened to be living near the red-light district with their old mother, where rent was cheap. Creel described in chilling detail what would have happened to the sisters after Roche arrested them. Without formal charges for anything other than vagrancy and with or without their consent, they would have been tested for venereal diseases and held until their results returned. If negative, they would be released. If positive, they would be treated (again, with or without their consent) with the then-standard—but we now know to be poisonous—treatment, mercury.[46] This process could take weeks, so if the women had jobs, they would have lost them, along with their reputations, personal dignity, and, perhaps, the ability to bear children. Yet none of the progressives at the time, or in Creel's biography that he wrote thirty years later, expressed any qualms about violating these women's civil rights in this intensely undemocratic process.

Progressives attacked more than just prostitution. In another newspaper article, worded in a way clearly meant to bemuse rather than infuriate, Roche demanded that a theater owner stop showing a western movie to young boys. At the exact moment Bob Ford shot Jesse James in the back, "in came Miss Roche, whose duties include the inspection of picture theaters."[47] Roche said, "Hi there, Bob Ford, cut it out this minute. Do you hear me?" Then, she "pranced down the middle aisle giving orders as she advanced upon the desperadoes. She flashed her star and the desperadoes vanished from the stage. In their place appeared a sign, which read: 'The Wages of Sin is Death.'"[48] Roche ordered the movie stopped and forbade the owner from showing it to children.

Denver's progressives might have gotten away with such heavy-handed, undemocratic, moralistic actions if they only affected juveniles, prostitutes, the working-class, and blacks, since an article in Roche's file documents that most of the suspected prostitutes arrested were "negroes." (So much for white slavery.)[49] Roche, however, apparently attempted to extend her reach to almost every stratum of society. For example, anonymous complaints concerning "wholesale 'ragging'" (dancing), whist playing (a popular card game), and alcohol consumption "at a dance hall patronized by the well-to-do" prompted Roche to inspect the premises, which led the infuriated club owner to tell a reporter, "The police have no authority to declare what kind of dancing shall be allowed in my hall." Additionally, neighbors were "quite aroused by the prospect of an officer of the law, whose business is usually among the lower dance halls of the city, invading their precincts."[50]

It only took three months of this kind of policing to drive both Creel and Roche from office. In March, the fire and police boards pressured Creel to resign his police commissioner position. He not only left the job but he left Denver, never to return. Citing budgetary reasons, the same groups then fired Roche, but she sued, since her job, unlike Creel's, was a civil service position, and she had not received a proper hearing before her dismissal. Roche rallied Denver's clubwomen to her cause, and they organized a series of mass meetings, demanding her reinstatement.[51] Her attorney, Edward Costigan, the Progressive candidate for Colorado governor, defended Roche in court, but he only won Roche's right to remain in her position through August 1, when she resigned. So ended the career of Denver's first policewoman, Josephine Roche.[52]

I have examined Roche's brief policewoman career for several important reasons. Although previous Roche histories mention it in passing, celebrating it as a valuable first in women's history, Roche's policewoman stint illustrates well her maternalist identity and attitudes about the power, scope, and function of government. Therefore, Roche's stint as inspector of amusements demonstrates well the twin impulses of progressivism and social reform, but especially social control, complementary forces that shaped her lifelong worldview. Also, because two of the fattest folders in her archival collection are filled with her carefully preserved, clipped, mounted, and chronologically sorted policewoman articles, it must have been important to her. Last, examining Roche's policewoman career does something else, too. It shows that for most of 1913, as the violent phase of Colorado's 1910–1914 long strike escalated in Colorado's southern coalfields, Roche was not, as subsequent historians have contended, advocating for workers' rights. Instead, she was trying to end white slavery.

There is overwhelming evidence that Roche's Progressive associates, especially Lindsey and Costigan, were very involved in the long strike, but if Roche joined them, there is no evidence of it in her archival collection,

FIGURE 1.3. *This Josephine Roche head shot was attached to the 1915 United States State Department travel form authorizing her to travel overseas on behalf of the Belgian Relief Fund.*

although that lack of evidence could be the consequence of careful culling. When the strike ended in December of 1914, the UMW lost, and the union almost disappeared from the state. As the strike sputtered to a close, so did Progressives' influence. By 1916, Lindsey, Vincent, Costigan, and Roche supported Democratic nominee Woodrow Wilson for president.[53] They joined the nation in turning their attentions to the Great War, and in 1915, Roche left Denver to work, briefly, for the Belgian Relief Fund.[54] Although the State Department cleared Roche to work in London, a glitch prevented that,[55] so instead, she spoke to community groups in the United States, sometimes as often as three times a day, to raise awareness and funds for that humanitarian mission.[56] Next, Roche wrote a report for the NCL, "Wage Earning Women and Girls in Baltimore: A Study of the Cost of Living in 1918." Roche's hero, Florence Kelley, wrote its introduction, describing the study as "one modest link in the world-wide chain of reports, official and otherwise, made in the past twenty years," documenting the low wages of women and trying to combat the myths (such as the "pin money fallacy") that justified them.[57] This report shows that Roche was still focusing her maternalist work, not yet living her life to right the wrongs of Ludlow.

Roche next moved to Washington, DC, to again work for Creel, who headed the Committee on Public Information (CPI). During its 1917–1919 existence, Roche was the only woman to head a CPI department, a remarkable accomplishment. Contemporaneously, few understood the role the CPI played in generating pro-war propaganda, but historians since have shown how the agency's "100% Americanism" message generated not just pro-war sentiment, but also wartime hysteria, which led to widespread civil rights violations directed against those suspected of opposing the war, especially the IWW.[58] Roche's department was charged with communicating the CPI's message to recent immigrants. She and her staff wrote, coordinated, and disseminated information and press releases to fourteen non-English-speaking ethnic associations and 856 foreign-language newspapers throughout the country, as well as overseas.[59] Roche also coordinated the July 4, 1918, patriotic ceremonies that took place in thirty-three US cities, where immigrants professed allegiance to their new home country, a daunting organizational feat that demonstrates Roche's mastery of detail and delegation, as well as her flair for public relations.

Although Congress defunded the CPI in 1919, through 1923, Roche helped sustain the organization through precarious private donations. In one effort to secure stable funding, she wrote a pamphlet aimed at potential donors, explaining why "working with the foreign born" was so important. What her wartime work had shown, she wrote, was that the biggest problems immigrants faced in assimilating into the United States were not ideological but practical. Helping immigrants get good medical care and file their taxes correctly had done more to win hearts and minds during the Great War than any newspapers articles or pageants had ever accomplished.[60]

The agency survived and eventually morphed into the Foreign Language Service, but Roche resigned in 1923, perhaps because her soon-to-be ex-husband still worked there. Next, after an arduous application process, Roche was hired as director for the editorial division of the Children's Bureau, "the first female stronghold in the federal government."[61] Established in 1912, the bureau continued its progressive, white, middle-class, maternalist mission throughout the 1920s and, to some extent, the 1930s.[62] In 1925, however, the thirty-nine-year-old Roche cut short her promising governmental career and returned to Denver, moving in with her aging, sick parents. She managed their care until they died two years later, her father in January of 1927 and her mother in June. Roche also got her old job back with Judge Lindsey in Denver's juvenile court. Yet, back in Denver, instead of learning about her dying father's coal business, Roche embroiled herself in Lindsey's troubles.

The "Little Judge" had always been controversial, but in the 1920s, he faced new kinds of opponents unique to that decade: the revived Ku Klux Klan, outraged citizens, and Denver government officials. In 1924, appropriating the former CPI slogan "100% Americanism," Klan members or Klan-supported candidates won most elective offices in Colorado. The KKK fielded a candidate against Lindsey that resulted in a tie. Both candidates cried fraud, and the disputed election was fought in the courts for the next three years.[63] Even non-Klan sympathizers, however, were soon troubled by Lindsey's moral shortcomings. In 1927, Lindsey enraged the good people of Denver and much of the nation's general reading public with an article he wrote for *Red Book* magazine.[64] During the progressive era, Lindsey's byline frequently appeared in the *Survey*, the *Nation*, *Collier's*, *Harper's*, the *Outlook*, and *McClure's* on topics relating to child welfare, but by the 1920s, the magazine industry had changed dramatically, and Lindsey changed with it. He began writing for women's magazines filled with advertisements for the burgeoning cosmetics industry and articles about fashion, beauty, and movie stars, in which "almost every issue contained 'stories about the (often sexual) misconduct of college youth,'" and other sex stories, which became "a staple of journalism in the 1920s."[65]

Lindsey's desire to remain relevant in the public eye finally proved his undoing. His titillating articles about young people proved so successful that he compiled them into his 1925 bestselling book, *The Revolt of Modern Youth*.[66] Buoyed by that success, Lindsey continued writing for *Red Book*. In an article published in February of 1927, Lindsey advocated for a new form of matrimony, using a term he had recently coined, "companionate marriage."[67] Couples could get married, practice birth control, and wives could continue working outside the home, but if the marriage did not pan out, as long as there were no children, a judge could grant a divorce if the couple declared it wanted one. In 1927, except in states such as Nevada that specialized in quickie divorces, judges could only legally grant divorces if one party were proven to be at fault, and that fault was usually adultery. Probably the most controversial aspect of Lindsey's proposal was not even companionate marriage itself but the way he insulted organized religion when he wrote, "I have been receiving a good many letters of late asking me how I reconcile some of the views I am expressing in the articles with the Bible. I have one short and conclusive answer to that question. I don't reconcile them with the Bible. Moreover, I don't see why I should."[68]

Adding to Lindsey's miseries, in the summer of 1927, the Colorado Supreme Court, presided over by Judge Greely Whitford, ruled that Lindsey had lost his 1924 election challenge. Additionally, it ordered Lindsey to repay his past three years of salary.[69] Lindsey believed, probably correctly, that Whitford's ruling was political payback, because in 1911, during the long strike, he and other Progressives had tried to get Whitford impeached over a restrictive injunction he had issued that landed sixteen northern coalfield UMW organizers, including Ed Doyle, in jail.[70] Whitford's injunction was so unpopular, Doyle testified in the 1915 US Industrial Commission hearings that it led to a Denver protest meeting attended by at least eighteen thousand.[71] The impeachment effort failed, however, and in 1927, Whitford must have delighted in punishing Lindsey.

Whitford ordered Lindsey to vacate his office immediately and turn over the juvenile court records to the new judge, and an outraged Roche leapt to her boss's defense. She wrote a press release, which all the juvenile court employees, including Oscar Chapman, signed. It proclaimed that, for over a quarter of a century, Lindsey had ceaselessly defended the interests of women and children and, using a favorite progressive phrase, had "never for an instant weakened in his overwhelming task of championing human rights against property rights."[72] Not only did Lindsey refuse to surrender the juvenile court records, in an effort to bring public attention to his plight, he, his wife, and two court officers ceremoniously burned them.[73] (Although newspapers did not specify whether or not Roche was among the record burners, she probably was.) Then, all of Lindsey's employees quit. In spite of these theatrics, however, no groundswell of support for Lindsey emerged.

During this controversy, Roche wrote to William Chenery, asking for his help. By 1927, Chenery edited *Collier's* magazine, but in his earlier life as a Denver newspaper man, after the April 20, 1914, Ludlow deaths, Chenery had written a passionate editorial in the *Rocky Mountain News* condemning the state for the strike violence. In fact, Chenery was the first person to use the term *Ludlow Massacre*.[74] Roche soon discovered that their old progressive ally was no longer in their camp. In his response to Roche, Chenery wrote that although Lindsey had served a valuable purpose in his early years, he should have retired about twenty years earlier. Furthermore, if a juvenile court was unable to function without the personality of one specific individual, then maybe it deserved to die.[75]

Chenery, of course, was right. By 1927, the juvenile court had become an institution that could function perfectly well, probably better, without the flamboyant Lindsey. Importantly, this Lindsey scandal tells us much about Roche. Even in her sick parents' final days, Roche was swept up in Lindsey's drama, and her first loyalty was to the person, Lindsey, not to the institution, the juvenile court. Roche learned that the muckraking techniques that had so effectively rallied public opinion during the progressive era no longer worked. Roche probably learned additional lessons, too, since soon after this extremely public fiasco, the relationship between her and Lindsey completely soured. I have some educated guesses why, but neither left documentation explaining their split, a fissure that demonstrated Roche understood when to fish or cut bait.

Most of Lindsey's former progressive allies deserted him as his former enemies piled on. Some sought to disbar him, which Oscar Chapman, now an attorney, fought, unsuccessfully, for two years.[76] Disbarred, dejected, and abandoned, Lindsey did what so many others before and since have done; he moved to California to reinvent himself. As a judge there, he granted the first major celebrity divorce (between Douglas Fairbanks and Mary Pickford) and established the nation's first family court.[77] Over two decades after Lindsey's death, in 1969, California became the first state to enact an updated version of companionate marriage. By then, it was called no-fault divorce.[78]

Although Lindsey had to leave the state to reinvent himself, Roche reinvented herself by remaining in Colorado. When her father died in January of 1927, Roche inherited his half of the RMFC. A month later, Roche hired former Progressive ally Merle Vincent to represent her company interests. Although it is unclear to what extent Roche controlled the company's board, she was powerful enough to make Vincent the RMFC's vice president, general manager, and spokesperson.[79] Immediately, Vincent began making changes. He fired Jesse Northcutt as the RMFC's legal counsel and took over that position himself, a position for which he was well qualified, since before coming to work for Roche, he served as president of the State Bar Association. Northcutt was also an excellent attorney, but his anti-union notoriety, dating back to the 1910–1914 long strike era, doomed his RMFC future. After digging through the RMFC's troubled finances, Vincent discovered another notorious long strike connection: Walter Belk had been on the RMFC payroll as a spy since 1919. Since Belk had worked as a spy during the long strike and probably pulled the first trigger that killed the first strike victim, Vincent fired him, too.[80]

A few months later, in June, Roche's mother died, and in July, Lindsey was ousted from his judgeship. In early August, a brief Sacco and Vanzetti sympathy strike broke out in Colorado's southern coalfields, not in the northern fields where most of the RMFC properties were located, and Vincent remained silent, since the walkout did not directly affect the RMFC. However, when most RMFC coalminers joined the statewide walkout on October 18, Colorado newspapers covered Merle Vincent's statement, delivered on behalf of *all* the state's coal operators. Their position was clear: The strike was illegal, all the state's coal operators opposed it, and coalminers needed to return to work.[81] So began the RMFC's aggressive resistance to the 1927–1928 Colorado Coal Strike that would soon change the course of Roche's life, yet even as the strike began, she was not yet living her life to right the wrongs of Ludlow.

2

Powers Hapgood

Becoming a Working-Class Hero, 1899–1928

During the 1920s and 1930s, Powers Hapgood's Forrest Gump-like ubiquity within the organized labor movement, paired with his frequent, archived correspondence, makes him an atypical, but important, participant/observer for historians. For much of the 1920s, alongside his mentor, John Brophy, Hapgood strove to democratize the UMW from within. Their Save the Union campaign would be the last meaningful effort to unseat John L. Lewis as president. That is why Hapgood's 1920s activities, which included work with several insurgency coalminer movements and the American Civil Liberties Union (ACLU), provides critical context explaining why the 1928 contract at the RMFC would become such a hopeful anomaly for the UMW.

Since Robert Bussel already wrote an excellent Hapgood biography, the following provides only a brief summary of his early years.[1] Born in 1899 in Chicago, Illinois, Powers Hapgood was an only child. When still a small boy, the family moved to Indianapolis, Indiana,[2] where the family's wealth provided his mother, Eleanor, free time to dote on her son[3] while Hapgood's

https://doi.org/10.5876/9781646423026.c002

father, William Hapgood Jr., owned and operated the Columbia Conserve Canning company (known as the CCC), which, by the 1920s, was praised as an exemplar of industrial democracy.[4] William shared the company's stock with his older, more famous brothers, Norman and Hutchins Hapgood. Norman penned muckraking articles during the progressive era and eventually edited both *Collier's* and *Harper's* magazines, and Hutchins mostly wrote fiction while hobnobbing with the bohemian Greenwich Village crowd. Like his father and uncles, Powers Hapgood went to public schools as a young boy, then attended Phillips Academy, followed by Harvard.[5] Except for sports, however, university life for Powers was a slog.

Between his junior and senior years, Hapgood took a break to hobo in the West, to see for himself what working-class life looked like. He first encountered the IWW while riding the rails and discovered, surprisingly, that many Wobblies were not the wild-eyed monsters portrayed during the World War I red scare, but thoughtful, well-read workers eager to debate big ideas.[6] Even though he admired them, Hapgood did not join the IWW, because he did not believe, as the IWW preamble stated, that the working class and the employing class had nothing in common. His own father's company was proving just how wrongheaded that class-based philosophy of industrial democracy could be.[7]

The diary Hapgood kept during his hobo summer provided information for "Paternalism vs. Unionism in Mining Camps," an article published in the May 4, 1921, issue of *The Nation*.[8] Ludlow's narrative had been such a powerful draw, it inspired him to visit southern Colorado, where he observed the Rockefeller Plan in action. After the massacre, John D. Rockefeller Jr. worked alongside future Canadian prime minister Mackenzie King to develop a plan that would provide Colorado Fuel and Iron (CF&I) workers a voice in the workplace. More importantly, a CF&I union would keep the UMW out. Critics claimed the Rockefeller Plan union was nothing more than a company union that did not represent workers at all. Hapgood's observations convinced him that, although CF&I coalminers had better housing, education, and working conditions than the UMW coalminers he had worked alongside in Montana, the UMW miners exhibited a greater sense of personal autonomy in their lives. The UMW's vision of industrial democracy so enthralled Hapgood that he joined the union, earnestly participating in its secret initiation ceremony that bound him to all UMW coalminers in life, work, and death.[9]

Hapgood's article was published the year he graduated from Harvard,[10] and his senior thesis, "The Works Council Movement in the United States,"[11] also reflected his intellectual interrogation of industrial democracy. The works council movement flourished in Great Britain during the Great War, but in the United States, a less formal version of wartime cooperation developed among government, businesses, and organized labor, a model the federal government abandoned when the war ended. Thereafter, reformers interested in industrial democracy experiments looked to the private sector for inspiration. Companies leading the way included Filene's department stores in Boston, Nash Cash Register (NCR) Company in Cincinnati, and his father's CCC. Hapgood's highly seasonal enterprise (picking, processing, and canning tomatoes for soup) never employed more than three hundred people during the peak season in late summer and early fall, and most of the year, it only employed about one hundred full-time workers. In spite of its small size, the CCC exemplified what W. Jett Lauck gushingly called "probably the most complete and perfect illustration of direct industrial democracy which exists today."[12]

Lauck's laudatory pronouncement appears in his book, *Political and Industrial Democracy, 1776–1926*. In it, Lauck analyzed several companies' experiments with industrial democracy, and he evaluated their varying levels of success. Lauck was a scholar, but his ideas achieved their greatest impact through his work with John L. Lewis. From 1919 to 1939, Lauck served as Lewis's chief economic advisor, publicist, and ghostwriter.[13]

In 1925, Lauck penned the only book ever credited to Lewis, *The Miners' Fight for American Standards*. The book presents several important themes to which Lewis adhered, not just in the 1920s, but throughout his forty-year UMW presidency.[14] The title and contents make the explicit claim that the UMW was a patriotic force for good. That argument directly challenged propaganda promulgated by reactionary organizations that equated organized labor with communism. Patriotic zeal promoting 100 percent Americanism proliferated during World War I, with much of it generated by the CPI that had employed Roche. In 1919, the year following the war's end and two years after the Russian Revolution, a massive strike wave swept the United States and close to one in seven workers joined a walkout. In 1921, the National Association of Manufacturers (NAM) spearheaded a coalition that declared war on newly unionized workers. Their massive public relations campaign promoted the term *American Plan* to describe non-union workplaces, which allowed employers to swaddle their union-busting ways in the American flag and denigrate union leaders and members as un-American.

The Lewis book directly challenged those claims. Lewis makes no effort to define industrial democracy and he even ridicules the term as one of many—including shop councils and employee representation plans—whose "richness in words is as marked as its poverty in performance."[15] Even so, Lewis did promote a vision of industrial democracy to which he consistently adhered that promoted the "sanctity of the contract" negotiated between businesses and independent trade unions. However, since the only union Lewis really cared about was the UMW and the only contract terms that mattered were the ones he negotiated, his vision of industrial democracy was never very democratic. In his book, Lewis acknowledged that coal was a "sick" industry, but he argued it could be healed by following the economic laws of supply and demand and by adopting principles of scientific management. He also argued that it was the proliferation of small, non-unionized coal operations that led to the overproduction of coal. As these independent operators degenerated into cutthroat competition, they were forced to cut wages simply to stay in business.[16] Therefore, small, inefficient coalmines need to be eliminated. Large, efficient, and unionized coalmines would remain, and they could afford to mechanize, which was not only inevitable, but preferable. Mechanization would reduce the numbers of coalminers, but the jobs that remained would be safer and well paid, because those workers would be represented by the UMW.

Because Lewis believed small, non-unionized coal operations should close, when he declared a UMW strike on April 21, 1922, for practical and rhetorical reasons, he only *appeared* to support the non-union coalminers who joined the official strike. They helped make the strike more effective, because fewer working coalminers and less available coal would help force recalcitrant coal operators to the bargaining table.[17] Lewis's effusive public praise, yet lack of actual support, for non-union walkouts sent mixed messages to coalminers who desperately needed to believe that Lewis backed their primary demand: union recognition. This was the fray into which Powers Hapgood inserted himself in 1922.

After graduating from Harvard, instead of going to work for his father's much-heralded company as was probably expected, Hapgood decided to dedicate his life to the working class. In the way only a rich young man with options could do, he spent several months earnestly interviewing prominent family contacts about potential career choices. During this process, Roger Baldwin, who headed the future American Civil Liberties Union (ACLU), became a close friend and mentor, but the most important person Hapgood met during his months-long career fair was John Brophy.

In 1917, John Brophy was elected president of UMW District 2 in central Pennsylvania. Although he repeatedly implored Lewis to send organizers, even during that heyday of World War I organizing, Lewis refused, because Lewis instead focused on consolidating already unionized coalfields.[18] In July of 1921, Brophy asked Hapgood if he was willing to get a job mining coal in his district and write about his experiences. Hapgood agreed, but he soon did more than write. He agitated, organized, and helped lead a two-year strike in Somerset and Cambria counties, funded not by the UMW, but by the district itself and rich friends of Hapgood's, including Baldwin.[19] This strike helps prove that the 1920s was *not* a quiescent era for workers, especially for coalminers.[20]

When the strike ended, although existing UMW contracts were renewed, nationwide, UMW memberships plummeted. Bitterness among non-unionized coalminers toward Lewis's rhetorical encouragement, yet lack of actual support during, but especially after the strike, and his increasingly dictatorial leadership led to a showdown at the 1922 UMW convention. His most effective challengers were the supporters of Alex Howat, the wildly popular District 14 (Kansas) president who, "at his best, exemplified the militancy, flavor, and courage of rank-and-file miners."[21]

Lewis officially became UMW president in 1920, but he began his ascendancy in 1917. That year, he test drove policies that would provide a blueprint for his complete consolidation of UMW power in the 1920s. Lewis first applied those policies in Colorado and next in Kansas, states that shared a border and several common characteristics. Both states' coalminers were led by charismatic, militant UMW organizers, and state legislatures had responded to that militancy by creating industrial commissions, Colorado in 1915, and Kansas in 1920. Although Kansas called its structure a court, both institutions served as mandatory arbitration boards. Theoretically, they shared a similar goal, eliminating industrial conflict, but in practice, both made it almost legally impossible for workers to go on strike.

Although Colorado politicians created the state's industrial commission in direct response to the violent 1910–1914 long strike and the Ludlow Massacre, Kansas created its industrial court in response to Howat's repeated wildcat strikes (strikes that are not authorized by a union). Before, during, and after that court's creation and implementation, Howat both condoned and led wildcat strikes, often getting jailed for his efforts. Howat also filed a lawsuit, charging that the industrial court was unconstitutional. In 1922, Supreme Court Chief Justice William Taft wanted to hear the case, but since it had been "disposed of in the State courts on principles of general and not Federal law," the court had no choice but to dismiss it.[22] This widely reported statement surely prompted the ACLU, the IWW's General Defense, and later, the International Labor Defense (ILD) to begin framing their lawsuits not as state law challenges, but instead as federal, Constitutional challenges, especially using the first amendment.

Lewis despised the Colorado and Kansas industrial commissions, but he thought they should be obeyed, so on October 14, 1921, charging Howat with insubordination to both Kansas law and UMW directives, Lewis ousted Howat from his District 14 presidency. As we shall soon see, he had done this first in Colorado, in 1917 and 1918 when he "appropriated" the district, which meant placing it under UMW national control. Lewis told reporters that all loyal Kansas coalminers should recognize the measures he had put into place, but Howat told reporters that Lewis should go to hell.[23] Instead of going to hell, Lewis sat tight at the UMW headquarters in Indianapolis and sent one of his top lieutenants, Van Bittner, to run the district. Bittner said he was prepared to suspend the UMW memberships of the four thousand striking coalminers who continued to support Howat by remaining on strike, and he mostly followed through with his threat, suspending many, but not all, of Howat's supporters.[24]

Angry about the district takeover, Kansas coalminers' wives organized a Women's Army that raided mines where scabs worked, beating the strikebreakers and pelting them with rocks. Initially, local police ignored the women, but that deference did not last.[25] As the Women's Army grew, so did local police response. By December, newspapers began calling the women's group, now several thousand strong, an "army of Amazons." One woman later remembered she had been one of approximately seven thousand women who converged upon the Girard, Kansas jail, where Howat was held prisoner.[26] The *New York Times* reported that the women entered the town in a formation headed by American flags and banners, paraded several times around the town square, then marched to the jail, raucously demanding to see Howat. The sympathetic sheriff, who had allowed Howat "all the privileges and comforts he wanted," stood in solidarity next to Howat as he addressed the crowd for over an hour.

Girard was a hotbed of radicalism. The leading Socialist newspaper in the United States, *The Appeal to Reason*, was published there, and Mother Jones frequently visited the area, attempting to encourage militancy among not just the coalminers, but also among some of the Mine Mill zinc and lead miners who worked nearby.[27] The day after Howat's speech, state officials transferred Howat ten miles away to Pittsburgh, an anti-union town that, for years, supplied strikebreakers to Colorado.[28] Probably fearing the Amazons would march on the jail as they had in Girard, the Pittsburgh sheriff "frantically assembled a deputized force of one thousand men and recruited veterans who stockpiled rifles and guns in a local hotel."[29] Three troops of National Guard cavalry arrived and fanned out to quell the militant rumblings in nearby local mining communities. Forty-nine women were arrested and charged with unlawful assembly, disturbing the peace, and assault. Unlike the striking men who had been arrested and whose bonds had been set at $200, the women's bonds were set at $750.[30]

The battle at the 1922 UMW convention was not just over Lewis' leadership but over what form industrial democracy would take in the union. Labor leaders like Lewis "ingratiated themselves with operators and politicians, while Howat gloried in the role of class warrior, the man who would risk prison before selling out workers to their employer or public officials."[31] Although Howat's rowdy supporters were strong enough to force his expulsion and District 14's takeover to a roll call vote, Lewis's presidential power allowed him to move the vote to the final business item of the convention. Before voting began, Lewis forcefully pronounced his conviction that the UMW members' best interests could *only* be protected by honoring the "sanctity of the contract," and he warned that if other militant UMW leaders followed Howat's undisciplined example, no operators would ever agree to sign binding contracts with the UMW in the future.[32]

Brophy stunned conventioneers when he voted with the Howat faction, a vote that surely sealed the outcome of the ongoing Pennsylvania strike

FIGURE 2.1. *John Brophy addresses a crowd in 1924, after the failed Pennsylvania strike but before the official Save the Union campaign began. Photograph from Catholic University Special Collections, The Catholic University, Washington, DC.*

and his own UMW political future. Although the vote was close, in the final—perhaps fraudulent—tabulation, Lewis won, probably because he controlled the votes from the newly appropriated Colorado and Kansas districts, where Lewis's loyalists served as convention delegates.[33] Soon after his vote, when it became clear that support from the UMW would never arrive, Brophy called off the Pennsylvania strike.

After the strike ended, Hapgood traveled abroad for a year, visiting England, Wales, Germany, and the Soviet Union. On his working vacation, he easily made friends everywhere he went, especially among unionized coalminers.[34]

When he returned to the states, he was demoralized to see how much the central Pennsylvania coalfields had deteriorated during his absence. Once again, he joined forces with Brophy. This time, they would directly challenge Lewis in a movement they called Save the Union.

In 1925, Brophy and Hapgood officially began their Save the Union campaign with the ultimate goal of building a movement strong enough for Brophy to defeat Lewis for the UMW presidency in 1927. Brophy's objections to Lewis had begun even before the ill-fated Pennsylvania strike. In 1921, Lewis ran, unsuccessfully, against Samuel Gompers for the presidency of the AFL, and to broaden his appeal, Lewis professed his support for nationalizing the coalmines. Lewis appointed Brophy and two other UMW officials who strongly supported nationalization to a committee charged with studying, then creating an action plan to promote that policy. Lewis lost, and as political winds shifted, Lewis not only buried Brophy's committee work, he also cultivated a close relationship with Republican Secretary of Commerce Herbert Hoover. Brophy soon realized that Lewis only supported nationalization when he thought it would help him politically, and in his 1964 autobiography, he wrote that by the mid-1920s, Lewis's "economic and political thinking was, if anything, to the right of Hoover's."[35] In fact, it had been Hoover who recommended that Lewis negotiate a long-term UMW contract, advice he followed in 1924. That three-year contract established the Jacksonville scale, a guaranteed wage for UMW coalminers. Almost immediately, however, operators began breaking the agreement, which led Brophy to question its strategic or even political value.

Contemporaries and historians alike have pondered whether Lewis was a pragmatist or an opportunist because he readily adopted almost any position or ally if it benefited him and the UMW. Like Roche, Lewis was a deeply private person who left almost no personal records, but his rhetoric and actions demonstrate that he understood power and valued personal loyalty. Lewis knew how to make headlines and eventually won over the hearts and minds of most coalminers. The nattily dressed, barrel-chested, charismatic Lewis exuded strength. Prominent jowls and shaggy eyebrows accentuated his powerful, booming voice's infinitely quotable pronouncements that are still delightful to read but must have been even more thrilling to hear in person or over the radio. Lewis knew when to play the class warrior and when to cut deals in the back room with coal operators and politicians. As Lewis began his UMW ascent, he promoted himself as the indispensable man and the UMW as the embodiment of industrial democracy. He did not want the public to view coalminers as violent, immigrant, wild-eyed revolutionaries who used their women and children in undisciplined labor fights. Instead, Lewis portrayed the UMW as a patriotic organization whose only purpose was to seek stable contracts that could produce decent wages and safe working conditions sufficient enough for a hard-working, male coalminer to support his family. Such working conditions would also benefit operators by stabilizing the coal industry. Strategically, Lewis held especially dear the Central Competitive Fields (CCF), consisting of Indiana, Illinois, Ohio, and western (not central) Pennsylvania. Historically, the CCF represented the first major organizational win for the UMW in the late 1800s. Practically, the CCF produced almost half of the nation's coal. Only after CCF operators threatened to cancel their contracts had Lewis called the 1922 strike, and when the strike ended, only those CCF contracts were renewed.[36]

Brophy not only disagreed with Lewis's strategic policies, he also regarded Lewis as a bombastic, lying, unethical, power-grabbing, dictatorial opportunist. Instead of attacking Lewis, however, Brophy's Save the Union campaign promoted his own competing vision of industrial democracy for the UMW.[37] Brophy rejected Lewis's claim that the sick coal industry could be saved by applying the principles of supply and demand and scientific management, and he did not think the proliferation of non-union coalmines or even overproduction caused low wages and bad working conditions. *Employers* caused low wages and bad working conditions and would continue to do so, because that was the nature of capitalism. While Lewis professed to be both pro-business and a registered Republican, Brophy leaned toward Socialism. Not only did he believe the US should follow Great Britain's example and nationalize coal, he also advocated forming an independent labor party, too. Brophy contended that Lewis's protectiveness of the Competitive Coal Field did not reflect changing conditions, because by the 1920s, the percentage of CCF coal represented under forty percent of the nation's total and it continued to drop.[38] Instead of protecting only current UMW coalminers, Brophy proposed organizing unorganized coalminers, and he knew it could be done because he had done it. The Pennsylvania strike he and Hapgood led even now remains the largest in UMW history, since over half a million coalminers joined.[39] Brophy faulted Lewis for failing to channel the militancy of non-UMW coalminers. For example, in

West Virginia, when coalminers waged a strike to achieve UMW recognition, their fight included the 1921 Battle of Blair Mountain, where an estimated ten thousand striking miners defied anti-union repression.[40] Instead of supporting local organizing efforts, however, Lewis sent Van Bittner from Kansas to West Virginia to reorganize coalminers there, appropriating yet another district and replacing its militant leaders with his own lackeys. In 1922, in Illinois, unorganized striking coalminers brutally assassinated twenty scabs, guards, and bosses, in what came to be known as the Herrin Massacre.[41] Brophy blamed Lewis's mixed strike messaging and his refusal to send organizers for that shocking violence, which shifted public opinion against the walkout. Finally, Brophy advocated a more democratic structure for the UMW that would begin by organizing unorganized coalminers at the grassroots level, then developing union leadership at workers' colleges such as Brookwood in New York. Brophy's vision of industrial democracy encouraged the development and nurturing of a diverse cadre of union leadership, a far cry from Lewis's increasingly centralized UMW control.

Because Brophy was wildly popular with the rank-and-file, the Save the Union campaign aimed to cobble together enough votes among them to win since UMW officers were already too intimidated by Lewis to publicly support any challenger. Brophy knew that Lewis would attack him, but he did not know how. Devoutly Catholic, deeply principled, personally moral, Brophy himself was beyond reproach. When the attack arrived, it came at the 1926 AFL convention, where Lewis waged his proxy war against Brophy by attacking Hapgood.[42] Lewis charged that Hapgood had duped Brophy into a "'Bolshevik Plot' to take over American labor," and as proof, Lewis read aloud a letter that Albert Coyle, a "left-leaning" editor of *The Journal of Locomotive Engineers*, had sent to Hapgood.[43] In the letter, Coyle requested permission to use Hapgood's name on the letterhead of a group of Illinois coalminers who wanted to create a periodical outside the reach of Lewis and the UMW. If Brophy won the UMW presidency, Hapgood would then edit that periodical. Although Hapgood claimed he never got the letter, whether he did or not was really beside the point. Lewis asserted Coyle's letter was proof not of coalminer resistance to Lewis, but that Communists were trying to infiltrate the UMW by "boring from within," an official American Communist Party policy at that time created to take over unions from the inside. In keeping with the convention's anti-Communist tenor, AFL delegates also voted down a resolution extending recognition to the USSR and a "proposal to send a labor mission to Soviet Russia."[44]

It was within that redbaiting atmosphere that Brophy officially ran against Lewis for the presidency of the UMW in 1927. Although both Brophy and Hapgood would challenge the results as fraudulent, Lewis claimed he won in a landslide, a victory that demonstrates Lewis's tightened grip over the UMW. Only five years earlier, when Howat's supporters challenged Lewis from the convention floor, they were strong enough to force a floor vote that Lewis purportedly won with a slim margin. By the time Brophy ran for president, Lewis dominated the proceedings so completely that when Hapgood, a UMW member in good standing, rose to speak, Lewis goons beat him up on the convention floor. Hapgood still refused to shut up, and the goons surprised him in his hotel room, beating him even worse. Those beatings produced the unintended consequence of turning Hapgood into a working-class hero, a symbol of anti-Lewis resistance.[45] After the convention, as he had done so many times before, Lewis arranged for the expulsions of his rivals, Brophy and Hapgood, from the UMW, which barred both from future work in union coalmines.

When Hapgood joined the UMW, he was an idealistic college student who believed that unions represented the ideal vision of industrial democracy. During the 1920s, after experiencing Lewis's policies and increasing authoritarian control over the UMW, he and John Brophy tried to return the union to what they believed were its democratic roots, but their efforts failed and afterward, Lewis turned both into UMW pariahs, unemployable in any UMW coalmine.

Brophy turned his attentions to his work at Brookwood and then toward establishing a new labor college in Pittsburgh, while Hapgood re-dedicated his life to the working class, this time by collaborating with Roger Baldwin and the ACLU. During the Great War, Baldwin had been jailed for opposing and refusing conscription. Serving time alongside Wobblies, he even joined the IWW and adopted the union's first amendment positions toward free speech and assembly. In 1917, he co-founded the civil liberties organization that in 1920 changed its name to the ACLU. Throughout the 1920s, the organization focused on defending first amendment civil liberties for organized labor. By 1927, after his UMW expulsion, Hapgood began working with Baldwin and the ACLU to test the legal limits of the first amendment.

His first test arrived in August of 1927, in Boston, where police arrested Hapgood four separate times during Sacco and Vanzetti protests.[46] Nicola Sacco and Bartolomeo Vanzetti were Italian-American immigrants living in Massachusetts who were charged and convicted of murder in 1921. Throughout the decade, the pair transformed into a worldwide cause célèbre as leftists rallied around them, declaring their arrests and convictions had more to do with their immigration status and unpopular political beliefs than with evidence. Like sympathizers all over the world, including Colorado coalminers, Hapgood believed if enough people protested, Sacco and Vanzetti's lives might be spared, or at the very least, they might get new trials. Hapgood's final Boston arrest was on August 22, the day before Sacco and Vanzetti's scheduled executions. Exhibiting behavior so erratic, police so oppressive, or both, Hapgood was delivered not to jail, but to the Boston Psychopathic Hospital, where he was kept on a twenty-four-hour lockdown. By the time ACLU attorney Arthur Garfield Hays arranged Hapgood's release the following day, Sacco and Vanzetti were dead. Later, in a hearing for his arrest, a judge asked Hapgood why he had come to Boston. Hapgood replied that "he believed Sacco and Vanzetti were innocent and he was willing to do or suffer in their behalf."[47] Although Hapgood did not know it yet, those executions would change the course of his life.

3

A. S. Embree

Becoming an IWW Organizer, 1876–1926

A. S. Embree rarely appears in history books, and when he does, he is usually being "deported" from Bisbee, Arizona, in 1917. Those deportation accounts tell us as much about the wartime hysteria surrounding the Great War as they do about the construction of dominant historical narratives. Although most historians abandon Embree in 1917, his significance and influence as a labor leader, which includes his leadership of the 1927–1928 Colorado Coal Strike, began before the deportation and continued through the 1950s. Although his attitudes moderated over time, what consistently drove his missionary-like zeal was an egalitarian vision of industrial democracy that aspired to a complete reordering of society that included racial, ethnic, and sometimes gendered equality. Throughout his six decades in organized labor, Embree worked to create a world in which the IWW refrain, "we are all leaders," might someday be true.

Adolphus Stewart Embree was born on December 15, 1877, in Blackhead, Newfoundland. Closer to Europe than to western Canada, Blackhead is almost

https://doi.org/10.5876/9781646423026.c003

the easternmost point of Canada. Around the turn of the nineteenth century, Napoleonic war blockades created an increased demand for Newfoundland cod, which spawned permanent coastal settlements like Blackhead.[1] Fishing was, and remains, dangerous, grueling, and seasonal. Newfoundland fishermen worked whenever the water was not frozen, usually between March through October. When fishermen went out sea, women ran the households, and when (and if) the men returned, the entire family helped process the fish for market.[2]

Embree's father was a Methodist pastor who ministered to these families. The year Embree was born, 1876, the census lists his father as the village's only non-fisherman.[3] Although Blackhead was the oldest established Methodist community in what is now Canada, it was also isolated, which explains why Newfoundland was the last province to join the Dominion of Canada in 1949. Those two factors—its early founding and geographical isolation—suggests why Blackhead Methodists stayed true to their original evangelical practices. They did not drink, smoke, play cards, or dance (or they were not supposed to, anyway). Fiercely democratic, they practiced "a disciplined commitment to holy living and social duty,"[4] and Embree's labor leadership and vision of industrial democracy reflected those Methodist roots. Whenever he led a walkout, strikers were forbidden to drink alcohol or gamble (or they were not supposed to, anyway), and like many Wobbly leaders, he exhibited a utopian, democratic vision for society. He championed the underdog, railed against corrupt bosses and corporations, and envisioned a society controlled by workers. During his long marriage to Lucy, he tried his best to be a good father to his two children, although his family, like any missionary's, often lived in poverty and endured his long absences from home, all for the greater good of the working class. His vision of industrial democracy sought nothing less than an entire reordering of society, and in his earliest days, even revolution.

How did a preacher's kid from an isolated fishing village transform himself into a migratory IWW leader who advocated industrial revolution? Little specific evidence about his childhood survives, but he did leave traces by which we might imagine his likely path. Embree probably received his most important education from his parents, but he also went to Mount Allison University in Sackville, New Brunswick. The school housed a separate boys' and girls' academy for younger students and a university for the

FIGURE 3.1. *Here is the first picture I have found of Embree, taken in 1895 at Mount Allison. In a group shot of the gymnastics team, an eighteen-year-old Embree stands farthest to the left. ("Mount Allison University gymnastics team, 1894–1895," Picture Collection, courtesy of Mount Allison University Archives, Sackville, New Brunswick, Canada.)*

older male students. College records from 1896 show that Embree wrote for the school newspaper and served as recording secretary for the debate club. Character hints flash throughout college newsletters, including joking references to his wild, unkempt hair and his passion for Shakespeare but little else academic.[5]

Although he was probably expected to, Embree did not study for the ministry but instead studied metal assaying. In 1897, the twenty-year-old Embree, youngest (and smallest) in his class, graduated and immediately headed west, seeking his fortune in the Klondike gold rush. We have some clues how that went, since Embree updates appeared in the university newsletter over the following six years. Almost immediately, he fell critically ill on a prospecting trip heading up the Peace River,[6] and after a year's convalescence, he tried reaching the Yukon again, although the newsletter never reported if he made it to the goldfields or not.[7] Photographs taken during the Yukon gold rush reveal fascinating evidence of the almost unbelievable hardships potential prospectors experienced,[8] and in 1897 and 1898, Embree joined thousands of men (and hundreds of women) who trekked the unforgiving trails where sudden blizzards and temperatures plunging to minus-forty degrees Fahrenheit could kill even the most well-prepared party.

By 1900, Nome (Alaska) fever supplanted Yukon fever, but when that last gold rush ended, so did most prospector dreams. The easy pickings were gone, and big businesses soon dominated hard rock mining operations. What gold remained had to be extracted, which required smelting, a complex chemical and mechanical process only corporations could afford. As mining and smelting technology improved, companies' needs for skilled labor decreased, and employers began cutting their labor costs because they could. The Western Federation of Miners (WFM) arose to combat those wage-cutting efforts and improve working conditions. Embree joined the WFM in 1899, so beginning his long career in organized labor.[9]

The WFM and UMW shared important similarities and differences. They were formed around the same time (the UMW in 1890, the WFM in 1893), but their workers mined different kinds of rock. UMW members worked with soft rock (coal), but WFM members mostly mined hard rock (often quartz that contained metals such as silver, gold, copper, and lead). The UMW's earliest victories occurred in the Central Competitive Fields east of the Mississippi, but most WFM miners worked west of the Mississippi. In 1892, the Idaho governor's heavy-handed tactics during a Coeur d'Alene strike motivated silver and lead miners there to join forces with gold miners in Colorado and the already unionized copper miners (who footed the bill for the new union) from Butte, Montana, to create the WFM in 1893.[10] Both the UMW and WFM organized industrially, which meant everybody working at the mine joined the same union, regardless of the specific job he did. Although the UMW belonged to the AFL, most AFL unions did not organize industrially but by craft or specific skill. Although the UMW and the WFM shared many commonalities and they briefly united twice, their half-hearted efforts to merge proved unsuccessful.

After a series of violent labor strikes, WFM leaders decided to form an organization to compete against the AFL, so on June 27, 1905, in Chicago, WFM secretary William "Big Bill" Haywood called to order "200 delegates from thirty-four state, district, and national organizations—socialists, anarchists, radical miners, and revolutionary industrial unionists" and formed the IWW.[11] The much-quoted IWW preamble began with this: "The working class and the employing class have nothing in common." By 1908, the amended preamble added that "between these two classes a struggle must go on until the workers of the world organize as a class, take possession of the earth and the machinery of production, and abolish the wage system." Furthermore, "It is the historic mission of the working class to do away with capitalism," and "by organizing industrially we are forming the structure of the new society within the shell of the old."[12]

Those words struck terror in the hearts of both progressives and the AFL, who both hated the IWW, but for different reasons. Progressives wanted to regulate, not destroy, capitalism. They also wanted to mitigate class conflict, and some even denied that class existed at all. The AFL hated the IWW because they competed with them for members. As the United States prepared to enter the Great War, the AFL also wanted to distance itself from the IWW because Wobblies made *all* organized labor look radical, an increasingly untenable image as 100 percent Americanism-style patriotism swept the country. Labor leaders, including AFL president Samuel Gompers and future UMW president John L. Lewis, hoped that if organized labor promoted a vision of industrial democracy that emphasized contractually negotiated, bread-and-butter issues, their co-equal status with businesses and the federal government might continue after the war ended.

A mere six months after the IWW's creation, hatred and fear of the IWW and, perhaps, guilt led to the arrest of Wobbly front man Bill Haywood for the murder of the former Idaho governor whose harsh persecution of the striking miners had led to the formation of the WFM.[13] Although Clarence Darrow won Haywood's acquittal, the cost of the defense (paid for by the IWW) power struggles between Haywood and his two co-defendants as the two-year trial dragged on, and Haywood's absence through 1907 robbed the fledgling IWW of money, momentum, and leadership. Partially because of these conflicts, the WFM quit the IWW in 1907 and four years later joined the AFL, only to quit again soon afterward.[14] In 1916, the union abandoned its WFM name altogether, probably hoping to leave its militant past behind. It rebranded itself the International Union of Mine, Mill and Smelter Workers, but since that name hardly rolls off the tongue, everybody just called it Mine Mill. The name change did not revitalize the union, however, and it almost withered away until leaders revived it in the early 1930s.

During the progressive era, Haywood symbolized labor radicalism, a status that accelerated his geographic and ideological mobility.[15] After his Idaho acquittal, he traveled and spoke frequently, then spent time in New York's Greenwich Village, where he held forth in Mabel Dodge's salon and helped lead (or, at least, took credit for leading) two East Coast IWW strikes.[16] Although the 1912 Lawrence, Massachusetts, strike succeeded, the 1913 Paterson, New Jersey, strike failed. After a trip to Europe and more traveling, Haywood returned to Denver, the headquarters of the WFM. Later, he moved to Chicago, headquarters of the IWW, to preside over that organization. He was simultaneously a member in good standing of the WFM, the IWW, and the Socialists. Mother Jones and A. S. Embree also exhibited similar geographic and ideological flexibility. Mother Jones agitated for the UMW, got fired, spoke and organized for the Socialists, helped found the IWW, quit the Socialists, then returned to UMW work. She traveled from West Virginia to Colorado to Mexico, to West Virginia then back to Colorado, and many places in between.[17]

Embree joined the WFM in 1899 in Greenwood, British Columbia, a Kootenay Mountains copper boomtown ten miles north of the Washington state border.[18] He served as local WFM secretary, edited the local newspaper,[19] and in 1908, married Lucy Mackenzie.[20] Embree joined the IWW in its first year of existence, 1905, and by 1907, he worked as an IWW organizer in Nome, Alaska, where he also edited The *Nome Industrial Worker*.[21] Even after the WFM quit the IWW, Embree continued belonging to both and saw no conflict in his dual memberships. Although he traveled widely, Embree usually lived in the West, including British Columbia; Nome, Alaska; Coeur d'Alene, Idaho; Butte, Montana; San Diego, California; Bisbee, Arizona; and Denver, Colorado.

Perhaps seeking stability for his new son, from 1910 to 1915, the Embrees probably lived in San Diego where they grew lettuce and A. S. worked as a grocery store clerk.[22] However, it is hard to imagine Embree contentedly settling into a life of domestic tranquility, especially considering what transpired nearby. On October 10, 1910, labor radicals set off a bomb in the *Los Angeles Times* Building. The explosion and subsequent fire killed twenty-one employees, an incident so terrifying, it sparked the formation of the United States Commission on Industrial Relations. The next month, the Mexican Revolution officially began, although many unofficial battles had already been fought, including one in Cananea, Sonora. In 1906, as part of its strategy to recruit more Mexicans,[23] the IWW (working through the WFM) led the Cananea strike that resulted in at least thirty and perhaps as many as 100 miners being killed by 1,500 Mexican soldiers and 270 Arizona rangers who had ridden on horseback the forty miles from Bisbee, Arizona, to help suppress the strike.[24] Mexican copper miners rebelled because they earned half of what whites were paid and because American and other foreign interests owned and managed 75 percent of the mines (like Cananea) and railroad lines throughout Mexico. Such disparities understandably created huge resentments among the Mexican people, most of whom were desperately poor. The political consequences of Cananea and textile strikes the following year contributed to the growing groundswell of discontent toward President Porfirio Díaz, who had held office since 1876 and was accused, accurately, of granting greater protections to American corporations than to Mexican citizens.[25]

In 1911, a splinter group fighting in the Mexican revolution, led by an American Wobbly and thirteen Mexicans, took over the town of Mexicali, while another group took over the border town of Tijuana only twenty miles south of San Diego in what came to be known as the Baja Revolution.[26] The ideological leaders behind the Baja invasion were the anarchist brothers Ricardo and Enrique Flores Magón. Starting in 1905, they led the *Partido Liberal Mexicano* (tied to the IWW) in attacks against Mexican dictator Porfirio Díaz. Díaz jailed them, they escaped, and by 1910, they had moved their headquarters to Los Angeles. From there, they tried to wrest control of the Mexican Revolution from Francesco Madero (who headquartered his movement in San Antonio, Texas) during the first year of the Mexican Revolution, but after the Baja Revolution failed a year later, so did they. When the Flores Magón brothers were put on trial in San Diego in 1911 for their revolutionary activities, rowdy Wobblies filled the courtroom during the proceedings.[27] We cannot know if Embree was in the courtroom or not, although he certainly was there in spirit if nothing else.

The Baja Revolution and trial also coincided with an IWW free speech fight in San Diego that attracted Southern California Wobblies, itinerant IWWs, as well as radical "stars" like Emma Goldman, who came to town to speak, agitate, and fundraise for both the Wobblies and the Mexican anarchists.[28] Joyce Kornbluh writes that "between 1909 and 1913, there were at least twenty major I.W.W. free speech fights throughout the country. All of them involved the right of the organization to recruit members at street meetings."[29] IWW speakers agitated not just for the right to organize workers, but also for their first amendment rights of speech and assembly, protests which influenced the future founder of the ACLU, Roger Baldwin, to take up their cause, at first, strictly on behalf of labor, and later, on behalf of anyone who had something unpopular to express.[30] So, while the Wobblies espoused social and industrial revolution, they also claimed it was their American, constitutional, first amendment right to do so. It is hard to imagine Embree sitting on the sidelines as these activities swirled around him in Los Angeles, San Diego, and Baja California. At the very least, the ongoing militant activities must have convinced him that the grocery business was not his calling.

Other sources place Embree in Colorado during the 1910–1914 long strike.[31] If true, along with other mostly California Wobblies, Embree came to Denver between 1912 and 1913, when the IWW waged its longest free speech battle of all.[32] That two-year period coincided with the peak of progressive political dominance in Denver. Even though much has been written about the Wobblies, their free speech battles, and the long strike in Colorado, it is worth pointing out the obvious: The IWW free speech battle in Denver took place during the 1910–1914 Colorado Coal Strike. Since one purpose of the free speech battles was to recruit new members in cities before they dispersed to remote job sites where workers were harder to organize, the timing of Denver's battle indicates that, to some extent, the IWW was involved in the UMW-led strike. Furthermore, the WFM was deeply involved in the long strike, and Embree probably was one of many dual members of both the WFM and the IWW.[33] As early as 1910 and continuing through the strike's end in 1914, Colorado coal companies recruited strikebreakers from other states and even from other countries, trying to keep the mines open. Those scabs would have arrived by train to Denver before transferring to trains delivering them to outlying coalfields. The Ludlow tent colony was established, purposely, near a train track, so that while the men were away, women and children could harass newly arriving scabs, to prevent their disembarkation.

In Denver, Wobblies soapboxed—literally standing on soapboxes, delivering speeches and acting out plays—outside Denver's Union Station, the city's train hub. Unlike San Diego and other cities, where city boosters and officials violently suppressed the Wobblies' speech, Denver's police chief George Creel remembered directing the police to let the Wobblies speak all they wanted.[34] However, Philip Foner's *Fellow Workers and Friends: I.W.W. Free-Speech Fights As Told by Participants* includes three Denver first-person accounts describing mass arrests, police beatings, and an IWW hunger strike in jail, accounts that sharply contradict Creel's recollections.

Additional evidence also suggests Wobblies played a role in Colorado's long strike. In 1908, the "overalls brigade" staged a successful coup and took over IWW leadership, and their uniforms included red bandanas. Red bandanas soon became the uniform of striking coalminer solidarity during the long strike, too, which led opponents to label the coalminers *rednecks* (a surprisingly different meaning of the word than its modern-day usage), an intended insult that backfired after miners proudly appropriated the name for themselves. Bandanas grew so central to strikers' identities that they wore them as symbols of their militance when posing for photographs and referenced them in their strike songs. Red bandanas also represented the "uniform" unorganized strikers wore in the 1921 Blair Mountain strike in West Virginia, which indicates that red bandanas—cheap, simple, and easily identifiable—symbolized worker solidarity more than labor organization affiliations.

Between 1910 and 1916, Embree *may* have been in Southern California, Mexico, Colorado, and God knows where else, but in 1917, Embree *definitively* surfaced in the copper mining town of Bisbee, Arizona. In fact, this is the first, last, and only time most historians mention Embree, because he was a key historical actor in the Bisbee deportation, one of the most infamous violations of civil rights during World War I. When historians abandon him there, however, their histories reinforce dominant narratives that falsely claim the IWW disappeared after the war and the 1920s was a quiescent era for organized labor.

On April 1, 1917, the United States formally entered the Great War, and on June 27, 1917, the IWW declared a strike at Bisbee's Copper Queen mine. In a predawn sweep on July 11, a vigilante committee rounded up over 2,000 strikers and sympathizers, corralling them into the town's baseball field. By 11:00 a.m., after their captors' questioning—Will you go back to work if you're released? Are you an American?—thinned the ranks, approximately twelve hundred remaining strikers were marched through a gauntlet of armed men (with Winchester rifles the weapon of choice), forced onto waiting cattle cars (conveniently provided by Phelps-Dodge, the company against whom workers were striking), and "deported" to Columbus, New Mexico, where federal troops held deportees captive, without charges, for two months.[35]

FIGURE 3.2. *This is just one of many photos taken during the 1913–1914 phase of the long strike, and the proud, red bandana–wearing striker is identified only as "A Greek Leader at Ludlow." (Photo courtesy of Denver Public Library Digital Collections.)*

Although Bisbee was neither the first nor last labor deportation, since it was the *largest*, it has received significant historical attention. Those accounts—and the ways they fit within a larger national labor narrative—help explain why historians have remembered Ludlow and forgotten the Columbine. Like the Ludlow Massacre or the Triangle Shirtwaist Fire, the Bisbee deportation took place as the progressive era drew to a close. Contextually, it provides another dramatic, outrageous example of corporations victimizing workers, especially those trying to unionize. The Bisbee deportation also demonstrates wartime hysteria and the demise of the IWW.

FIGURE 3.3. *A local photographer captured the Bisbee roundup of strikers in the ball fields where they were initially questioned and sorted out. ("The Bisbee Deportation: A University of Arizona Web Exhibit," courtesy of University of Arizona, Tempe, 2005.)*

FIGURE 3.4. *Armed townspeople marched strikers to waiting trains. ("The Bisbee Deportation: A University of Arizona Web Exhibit," courtesy of University of Arizona, Tempe, 2005.)*

FIGURE 3.5. *Strikers were kept for two months in Columbus, New Mexico. Embree is third from the left. He led the strikers in Bisbee and led the deportees during confinement. (Courtesy of Arizona Memory Collection, Arizona State Library, Archives and Public Records, History and Archives Division.)*

Melvyn Dubofsky, James W. Byrkit, James McCartin, and Katherine Benton-Cohen all have incorporated Bisbee into their histories. In turn, their histories have been incorporated into the dominant US narratives. In Dubofsky's sweeping IWW survey, *We Shall Be All*, Bisbee is contextualized within the wave of 1917 IWW walkouts that included copper strikes across Arizona and Montana as well as lumber strikes in the Pacific Northwest. Overall, Dubofsky argues that the IWW was a uniquely Western phenomenon that originated in response to rapid industrialization between the Civil War and World War I. He also argues that wartime persecution essentially killed the organization, but not its ideals. Dubofsky identifies Embree as an important IWW militant who led Bisbee's organizing efforts and kept deportees unified during their two-month post-strike imprisonment.[36] During their captivity, Embree served as a spokesman, but above all else, he *wrote* flurries of telegrams and letters to local governmental officials, to IWW leader Bill Haywood, to US president Woodrow Wilson, and to the secretaries of labor and war, pleading for blankets, food, constitutional rights, aid to the men's families back in Bisbee (including his own), and transportation out of Columbus, New Mexico.[37] Dubofsky even chose an Embree quote as the last sentence in his book, to serve as the IWW's most fitting epitaph: "The end in view is well worth striving for, but in the struggle itself lies the happiness of the fighter."[38]

In *Forging the Copper Collar: Arizona's Labor-Management War, 1901–1921*, James W. Byrkit argues that the 1917 IWW-led Bisbee strike was neither militant nor radical, which explains why Byrkit describes Embree as a pragmatic unionist, not a doctrinaire Wobbly.[39] Byrkit argues that Phelps-Dodge, the copper company against whom the strike was directed, only *portrayed* the strike and strikers as radicals so that *all* organized labor could be painted red and crushed in the 1920s. Joseph A. McCartin includes Bisbee, "the most infamous episode to come from the first year of the war," in *Labor's Great War* to exemplify the massive civil rights' violations that transpired during World War I.[40] Although Embree does not appear by name, he appears by type, representing one of the three visions of industrial democracy exhibited by enlightened employers, AFL advocates, and revolutionaries that competed for dominance during the war. Unlike competing visions that advocated for the adoption of scientific management principles in the workplace or the AFL's bread-and-butter-style unionism, Embree's vision called for a complete restructuring of society. That vision proved so threatening, it led to the IWW's wartime persecution and, McCartin and most other historians agree, consequent disappearance.

Katherine Benton-Cohen makes the Bisbee deportation the turning point in *Borderline Americans: Racial Division and Labor War in the Arizona Borderlands*, a study exploring constructions and reconstructions of racial, gender, and national identities in southern Arizona from the late 1800s through the 1930s. She asks, "Which borderline Americans became, in the minds of their neighbors and employers, 'white Americans,' and which ones did not?"[41] Her answer is that the deportation marked a redefinition of whiteness for the community that, by the time the New Deal arrived, excluded Mexican Americans. As evidence that this shift was already underway during the 1917 Bisbee strike, Benton-Cohen quotes a letter Embree wrote in which he "saw Mexican workers as 'a sure bet [to join the strike],' as we are demanding a minimum of $5.50 for all topmen."[42] She concludes, however, that this formal strike demand was "never a main priority,"[43] a conclusion with which I disagree.

Embree's vision of industrial democracy included championing the rights of all ethnicities. Benton-Cohen claims that wage equality for Mexican workers was never a strike priority, but in the 1950s, Embree remembered that the two main causes of the Bisbee walkout had been discrimination against Mexicans and the speedup. Because Mexicans were not allowed to work underground, they got paid two to three dollars less per day than all the other copper miners; the speedup had increased the rate of work beyond the point of safety.[44] Additional evidence that Embree meant what he had written about equalizing pay for Mexicans, whether United States citizens or not, is this: After Bisbee, in 1920, Embree and other IWW organizers specifically recruited Mexicans coming into the US through El Paso "enroute to the Colorado beet fields."[45] As the next chapter will show, during the 1927–1928 Colorado Coal Strike, Embree continued recruiting Mexicans as central figures in the strike. As chapter 9 will show, he influenced future labor leaders to do the same.

Although most historians abandon Embree after the Bisbee deportation, he continued to fight on behalf of workers and organized labor. After being held captive for two months in New Mexico, the deportees, including Embree, were finally released. Embree made the long walk home to his family in Bisbee, but local law enforcement authorities arrested him upon his return.[46] They jailed him until December of 1917, when he stood trial for inciting a riot. He was acquitted. None of the other deportees was ever convicted of any strike-related crime, either, which suggests that the real purpose of the deportation had been to break the strike. Those efforts succeeded.[47]

After his acquittal, Embree moved to Butte, Montana. The sister cities of Bisbee and Butte shared workers, organizers, technology, information, and in 1917, they also shared the distinction of producing more copper than anywhere else in North America.[48] While copper was used for plumbing and light bulb filaments, it also sheathed bullets, which were in high demand. The US economy boomed with the outbreak of war in 1914, corporate profits rose astronomically, and so did workers' wages, although wages did not keep pace with wartime inflation. Even with AFL promises made to the federal government and corporations that workers would forgo strikes during the war, that discrepancy fueled a 1917 strike wave that included Bisbee and Butte.

Mining corporations in both cities used wartime hysteria to crush organized labor, but workers stoked conservatives' worst fears, too. In Arizona, many miners openly sympathized, aided, and fought for the Mexican Revolution's radical working-class goals. Although Butte mine operators could not blame a nearby Mexican revolution for upheavals, they did assign the unpatriotic actions of striking miners to an interchangeable cast of radicals.[49] For example, when the federal government proclaimed June 2, 1917, national conscription day, on June 5, Finns, Irish patriots, and Wobblies marched together down Butte's main street in a raucous anti-conscription parade. Protestors had ample opportunity to plan their march, since the groups shared the same meeting hall and many of the same leaders.[50]

Although Butte built upon a much stronger labor tradition than Bisbee, in the summer of 1917, the arrival of federal troops inflamed already volatile labor-management relationships. Furthermore, federal government officials began targeting Wobblies not just in Bisbee or Butte, but nationwide, and the fledgling US Justice Department Bureau of Investigation, renamed the Federal Bureau of Investigation (FBI) in 1935, helped lead these anti-IWW efforts. A young, energetic agent, J. Edgar Hoover, rose to power during this red scare campaign,[51] and Justice Department records in the National Archives are filled with spy reports on IWW organizers, including Embree.[52] Hoover became head of the future FBI in 1924, and he continued the same kinds of policies that had propelled him to power until his death in 1972.

On September 5, 1917, Justice Department officials, with the help of local policemen, raided every IWW office and most IWW leaders' homes across the country, ransacking but also confiscating everything they could find.[53] In 1918, federal prosecutors used these materials as evidence against Wobblies who stood trial in the government's first showcase trial in Chicago, where 113 leading Wobblies were charged with conspiring to undermine the US war effort. That trial set a precedent for other federal IWW trials that followed in Sacramento, Fresno, Omaha, and Wichita.[54] During and after the four-month Chicago trial, Embree divided his time between Chicago and Butte.[55] In Chicago, Embree testified and helped coordinate defense efforts, which IWW leaders seemed determined to turn into a circus, just as they had used their earlier, histrionic free speech fights to spread the IWW gospel. Witness after witness, including Embree (who testified about the Bisbee deportation), chronicled the deplorable conditions the working class faced across the country. Although producing high entertainment value, the IWW defense strategy utterly failed. Almost all the Chicago defendants were found guilty, and the judge handed out maximum sentences to most, including twenty years for Big Bill Haywood. Facing ill health and a lifetime in prison, Haywood

FIGURE 3.6. *Visiting Frank Little's Butte grave turned into an important IWW pilgrimage. The ever-rumpled Embree, standing farthest to the right, brought his son (standing in front of him) to that holy site. Photo from the Fred Thompson papers, Walter P. Reuther Library, Wayne State University, Detroit, Michigan.*

jumped bail and took refuge in the USSR, where he remained until his 1928 death. After the verdicts, once again using his writing talent, Embree wrote the introduction to an IWW-published book intended to defray the costs of the trial and raise money for appeals and bail. The book provided excerpts of trial testimony that Wobblies wanted to publicize, including examples of their persecution, the itinerant habits they were forced to adopt in search of seasonal work, the unfairness of brutal bosses, and the excesses of the idle rich who, for example, thought nothing of conducting elaborate weddings for their jewel-encrusted dogs, all paid for by exploiting workers whose hardships they blindly ignored.[56]

After the Chicago trial ended, Embree returned to Butte and organized strikes there in 1918, 1919, and 1920.[57] In 1917, while Embree was being held captive in New Mexico, a much worse fate had befallen IWW organizer Frank Little in Butte. On August 1, Little was abducted from the IWW hall, dragged from a car, beaten, and hanged from a bridge. That brutal lynching death turned him into an important IWW martyr, second only to Joe Hill in IWW lore. In 1915, Joe Hill, the IWW songwriter, organizer, and activist, had been executed by a Utah firing squad after being convicted—framed, IWW fellow workers claimed—of murdering a grocer during a robbery gone bad. The extralegal Bisbee deportation and Little's lynching convinced Justice Department attorneys they needed a *legal* federal strategy for controlling political dissidents, especially the IWW. Their solution produced the federal IWW trials.[58] The government also expanded its powers by sending federal troops to protect copper production during the war. A year after the war ended, in 1919, remaining troops bayonetted strikers in the IWW hall and on the picket line, actively helping to suppress the IWW strike that year. Furthermore, federal soldiers remained in Butte through January 8, 1921.[59] Nevertheless, Embree and other Wobblies continued organizing.[60]

A 1920 *McClure's* magazine article described Embree as the IWW's "ablest tactician,"[61] an assessment supported by Embree's inventive organization in Butte. He urged workers to pursue dual memberships, so the IWW could have a voice within all active labor organizations. He helped craft strike demands that focused on "bread and butter" issues but also included items such as the release of IWW political prisoners from jail to link those conservative demands to more radical Wobbly goals.[62] Surely learning from the anti-patriotic hysteria directed against the IWW in Bisbee, Embree encouraged strikers to promote their patriotism. For example, he urged veterans to wear their uniforms on the picket line.[63] He also consistently assured workers that the first amendment protected their rights of speech and assembly.

In the walkout that began on April 20, 1920, the following day IWW organizers, including Embree, carried out "dry squad" raids on all Butte saloons and card rooms. That was because, during a strike, there was supposed to be no drinking and no gambling, not even any card playing.[64] The same day, Embree led picketing on the Anaconda Road, outside the main entrance to the Neversweat Mine. The Butte sheriff tried breaking the pickets up, but picketers refused to budge. They declared they had a right to assemble there because it was a public road paid for with road taxes; they even produced their road tax receipts as evidence.[65] Accounts vary about what happened next, but as guards, local law enforcement officials, and picketers began fighting, a barrage of gunshots rang out, and sixteen men were wounded, all picketers shot in the back as they tried to run. One of them, Tom Manning, soon died. Afterward, over two hundred more troops were sent to Butte, intensifying the already oppressive atmosphere. As would be the practice for the next decade or so, a coroner's jury, which functioned to some extent as a grand jury, was convened to investigate Manning's death, and in spite of overwhelming evidence, including an eyewitness who identified the shooters, the jury failed to recommend criminal charges be pursued. On May 12, the strike ended. The miners lost, and for the remainder of the decade, Butte's unions disintegrated, miners' wages fell, and their legendary worker solidarity waned.

After testifying before the coroner's jury, Embree traveled to Idaho to raise bail money and testify on behalf of Wobblies on trial there. In spite of his prominence as an IWW leader, Embree had been remarkably adept at staying out of jail. After his Bisbee acquittal,[66] he dodged espionage and sedition charges in all of the 1918 federal trials. In Spokane, Washington, in April of 1919, he was again indicted alongside twenty other Wobblies, but again, not convicted.[67] His luck, however, was about to run out.

Embree's freedom deeply frustrated Justice Department agent E. B. Sisk, who wrote a letter to his boss suggesting the easiest way to get rid of Embree might be to deport him, since Canadians were British Commonwealth citizens.[68] Although Embree had started the process of applying for American citizenship, taking out his first papers in Nome in either 1909 or 1910, he had not completed it.[69] He started the procedure again in San Diego, but with no witnesses, his paperwork was deemed invalid.[70] Records from the 1917 Bisbee deportation show that Embree had bought Liberty bonds and registered for the US draft, but at the age of forty-two, the married father of two must have understood he was unlikely to be drafted.[71] None of Embree's sporadic efforts made him a citizen, though, which meant, legally, he could be deported.

The biggest problem with the Justice Department's deportation plan was that the Immigration Department, within the Department of Labor, refused to cooperate. A month after Sisk suggested the deportation route for Embree, Sisk again wrote his boss, disappointed, because he had just learned that Immigration officials were instructed *not* to deport anyone solely based upon their IWW membership,[72] a policy that made that department an outlier. From 1917 to 1920, the following entities enthusiastically shared information about Embree, case number 109390: Justice Department officials and agents; local law enforcement agents in Arizona, Montana, Illinois, Washington, and Idaho; the US Postal Service; and Army officers.[73] Through spying, opening mail, and devising any other methods they could think of, this network of governmental officials attempted to gather and share enough evidence to make an arrest stick or to convince Immigration that Embree deserved deportation.

With Immigration flatly refusing to cooperate, Justice Department agents hatched another plan to jail Embree. They would entice him into Idaho, a state with an extremely hostile attitude toward Wobblies, and state officials would arrest him there.[74] When the federal government brought charges against Wobblies, it used federal sedition and treason statutes, but when states brought charges against Wobblies, they invoked state criminal syndicalism violations. Idaho passed the first such law in 1917, and twenty other, mostly Western, states followed suit by 1920.[75] Those laws outlawed individuals associating with others for criminal purposes, but the real intention was to ensnare Wobblies.

Embree was ensnared. On May 25, 1920, in Idaho, immediately after testifying on behalf of Wobblies charged with criminal syndicalism, he himself was arrested for that crime. Afterward, a federal agent contacted the prosecuting attorney, offering to share all the information the Justice Department had amassed on Embree, but the prosecutor politely refused his help. If the case went to trial, he would certainly avail himself of that offer, but "we have not a strong case against Embree, for the reason that it is necessary for us to prove that he organized or attempted to organize the I.W.W. in this county. The officers were over eager and arrested him before he had fairly started."[76]

Meanwhile, Embree's arrest left his family in dire financial straits back in Butte, which created a situation allowing historians a rare glimpse of Embree's home life. With her husband's unexpected absence, Lucy Embree's situation grew so desperate, she asked for and received twenty dollars for grocery money from county officials. The *Butte Post*, friendly to the Anaconda Copper interests, then published an article detailing how the wife of A. S. Embree, "the I.W.W. leader who took a prominent part in the riot on Anaconda Road on the afternoon of April 21, and who testified at the inquest on the body of Thomas Manning, had become a county charge."[77] The article so incensed Lucy, she fired off a response published the following day in the labor-friendly newspaper, The *Butte Daily Bulletin*.[78] Apparently, those two articles triggered a visit from Special Agent D. H. Dickason.

Dickason, misrepresenting himself as a county official, tricked his way into the Embrees' home. He had been instructed by the Butte agent in charge of the Embree investigation to "ascertain the manner in which Embree has provided for her, if ever, by work and so forth."[79] Dickason described Lucy Embree as a nervous, seventy-one-pound woman who held the same radical beliefs as her husband. (How he discovered her weight, his report does not say.) They had two children, a ten-year-old boy and a baby girl. The agent reported that Lucy Embree believed her husband "'got in bad' with the police by trying to stop the boot-leggers," because they were on the take from them. Her husband had been blacklisted as a miner since Bisbee, where she had lost a baby because of the terrible company doctors there. She showed the agent the baby's picture, cried, and "as any mother says," told him that baby "was the sweetest of all." During the interview, the telephone operator called, delivering a telegram from Embree because it was their wedding anniversary. The message was, "Love to the children. I'm all right." The agent ended his report with the following assessment: "She is absolutely loyal to him in every way and entertains his views without reservation. There is no literature nor propaganda work of any kind around the house, just a meagerly furnished poor couple of rooms in an undesirable location. She and the children were poorly dressed. Investigation concluded."[80]

As the special agent snooped around their home, Embree was being released on bail. In spite of its weakness, the prosecutor did not drop Embree's case. In his absence, Justice Department informants "circulated rumors among I.W.W. members that Sam [the name he had begun using] Embree was a 'stool pigeon and a traitor,'"[81] and the whispering campaign seemed to work, since upon his return, he was removed from the Butte IWW organizing committee.[82] Over this year-long period that Embree awaited trial, correspondence between the Wallace County, Idaho, prosecutor and Justice Department agents continued. Agent F. W. Kelly sent the prosecutor photostats of Embree's courtroom testimonies over the years, including the Manning coroner's report. Kelley advised the prosecutor that "Embree is an experienced and cautious witness," so he should be careful if he put Embree on the stand to testify.[83] Not only did federal agents ply the district attorney with information, significantly, a "representative of the Bunker Hill and Sullivan mining company instructed local officials to 'spare no expense in their prosecution of Embree.'"[84]

In 1921, Embree returned to Idaho to stand trial. He was convicted and sent to the Idaho state penitentiary to serve a twenty-six-year sentence. Soon, however, wartime hysteria died down, but more significantly, several excellent defense organizations—including the ACLU and, by 1925, the ILD—were created in reaction to the widespread civil liberties violations that had transpired during the WWI era, and their efforts helped liberate most Wobblies by 1925. Embree was released in 1924, the last Wobbly freed in Idaho.[85] He was on probation for a year, time spent in abject poverty, since he was forbidden to organize, and nobody would hire him. Fortunately, friends offered the family a free place to stay.[86]

In spite of those hardships, Embree remained a dedicated Wobbly, and as soon as he was able, he resumed his IWW career. As he was about to learn, however, while he had been in jail and on probation, the IWW had become a very different organization. After Embree and his family moved to Chicago, the IWW headquarters, they hoped to settle down. Instead, in March of 1926, the IWW General Executive Board (GEB) sent Embree to Colorado to join other IWW leaders who had begun organizing efforts the previous year. His success in organizing Colorado's coalminers would surprise him as much as it did his bosses.

4

The 1927–1928 Colorado Coal Strike

March 1926–October 18, 1927

Soon after his arrival in Colorado in March of 1926, Embree wrote a lengthy report to his IWW bosses. He unequivocally expressed his desire to move back to Chicago, then he assessed Colorado's organizational strengths and weaknesses. Embree recommended several possible organizers who could replace him and do a good job "among the Italians and Slavs who were formerly members of the UMWA," although the "main work is to be done among the Mexicans," since the "Americans and Welsh who are working in the mines are mostly loyal slaves of the companies and it will be practically impossible to line them up in any union except that approved by the boss. But they do not figure largely numerically."[1] He estimated there were 14,000 coalminers in Colorado, although most newspapers reported closer to 12,500. Almost two-thirds of coalminers worked in the southern fields, and "they have proven that they are good material as union men by the battles they have fought in 1913–1914 and other years. Their betrayal by international officials of the U.M.W.A. in 1921–1922 has disgusted them with that organization and they are now willing to listen to what the I.W.W. has to offer."[2]

https://doi.org/10.5876/9781646423026.c004

Remember that when John L. Lewis called the 1921 UMW strike, his primary goal was to pressure operators in the Central Competitive Fields to renew their contracts, although he rhetorically encouraged non-UMW coalminers to join the strike too, because they strengthened his bargaining position. Unorganized coalminers, including those in Pennsylvania and Colorado, went on strike, but when the strike ended and only CCF contracts were renewed, unorganized coalminers felt betrayed. The betrayal Embree referred to resulted in a steep plummet in UMW power and membership, not just in Colorado, but also nationally. In 1920, UMW membership stood at 785,000. By 1928, it had dropped to 80,000,[3] and most of that decline happened after the UMW's 1921–1922 strike.

Even before its nationwide decline, the UMW had mostly abandoned Colorado coalminers after losing the 1910–1914 long strike. Those consequences are described in explicit terms in a December 19, 1924, letter written to John L. Lewis from Frank Hefferly, who had been charged with assessing Colorado's District 15. Hefferly wrote, "As you are doubtless aware, the organization in District Fifteen has dwindled away until it might safely be said that even the district organization, to say nothing of the local unions, has practically ceased to function." The union could account for only two hundred dues-paying members, and even they would not show up for the meetings he tried to convene. Therefore, "As a result of our observations we have arrived at the conclusion that at present very little can be done in the way of building up the organization in District Fifteen."[4]

The IWW sent organizers to Colorado in 1925, and there was enough interest to send Embree in 1926. In June of that year, however, Embree got his wish and returned to Chicago, where he began editing the IWW newspaper *Industrial Solidarity*. He did not last long in that job, however, because the GEB determined he was "incapable of detecting the subtle propaganda" Communists were successfully slipping into the periodical. His bosses said that after being in jail and out of circulation for so long, through no fault of his own, Embree was simply unable to understand the subtle ideological battles that had gone on in his absence. So, once again, the board sent Embree to Colorado.[5]

John S. Gambs's 1932 book, *The Decline of the I.W.W.*, details the IWW's ideological battles that climaxed in the union's 1924 split and its organizational struggles following that division. Gambs also offers his own interpretation of why the GEB sent Embree to Colorado, and we have good reason to trust him on this. He was a PhD economist who taught at Columbia, and his book was a follow-up to the well-regarded 1920 IWW study written by another Columbia PhD economist, Paul F. Brissenden.[6] Gambs could access Brissenden's voluminous research notes on the Wobblies from their origins through 1920 (which, unlike most IWW documents, were *not* confiscated or destroyed during the WWI-era red scare), and he also interviewed many Wobblies in the twenties, probably making him the only researcher studying the IWW in that decade.[7] The following is what Gambs had to say about Embree: "A. S. Embree was looked upon as too strong a man to have near general headquarters in Chicago. He had recently been released from prison; he had a personal following: he was, therefore, a threat to office-seekers and office-holders. Embree was sent to Colorado, presumably, because it seemed a hopeless place to go. It is further alleged by interviewees, that when Embree proved himself to be a successful agitator in Colorado, he was immediately withdrawn from the scene."[8]

My research completely supports Gambs' assessment.[9] Whether or not Embree suspected he was being set up for failure, Embree loyally returned to Colorado, and fellow worker Kristen Svanum soon joined him. After their efforts showed promise, the IWW sent even more organizers, including Paul Seidler and Byron Kitto, although Embree and Svanum remained the nucleus of IWW organization.

Embree and Svanum began their organizing with "missionary work," quiet, door-to-door, person-to-person organizing, easiest to do where coal-miners owned or rented their own homes. "Closed camps"—company towns—were hard to penetrate, since company officials and guards kept those men and their families under close supervision. Strangers were easy to spot, so Embree needed at least one delegate, or organizer, living within each camp, and that delegate needed to be stealthy, or he would get fired. He also needed to speak whatever languages the men in the camps spoke, and increasingly, that meant Spanish. One historian estimates that IWW pamphlets and flyers published in Spanish and English (as they often were) would have reached 86% of the literate coalminers (35% could not read), and organizers who spoke English and Spanish could communicate with 95% of the coalminers.[10] The flood of southern and eastern European immigrants who comprised the majority of workers in Colorado's 1910–1914 long strike

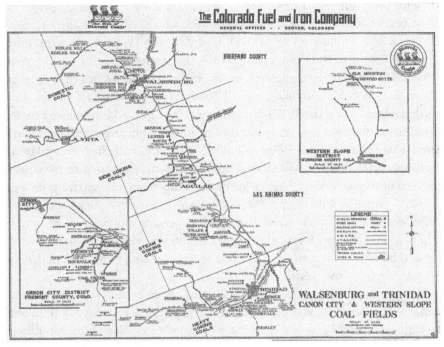

FIGURE 4.1. *This 1931 CF&I map of its coal properties illustrates that the company had already begun to showcase its newly created brand name, Diavolo.*

slowed to a trickle at the outbreak of WWI, then practically dried up with the passage of 1920s' restrictive federal immigration legislation, especially the 1924 National Origins Act. Western agribusinesses, including Great Western Sugar, successfully lobbied politicians to exempt Mexicans from the 1924 act, which led Mexican immigration into the US to explode in that decade, especially in the American Southwest.

Embree first concentrated on organizing Colorado's southern fields' coalminers and chose a Walsenburg storefront for the IWW's headquarters. As membership grew, meetings usually took place after work or on Sundays, the miners' day off, not in the IWW office, but open-air, often at the Ludlow Memorial. Ever since its 1918 dedication through today, the monument has consolidated, reshaped, and rekindled memories of past struggles, providing inspiration for the present. Conversely, for many in Colorado's southern fields, the Ludlow monument also symbolized their betrayal by the UMW. More prosaically, it provided an unsupervised meeting place for people who lived nearby in closed camps. The early 1930s' map below shows the southern Colorado CF&I coalmining region, including Ludlow's location.[11]

By December of 1926, Embree and Svanum had succeeded enough to transition their organization efforts from private to public. To initiate this new phase, they invited Elizabeth Gurley Flynn to speak in Walsenburg, Aguilar, and Pueblo. The thirty-six-year-old Flynn was still known as the Rebel Girl; a nickname Joe Hill gave her in 1915 when she visited the IWW organizer and songwriter in a Utah jail shortly before his execution. Utterly smitten, Hill wrote the song "Rebel Girl" with Flynn in mind, to glorify strong women in the labor movement.

For over twenty years, Flynn spoke on behalf of the Wobblies, following in Mother Jones's footsteps. During Colorado's long strike, the fiery oratory of Mother Jones proved so effective, coal operators collaborated with local law enforcement, who kidnapped and jailed her, to keep her from speaking. She inspired the men, but especially the women and children, to follow her militant example. By the 1920s, as Flynn grew older, times had changed. The oratory she had spent years perfecting grew obsolete as microphones, radios, and motion pictures created new, more intimate methods of communicating with large groups of people. Tiring of the tenuous life of a migratory agitator, Flynn settled down in her hometown of New York City, and instead of agitating from soap boxes or street corners, Flynn formulated policy in boardrooms for the ACLU (which she helped co-found), the ILD, and the IWW's General Defense organization.

Apparently, Flynn could still be persuaded to whip up a crowd as she had in the old days, because she delivered a rousing stem-winder in Walsenburg on December 6, 1926. Afterward, Embree coolly observed that Flynn "gave us a good organization talk in connection with the defense spiel and woke up our members besides enabling us to gather in a few new ones."[12] After her dramatic finale, Embree ceremoniously collected twenty signatures at a midnight business meeting and officially established Colorado's first new IWW chapter.[13] Those members comprised the IWW's core and corps during the strike.[14]

By the summer of 1927, it was time for the IWW to go completely public. By then, close to one thousand Wobblies filled the southern coalfields. Through its spies, CF&I uncovered the identities of many of the organizers and members and began firing them,[15] but as seen on the flyer, the firings and blacklistings were turned into a rallying cry to attract new members.[16] By July, Embree had so successfully organized Colorado's southern fields that he was elected to the IWW General Executive Board, the board that only a year earlier had fired him from editing *Industrial Solidarity*.[17] That same month, Embree served as recording secretary for a district IWW conference in Walsenburg, attended by 167 members representing thirty-six different coal camps, including five in New Mexico. Notably, Embree recorded, but did not lead the meeting. Consistent with Embree's democratic vision of industrial democracy, a central purpose of the meeting was to develop new leaders by training members on how to run meetings, educating new recruits on IWW ideology, and defining the goals for the upcoming strike.

The conference recorded nine resolutions, and significantly, only one related to bread-and-butter issues such as pay and working conditions. The first two resolutions related to John L. Lewis and the UMW. On April 1, 1927, when coal operators refused to renew their UMW contracts, Lewis had called a UMW strike in Pennsylvania, West Virginia, and Ohio, the CCF strongholds of the UMW organization. The IWW resolution declared the strike was going badly because "Eastern owners are shipping western coal [from western Canada, Washington, Montana, Wyoming, Utah, Colorado, and New Mexico] to break the strike."[18] Therefore, the "policy being followed by Lewis and the UMW of A in the present strike," which "tends to divide the coal miners, some of the union districts working, while other union districts are striking," had forced "union men to scab on their brothers," making it "harder for those on strike to resist a cut in wages."[19] *All* coalminers needed to stick together, not follow the suicidal "divide and conquer" tactics that Lewis was responsible for; "Save the Eastern miners and you save yourselves."[20] Resolutions three through six, as well as eight and nine promoted IWW goals: freeing Sacco and Vanzetti, patronizing only union establishments, advocating the six-hour workday, paying their IWW dues, and so on. Only resolution seven, subdivided into five separate items, related to pay and working conditions in the mines.

Less than a month after this conference, coalminers in Colorado's southern fields staged a three-day walkout, and historical interpretations of that strike's significance have surely been shaped by New Labor historian David Montgomery. In *The Fall of the House of Labor*, Montgomery describes post-1922 workers as quiescent, to a large extent because corporate management programs, epitomized by the Rockefeller Plan, had successfully suppressed militant labor unions. In the book's final pages, Montgomery writes that in spite of this quiescence, "There was one issue that linked the beleaguered Left to the sentiments of millions of working people, and that was the defense of Sacco and Vanzetti. By the summer of 1927, when the campaign to prevent execution of the two Italian anarchists by the state of Massachusetts reached a fever pitch, they had come to symbolize for foreign-born workers and their children the contemptuous treatment dealt them by Anglo-Saxon America. . . . *Even* [my emphasis] the miners of Colorado Fuel and Iron struck en masse at the behest of the IWW in protest against the pending execution."[21]

This southern Colorado coalminer walkout was not, however, the anomalous spike of militancy exhibited by submissive workers beaten down by the Rockefeller Plan that Montgomery describes. Instead, this three-day Sacco and Vanzetti walkout signaled the opening salvo of the 1927–1928 Colorado Coal Strike, and because of its scope and effectiveness, this strike, led by the IWW, has been called the most successful strike in Colorado history.[22] I agree. Most coalminers joined, a remarkable statewide unity not seen before or since, and strikers, albeit temporarily (until 1931), won most of their demands, including higher wages and safer working conditions. Their victories were as substantial as they were unusual for the time period.

The Sacco and Vanzetti walkout began on August 8, 1927, and the state's newspapers reported it as "spontaneous." CF&I officials feigned shock, although their blacklists prove they already knew Wobblies were organizing in their camps, and as the poster shows, the IWW used those blacklists as an organizing tool.[23] Internally, they judged the IWW too weak to stage a walkout,[24] and even Embree was unsure of the IWW's strength. Therefore, the Sacco and Vanzetti walkout, while genuinely reflecting workers' passions, also served as a stress test, to gauge organizational strengths and weaknesses.

That test proved that not all of Colorado's coalminers were solidly behind the IWW.[25] Divisions surfaced during the meetings held to vote on the August 8 walkout. In Pueblo, headquarters of Rockefeller's CF&I, state industrial commissioner W. H. Young "attempted to sway the miners from striking" by suggesting that donating four days' pay to the Sacco and Vanzetti defense efforts would be more effective than a walkout. Embree followed

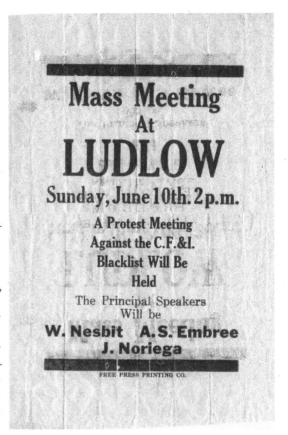

FIGURE 4.2. *Before the "spontaneous" Sacco and Vanzetti walkout in early August, the CF&I already knew there were IWW organizers in its camps, because the company fired and blacklisted them. As the poster shows, the IWW used those blacklistings to strengthen their organizing. ("Mass protest meeting flyer," INR1300-7, Steelworks Archives, Courtesy, Steelworks Center of the West; henceforce referred to simply as Steelworks.)*

Young and told the crowd, "Sacco and Vanzetti don't want your money. They want action."[26] After Embree's speech, the Pueblo crowd voted to walk out. Therefore, the majority of coalminers represented by the Rockefeller Plan seemed ready to join an IWW strike.

Remnants of the UMW were not. As reported in The *Pueblo Chieftan*, "Meeting in the grandstand near the monument which was erected to victims of the Ludlow strike of former days, 1,000 I.W.W. miners and sympathizers, representing eight different camps, this afternoon voted to postpone for 30 days action on the proposed strike in protest against the hanging of Sacco and Vanzetti." E. J. Penno of the *Trinidad Free Press*, "official paper of the United Mine Workers in Southern Colorado," spoke to the crowd, imploring

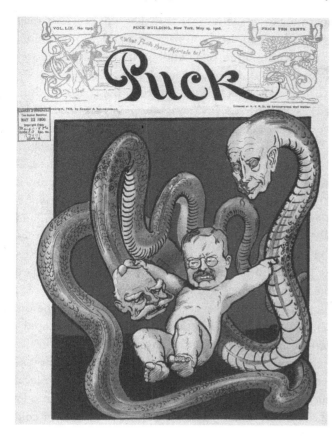

FIGURE 4.3. *In this 1906* Puck *magazine cover, the snake personifies Standard Oil and Rockefeller Sr.; President Theodore Roosevelt wrestles for control. (Frank A. Nankivell [Frank Arthur], "The Infant Hercules and the Standard Oil Serpents,"* Puck, *May 23, 1906, NY: J. Ottmann Lith. Co., Puck Bldg., access through the Library of Congress.)*

them to follow the thirty-day strike notice required by the state's industrial commission and to support Governor Billy Adams, who had recently been elected with their votes.[27] His arguments carried the day, so Embree and Svanum still had work to do. That required addressing Penno's spoken and unspoken appeals to memories and consequences of the long strike, the legal requirements of the Colorado Industrial Commission, and 1920s state politics.

Colorado's long strike began in 1910, after the Northern Coal Company refused to renew its contract with the UMW. The strike so distressed the company's finances that John Roche, Josephine Roche's father, and a partner acquired the struggling company, which in 1911 they renamed the Rocky

Mountain Fuel Company. They made it clear that, like the previous management, they also intended to run their company as an open (non-union) shop.[28] By 1913, after two tumultuous years and spirited internal debates within the UMW headquarters, UMW organizers John R. Lawson and Ed Doyle were directed to shift their strike efforts south, to the coalfields dominated by the state's largest coal producer, CF&I, whose largest shareholder was John D. Rockefeller Jr. Labor leaders, progressives, and the general reading public already reviled John D. Rockefeller Sr., thanks to Ida Tarbell's methodically researched book, published in 1904, *The History of the Standard Oil Company*, one of the era's most influential exposés. Tarbell documented how Rockefeller's ruthless business practices consolidated his monopoly over the entire US oil industry, and the name Rockefeller became shorthand, signifying concentrated power in the hands of a few. Progressive outrage against Rockefeller and Standard Oil inspired President Theodore Roosevelt to target the company for federal investigation.[29] By 1909, most of Standard Oil was dissolved, along with Rockefeller Sr.'s reputation.

John D. Rockefeller Jr. actually viewed himself as a progressive. Before the strike, at the CF&I, he had built model company housing and created a sociological department aimed at improving the physical and mental health of employees and their families. As soon as CF&I coalminers joined the strike in 1913, however, local company officials, working closely with local politicians and law enforcement, quickly evicted residents from their model company houses, and the UMW moved the newly homeless into tent colonies for the duration of the strike.

The winter of 1913–1914 was one of the snowiest on record, with areas of the state receiving over forty-five inches of snow. In spite of, or maybe because of, those harsh living conditions, striking coalminers and their families formed strong community ties, bound together by a strong sense of solidarity. Furthermore, both sides of the conflict were armed to the teeth, with Winchester .30-30s as the weapon of choice, which helped turn the walkout into probably the deadliest strike in the nation's history. The most infamous incident during the strike remains the Ludlow Massacre, and after it, the same forces that had vilified Rockefeller Sr. began vilifying his son. In spite of the Ludlow publicity, when the strike sputtered to an end in December of 1914, coalminers lost all their demands, including their central one, representation by the UMW.

FIGURE 4.4. *One young boy living in the Ludlow tent colony posed for this photo after the record-setting snowstorm that made the lives of strikers and their families more miserable, strengthened their resolve, or perhaps both. ("Ludlow Massacre—Tent Colony," courtesy of Denver Public Library Digital Collections, X-60352.)*

That strike loss and the Great War led to a complete shift in UMW policies and leadership, a transformation that can be traced through the pages of *The UMW Journal* between 1916 and 1918. For example, in 1916, almost every issue included at least one article opposing militarism and a page devoted to public service announcements, including notices from UMW members looking for lost union cards, or occasionally, wives looking for their lost UMW husbands. By 1917, the journal expanded from twenty to almost thirty pages per issue, and slicker production values paralleled slicker content. Most of the personal announcements disappeared, and cautiously patriotic articles replaced the stridently anti-militaristic ones. These shifts in the *UMW Journal* reflected new national attitudes as super-patriotism swept the country, but more significantly, they document the meteoric rise of John L. Lewis. In 1920, UMW vice president Lewis assumed the office of UMW president after the resignation of president Frank Hayes, who helped lead Colorado's long strike. In their excellent Lewis biography, Melvyn Dubofsky and Warren Van Tine analyze how Lewis began, then consolidated his control over the UMW when, beginning in 1917, Lewis oversaw the content of the *UMW Journal* and worked alongside AFL president Samuel Gompers on

World War I policies. Dubofsky and Van Tine document how, after Hayes's resignation in 1920, Lewis consolidated his power by "appropriating" United Mine Workers districts, which meant the UMW headquarters took over the local district's finances and replaced its leadership with Lewis's hand-picked officers. Ironically, as Lewis consolidated his power, he increasingly had less to control, since UMW membership plummeted throughout the decade, declines that, to a great extent, were a consequence of his increasingly dictatorial policies.

What Dubofsky and Van Tine omit is that Lewis began that appropriation policy in Colorado before he was even UMW president. On February 15, 1917, the *UMW Journal* ran a long, positive article, including a distinguished-looking headshot, that introduced readers to Lewis, the UMW's new statistician. On page 11, almost buried in the fine print, the journal also published the UMW's new policy:

International Organization Takes Over Dependent Districts

In accordance with the action of the international executive board, the international organization has assumed direction of all the districts under its jurisdiction that are not self-supporting.

Efficient organizers have been selected to take charge of the officers of these districts and to carry forward a campaign looking toward complete organization.

Vice-President Hayes, International Statistician John L. Lewis and International Board Member Robert H. Harlin are now in Colorado and will co-operate with those in the district who desire to bring about full and complete organization of the miners there. Other competent organizers will be selected by the committee of internationals officials to further the work toward unionism.[30]

Of course, the reason Colorado's District 15 was broke was because, for four years, it had been waging the UMW-authorized long strike. At any rate, UMW vice president Hayes, Lewis, and Robert Harlin took over District 15's finances. In a power-grabbing, unethical process too byzantine to explain here, they also finagled the removal of John Lawson and Ed Doyle, District 15 president and secretary-treasurer, respectively. Although revered by coalminers for their fearless leadership during the long strike, the UMW headquarters' team replaced them with out-of-state appointees. In the April 14 *Journal*, six days before the Ludlow commemoration would take place, a long article ran, praising the Hayes-Lewis-Harlin trio for "bloodlessly" negotiating a three-year contract with the Victor-American Fuel Company, the second largest coal company in the state. It sunnily predicted this new agreement would soon bring a new day in the Colorado coal fields and replace the Rockefeller Plan.[31] Yet less than a month after that contract was signed, on April 27, 1917, an explosion killed 121 coalminers working at the Hastings coalmine near Ludlow, a Victor-American property.[32] It was the worst coalmining accident in the state's history. Not only had the new UMW contract failed to create a new day in Colorado's coalfields or replace the Rockefeller Plan, it also had not improved safety conditions at the Hastings mine. Furthermore, newspapers reported that John Lawson, recently deposed and humiliated by UMW headquarters, rushed to the scene to help with recovery efforts. No mention was made whether UMW officials arrived from Indianapolis to provide aid. After that tragedy, the UMW's grand promises for Colorado quietly disappeared from the journal's pages, and Victor-American did not renew its UMW contract when it expired.

Soon after the Hastings deaths, which went un-commemorated, the UMW began a widespread campaign encouraging members to contribute to a monument that would be built at the Ludlow Massacre site. Eleven months later, the monument was complete. In 1918, the dedication ceremony took place *not* on April 20, the anniversary of the massacre, but on the Civil War commemoration day, Memorial Day. Most of the Ludlow strike leaders—including John Lawson, Ed Doyle, and Mother Jones—did not attend the ceremony, surely because they had not been invited. A few months before the dedication, in reaction to their undemocratic ouster from their UMW leadership positions, Lawson and Doyle had formed a local, independent coalminers' union, and for that betrayal, they were permanently expelled from the UMW.

Although Mother Jones was not fired—at least not officially—from her UMW organizer position, there was no love lost between her and Lewis, whom she called "the general Jesus of the movement" and "an empty piece of human slime." She hated him and the style of unionism he represented, saying that "If the organization ever gets into the hands of this fella that is the end of the miners."[33] Lewis had little use for Mother Jones, either, or for other militant women who had been so important during the Ludlow strike.

FIGURE 4.5. *Although this photo is undated, it is clear from the surroundings that the monument has just been built.*

The Ludlow tent colony had been constructed next to a site where scabs disembarked from trains, and while the armed, striking coalminers were away skirmishing with their foes, women and children were charged with intimidating potential strikebreakers from disembarking, which often meant throwing rocks, or worse, at them. Yet the Ludlow Monument permanently portrays an idealized version of UMW-style domesticity that Lewis consistently promoted. A strong man stands proud and independent, clothed not in mining gear, but in everyday work clothes. Off to his side cowers a classically garbed, submissive everywoman (with great gams), who hovers protectively over their child.[34] Clearly, by May of 1918, with the quick construction and dedication of the Ludlow Monument, Lewis and the UMW had already begun reappropriating the memories of Ludlow.

After Ludlow, the Colorado Democrats and Republicans, bereft of any constructive plans of their own, deferred to the Progressives, led by reformers including Costigan, Vincent, Lindsey, and Roche, who absolutely brimmed with ideas. In their 1914 Colorado party platform, they recommended establishing a group of experts who would mediate labor disputes, so violence like the Ludlow Massacre would never happen again.[35] The commission would consist of three people chosen by the governor to represent the three perceived interests involved in labor disputes: business, labor, and the public. Furthermore, rules would specify how, when, and under what conditions workers could strike or employers could raise or lower wages. Colorado Progressives hoped the new commission would become a model for achieving industrial democracy.

Unsurprisingly, the technocratic ideal of reasonable, dispassionate experts determining fair labor policies failed, and fairly quickly, too. Just five years after its creation, the commission did not prevent the bloody 1920 Denver Tramway strike, in which city and state officials provided guns to professional strikebreakers who subsequently shot into a crowd, killed seven innocent bystanders, and wounded many more. Holdover World War I-era hysteria helped fuel that overreaction, since Denver's mayor enlisted the American Legion to aid the strikebreakers, and the tramway company produced widely circulated, incendiary pamphlets blaming the strike on the IWW, which apparently played no role in the strike.[36] The same governor who helped crush the tramway strike, Republican Oliver Henry Shoup, successfully pushed the passage of a 1920 law that outlawed picketing, and he also created a state military police force everybody called the "Rangers." Subsequently, the Rangers helped suppress the 1921–1922 coalmining strike in Colorado, another outrage the industrial commission did nothing to prevent.

In the 1926 gubernatorial election, most industrial workers supported Adams because he ran against former governor Shoup. Probably since little else differentiated them—both candidates were "dry" (supporting prohibition) and fiscal conservatives—Adams revived Shoup's anti-labor record, especially his creation of the Rangers, and that helped rally workers to his

FIGURE 4.6. *The photo shows the procession of fully robed Klansman marching to their 1926 convention. ("Parade in Denver preceding a convention of Klansmen," May 31, 1926, courtesy of Denver Public Library Special Collections, X-21543.)*

behalf.[37] Workers also supported him because, as a Democratic state senator and minority leader, Adams had mobilized enough votes to keep newly elected KKK politicians from achieving much legislative success during their heyday. In 1923–1924, Colorado voters elected a wide swath of Klan members, including a federal senator, a governor, and the Denver mayor, who, in turn, used his authority to appoint a Klan police chief. Serving from 1925–1927, Governor Clarence Morley's campaign slogan had been "Every Man under the Capitol Dome a Klansman,"[38] and in 1926, he even led a procession of five hundred fully robed Klansmen down Denver's 16th Street, the city's main civic thoroughfare.

Although Morley tried rewarding his KKK supporters with plum political appointments, the state's strict civil service rules (enacted by Progressives) severely thwarted his efforts. On June 10, 1925, however, he "evoked a forgotten antiliquor law and commissioned fifty-two prohibition agents" that ballooned to a force of almost two hundred men by year's end. Publicly, he created the prohibition police to enforce state and federal prohibition laws. Privately, he created the force to "repay campaign debts, provide employment for jobless Klansmen, and to honor the realm's leading men."[39]

The prohibition officers quickly turned into a secret police force. In Denver, they harassed political opponents. Farther afield, in the southern coalfields near Trinidad, they "battered in the doors of fifty homes without identifying themselves, drew revolvers, and lined up the frightened men and women for search," actions they repeated in Weld County, the location of the northern coalfields and Great Western Sugar beet fields worked by Mexican contract labor.[40] By December 31, 1925, public indignation forced the governor to disband the prohibition police, although Morley still retained their services as an honorary, non-salaried guard. When Adams became governor, he very publicly disbanded this much-hated group, although, as we shall soon see, the governor's executive authority to reconstitute the officers remained in place.[41]

In August of 1927, E. J. Penno was able to convince coalminers not to join the Sacco and Vanzetti walkout by imploring them to support Governor Adams and urging them to adhere to the rules required by the state industrial commission. In an organizing move clearly meant to appeal to those resistant workers who heeded Penno's appeals, IWW leaders meticulously followed the rules of the Colorado Industrial Commission (CIC) when preparing and submitting their strike announcement, which they revealed at a conference on September 4, chaired by Kristen Svanum. Members laid out their demands, which carefully included only the bread-and-butter demands from their July list and omitted anything that referred to the IWW, Lewis, or the UMW.[42] As required by law, the group submitted the strike petition thirty days in advance. The petitioners, however, did not identify themselves as representatives of the IWW, surely because there was so much prejudice against that union. Instead, they called themselves the All State Conference of Colorado Coal Mines.[43]

Although the petitioners scrupulously followed CIC rules, commissioners rejected the petition. Furthermore, Governor Adams turned out not to be such a friend of labor after all. After his victory, Adams appointed Thomas Annear, the head of the state Democratic Party, to chair the commission.[44] Although Annear was considered sympathetic to labor, appointing any political operative represented an act of pure political patronage, the opposite of the technocratic ideal Progressives envisioned in 1915 when they tried to civilize capitalism with their proposed industrial commission. All three commissioners, including Annear, agreed that the committee presenting the petition did not legally represent the coalminers, because it was a front for the IWW, which was not a bona fide (code for AFL) labor organization. Therefore, *any* petition it presented to the commission would *always* be illegal, whether submitted legally or not.[45]

The commissioners' intransigence consolidated worker solidarity among coalminers still loyal to the UMW, and it also gave the IWW the gift of time. Organizers moved the strike date from October 8 to October 18. "Ostensibly, the reason for the change was to allow time to take a strike vote. Actually, the committee planned to use the time organizing the northern field, and thus increase the scope and effectiveness of the walkout."[46] As they had in the southern Colorado coalfields, IWW organizers in the north tailored their messages to Mexicans, which included not just those who mined coal, but also the newly recruited families who labored in the nearby beet fields. On October 11, the *Daily Camera* in Boulder ran an article describing IWW literature circulating in Spanish and English "that tells the Mexican field workers that they were the first owners of this western land, that they got here before the English, and that they could take it back. All they need do is organize. They are being organized, too."[47]

Events escalated quickly. Coal operators submitted a petition to the CIC to raise coalminer wages and, on October 14, the commission approved a sixty-eight-cent a day raise,[48] but it was too little too late, since coalminer discontent concerned far more than wages. For example, four days before the walkout officially began, in Lafayette (the northern strike headquarters,) Mrs. McCready, the Lafayette High School music teacher, was kidnapped, driven around with a bag over her head, and dumped on the side of the road. The Boulder *Daily Camera* reported the incident was believed to be "the outgrowth of bitterness that exists in Lafayette from activities of the late Ku Klux Klan of which McCready is said to have been a member."[49] According to a 1970s Lafayette oral history, McCready's husband, Lafayette's school superintendent, was also a Klan member, as were most of the town's prominent citizens, including all the school board members and several teachers, affiliations that the first and increasingly second generation of immigrant parents and their children clearly loathed. Just a few years before the 1927–1928 strike,

Klan members burned crosses in front of Lafayette's Catholic church, as well as in the company town of Serene, where many immigrants lived.[50] Stories circulated of KKK members kidnapping their victims, putting bags over their heads, and scaring the daylights out of them, so it appeared the Klan's former targets were giving their former tormentors a taste of their own medicine. No hard proof exists that IWW organizers condoned scaring Mrs. McCready, but upon her release, she did renounce her Klan membership. Clearly, less than a week before the strike officially began, the northern Colorado community could feel the power structures shifting over issues relating to much more than coalminer pay.

Local power structures began shifting in the southern fields, too. On October 17, Walsenburg mayor John Pritchard led a mob of seventy-five businessmen to the town's IWW's headquarters. Someone in the crowd tossed a brick through the plate glass window, and the group ransacked the office. They "burned all the literature and office records and books found in the building" in the street, then posted a resolution on the door, ordering the organizers to leave town immediately.[51] Just a decade earlier, such actions would have constituted official federal government policies, but this lawless raid only solidified support for the strike vote the following day. In Lafayette, the meeting grew so large that Embree relocated it from the old UMW hall, newly re-christened the IWW hall, to the local ballpark to accommodate the estimated four thousand people who converged to cast their ballots.[52] Both fields, north and south, voted to go on strike the same day, a unity never achieved during the 1910–1914 long strike. The next day, coalminers across the state walked off their jobs, officially beginning the 1927–1928 Colorado Coal Strike.

5

The 1927–1928 Colorado Coal Strike

October 18, 1927–November 4, 1927

The first day of the strike, Colorado State Federation of Labor president Earl Hoage acknowledged that the coalminers had legitimate grievances, but said since the IWW was a "renegade, radical organization," the federation, which represented AFL unions (including the UMW), would take no part in the strike.[1] On October 19, Thomas Annear, the state industrial commissioner appointed to represent labor, made a statement on behalf of the entire commission. It declared the northern Colorado strike illegal, because coalminers did not provide thirty-days' notice to the commission. Although the southern coalfield miners *had* provided the required notice, their petition was deemed illegal because an investigation indicated those who signed did not represent the coalminers.[2]

The coal operators agreed with the commissioners. On October 19, Merle Vincent released a statement, delivered on behalf of *all* Colorado coal operators. The statement agreed with the findings of the state industrial commission's investigation. The IWW did not represent the miners. Alluding to the Walsenburg raid, Vincent acknowledged it was "regrettable" that citizens

https://doi.org/10.5876/9781646423026.c005

had "seen fit to take the law into their own hand," because those actions not only violated "law and order," they also undermined "confidence in our public officials" that "naturally invites resentment and encourages retaliatory acts of some kind." Such "lawlessness immediately aroused widespread sympathy for the I.W.W. among miners who do not belong to the I.W.W. and oppose its methods." Vincent stated that Colorado coal operators intended "to observe the law," which outlawed both the strike and picketing, and he hoped the striking coalminers would do the same.[3]

It is especially significant that Vincent delivered the coal operators' statement. Not only did he work for Josephine Roche, who future historians would assert did everything in her power to prevent violence during the strike, it appears that Vincent himself wrote most of the 1914 plan that Progressives proposed for establishing the CIC.[4] Perhaps Vincent was so invested in the CIC's success that he could not see it had already failed to achieve its original purposes, arbitrating labor disputes and preventing labor violence. Ignoring the declarations from Colorado's AFL, the CIC, and coal operators, who all declared the strike illegal, on October 19, the majority of Colorado coalminers did not report for work.

When the strike began, Denver's two major dailies, the conservative-leaning *Denver Post* and the progressive-leaning *Rocky Mountain News*, were in the throes of a circulation war, so trying to out-sensationalize the other for much of the strike's four-month duration, news of the walkout appeared on the front pages of both, often accompanied with elaborate photo collages or political cartoons about the walkout or its leaders. Locally, as well as nationally, newspapers showed particular fascination with the strike's militant women, often labeling them "Amazons."

Labeling militant women *Amazons* was nothing new. As early as the late 1800s, newspapers used the term in attempts to condescendingly transform rebellious women from threats into jokes, and this strike proved no different.[5] On October 21, the *Daily Camera* in Boulder, the major town in the northern coalfields, reported that out of sixty pickets arrested in southern Colorado, twenty were "chattering women," one with a "suckling babe at her breast" who "led the strikers' 'victory' chorus in the plaintive strains of 'Solidarity,' battle cry of the radicals."[6] By the next day, the newspaper described those same women as rock-hurling Amazons.[7] Fifty more southern coalfield arrests followed two days later. Santa Benash, identified as an Amazon, led a group of protestors up Berwind Canyon, the location of many closed camps, and they were arrested after they "staged a riot."[8] Newspapers also labeled Benash's older sister, Milka Sablich, an Amazon, but the press soon assigned her more personalized nicknames, including "The Girl in Red" and "Flaming Milka," reflections of 1920s' celebrity culture. In the melee described above, sheriffs on horseback trampled Sablich, breaking several of her bones. On October 29, the *Denver Post* ran a photograph of the hospitalized, smiling, yet defiant Sablich on the front page superimposed next to Byron Kitto, a young, attractive male IWW organizer, falsely suggesting they were romantically linked.[9]

Sablich and Kitto certainly would have made an odd couple. Kitto was a law student in San Francisco when he joined the IWW. He moved to Boston to work on the IWW's Sacco and Vanzetti defense committee, then was sent to Colorado. Although newspapers called him a publicity man, all IWW organizers did whatever was needed, including speaking. We have no copies of speeches delivered during the almost-constant mass meetings during the strike, but listeners noted that Kitto's style differed from other IWW speakers. Older Wobblies, including Embree, developed their speaking chops during the free speech movements when, literally standing on soapboxes, they projected loudly and dramatically to attract and hold a crowd's attention. Over a decade later, Kitto spoke in a more intimate way, incorporating 1920s' slang that made him sound modern.[10] His speech, education, good looks, and charisma made him an important new IWW leader during the strike.

Sablich emerged from a very different background. The seven-year-old had lived in the southern Colorado RMFC coalmining company town of Forbes with her parents before moving to a tent colony during the long strike. (In the Ten-Day War following Ludlow, coalminers attacked Forbes and killed at least eleven strikebreakers there. During their rampage, their reported battle cry had been, "Remember Ludlow!")[11] Sablich would have heard oft-repeated stories of the long strike, but she had been old enough to form her own strike memories, too.[12] When the IWW walkout began, Sablich worked in a laundry, the kind of low paid, domestic work coalminers' daughters often did before marriage, frequently for other coalminers.[13] The strike, however, lifted Sablich out of her mundane existence, revealing untapped leadership qualities. Sablich-led protests usually began at the Ludlow Monument

FIGURE 5.1. *Although newspaper descriptions titillated readers with stories of wild, riot-inducing Amazons, this photo taken of women marching in Lafayette during the strike looks pretty tame.*

before proceeding up Berwind Canyon, where the Ten-Day War had raged, so she directly linked the past to the present by becoming a fascinating and fearsome symbol of the strike.

Militant women of the 1927–1928 Colorado Coal Strike followed in the footsteps of women including Elizabeth Gurley Flynn but also, more importantly, Mother Jones. When Mother Jones was jailed during the long strike, women in Trinidad staged a protest parade that devolved into the "Mother Jones riot." Photographs taken by a UMW organizer document guardsmen on horseback charging into the procession of marching women, which made the soldiers look like fools and bullies.[14] No wonder Sablich had stood her ground when confronted by soldiers on horseback who charged into their demonstration. How could she do less than the women from the long strike?

Whether accurate or not, the portrayal of women in the 1927–1928 Colorado Coal Strike as Amazons was hardly a localized phenomenon.[15] Newspapers in Chicago, New York City, and perhaps other cities ran stories about the strike's Amazons. For example, a *New York Times* story about the riot at the Ideal

Mine reported that "ten women advanced on a group of twelve mounted and armed guards" at the mine, "hurling stones and daring them to 'start something,' . . . [as] thirty men pickets remained behind in motor cars while the Amazons took the offensive."[16] The article concluded by describing an especially active picketer, a "20-year-old bobbed haired Mexican girl, known as Rosia," like this: "A dirt-begrimed brown felt hat pulled down over her shorn tresses, she has trudged forth daily to help wage the conversational battle that has kept scores of men from the mines. Two of her brothers were killed in the bloody days of the 1913–1914 Colorado coal strike." In other words, Rosia, a dirty, Amazon, Mexican flapper convinced strikebreakers not to scab based on her memories of Ludlow. Remember Ludlow, indeed.

Ten days into the strike, an unusual story appeared in the *Denver Post*, and it shows Roche's earliest public relations efforts to spin strike coverage in her favor. By 1927, her WWI Committee on Public Information and Children's Bureau work had turned Roche into a seasoned public relations specialist, and this article had her fingerprints all over it. The title established the feature's bifurcated premise: "Strikers Hear Rival Calls of Two Women: 'Girl in Red' Urges Them to Attack Mines, While Josephine Roche, Owner of the Fuel Company, Invites Them to Parley on Wages."[17] Note that Roche is identified as owner of the RMFC, a distinction worth keeping in mind since Roche herself, future press releases, and historians would claim that Roche did *not* control the company at the time of the Columbine Massacre. The battle lines between the two women and what they represented were clear:

"Carry on!" shouts the Polish radical, Milka Sablicsh [*sic*], to the coal miners of the southern fields.

"Come let us confer together!" says the American, Josephine Roche, to the coal miners of the northern district.

Which will win? The contest is as clearly between two women as between striking miners and mine operators.[18]

Polish or American? Radical, nineteen-year-old strike leader or forty-year-old "college graduate, social worker"? An unknown teenager, whose last name the newspapers misspelled, or a woman "with a long record of public service and of personal fortitude"?[19] Not just who but where would the battle be decided? In the Southern coalfields (which were implicitly militant since that was where the Ludlow Massacre had taken place) or in the northern (and implicitly more conservative) coalfields? Which archetype of woman-hood would prevail, the lawless Amazon Sablich, or the anti-Amazon Roche?

Two days before the Roche feature appeared in the *Denver Post*, on October 26, Governor Adams issued his first official statement on the walkout, and it was a convoluted mess. He said, "An unfortunate condition exists in the coal fields of the State by reason of the I.W.W., an un-American organization, having attempted to bring about a strike, and in this attempt has openly and publicly advocated and practiced defiance and violation of the law." Like the industrial commissioners and operators, Adams denied the ongoing strike was even taking place, yet he added, "Picketing and intimidation are unlaw-ful." He was correct. Picketing was illegal because the state outlawed it in 1920, during the anti-labor administration of Governor Shoup. Adams next made what was a startling statement coming from a politician who had cam-paigned for governor as a friend of labor: "Every man has a right to quit work if so inclined. Every man has an equal right to work and is entitled to protection in that right." Adams concluded his tortured statement with an ominous threat. If at any time the local officers were unable to main-tain peace, "the State stands ready and will give them any and all assistance necessary, and use every instrument within the power of the Governor to both enforce the law and protect life and property."[20] Unfortunately, Adams simply did not have many instruments within his power to use, since, at his urging, the state budget had been slashed to the bone. If he chose to call up the Colorado National Guard as Colorado Governor Ammons had done in 1913 during the long strike, the state would have to pass a special bond to pay them. As it had during the long strike, a relatively weak state government, hampered by extreme fiscal conservatism, would soon lead to strike violence.

Much of what went wrong at Ludlow was tied to stingy state funding. When the state of Colorado could not meet its National Guard payroll, the regular guardsmen, understandably, went home. By the spring of 1914, the newly constituted National Guard consisted of an agglomeration of mine guards, out-of-work cowboys, private Baldwin-Felts guns-for-hire, local sher-iffs, and Guardsmen willing to work without pay, and the motives of men who *wanted* to work without financial remuneration should have been a flag big and red enough not to hire them.[21] As the saying goes, you get what you pay for, so had Colorado been willing to pay for a professional, relatively unbiased National Guard to work in the strike zone, perhaps things might have gone differently during the long strike.

That Colorado stinginess had not changed appreciably since 1913. Governor Adams promised fiscal conservatism, and to that pledge, but not so much to others, he stayed true. He supported the state when it aggressively slashed corporate taxes, even for enormously profitable companies. For example, Great Western Sugar protested the Boulder County assessor's valuations in 1925, 1926, and 1927, and each of those years, the state equalization board overrode the county, reducing the corporation's tax bill by almost five million dollars over that three-year period.[22] Even in flush economic times, Colorado simply did not have much money. Furthermore, at Adams's request, the state legislature passed a stripped-down, two-year appropriations bill coinciding with his term. Part of that budget allocated $18,400 annually to fund a state police force in case of emergencies.[23] Adams would soon discover, as had Ammons before him, that lack of funds would lead to tragedy in the coalfields.

From day one, Adams tried to fight the strike on the cheap. At first, that meant leaving all strike control measures in the hands (and budgets) of local law enforcement agencies and coal companies. For example, when four thousand people met in the Lafayette ballpark for the strike vote, not everybody went home after the meeting. Some camped out around the Columbine, and their campfires so unnerved the Weld County sheriff that the next day he authorized twenty "special deputies" to guard that coalmine.[24] Even with the extra men, the sheriffs were overwhelmed, understaffed, and underfunded, and as the strike continued, local resources would grow increasingly strained, especially as IWW protests escalated.

Between the first day of the walkout, and the day coalminers voted to end their strike on February 19, 1928, A. S. Embree and other Wobblies used tried-and-true organizing methods and invented new ones to close the coalmines, keep supporters' morale high, and expand their strong coalition of strike supporters. Old organizing methods included picketing and mass rallies, but with a modern twist, since widespread use of telephones and automobiles allowed quick communication and mobilization.

The main purpose of picketing is to discourage—or as its opponents, such as Governor Adams or coal operators would say, intimidate—strikebreakers from going to work and breaking a strike. Picketing also builds morale and solidarity. Relatively few mines stayed open during the strike, but where they did, pickets congregated. In the north, the RMFC's Columbine was the only large coalmine that remained open, and it was surrounded by the company town of Serene. Unlike most southern closed camps—geographically isolated from nearby Trinidad, Walsenburg, or Pueblo—Serene was within walking distance of several towns, including Lafayette and Erie, and connected by good roads to nearby Boulder, Denver, and Longmont. Picketers could converge on foot or by car as strikebreakers were readying for work at the Columbine and then go home, something much harder for picketers in southern Colorado to do.

The first two weeks of the strike, coal companies determined their own policies toward picketing and made their own arrangements with local law enforcement. Operators, including those at the RMFC, pressured strikebreaking coalminers to become mine guards, although at least some resisted those reassignments.[25] Even with extra guards, CF&I could not stop picketing, so company officials closed coalmines where it occurred.[26] Surely, the history surrounding the Ludlow Massacre entered into the company's decisions. Although the RMFC did not directly challenge the pickets—not at first—company management chose to keep the Columbine open by employing scab labor, even as the crowds marching through Serene grew larger, more raucous, and increasingly effective at converting strikebreakers into strikers. Furthermore, local Weld County sheriffs did not fight the strike very aggressively. For example, on November 4, carloads of pickets parked on the highway outside the Columbine turnoff, blocking commuting strikebreakers from entering the compound for their morning shift. By the time the sheriffs arrived, the pickets were gone, and even though the sheriffs almost certainly knew who the picketers were, they did not pursue them.[27] Sheriffs probably were sympathetic to the strikers because many had previously mined coal and they did not want trouble with their neighbors.

Although Colorado outlawed picketing in 1920 and the United States Supreme Court did not decide that picketing was constitutional until 1940,[28] strikers and their supporters, especially during mass meetings, were constantly reminded that the first amendment allowed free speech and assembly. IWW organizers' reasoning went like this: Marchers had a right to march, and drivers had a right to drive on public roads. Strikers and their supporters also had the right to hold meetings where even private roads led to facilities

FIGURE 5.2. *Even with the poor quality, this photo shows a very diverse student population of public-school students who attended school inside the Columbine coal camp. (Courtesy of "Joe Bear" Beranek and Betty Shapowal Beranek when I interviewed them in 2004.)*

that included public buildings. Since almost all the coal camps had federal post offices and public schools, including Serene, built around the Columbine coalmine, not only did Wobblies have the right to hold meetings and parades inside the camps, they were also patriotically exercising their constitutional rights when they did.[29] The IWW reinforced that patriotic appeal by making sure American flagbearers led all their picketing and American flags festooned their meetings and automobiles.[30]

The 1920s proved a landmark decade for establishing first amendment rights, and most of the significant cases that came before the Supreme Court related to civil liberties violations were brought by groups representing organized labor. In 1925, in the first case the ACLU argued before the Supreme Court, *Gitlow v. New York*, the justices incorporated the first amendment. Incorporation is the "constitutional doctrine through which the first ten amendments of the United States Constitution, the Bill of Rights, are made applicable to the states through the Due Process clause of the Fourteenth Amendment."[31] This incorporation doctrine revolutionized civil liberties. On May 16, 1927, in *Fiske v. Kansas*, again using incorporation, the Supreme Court held that Wobblies' first amendment rights had been violated when state criminal syndicalism laws assumed criminal intent flowed from the IWW preamble. Had the Supreme Court made that ruling during the World War I red scare, neither Embree nor hundreds of other Wobblies would have been convicted and jailed. Unfortunately for the IWW organizers in Colorado, although judges seemed aware of *Fiske*, everybody else mostly ignored it. Therefore, the IWW's constitutional arguments worked only slightly better for them in 1927 and 1928 as they had during the progressive era and the World War I-era red scare. No matter how many American flags they carried in their parades, waved at their rallies, or draped on their cars, during the strike, the CIC, Governor Adams, the coal operators, local sheriffs, the strike police, and outraged private citizens' groups regarded the IWW as un-American and their actions as violations of the law.

Along with using tried-and-true methods of picketing and rallies, Embree employed new organizational tactics during the strike. Perhaps his most significant innovation was assembling a powerful strike coalition that worked alongside the IWW. Coalition members included the ACLU, the ILD, and their network of allies. Reverend A. A. Heist headed the Colorado ACLU, and he worked closely with the IWW throughout the strike.[32] Heist had begun his pastoral career with the Methodist Federation for Social Service, and Grace Community Church in Denver hired Heist away from his Washington state pastorate, where he made a name for himself advocating for Wobblies during their Pacific Northwest WWI-era persecution. Heist's Colorado network included Ben Mark Cherrington, founder and director of the Social Science Foundation at the University of Denver, and Cherrington's students, who conducted field research during the strike, interviewing at least 250 striking coalminers, as well as coal operators, including Vincent.[33] Heist also directed the Denver Labor College, which held its classes at Grace, and two of its teachers included John Lawson, the former long strike hero, and Frank Palmer, who wrote for and edited the *Colorado Labor Advocate*, which published news about the state's AFL unions.

FIGURE 5.3. *This photo features several members of the 1927 "B team" labor delegation that visited the USSR. Written on the bottom of the photo is: "Back row: Bob Dunn, Interpreter, Jas. Fitzpatrick, Frank Palmer [note that he is wearing a Russian-style shirt]; Front Row—Paul Douglas, Jas. Maurer, Jno. Brophy, Albert Coyle—Russians." (Courtesy of John Brophy papers, The American Catholic History Research Center and University Archives, Box 60, Folder 40, The Catholic University of America, Washington, DC.)*

Remember, at the same AFL convention where John L. Lewis rebaited Powers Hapgood, Lewis also condemned the proposed labor delegation slated to visit the USSR the following year. His attack led the "A team" delegates to withdraw from the delegation, but a "B team" took their place and made the trip in August of 1927. That group included Albert Coyle (whose letter to Hapgood Lewis "leaked" to the convention), John Brophy, future FDR "brain truster" Rex Tugwell, James Maurer (former president of Pennsylvania's State Federation of Labor and a prominent Socialist Party member), and Frank Palmer.[34] Sandwiched between meetings with Trotsky and Stalin, Maurer, Brophy, and Palmer visited former IWW leader Big Bill Haywood in Moscow, reminisced about old times, and caught up on news about common acquaintances from Denver.[35] When the committee returned to the United States, Hapgood served as the master of ceremonies when members presented their findings at Madison Square Garden, and the delegation also published a book about its trip.[36]

FIGURE 5.4. *Although the person speaking, and the location of the meeting are unidentified, this photo was taken during the 1927–1928 strike, probably early in the strike, because the crowd is so small. (Courtesy of CFI_IND_0001-web, Steelworks Museum.)*

After the USSR trip, Palmer returned to Colorado, and although he was no Wobbly, he immediately threw himself into speaking at IWW mass meetings and working on the strike's behalf, especially coordinating efforts with Heist, who served as vice chairperson for strike relief.[37] Communist fears still ran rampant because a big rumor, printed as fact in the *Pueblo Chieftan*, was this: Haywood had smuggled Russian gold into Mexico, where Palmer arranged for it to fund the strike.[38] IWW financial records of the strike show no evidence to support this wild claim, but the rumor does demonstrate how scared people were of the IWW.

Holding frequent mass meetings was an old IWW organizational tactic. Meetings also doubled as the strike's governance mechanism. Following the Sacco and Vanzetti walkout, Embree and other organizers switched from using conferences for decision-making to using mass meetings instead, because they were cheaper and quicker to organize. These meetings exemplified Embree's vision of industrial democracy, and they constituted the governance structure for the remainder of the strike.[39] That much direct democracy is messy, and it often led to competing and inconsistent tactics during the remainder of the strike, especially after the original IWW strike leaders were jailed in early November.[40]

Also representing the IWW's egalitarian vision of industrial democracy, a strike committee representing the main nationalities comprising the striking coalminers—Americans, Mexicans, Spanish, Greeks, Italians, Slavs, and Negroes—coordinated strike activities.[41] Spanish, also called Old Mexicans, was a term used to describe miners whose families had lived in the Southwest for generations dating back to the 1500s, while Mexicans was a term used to describe newer immigrants, sometimes citizens, sometimes not. By the late 1920s, the distinction between Spanish and Mexicans was beginning to fade, at least among those who self-identified as white, since Mexican had become a blanket term determined by name and skin color, not citizenship. However, the cultural distinctions were important enough among the striking coalminers that they consciously created separate ethnic categories to identify themselves, to provide each group a democratic voice in decision making.

Aside from their governance function, mass meetings encouraged recruitment, discouraged scabbing, and probably most important of all, provided entertainment, inspiration, and indoctrination for idle workers, their supporters, and community members. The IWW held meetings constantly, with the Sunday rallies always the biggest of all. Coalmines, like all businesses, closed on Sundays, so IWW meetings attracted people looking for something to do. Revival-like in structure, meetings included a heady combination of local and national speakers interspersed with generous musical interludes that featured local musicians, soloists, and group-led singing of IWW favorites, often from the *Little Red Song Book* (still little, still red, but reissued in 1923 and again in 1927 under the new title of *Songs to Fan the Flames of Discontent*).[42] Additionally, strikers also updated new, popular, Tin Pan Alley songs with pro-worker lyrics. Although the middle of the meetings changed, every meeting began and ended the same. The Rebel Girls (an interchangeable group of local, singing girls) would open, usually singing "Solidarity Forever." Then, a big cheer closed the meeting, and it went like this:

Rang-a-tang, Rang-a-tang
Zip, boom, bah!
Who in the heck do you think we are?
Wobblies, Wobblies, ha, ha, ha!

We are rough, we are tough,
We never take a bluff,
Of free speech we never get enough,
Who? We! Wobblies! Wobblies! Wobblies![43]

What transpired between the Rebel Girls and the final cheer could last anywhere from thirty minutes to over three hours, and Sunday meetings could run even longer. Experienced speakers, including Embree, Svanum, Palmer, and James Cannon from the ILD, expertly invigorated the crowds and whipped up "the old rang-a-tang." Since mass meetings promoted IWW goals such as ethnic, racial, and gender egalitarianism, local speakers, such as Milka Sablich, who knew their audience well, moved the crowds with their personal testimonies. Important bilingual speakers emerged, since Spanish, and other dominant languages, were always part of the program. As one IWW reporter wrote, "One couldn't call any of them gifted orators or 'able speakers.' As a matter of fact most of them murdered the English language,—and more power to them for that. They were earnest, sincere, and they spoke the language of the mass. They voiced the hopes, the aspirations and the determination of their fellow worker miners now on strike."[44]

Embree and other IWW leaders recruited and developed local strike leaders, because diffused leadership aligned with the IWW's vision of industrial democracy. Also, such leaders dispelled the stereotype of Wobblies as transient, "footloose" single men with no community ties.[45] Enthusiastic IWW supporters, such as the Beranek family, helped meet that organizing goal. Joe Beranek had migrated to Lafayette from Bohemia in 1913. Surely imported as a strikebreaker, like many others recruited for that purpose, he joined the strikers instead.[46] Over the next decade, he returned to his home country several times, to bring his wife, Elizabeth, and their oldest son to Colorado. By 1928, the Beraneks had seventeen children, with all but their oldest born in the United States. This was an enormous family even by coalmining community standards, so everybody knew who the Beraneks were. Joe, and later

FIGURE 5.5. *Joe Bear gave me a copy of this family photo taken in 1914, which he said was taken to celebrate his parents becoming citizens of the United States. (Courtesy of Mr. and Mrs. Beranek during my interview of them in 2004.)*

his sons, mined coal, while the girls did domestic work, either at home or for hire, with local, wealthier families.

Coalmining in the northern Colorado coalfields was seasonal work, because the bituminous coal was a soft lignite that did not store well; if the mined coal was left outside, it turned slack, meaning it would not burn, although it did occasionally, spontaneously, burst into flames, creating local excitement when it did. Therefore, northern Colorado coalminers dug coal only during cold months, usually from October to March, a coalmining season that aligned with the 1927–1928 Colorado Coal Strike, when people needed coal to generate heat and electricity for their homes and businesses.

When the men were not mining coal, in the warm months, the entire Beranek family had worked in the sugar beet fields, until contract Mexican labor began replacing them. From the early 1900s through World War I, most beet labor had been supplied by eastern Europeans, especially Russian-German workers.[47] At first, growers preferred single men, but over time, beets evolved into family work, and the bigger the family, the better.[48] I interviewed "Joe Bear" Beranek, one of the youngest of the brood, and he described what beet work had been like.[49] His mother would position herself at one end of a row, his father at the other, and they would distribute the children between them, with everybody working who was able. Lewis Hine documented how dangerous that work could be, and his photographs of young children in Colorado's beet fields, posing with their dangerously sharp beet-topping tools, helped get the Owens-Keating Act prohibiting child labor passed in 1916.

Clearly, Joe and Elizabeth Beranek would never have joined the IWW had they believed it unpatriotic to do so. As well-known community members, the Beraneks, and other families like them, helped build a strong, democratic movement at the local level. In fact, one of the first reasons I became interested in the 1927–1928 Colorado Coal Strike was because local histories of the strike placed Elizabeth Beranek on the frontlines during the Columbine Massacre, a version of events corroborated by a *Rocky Mountain News* article published the day after the shootings that cited her by name.

Also cited by name was William Lofton. In many ways, he was the perfect Wobbly, but because he was also black, that might account for his absence in oral histories collected fifty years after the strike, when fewer than 1 percent of local residents self-identified as African-American. Like the Beraneks, Lofton was a local resident who understood the northern coalfield community well. IWW newspaper photos show he was handsome and noted that his beautiful tenor always "made a hit with the crowd," so surely, some people attended IWW rallies just to hear him sing. Unlike the Beraneks, who struggled with English their entire lives, Lofton was a powerful speaker. IWW leaders recognized his talents, and arranged for him to travel widely across the state during the strike, telling crowds he was on strike to "try to give my children the advantages that I didn't get."[50] Combating the image of Wobblies as irreligious, he often led mass meetings in a prayer, although the *Industrial Worker* reported that "Lofton said he does his praying in church, his organizing on the job, and his voting in the union hall."[51] He clearly demonstrated his rhetorical skills by always closing his portion of the program with this: "My skin is black, my heart is white, my card is RED."[52]

Along with the old-school organizing methods of picketing and staging almost constant mass meetings, Embree and other IWW leaders created

FIGURE 5.6. *Although the caption does not identify when or where this photo was taken, the descriptor says, "Members of the Junior Wobblies Union Local 1 pose for a group picture." Since the IWW GEB reported that the very first Junior Wobblies were started by Embree during the 1927–1928 Colorado Coal Strike, this photo of Local 1 must be from the strike. ([4943] "Children, Organizing, Junior Wobblies, 1920s," Courtesy of Industrial Workers of the World Image Gallery, Walter P. Reuther Library, Wayne State University, https://reuther.wayne.edu/node/11658.)*

new tactics to support the strike. One included the creation of the Junior Wobblies, who staged local dramatic performances in the Denver area to raise strike funds and even organized their own strike in Frederick after a teacher criticized the walkout.[53] They also got their own section of the *Industrial Worker* that they wrote themselves. Another novel IWW tactic grew out of the CIC's refusal to recognize the IWW. Since commissioners had declared that anything the IWW did was illegal, Embree recruited strikers on behalf of the Colorado Striking Coalminers. As he had in Bisbee and in Butte, Embree used dual unionism to its fullest potential, but this time, the dual union was a façade so complete that the fake union even issued its own white strike cards. Perhaps Embree thought those cards, instead of the easily identifiable red IWW membership cards, provided better protection in case of an arrest. Perhaps another purpose was to overcome residual loyalties to the UMW, because if coalminers traded in their old UMW cards, they got the new white cards for free, without having to pay an IWW initiation fee.[54]

The Colorado Striking Coalminers committee even elected its own governance committee. Its chairperson, Lafayette grocer Karl Clemens, represented the striking miners even though, as Denver newspapers correctly reported, Clemens had never worked a day in the mines. On October 27, Clemens and eight other committee members, including a woman, representing both the southern and northern coalfields, smiled, shook hands, posed for pictures, and conferred with Governor Adams in his office about the strike. A photograph of the parley appeared on the front pages of Denver's two leading newspapers, and as the *Denver Post* caption correctly stated, "it was the first time the I.W.W. ever has been accorded official recognition," even though the governor had officially met with the Colorado Striking Coalminers committee.[55]

The meeting produced mixed messages, however. A few days afterward, the governor told reporters that Clemens's takeaway of what they had discussed was "absurd."[56] Yet even after Adams's insult, Clemens and other committee members earnestly presented to coalminers the plan they believed they had discussed and agreed upon with the governor, which was this: If each coal camp authorized its own strike committee, then signed petitions and presented them to the industrial commission, surely the CIC would declare the strike legal. In a good faith move, since the union was hardly flush with cash, the IWW paid for over twenty thousand petitions to be printed and members began circulating them in the northern coalfields.[57] However, when Clemens and other committee members tried entering the southern field's closed camps to circulate the petitions, CF&I mine guards blocked them, so the petition idea quickly fizzled.[58]

In a tactic that reflected either the inconsistencies flowing from the IWW's direct democracy or a shrewd move calculated to pressure Governor Adams, on October 26, two days before Clemens's committee met with the governor, northern coalminers and their supporters began a fifty-car convoy from Lafayette to Fremont County in the southern field, an event well documented in state newspapers. Each vehicle was packed with enthusiastic supporters and festooned with American flags, with the lead and tail cars flying the largest flags of all.[59] At Fremont, the participants camped out near the still-working mines, and the following day, the caravan converged with

FIGURE 5.7. *This photo shows what a "parade," this one through Walsen camp in the southern fields, looked like. ("Strikers and sympathizers marching through the streets of Walsen Camp, 1927," cfi_min_wal_0023, courtesy of Steelworks Museum, https://steel works.pastperfectonline.com/photo/E8DCA699-2ABA-43CD-BDD5-357339143905.)*

an even bigger one hundred-car convoy that had formed near Florence (also in Fremont County). The groups then held a mass meeting that evening in Trinidad. At this and other nighttime meetings, people parked their cars in a big circle, with their headlights pointing toward the center, providing not just illumination of the speakers, but additional drama. Clearly, cars allowed the quick formation of "flying squadrons" that could easily drive between coalfields and address "hot spots" of resistance.

Even after this well-publicized convoy, Adams agreed to meet with the strike committee on October 28, indicating he continued to hope the strike could be settled without incident. To Adams, however, without incident meant that *all* forms of picketing would stop, and the IWW would never agree to that. Adams viewed the IWW's stance toward picketing as openly defying the law, a position supported by his attorney general's lengthy legal opinion issued early in the strike.[60] IWW organizers obviously disagreed. After the Colorado Strike Committee conferred with Adams, the Wobblies did make a concession, however. They stopped using the word *picketing* in public (although they continued using it in their newspapers) and began using more euphemistic terms for their actions. Car convoys were no longer designated as picketing operations; instead, they became car caravans. Wobblies suddenly stopped picketing the coal camps and began holding parades.

Parades were festive affairs that ranged from a few hundred men, women, and children to one gathering at the Columbine estimated at a thousand participants. In the northern field, paraders would converge in a nearby town such as Lafayette or Erie, sometimes treated to coffee and donuts by a local merchant, then march together to Serene. They would arrive between six and six thirty in the morning, when the men living in town—married men in family homes and single men in the boarding houses—would have been preparing for work. Once inside the camp, paraders would march behind an American flagbearer, singing "Solidarity Forever" and other songs. On as least two occasions, perhaps more, a fife player and drummer followed closely behind the flagbearer, recreating a "Spirit of '76" patriotic display. Parades usually lasted about half an hour, then the crowd would disperse, going home, to school, to other organizing activities, or to meetings later in the day.

In the first two weeks of the strike, mass meetings and picketing in both the northern and southern fields grew larger and increasingly effective. On November 3, Milka Sablich led an all-night meeting in Aguilar, and at dawn, attendees paraded at the Morley and Berwind mines near Ludlow. The next morning, however, for the first time, CF&I officials flatly stated that they would do whatever it took to protect their property.[61] Driving that decision was this: Even though CF&I publicly claimed production at its mines had increased since the strike had begun, on November 3, the company laid off 2,500 workers, about half the workforce, at its Pueblo steel works, because there was not enough coal to run the plant.[62] Finally, when the coal strike affected CF&I's steel production, Governor Adams decided to intervene, and that changed the course of the strike.

6

The 1927–1928 Colorado Coal Strike

November 4, 1927–February 19, 1928

On November 4, with the stroke of a pen, Governor Adams revived Governor Morley's much-hated prohibition force that he had campaigned against. He did, however, change the force's name to the state strike police. Denver's *Rocky Mountain News* wrote that Adams revived the state police "to avoid the friction which might arise if guardsmen in uniforms were called out,"[1] but the Boulder *Daily Camera* surely was more accurate when it reported Adams wanted to "enforce state laws in the strike zone without going to the heavy expense of calling out the National Guard."[2] Since the original purpose of the prohibition police had been to reward Klansmen, many coalminers, often immigrants and Catholics, had already experienced negative run-ins with those very same officers. Compounding those bad associations, the leader of the new state police, Louis Scherf, had served under Pat Hamrock, the former Colorado Ranger who helped break up the 1921–1922 Colorado coal walkout, and he had also served in the National Guard during the Ludlow strike.[3] Scherf and these former prohibition officers further complicated the strike, not only because they escalated the conflict, but also because both

https://doi.org/10.5876/9781646423026.c006

the strikers and the police had old scores preceding the walkout to settle. When Adams activated the strike police, he surely believed they would bring a quick end to the walkout, but instead, their violent actions changed the course of the strike.

Adams and the coal operators believed that if the strike leaders were arrested, the strike would end, but they were wrong. By November 6, most of the IWW organizers, including Embree and Svanum, were jailed in Walsenburg, none charged with any crime. In the dead of night, they were moved to a more secure jail in Pueblo. Walsenburg Wobblies reacted to the arrests by holding a mass meeting that spooked local residents, who reported seeing "signal fires and rockets flaming from nearby hills." Those sightings (or rumored sightings) prompted local officials to increase their patrols and install machine guns at the courthouse that housed the jail. Fearing carloads of Wobblies were on their way to break their leaders out, one hundred armed deputies guarded the jail through the night. The following evening, the city doubled the number of deputies, "armed [them] with tear bombs and machine guns," and parked three fire engines as a barricade in front of the building.[4]

Because the governor ordered all strike leaders to be arrested, strike police must have assumed anyone who spoke was a leader. On November 6, at the Berwind camp, Scherf and seventeen other state policemen arrested seven speakers "as they climbed the steps of the post office to address the crowd." In the melee that followed, the police attacked the crowd with "clubs and fists." In newspaper accounts that shock modern readers, reporters gleefully describe this encounter, even praising the police for their restraint. Although under strict orders not to shoot, police were vastly outnumbered and armed with pistols, which the National Guard adjutant general, an observer sent by the governor, noted with concern.[5] That same day in the northern fields, Denver newspapers reported at least one thousand convened for a Lafayette rally, and afterward, approximately two hundred marched to the Columbine.

On November 7, Adams authorized the creation of twenty more strike police and sent them all into the southern fields. When added to the already deputized locals, that put sixty men under Scherf's control. When three thousand people assembled at the Ludlow Monument for a rally, four airplanes, one armed with bombs, buzzed the meeting, causing people to flee into the surrounding hills in terror. That day, CF&I installed machine guns in all its camps.[6] In the north, carloads of protestors blocked the road entering the Columbine mine, and for the first time, closed all production there.[7]

On Tuesday morning, November 8, the IWW newspaper reported a patriotic, festive parade at the Columbine, although the Boulder *Camera* described an entirely different scene in which an unidentified Amazon urged eight hundred protestors, including women and children, to destroy the tipple. Local sheriffs tried arresting a few paraders, but the crowd surrounded their car, which allowed the detainees to melt back into the crowd. The parade achieved its goal because strikebreakers joined both the procession and the strike. Since the strike began, the number of coalminers working at the Columbine had dropped from a pre-strike average of 350 down to 75. The *Camera* reported that "no warrants have been sworn out for leaders of the picketing parties today, according to authorities, because of the reason that there appear to be no leaders. The crowd of picketers resembles a herd of sheep in that it mills about, following anyone who starts to do something."[8]

Governor Adams and the operators had assumed, mistakenly, that after IWW leaders were arrested, the strike would end. Instead, it intensified, which suggests the leaders had served as moderating influences. Furthermore, although the IWW did have leaders, including organizers such as Embree, it disdained the strong, centralized leadership exercised by officials such as the UMW's John L. Lewis. Wobblies often have been criticized for having no consistent ideology, but at least two characteristics of every IWW strike included the singing of "Solidarity Forever" and the repetition of the slogan, "We are all leaders." Both the song's lyrics and the chant embodied their deeply democratic vision of industrial democracy as well as any statement of principles ever could.[9]

On Wednesday, November 9, when a mass meeting at Walsenburg began, police rushed the stage, arresting speaker after speaker, but no matter how many speakers police arrested, a new speaker took the stage. In the early 1960s, this would be the tactic black civil rights protestors used when conducting their lunch counter sit-ins. According to The *Rocky Mountain News*, the Walsenburg crowd attacked the police with knives, chairs, and spades, although that seems unlikely, since only two policemen suffered minor injuries. The following are the names of the most seriously injured, all of them

Wobblies: Carmello Martinez, Jose Camachio, Panciano Sloriano, Pablo Trujillo, Andy Archuletta, Juan Alvarado, Pablo Espinosa, Ruqino Garcia, Jose Sciof, Cahilla Ciruria, and Casimirio Valdez.[10]

Since the 1910–1914 long strike, which CF&I public relations apologist Ivy Lee blamed on violent Greek immigrants, a significant demographic shift had taken place in Colorado that reflected changes taking place across the Southwest.[11] In 1920, Colorado had 14,340 residents the federal census described as Mexicans. By 1930, it had 57,676. However, almost 80 percent of people classified as Mexicans were born in the United States.[12] Out of a partial list of eight hundred IWW members amassed by CF&I officials, although twenty different nationalities were documented, only forty members were classified as Americans, with even fewer Greeks. Unlike the long strike, eastern and southern European immigrants no longer comprised most of CF&I's striking coalminers. Over half had Spanish names, the same percentage as in the northern field.[13]

Newspaper evidence tells us that Mexicans were key participants and leaders in the strike, but their stories are almost impossible to find, and this massive historical silence is the greatest omission from the strike records. Who were these strikers and their families? Were they mostly new immigrants, or had they lived in the Southwest for generations? Did they strike because they were tired of holding the lowest paying jobs and living in the most decrepit company housing? Were they apolitical, or had they been radicalized in the Mexican Revolution? Did the coalminers know the sugar beet workers? These are just some of the questions I would love answers to, but they were not asked during the strike, just as they were not asked fifty years later during oral interviews of the old-timer, English-speaking strikers, either.

I have spent a lot of time imagining who these strikers were based on the limited evidence available. For example, here is in intriguing nugget: When Kristen Svanum wrote a letter of introduction on behalf of organizer Ramon P. Gonzalez, a letter only available because it was intercepted by a CF&I company official working to thwart the strike, Svanum highly recommended Gonzalez because he had "shown his reliability in the Mexican Revolution as a member of the Magon group and in the 1917 [Bisbee] strike of the I.W.W. in Arizona." Svanum wrote that Gonzalez was "our most competent job delegate in Aguilar," which explained the IWW's success in Las Animas County. He spoke Spanish, invaluable for the strike, and would excel at any kind of organizing "work he may offer to do."[14] How many more organizers were like Gonzalez? Unfortunately, it is impossible to know.

Several historians have hinted at legacies these organizers and strikers left behind. The following is Vicki Ruiz's dedication in *Cannery Women, Cannery Lives: Mexican Women, Unionization, and the California Food Processing Industry, 1930–1950*: "In memory of my grandfather, Albino Ruiz, beet worker, coal miner, Wobblie."[15] In response to my questions, Ruiz emailed me that her grandfather played all three roles in the 1927–1928 Colorado Coal Strike. Those memories, conflicts, and grudges within her family—over which family members went on strike and which ones scabbed—still created tensions at her mother's funeral in 1971, decades after the strike ended.[16] Clearly, Ruiz family activism influenced her career choice, since as a historian, she has spent most of her career looking for other silenced stories within the Mexican American community.

Ruiz's grandfather could not have been the only Wobbly coalminer and beet worker. I have never found "smoking gun" evidence, but longtime locals whose families worked both coal and beets have told me that "everybody" knew coal operators wanted to replace coalminers with Mexican beet workers. Both were cheap, but beet workers were cheaper. One of the IWW strike demands was a minimum $7.75 daily wage, which in good years could yield $1,000 to $1,300 annually. Beet workers, contracted and paid as families, made $250 per season.[17] Mexicans were also easier to control. Most did not know English, wage theft was common, and if they complained or tried to organize, since most were contract workers, they could be deported. As the early 1930s repatriations showed, even citizens got deported, too. Coal and beets were both seasonal, but in opposite seasons. Coalminers worked when it was cold, from October to February or March, and beet workers worked when it was warm, from April through September. Obviously, if bosses could replace coalminers with contract workers, beet farmers *and* coal operators could employ cheap, compliant labor all year long.

Wobblies needed beet workers to join the strike and beet workers needed representation, so on November 11, the IWW held a "monster mass meeting" at Fort Lupton (about ten miles east of the Columbine). As they had in early October, speakers urged beet workers to join the strike. Approximately two thousand striking miners fanned out into the fields and even entered the processing factory to recruit new members.[18] Although newspaper accounts reported the beet workers did not join the strike, Sarah Deutsch, in *No Separate Refuge*, and Zaragosa Vargas, in *Proletarians of the North*, cite evidence that they did. Deutsch quotes an organizer who said that by January of 1928, the IWW founded fourteen sugar beet locals with seventeen hundred members.[19] Vargas writes that by 1928, "Mexican sugar-beet workers had organized *La Liga Obrera de Habla Española* (Spanish-Speaking Workers' League) with the help of the militant Industrial Workers of the World, and that the influence of *La Liga* was widespread. It extended into northern Colorado, the Denver area, and into northern New Mexico among a workforce that was largely migratory." That union's influence, he argues, spread to the industrial Midwest in the 1930s and helped fuel the rise of the CIO.[20]

Even with their leaders jailed and the newly authorized state strike police trying to stop them, the "Solidarity Forever"-singing, "We are all leaders"-chanting, multi-ethnic strikers and their supporters escalated their resistance. On Friday, November 12, an estimated one thousand men, women, and children paraded inside the Columbine, marching behind a flag bearer and a drummer, at the extraordinarily disruptive hour of four in the morning, doubtlessly jarring awake the strikebreakers.[21] On Saturday, Judge J. Foster Symes of the US federal district court in Denver agreed to hear, on Friday, November 18, the writ of habeas corpus application for eight of the jailed IWW leaders, including Embree. On Sunday, November 13, Wobblies held their biggest and most visible mass rally to date in downtown Denver.[22] Sponsored by both the ACLU and the uncredited ILD, the meeting was scheduled for Reverend Heist's Grace Community Church. It filled fast, so the overflow crowd walked several blocks to hold a second meeting at the Greek Theater, part of the Civic Center complex between the state capitol and the Denver city government building. Frank Palmer, probably the AFL able speaker referred to on the flyer, orated at Grace, and Adam Bell, a local, northern IWW leader, addressed over two thousand who gathered to hear him and others decry the massive violation of civil liberties in Colorado's coalfields.[23]

The rally so "fanned the flames of discontent" that the Boulder *Daily Camera* reported at least forty-seven carloads of strike supporters drove directly from the Denver meeting to Boulder, continuing to demonstrate

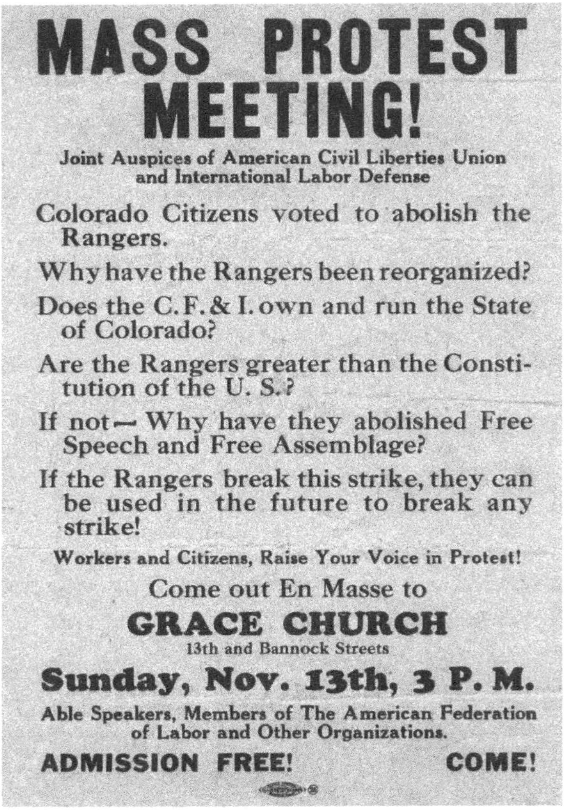

MASS PROTEST MEETING!

Joint Auspices of American Civil Liberties Union and International Labor Defense

Colorado Citizens voted to abolish the Rangers.

Why have the Rangers been reorganized?

Does the C. F. & I. own and run the State of Colorado?

Are the Rangers greater than the Constitution of the U. S.?

If not — Why have they abolished Free Speech and Free Assemblage?

If the Rangers break this strike, they can be used in the future to break any strike!

Workers and Citizens, Raise Your Voice in Protest!

Come out En Masse to

GRACE CHURCH
13th and Bannock Streets

Sunday, Nov. 13th, 3 P. M.

Able Speakers, Members of The American Federation of Labor and Other Organizations.

ADMISSION FREE!   COME!

FIGURE 6.1. *The poster credits the ACLU and the AFL (but not the ILD) for sponsoring the Denver rally, where the former prohibition police, newly commissioned as the state strike police, were condemned as "Rangers."*

their exuberant support for the strike. On Monday morning, November 14, paraders were back at the Columbine. Again, local Weld County sheriffs unsuccessfully tried arresting the perceived ringleaders, and again, the crowd swarmed their car, allowing the suspects to escape. Apparently, that was the last straw. Afterward, strike policeman Sam Lee "told newspaper men that the state police were going to make a radical change of policy in Weld county," and from now on, "law enforcement officers were to cooperate with mine guards in attempting to keep picketers off the property of the Columbine."[24]

The next day, Tuesday, November 15, the Columbine closed so that it could be fortified. Governor Adams transferred twelve state police from the southern to the northern fields, and when the Columbine reopened Wednesday, a total of thirty-five armed men occupied the compound. Also added were two machine guns, one mounted on the back of a truck and the other atop the tipple, which was now surrounded by a barbed-wire fence labeled "high voltage." Since the tipple was the highest point in the camp, it could provide shooters with a bird's-eye view both inside and outside the compound. Vincent and Adams knew that to defend the Columbine, the tipple—which resembled a wooden oilrig and functioned as the heart of all coalmining operations—had to be protected. Coal was lifted from elevator shafts below ground up through the towering structure, where topmen would sort and clean the coal and checkweighmen would record each coalminer's weights. Finally, coal would be tipped into empty train cars at ground level and sent on its way. Because coalminers were paid by the ton, one of their central strike demands had been the power to choose their own checkweighman (who would not cheat them on their weights).

When the thoroughly militarized Columbine reopened on Wednesday, mine officials told reporters that "mine guards would shoot the first picketer who attempted to set foot on the property Wednesday morning."[25] Furthermore, "Merle Vincent, vice-president and general manager of the Rocky Mountain Fuel company, said that every effort would be made to keep the mine open," and "if the military defense of the Columbine mine proves successful, other mines in the northern Colorado coal field will be reopened."[26]

Clearly, a mounting panic gripped Adams and the coal operators. Their plan to end the strike had failed and money was running out. Remember, the state legislature only allocated $18,400 annually to fund an emergency state police force. Since November 4, Governor Adams had spent $16,000. At that rate, Adams had two days of funding left, and the new state police allocation would not begin until November 30.[27] By Thursday, November 17, Governor Adams's police fund had dwindled to a few hundred dollars, and the IWW habeas corpus hearing was set for the following day. To halt the hearing, Adams instructed the southern coalfield sheriffs to file formal charges against the leaders since that would keep them in jail, at least over the weekend.[28] In spite of the Columbine's fortifications and mine officials' threats to shoot them, on Friday, November 18, 750 men, women, and children defiantly conducted another parade inside the camp.[29]

Sunday, November 20, the Wobblies held their mass meeting in Boulder, and over one thousand attended, including college students from the

University of Denver and the University of Colorado, as well as local Boulder residents interested in the strike.[30] Coalminers and their families were encouraged by this show of middle-class support, since they often felt that people in Boulder "treated them like rats" whenever they came into town.[31] The meeting lasted over three hours, and H. C. Duke, a new IWW arrival to Colorado, spoke for over half the rally. When IWW organizers had been jailed on November 6, the Chicago IWW headquarters issued a frantic appeal for all available Wobblies to come to Colorado. Duke was one of many to heed the call, arriving from California, where he had just gotten out of prison for helping lead the 1923–1924 San Pedro shipyard strikes.[32] After the rally, as they had a week earlier, many of the striking coalminers kept celebrating, which, in spite of prohibition, involved heavy drinking. The first week of the strike, their coalmining buddy Ray Jacques had been heavily fined for selling bootleg liquor, but they had no such fears now, since the prohibition police were now operating as the strike police.[33]

Around midnight, the mood turned increasingly sour as rumors began running rampant. Coalminers heard that uniformed strangers had come banging on the doors of strike activists and that afterward, many of their neighbors simply disappeared into the night.[34] Strike police heard that Wobblies planned on breaking into Serene, so they sent south for police reinforcements who arrived around three in the morning, bringing steel helmets, tear gas, and .44 pistols with them.[35] Families living inside the coal camp swore they heard the guards and police carousing during an all-night drinking party.[36] Everybody was on edge, anticipating trouble, which arrived early the following morning.

At dawn, at least five hundred people appeared at the gates of the Columbine. That morning, there was no festive singing of "Solidarity," and most of the women and children stayed home. For the first time, the gates surrounding Serene were locked. Inside the fence, strikebreakers and families slept, but not soundly. A cluster of local sheriffs, observers sent by the governor, and RMFC officials congregated nervously near the Columbine's office. A phalanx of twenty state police wearing tin helmets, knee-high boots, and pistols strapped to their sides faced off with protestors on the opposite side of the fence. There would be no parade today, Colonel Louis Scherf told them. Yes, there would, the crowd replied. Scherf asked who their leaders were, and the crowd responded, "We are all leaders!" Then, the confrontation began.[37]

The next day, Scherf testified before the Weld County Coroner's Inquest. He said the crowd had stormed through the gate, pushed down the fence, and attacked his men with knives and rocks. Ignoring verbal warnings to stop, the crowd pushed his men 150 feet back, forcing their backs against the water tower next to the tipple. He fired a warning shot into the ground, which only stopped the mob for a few seconds. He had no choice. He ordered his men to open fire. At last, the crowd fell back. His men stopped shooting, and Scherf called for medical help.[38]

Although the coroner had not summoned anyone in the crowd testify, many—mostly women—insisted their voices be heard. He allowed it, and they offered a very different version of events. They had wanted to march as usual at the Columbine, and they had a right to, because there was a post office and a school there. After Scherf asked them who their leader was and they replied they were all leaders, Scherf got aggressive and started yelling insults, profanities, and threats at them, which he had no right to do. Adam Bell got into a shouting match with one of the strike police, but when both climbed up their sides of the fence, the policeman yanked Bell over and beat him unconscious. The marchers had to break through the fence to save Bell's life, and they had not thrown rocks because there were none to throw. They did lob unexploded tear bombs back at the police, but the police had thrown them first. As repeatedly instructed throughout the strike, they carried no weapons of any kind, "not even a knife."[39] As the police attacked them with their fists and nightsticks, they fought back in self-defense. The police knocked down the flagbearer, broke the staff, and trampled the American flag. An eyewitness quoted in the *Rocky Mountain News* said that Elizabeth Beranek threw her body over the flagbearer, trying to shield him from further attacks. Somebody picked up the flag and continued marching, and that was when the shooting started. Bullets came so fast that World War I veterans in the crowd testified they could only have been fired from machine guns. Even when marchers began running away, the shooting continued. Soon, drivers returned to the site, their cars draped with white flags of surrender, to collect the dead and wounded. They drove them to the nearby doctor in Erie and waited all day outside his office, hoping for word. They learned that two men—John Eastenes and Nick Spanandakis—died immediately. Three more—Jerry Davis, Rene Jacques, and George Kovoitch—passed by nightfall. The last to die was Mike Vidovich, on Friday. At least twenty of the wounded were taken to local hospitals, but after news spread that strike police took Adam Bell to jail, not a hospital, injured people stayed home, too scared to seek medical attention.[40]

The violence on November 21, 1927, was soon known as the Columbine Massacre, and it was the turning point of the strike. The day after the Columbine, mainstream Denver newspapers published photographs of smiling, uniformed strike police wearing homemade arm slings. By November 23, however, stories shifted—hard—toward sympathetic coverage of the Columbine's victims. Jerry Davis, a local twenty-one-year-old striking coalminer, had been shot and trampled while carrying the American flag.[41] Thirty-six-year-old John Eastenes left behind a wife and six young children. The family was so poor that churches began collecting donations for them. A prominent Denver philanthropist sent the widow a check for one hundred dollars and offered to place her children in a Catholic orphanage.[42] Rene (Ray) Jacques, arrested by prohibition police in October, had been a war veteran. Newspaper stories described how Jacques's brother, also a veteran, had been killed in the coalmines his first day back from the Great War when a mule kicked him.[43] George Vidovich had been the last to die. Doctors tried saving his life by amputating first one leg and then the other, but he died of gangrene.[44] Vidovich had also served in the Great War and had been the first to volunteer from his hometown of Erie.[45] Both the American Legion and the Wobblies led the six-thousand-strong funeral procession through Lafayette before burying him in an unmarked grave alongside four of the others shot and killed that day.[46] Only Jacques's family could afford a headstone, and they buried him in a family plot in nearby Louisville.

Such stories dripping with pathos reflected changing attitudes toward the strike that, at last, pressured the CIC to hold public hearings, which lasted from December 23 through February 17. Reading Merle Vincent's annotated transcript of the hearings in Roche's papers, it would be impossible to glean any information about events that continued spiraling out of control outside the hearing rooms. Although they tried, striking coalminers and IWW lawyers were unable to include any of those outrages into that public record because commissioners insisted on keeping testimony narrowly focused only on wages and working conditions, information damning enough in its own right.

The Columbine Massacre also served as a turning point for the IWW. By November 21, A. S. Embree and the original IWW organizers had, to a large

True you have not won all your demands. But did you really expect to win them all? More than anything else you have won organization. With that power in your hands you can hold all other gains and prepare yourself for still greater advances . . . the slack season is upon us. It is foolish to strike when the bosses can meet the demands for coal by keeping a few scabs at work.

To protect yourselves, to maintain your organization, to win further concessions later on, you should get back into the mines at once. Union men must mine the coal in Colorado. . . . Remember the sacrifices made by your fellow workers. They gave their lives at Columbine and Walsenburg—for what? For organization and solidarity.

Do not mistakenly make their sacrifices of no avail by refusing to return to work now. Vote for solidarity. Vote for your organization. Vote to return to work at once. Take your splendid solidarity with you to your jobs.[61]

Although the workers overwhelmingly voted to end the strike, for Colorado coalminers, the IWW, Josephine Roche, the RMFC, John L. Lewis, the UMW, and future New Deal labor policies, the consequences of the strike were just beginning.

7

The Aftermath of the 1927–1928 Colorado Coal Strike

1927–1930

The aftermath of the 1927–1928 Colorado Coal Strike changed the personal and professional trajectories of Roche, Hapgood, and Embree. It also challenged their earlier visions of industrial democracy. The strike destroyed Embree's IWW career and accelerated the decline of his beloved union. In their efforts to gain legal and financial control of the RMFC, the strike's aftermath led Josephine Roche and her allies to create a mostly false narrative, premised upon remembering Ludlow but forgetting the Columbine, that promoted the RMFC as a noble experiment in industrial democracy. That powerful story helped lead Roche to negotiate a 1928 contract with the UMW with prospects so promising, it helped shape 1930s labor history. The contract's promise lured Powers and Mary Hapgood to Colorado in January of 1929. By the summer of 1930, however, Roche and the Hapgoods realized that the RMFC's promise did not match its messy reality.

When Roche inherited her father's half of the RMFC after his death in January of 1927, she hired former Progressive ally Merle Vincent to run her

https://doi.org/10.5876/9781646423026.c007

share of the company. The shock of the Columbine Massacre, however, prompted Roche to at last exert greater control over the RMFC, and her first priority was spin control. Building upon the skills acquired working in the Committee on Public Information and the Children's Bureau, Roche expertly created a compelling, but mostly false, narrative that portrayed her and the RMFC as blameless for the massacre. That tale, however, did not originate from her but from the national press, leftists, and sympathizers, who, after the Columbine Massacre and regardless of the evidence, could only see Ludlow.

On November 22, 1927, the day after the massacre, The *New York Times* ran an article about the conflagration. It mostly praised the strike police but also quoted Frank Palmer, who said, "No one less than John D. Rockefeller is responsible for the deaths of our comrades."[1] Lest there be any confusion about Palmer's reference, directly below the Columbine article ran a much shorter one summarizing the Ludlow Massacre. On Wednesday, November 23, Communist Party (CP) members in New York City picketed Rockefeller's Standard Oil Building at 26 Broadway, protesting the Columbine shootings. This led Rockefeller Jr. to issue a short, truthful statement: The CF&I had no connection with the Columbine. A CP secretary responded with this: "Mr. Rockefeller cannot hide behind any technicalities . . . in evading responsibility for the Colorado situation. One has only to know the violent labor-hating policy of Mr. Rockefeller's coal and iron corporation to know that they do not hesitate to employ thugs, gunmen and the State police and resort to violence and murder in order to maintain their tyrannous company union and to keep the miners enslaved."[2]

On November 24, Denver's *Rocky Mountain News* printed an Associated Press (AP) article that allowed Roche to gauge national Columbine Massacre coverage. She must have breathed a sigh of relief, since there was no mention of her or the RMFC. Locally, newspapers quoted regional activists, including Denver's Reverend A. A. Heist, who blamed Rockefeller, not Roche, for the Columbine. Perhaps such coverage emboldened Vincent to make the following RMFC statement on November 26:

> Until Monday morning, when the riot and loss of life occurred at the
> Columbine camp, this mine had been operating under an award of the indus-
> trial commission made after the commencement of the strike. Previous to

Monday picketing meetings and parades had taken place without disturbance.

Sunday evening Mr. Annear [of the CIC] and I called on Governor Adams to consider conditions at the Columbine camp.

Machine guns had been taken there, the governor stated, without his knowledge. We all agreed these should be removed and he gave orders that they were to be removed.

It had been from the first our expressed and fixed policy that there should be no violence or shooting. I informed the governor we would close the mine if necessary to avoid this. The officer in command was satisfied, the governor said that the situation could and would be handled without trouble or resort to force. This the governor and we believed. The riot which followed Monday and the loss of life resulted were entirely unexpected.[3]

Vincent's statement, made five days *after* the Columbine Massacre, contradicts newspaper accounts that described, in detail, the complete militarization of the Columbine five days *before* it. Nevertheless, Heist wrote a congratulatory letter to Vincent about his statement, noting it was especially important "you had previously expressed yourself as willing to close down the mine, rather than have any bloodshed." Heist also praised Vincent for "releasing" (firing) Ted Peart, the Columbine manager, and added, "I hope in the interests of future amicable relations between the miners and such fine spirited men as yourself, you will leave no stone unturned to fix the responsibility for the unnecessary killing by the state police."[4]

The narrative blaming Rockefeller but holding Roche blameless for the Columbine Massacre reached a wider audience on December 7, 1927, when *The Nation* published Frank Palmer's article, "War in Colorado." His lede, "Colorado again has paid in blood for the dominance in its coal industry of John D. Rockefeller, Jr.," set the tone for his entire polemic. Palmer claimed that the Rockefeller Plan had caused the 1927–1928 Colorado Coal Strike and, without evidence, intimated that Rockefeller might have conspired to incite the Columbine Massacre so he could buy Roche's RMFC shares on the cheap. He repeated the exact phrase Heist had written to Vincent, that the RMFC had made clear it would "close down the mine, rather than have any bloodshed." He further absolved the RMFC from blame when he wrote that "Merle Vincent, who had ordered the gates left open and the strikers given access to the property for their mass meetings, was not present on that fatal Monday morning. Ted Peart was; though he resigned his position on the following Friday."[5] Both Heist and Palmer referred to Ted Peart, but his name was Fred. That relatively minor error indicates just how closely the two were sharing and disseminating information, but also misinformation, about the strike.

Among Palmer's many reporting errors, the most egregious was this: Vincent *had* been at the Columbine the morning of the massacre. We know this because of the Weld County Coroner's Inquest held after the Columbine Massacre. The two-day inquest began the day after the massacre, and Peart's testimony was unambiguous. At five thirty in the morning, on November 21, Scherf had called him to come to the Columbine. Peart figured Scherf must have called Vincent next, since they arrived at the same time. Vincent even remarked to Peart, "That was pretty good time we made," since "it is now . . . ten minutes after six." Vincent asked Peart "if we 'had any visitors that morning' and I said 'yes, I think so.' I drove the car right behind him . . . but inside of the gate . . . I could see a crowd coming in; it was a dark dusk, so I drove . . . to the mine office, and I left the car by the [company] store, and walked over to the fence line that separates the store from the office of the mine proper," and "at that time the crowd had broken over the gate." Peart rushed into the Columbine office to call the governor, asking him to send airplanes "to see if he could not scare or quiet them down," but during his conversation, "I heard a lot of shots fired . . . I heard the 6:30 whistle blow right in the middle of it. Thru all that noise I could not get the Governor to understand."[6]

Peart's testimony reveals several important facts. It definitively places Vincent at the Columbine the morning of the massacre. It also indicates Vincent and Peart shared a comfortable working relationship and that neither did anything to prevent the massacre. Clearly, they were coordinating strike control efforts with the governor, who directed the strike police's actions, and perhaps with Scherf, who had called both men on the phone. Had Heist or Palmer attended the inquest, they would have heard Peart's testimony themselves, but local newspapers printed no inquest information other than its final verdict. Had Heist and Palmer investigated the strike with open minds, their findings might have removed their anti-Rockefeller blinders, but like the Communists picketing the Standard Oil Building, regardless of the evidence, all they could see was Ludlow.

No one ever took responsibility for militarizing the Columbine or for deploying the strike police there, decisions that led to the Columbine Massacre. Yet somehow the orders had been given. In *The Order Has Been Carried Out: History, Memory, and Meaning of a Nazi Massacre in Rome*, Alessandro Portelli analyzed an event from his childhood during World War II. On March 25, 1944, a newspaper in Rome published, and his mother read aloud to him, a press release from the state news agency. It reported that on March 23, "criminal elements," identified as Communists, had thrown bombs at a German police column marching along the via Rasella, killing thirty-two Germans. To prevent future attacks "from these heartless bandits," the Germans commanded that for every policeman who had been killed, ten Communists would be shot. Furthermore, "this order has already been carried out." Within twenty-four hours of the street bombings, Germans retaliated by killing 335 Italian prisoners in an abandoned quarry, a massacre remembered as the Fosse Ardeatine.[7]

Using newspapers and official documents, but especially oral histories, Portelli explores how the widely accepted historical narrative surrounding this event—that Germans implored the partisans responsible for the attacks to surrender, and only after they refused had the Germans retaliated at the Fosse Ardeatine—is still generally accepted among most Italian people, published in history books, repeated in Italian tour guides, and found on the Internet. This commonsensical narrative is not only false but it is a political distortion of memory, "perpetrated by the popular press, the media, the Church, and conservative political forces." Portelli explores how and why that historical reconstruction took place over time, a reinterpretation that began for him with a newspaper press release that concluded with the sentence, "The order has been carried out," a passive-voice construction that assigned no responsibility to whomever ordered the massacre.

Over time, Portelli explains, the historical narrative surrounding the Fosse Ardeatine massacre became decontextualized, generating its own boundaries of "acceptable reality": Nothing worth mentioning happened before the story began and nothing happened after it ended. Far from a single event, however, both the attack and the subsequent massacre comprised a larger pattern of German dominance and Italian resistance taking place in Rome late in the war that, for complex reasons, none of its participants wanted to remember. Furthermore, memories of the massacre shifted after the war, as conservatives began downplaying the significant role Communists had played in the Italian resistance movement and Italians grew ashamed of their passive reaction to such savagery. As much as Romans needed to forget the specifics of the conflict, as late as 1970, when city police arrived to evict homeless families, both the police and the squatters began yelling at each other in language that evoked the Fosse Ardeatine massacre, showing that thirty years later, the memory of those events still served as the "symbolic yardstick for the violence of oppression."[8]

Portelli's analysis yields important parallels worth considering regarding the Columbine Massacre. Like the Fosse Ardeatine, memories of the Columbine Massacre have become decontextualized. Today, if the massacre is remembered at all, it remains an example of an interesting but anomalous incident in local history or it is mentioned as brief background information about Josephine Roche. In fact, the massacre was part of a much larger uprising sweeping the nation's coalfields throughout the 1920s and early 1930s that demonstrates the weakness of the UMW and coalminers' resistance to Lewis's governance. The commonsensical, yet incorrect, historical interpretation of the aftermath of the Fosse Ardeatine massacre blamed the victims for not turning themselves in sooner, even though the order to kill them had already been given and carried out. Although Scherf gave the order to fire upon the Columbine protestors, many people, including Roche, share responsibility for creating the conditions that led Scherf's men to fire. Therefore, portrayals of Roche solely as a beneficent reformer who tried everything in her power to prevent the Columbine Massacre are false. The dominant story that emerged from the massacre is that Roche invited the UMW to unionize her coalminers, but the context for that invitation has largely disappeared. Like the Fosse Ardeatine, such a historical interpretation becomes a political distortion of memory, and as we shall see, the press, politicians, Roche, John L. Lewis, the UMW, and even the IWW helped create a dominant historical narrative about the 1927–1928 Colorado Coal Strike and the Columbine Massacre that served their own political purposes. All downplay the significance of militant workers and their supporters.

Portelli writes that the Fosse Ardeatine massacre became a symbolic yardstick for the violence of oppression, and so had the Ludlow Massacre. That memory helped Vincent and Roche divert attention from their own responsibilities for the Columbine Massacre. They first committed a sin of omission by remaining silent, allowing others, erroneously, to evoke Ludlow. However, they soon proved fully capable of committing sins of commission, beginning with their decision to fire Fred Peart. Peart's father had been a key anti-union figure during the long strike, and Roche, Vincent, and Edward Costigan all knew that Peart's name, like Rockefeller's, elicited memories of Ludlow. They willingly scapegoated Peart, because he knew too much and was willing to talk, but also because he reinforced the false yet powerful narrative about Jr. and the Rockefeller Plan causing the Columbine Massacre. Peart's firing contributed to constructing a new narrative that valorized Roche and her colleagues as progressive, pro-organized labor saviors.

Historians have declared, uniformly, that Roche did not control the RMFC before March of 1928, when she bought out the shares of her father's partner. Because Roche was such a master of public relations and her record keeping was so opaque, I do not trust those previous accounts that appear to be based upon RMFC press releases.[9] I do know that before the Columbine, Roche controlled the company sufficiently to delegate most RMFC control to Vincent, who fought the strike more aggressively than any other Colorado coal operator. As Vincent's boss, Roche could have overridden his actions. Even more damning, within the first two weeks after Palmer's *Nation* article was published, internal RMFC communications between Roche and Vincent show that Vincent wanted to set the record straight about being at the Columbine the morning of the shootings, but he had been overruled, probably by Roche.[10] As time passed and it became clear the circumstances surrounding the Columbine Massacre would never surface, Roche, and later Costigan, grew bolder. They embellished Roche's narrative about herself, the RMFC, the Columbine Massacre, Rockefeller, and the strike, repeating it so often that perhaps even they began to believe it was true.

On March 19, 1928, Vincent issued a press release on behalf of the RMFC stating that Roche had gained financial control of the RMFC, and the company would negotiate with any union affiliated with the American Federation of Labor (AFL).[11] The statement was both false and unnecessarily vague, since Roche never gained financial control of the company and the only coalminers' union in the AFL was the UMW.

The timing of that statement suggests it was made in an attempt to grab the UMW's attention. The Colorado coalfields were still volatile and dominated by the IWW, which, in its initial strike petition presented to the CIC, had expressed a willingness to bargain collectively with coal operators.[12] Additional evidence of the IWW's openness to collective bargaining can be seen in a flyer written and signed by Embree, which circulated throughout Colorado's coalfields after the strike. In the page-long document, he wrote that a UMW organizer was spreading rumors that "the Rocky Mountain Fuel Co. had offered to sign a contract with the I.W.W. and that A. S. Embree, I.W.W. organizer, has refused to sign." Embree referred to a meeting that he and the flyer's co-signers had attended with Roche, Vincent, and Costigan "to see if some understanding could be reached between the company and its employees," but he concluded he did not have the authority to negotiate anything without the members' approval.[13]

The petition and flyer raise as many questions as they answer, including the following: Did the IWW seek recognition as an exclusive bargaining agent for the coalminers? When Roche, Vincent, and Costigan met with IWW leaders, had they really proposed negotiating a contract with the IWW? If so, did Embree present that offer to members? Since there was almost no UMW presence in Colorado, was the UMW organizer spreading rumors in attempts to lure coalminers away from the IWW, which eschewed contracts, and into the UMW, which welcomed them? Finally, did the RMFC issue its March statement as a trial balloon to see if the UMW would send more organizers and a negotiator to Colorado? If so, the UMW did not respond, surely because its own ongoing 1927–1928 coal strike required the union's undivided attention. Only after that strike ended in a total defeat in June did UMW officials, in July, schedule meetings for August, to negotiate an RMFC contract.[14] This timing suggests that between March and July, Roche was actively searching for ways to suppress the Wobblies, which led to perhaps her most creative and brilliant move, hiring John R. Lawson.

Roche hired Lawson as general manager and co-vice president of the RMFC in June of 1928. Since his UMW expulsion, the Ludlow hero had struggled to make a living, a problem the RMFC was offering to solve. Furthermore, Lawson literally owed his life to Costigan, who got Lawson's Ludlow-related murder conviction overturned. Roche and her allies also knew that Lawson, still regarded as the hero of the long strike, could help win over the coalminers' conflicted loyalties. Lawson also worked with Palmer and Heist, strong

IWW supporters, at the Denver Labor College. Finally, if Roche really could negotiate a contract with the UMW, at long last, she would have fulfilled the central, unmet demand of the 1910–1914 long strike.

Whether or not this had been Roche's intention, hiring Lawson destroyed the IWW's carefully crafted strike coalition. This is evident from angry letters to the editor Embree and Heist addressed to each other in Denver's *Rocky Mountain News* in August of 1927, reprinted in the IWW's *Industrial Solidarity*.[15] When negotiations between the RMFC and the UMW began, Embree wrote a long letter to the editor, attacking Lawson as a has-been labor leader. In response, Heist fully defended Lawson, not just as the hero of Ludlow but as a man of unimpeachable character. Heist's enthusiastic Lawson defense signaled the end of his alliance with the IWW and his switched allegiance to Roche and the RMFC. Heist took his many allies with him, including Palmer, Cherrington, the Colorado ACLU, and the Denver Labor College.

As Embree witnessed his strike coalition dissolve, he was also challenged by enemies within the IWW. Remember that when Embree and other IWW organizers had been jailed in early November of 1927, new Wobblies, including Tom Connors, arrived in Colorado and began assuming strike leadership roles, steering the walkout in a different direction from its original organizers. In March, a month after the strike ended, Fred Thompson arrived in the state, and he quickly joined forces with Connors. Together, they began attacking Embree in earnest. As chapter 10 will explore, although Wobblies remained in Colorado's coalfields for years, stripped of their allies, internally divided, and faced with a new, closed shop RMFC contract that made UMW membership a condition of employment, the IWW, and memories of the strike, began to fade, even among those who had enthusiastically participated in the strike.

After the contract between the RMFC and the UMW went into effect on September 1, 1928, Roche and the RMFC still faced daunting problems, many of them legal. Over twenty-one lawsuits related to the Columbine Massacre had been filed against the RMFC, most filed by the ACLU.[16] One of the few non-ACLU suits was filed by the IWW General Defense Committee on behalf of the widow and six orphaned children of John Eastenes, killed at the Columbine. As the case wended its way through the court system for two years, Mrs. Eastenes received a paltry Mother's Pension (a reform passed during the progressive era) from Boulder County. The IWW General Defense Fund sent the family forty dollars a month until 1933, when it reduced its payment to ten dollars, because the union had so little cash in the bank.[17] We cannot know if the family's dire situation tugged at Roche's conscience, but we do know that Costigan aggressively and successfully fought the case and that the RMFC never paid the Eastenes family a single cent.[18]

The ACLU had much deeper pockets than the IWW, so it represented a greater threat to the RMFC, but thanks again to Costigan's legal skills, most of the RMFC's legal troubles were soon over. In October and November of 1928, a flood of letters and telegrams circulated among Roche, Costigan, and Roger Baldwin. In these missives, Roche, but especially Costigan, repeated and expanded the hardening narrative about Roche and the RMFC: Both were blameless for the Columbine because Roche did not control the company when it occurred. Furthermore, the time and money Roche was having to spend fighting lawsuits was depriving her of the resources she needed to convert the RMFC into a bold experiment in industrial democracy. Although no records exist of their conversation, Costigan and Baldwin even met in person to discuss the cases, and in November of 1928, Baldwin abruptly withdrew the ACLU as a plaintiff from all its lawsuits against the RMFC.[19]

In January of 1929, just four months after the contract between the RMFC and the UMW went into effect, Powers and Mary Hapgood arrived in Colorado. Their year-and-a-half in the state helps contextualize the significance of Roche's 1928 contract and also demonstrates Roche's ongoing, inventive, yet grasping-at-straws efforts to keep her company afloat.

After Sacco and Vanzetti were executed on August 23, 1927, more distraught than most were Powers Hapgood and Mary Donovan, who had served tirelessly as the secretary of the Sacco and Vanzetti Defense Committee. Over four intense months of shared protests, arrests, and trials, they fell in love, and on December 28, 1927, Hapgood's twenty-eighth birthday, Powers and the thirty-eight-year-old Mary married in a civil ceremony in New York City. Because of their spartan ways (and occasional checks tucked into their frequent correspondence from Hapgood's parents), the couple was able to live on their wedding cash over the following year and crusade together for social causes in which they passionately believed: promoting free speech and assembly; spreading the ideas of the Socialist Party; exploring the injustices that led to the deaths of Sacco and Vanzetti; and advocating for fair wages, better working conditions, and a democratic labor union for coalminers.

FIGURE 7.1. *The photo of Donovan, speaking in Boston Commons in 1927 on Sacco and Vanzetti's behalf, captures her dedication to that cause. ("Mary Donovan protests against the execution of Sacco and Vanzetti, 1927," Image ID: CPMWBF, Sueddeutsche Zeitung Photo/Alamy Stock Photo.)*

One reason Mary appealed to Hapgood was because, unlike him, she came from an authentic working-class background. Raised in an Irish-Catholic family near Boston, she worked her way through the University of Michigan at Ann Arbor, and after graduation, took a job as an inspector for the state of Massachusetts, monitoring adherence to their newly passed wage and workday regulations for women and children. Next, in Boston, Donovan organized on behalf of the Stenographers, Bookkeepers, Accountants, and Office Employees Union, although she was asked to resign because she spent too much of her time on the Sacco and Vanzetti cause instead of union business.[20]

Six days before their wedding, on December 22, 1927, after their final Sacco and Vanzetti acquittal, Hapgood chaired a meeting in New York City about the ongoing insurgent coal strikes in the Ohio, Pennsylvania, and Colorado coalfields, where he met Embree.[21] Embree and a few other strike leaders, including Milka Sablich, were in town raising strike funds and publicity, which landed them on the front page of the ILD newsletter. In a long letter to Mary, the following is what Hapgood wrote about Embree:

> Embree, the organizer, is a fine man. The meeting was organized by communists, and the local Wobblies didn't cooperate much. Embree, a member of the Executive of the I.W.W., told his followers there must be better cooperation and agreed with me that it was a crime for the various class conscious groups not to combine in the fight against capitalists and labor fakers who are sucking the life blood out of the labor movement. He was high in his praise of the work of communists and the I.L.D. in Colorado and refuses to make plans for his speaking tour except in cooperation with Jim Cannon. I was much surprised at him. He is one of the least sectarian and most tolerant and understanding of the temperaments of differing radical elements that I know. If there were more really broad leaders like him, concerned and interested not at all in personal conflict but only in the class war, the working class would make more progress.
>
> Embree told me a lot about the south-western coal fields. When he heard I had been planning to go to Colorado before the strike, he said that another good place to help was just across the line in New Mexico. There are about the same number of coal miners there as in Colorado and they are more concentrated—11,000 in four towns. The miners work everyday, so jobs can be had. The I.W.W. intends to strike New Mexico as soon as they finish with Colorado, and anyone already there can be of help. After New Mexico they intend to organize the coal camps of Utah and after that those of Oklahoma. Wouldn't it be wonderful, darling, to help and go through all that together? Do you think we could ever go so far? I don't know any place to help more than there.[22]

Embree was dreaming big, but so was Hapgood. They both hated Lewis and wanted to organize the unorganized coalfields, even if that meant working with Communists. Hapgood had already exhibited a romance with the West in his earlier hobo travels, and his letter made clear that the region still provided a strong pull, especially the idea of starting a new life there with Mary. Although the couple would not move to Colorado until a year later, clearly the idea was already brewing between them.

In early February of 1928, the month the 1927–1928 Colorado Coal Strike ended, the newlywed Hapgoods departed for the Pennsylvania coalfields where they worked, not with Brophy, but with insurgent coalminers and the ACLU. As in the 1921–1923 strike, non-union, militant coalminers once again organized themselves, waging a concurrent yet unauthorized strike along-side UMW coalminers who walked off their jobs on April 1, 1927. Once again, in Pennsylvania, UMW loyalists and insurgents battled for control of strikers' hearts, minds, and dues. In 1928, insurgents tried reviving the Save the Union movement, and at first, Brophy allied himself with the insurgents, although as the situation careened out of control, he quickly withdrew his support.

Hapgood sided with the insurgents and threw himself into the thick of the strike turmoil in which at least five people were murdered. Lewis backed UMW Pennsylvania District 1, whose miners worked the anthracite fields between Scranton and Wilkes-Barre. District 2, over which Brophy had pre-sided, was populated with Lewis-hating, bituminous-mining insurgents who made their headquarters in Pittston, southwest of Wilkes-Barre. Hapgood soon headed the defense committee for the three insurgents charged with murder. The ACLU provided the attorneys, and the ILD newspaper gener-ated most of the publicity, the same arrangement both legal groups followed during the 1927–1928 Colorado Coal Strike, except there, Wobblies also worked with the IWW's General Defense Fund. As the defendants awaited trial, Hapgood's friends, insurgent leaders Alex Campbell and Peter Reilly, were ambushed and killed on February 29, 1928.[23] A local judge banned public assembly after "angry muttering and audible threats of reprisal and retal-iation" arose "from a crowd of nearly 10,000 miners and their families as the body of Alexander Campbell, one of the local victims in the local mine union warfare, was lowered into a grave."[24] Although Baldwin tried nego-tiating with local officials for a speaking permit, the judge refused to grant one, so in silent protest, the Hapgoods and insurgent mine leader Pete Lichta, wearing black armbands, silently paraded in front of the hall they had already rented for their now-cancelled meeting. Powers's armband read "We Mourn Free Speech." Mary's and Lichta's read "Civil Liberty." Local police arrested them, charged them with inciting a riot, and the judge set their bail at one thousand dollars each.[25] Newspapers across the country covered their arrests, and after Hapgood's parents read about them in their local Indianapolis papers, they worriedly wrote their son, offering to pay his and Mary's (but not Lichta's) bail.[26] Hapgood urged his folks not to worry and to hold onto their money, and his reassurances proved correct, because on March 9, all three were released on bond provided by the ACLU.[27] In April, they were acquitted after the judge instructed the jury it would be impossible to convict them of inciting a riot since there had been no riot.[28] The legal situation did not go as well for Sam Bonita, one of the three insurgents charged with murder. Although charges against the other two defendants were dropped, on April 15, Bonita was found guilty of manslaughter and sentenced to prison.[29]

In June, the strike sputtered to a close. The District 1 president resigned, and a new president, more sympathetic to the plight of the insurgent Pittston coalminers, won election, a small victory for the rebels. Insurgents returned to work, having won little more than a new leader who promised not to openly fight them. Most District 2 coalminers abandoned their efforts to democratize the UMW from within and turned toward the Communists, who had recently formed the National Miners Union (NMU). When Lewis officially ended the strike on July 19, 1928, the *New York Times* headline accurately captured the disastrous, thirteen-month walkout's consequences: "Miners Abandon Jacksonville Scale: Union Leaves to the Districts the Rights to Settle with Coal Operators." Since each district was now "free" to negotiate its own contracts, the coalminers' race to the bottom on wages and work conditions intensified.

The day Lewis ended the strike, Pennsylvania insurgent coalminer Tony Minerich wrote a letter to Hapgood, trying to convince him to support the NMU. In the same letter, he also urged Hapgood to move to Colorado, because "The Colorado boy's [*sic*] want you to go out there and help them in their fight. They had a talk with rev. Hite or Hist [surely meaning Heist] or some name like that and he wants you to go there." Minerich added, "Powers you must come back into some mining district. I don't care which one but one of them you must work in. You are too well known and liked to stay in Indianapolis."[30] When Hapgood asked Brophy what he thought about Minerich's letter, Brophy advised Hapgood not to join the new union because Communists dominated it, which "condemned [it] to futility from the start."[31] Although Hapgood showed few qualms about associating with Communists, Socialists, the IWW, or any other organization, he took Brophy's advice and let Minerich know that although he could not support the NMU, he would attend their kickoff convention in early September, but strictly as an observer.

On September 1, the UMW showed signs of life when the contract Josephine Roche initiated at the RMFC officially took effect. Days later, Palmer wrote a long letter to Hapgood, answering his questions about the new contract, the

NMU's chances of success in Colorado, and Hapgood's personal prospects in Colorado. Palmer believed that, although Colorado coalminers had lost faith in the UMW after "John R. Lawson was robbed of the election as district president" and that their "confidence has never been fully restored," it was also unfair for radicals to label the newly constituted UMW at the RMFC a company union, which both the Communist and IWW newspapers were doing. Although the company union label was not completely unwarranted since Roche had largely dictated the terms of the contract, Palmer emphasized that Roche's recognition of the UMW represented "a radical step in Colorado, there being no other operator going even that far." Regardless of how the contract had been negotiated, it was a victory for organized labor, not just in Colorado, but elsewhere in the country, too.

Palmer opined that "If there were a new union, the coal camps would be divided into three groups instead of two; the wobblies are still here and making a desperate effort to survive; the UMWA will soon have 1,000 members in the RM [RMFC] and that will give it a foothold from which it will gather more." Palmer added that "if the new union could get a powerful enough start to make the Colorado miners believe that here was a movement that was going to swing things and be a real power, they might climb aboard the band wagon gladly to escape the battle between the IWW and the UMWA. But that seems rather too much for even its best friends to expect. Or is it?"

Palmer thought that "so far as you personally are concerned, there are plenty of independent mines in which work can be obtained so that the attitude of the RM [RMFC] would not be final. I doubt whether they would keep you out of their mines, though. That would be a bit strong, and would jar a lot of liberals who are now strong for them." Palmer left no doubt about

whether I still think you ought to come. I do, enthusiastically. I have a place of service open to you with a group of young folks (where you will not be "reachable" thru the Lewis machine) that is the most hopeful group I know about anywhere, but which seriously needs just the leadership that you can give. I am delighted to see that you are thinking of settling down in Colorado. I believe here is the opportunity for doing, rather slowly I'll admit the things that you folks will want to do with your lives. The field is small enough so that it can be encompassed; a given task can be accomplished. I am strong for your coming just as soon as possible.[32]

Palmer's letter prompted Powers to write this to Mary: "I do hope we can go to Colorado—for quiet work, and study, and rest. Perhaps I will be far more useful to the movement in the end than agitating for a new union."[33] Just four days after Palmer wrote his letter, Hapgood went to Pittsburgh to observe the new coalminers' union convention, which was "broken up by a combination of Lewis thugs and policemen before it even got started."[34] The *New York Times* reported that the street fight in front of the convention hall resulted in six badly wounded men, one critically, and a stunning 122 arrests.[35] Since Hapgood was neither a UMW member nor an insurgent, his new status as a complete outsider plunged him even deeper into despair. He wrote to Mary, "I feel so out of things. From one who used to be in the forefront of everything in the coal fields, I'm now considered dead."[36] The Hapgoods spent the fall campaigning on behalf of Mary's Socialist Party candidacy for the governorship of Massachusetts, mostly to continue speaking about Sacco and Vanzetti. Yet by October 5, they had already made up their minds to move to Colorado.[37]

Although Embree, Minerich, Palmer, and perhaps even Heist had urged Powers Hapgood to come to Colorado, within weeks of their arrival in January of 1929, the Hapgoods socialized with and worked exclusively for Roche. There is no correspondence proving it, but surely Roche had also invited the Hapgoods to Colorado. Roche's simple RMFC narrative had never reflected the company's messy realities, and in her ongoing struggles to keep the RMFC afloat, she needed them both. Throughout 1928, the Hapgoods expressed mixed motivations for moving to the state, but Roche's motives are easier to disentangle. She had big problems—with restive coalminers, the CIC, and money, always money—that the Hapgoods were in a unique position to help her fix.

Roche needed to win the Hapgoods over, and we know from the Hapgoods' frequent correspondence with his parents that she did, quickly, although the couple appeared oblivious to Roche's machinations. Within their first Colorado fortnight, the Hapgoods dined with Roche at least four times at her apartment. These discussion-filled evenings spent lingering over dinner included Roche's oldest and closest friends, Mabel and Edward and Costigan, Olive and John Lawson, Merle Vincent (whose wife rarely joined the group), and the newest additions, Edith and Ben Cherrington. This tight circle of intelligent, progressive friends quickly enveloped the Hapgoods into their world. In a letter to his father three days after their arrival, Powers wrote,

"The subject of conversation most of the evening was the Sacco and Vanzetti case, in which they all were much interested. We admire and like them all very much."[38] Although their hostess and her other dinner guests might have been expressing genuine interest in Sacco and Vanzetti, more likely they were gently patronizing the Hapgoods by engaging them about a cause to which they were deeply committed. On a different topic, Hapgood wrote: "I have said nothing to them about a job, beyond telling John Lawson some days ago that I was looking for one and hoped to get it in one of the Rocky Mountain Fuel Co's mines. They evidently thought it best not to give me one through the main office, and I believe they were right. I have tried about seventeen mines and finally today, got a job at the Industrial Mine at Superior, which is one of the Rocky Mountain Fuel Co's mines. I start work tomorrow [January 10, 1928] on the night shift (from 4 p.m. to 12 Midnight)."[39]

Within a week, the couple moved into a small miner's cottage in Lafayette, sharing the house with the Richards, an elderly couple who needed help around the house, which the young couple provided. No doubt the Hapgoods' rent for half the house and the garage in back helped the Richards financially, too.[40] After getting established with a new house and job, Hapgood wrote his father that "the mine doesn't work very often, only one day so far this week, but when it does run I can make more than in most of the other mines I've worked in."[41] So, although the new UMW contract brought above-average wages to the RMFC coalminers, it had not fixed the problem of short work, a term that described the sporadic, shortened hours many coalminers experienced. It did little good to earn a high daily rate if a miner only worked one to three days a week for six or fewer months out of the year.

By their second week in Colorado, not only was Powers Hapgood working for Roche, so was Mary. Roche had asked Mary if she would consider "making a scrap book from back numbers of the *Survey*, *Nation*, *New Republic*, and *Colorado Labor Advocate*. This, of course, can be done at home, but Miss Roche offered Mary $50 a week and handed her an envelope with $100 for two weeks work in advance."[42] Mary protested, insisting that she would be glad to do it for nothing, but "Roche insisted," something Roche seemed to do often with the Hapgoods. Powers believed that "I think later on, when the health and medical plans that she is working on for the miners' families become more advanced, she will want Mary to help her with that."[43] Under the new UMW contract, most coalminers only earned seven dollars a day, so

Mary would be earning more than Hapgood. Clearly, Roche was subsidizing the Hapgoods, but they seemed too guileless to notice.

Powers Hapgood thought Roche's friends were all wonderful people, but he was especially impressed by Lawson, who appealed to Hapgood for the same reason he appealed to almost all the coalminers: He remained forever the legendary hero of the 1910–1914 strike. Over dinners at Roche's, we can imagine Lawson regaling the Hapgoods with stories from the long strike. Hapgood also knew that Lewis had initiated the UMW's appropriation policy to take over District 15 and expel Lawson and Doyle from the UMW, the same mechanism Lewis employed throughout the 1920s to consolidate his control over the union and to expel him and John Brophy from the UMW.[44] Hapgood described Lawson as a "big, serious, kindly man" who "happened to meet Mary and me in the company store the other day and told Miss Roche later on, 'I saw our children in Lafayette today,' "[45] a remark that suggests Roche, Lawson, and probably her friends did not consider Powers and Mary Donovan Hapgood fully adult yet. More troubling, the Hapgoods seemed not to mind.

One of Roche's most compelling reasons for employing the Hapgoods related to her financial and legal problems, and ten months into his Colorado residency, Hapgood's father made Roche an interest-free twenty-thousand-dollar loan.[46] Was he supporting Roche's experiment in industrial democracy, thanking Roche for taking care of his troubled son, or both? Evelyn Preston, who knew Hapgood well and delighted in his company, had also loaned money to Roche.[47] We do not know if Preston asked Roche to hire Hapgood, yet Roche surely knew that doing so might delay, perhaps permanently, repaying Preston. Roche also might have hired the Hapgoods to fix her ACLU problems. For serving as first amendment guinea pigs, the ACLU owed both Powers and Mary Hapgood a great debt. When Costigan met with Baldwin in November of 1928, might they have struck a deal with Baldwin agreeing to drop the ACLU cases in exchange for hiring Hapgood? Since Baldwin was married to Evie Preston, whose money helped bankroll Roche but almost completely supported the ACLU, Baldwin also might have been double-dipping on his motivations, too.

It is equally plausible Roche recruited Hapgood to quell ongoing coalminer dissent. He had ties to the IWW, the NMU, Socialists, and Communists, and all were actively agitating in the coalfields. In the summer of 1928, when Roche had contacted the UMW about negotiating a contract at the RMFC, the district president wrote Lewis that before negotiations formally began, "the new management wanted the opportunity to weed out 'elements that [did] not believe in the trade union movement' so that unionization would proceed smoothly when a contract was signed."[48] Even after the contract went into effect, the RMFC continued trying to weed out dissidents. For example, in September of 1928, the *Industrial Worker* reported that although Charles Metz, a Wobbly, had been democratically elected as the Columbine's checkweighman, Merle Vincent had fired him and replaced him with a UMW member.[49]

Additional evidence of discontent is in a letter Hapgood wrote his father about the RMFC's hiring practices. In a discussion among Roche, Vincent, Costigan, Lawson, and the Hapgoods, they shared that one of RMFC's biggest quandaries was what to do with the Wobblies now that the company operated under a closed shop arrangement with the UMW. The Roche bunch were "remarkably understanding and anxious to do the right thing," Hapgood wrote, but

> often they are faced with the problem of doing what appears to be and is
> an injustice to an individual in order to do justice to the whole group. For
> instance a few Mexican I.W.W.s who were active in the last strike here haven't
> been able to get work because their places had been filled by old natives who
> had been black-listed from the strikes of 1915 and 1922. There certainly is no
> discrimination, however, even though some of the men affected think there is,
> and "quite naturally think so" in the words of Mr. Vincent.[50]

Employment records at the RMFC were spotty, so it is highly unlikely any kind of reliable list was available on which to base seniority decisions. More likely, the RMFC was using mandatory UMW membership to weed out Wobblies, NMU sympathizers, and Mexican-Americans in favor of hiring "old natives," all under the guise of fairness.

In February of 1929, Hapgood received a letter from Gerry Allander, who lived and worked in Frederick, a town just ten miles from Lafayette. Allander enthusiastically participated in the 1927–1928 Colorado Coal Strike, had recently been expelled from the Communist Party because he was a Trotskyite, and served as a delegate to the 1928 National Miners Union coalminers' convention that Hapgood observed and Lewis thugs broke up. Allander wrote that when he first heard Hapgood was coming to Colorado, he concluded that "if the R.M.F. [RMFC] openly and publicly invites Hapgood to work in its pits it is a clever maneuver to further disintegrate the organizational independence of the Colorado miners."[51] Allander seemed concerned that Roche had hired Hapgood to convince coalminers still loyal to the IWW or even the NMU to join the UMW. Maybe he was right.

In spite of his radical connections, Hapgood's actions in Colorado show that, above all, he desired re-admittance into the UMW. The gregarious, famous, much-admired Hapgood might be able to convince still-resistant coalminers that the UMW was not a Roche-dominated company union at all, but instead an institution still worthy of their allegiance. Hapgood's relationship to the UMW was still fraught, however. In February, contrary to Frank Palmer's earlier assessment, Powers discovered he was not outside the reaches of Lewis and the UMW at all. Lewis found out that the RMFC had hired Hapgood after Hapgood applied for reinstatement into the UMW, a situation that prompted Hapgood to seek advice from Brophy.

In a February 3 letter, Brophy counseled Hapgood to keep a low profile and force Lewis to make the first move. He also advised Hapgood, even if asked, not to quit his job. "If you are to go make them give reasons. Even though there is a closed shop at the mine at which you are working and the worst happens, it would place the local union and the coal company in the position of co-operating with Lewis in blacklisting Lewis' inter union political opponents. I don't think Josephine Roche or the others associated with her will want to get in that position. If you play your cards carefully, Lewis will not be able to push you out."[52]

Hapgood clearly ignored Brophy's advice, because on February 13, 1929, the *Denver Post* featured a half-page photo collage about Powers and Mary, and its captions read as follows:

"Here's your lunch," says the first woman candidate for governor of Massachusetts to her Harvard graduate husband, and the picture at the bottom shows that the said husband grins a happy reply and is all ready for a night's work digging coal. The gubernatorial candidate is Mary Donovan Hapgood and her husband is Powers Hapgood, scion of a famous literary family. There are living in Lafayette and Hapgood is working as an ordinary miner at Superior, Colo. At the upper left is a glimpse of the little frame house which the Hapgoods occupy with another family. In the center is a closeup of the miner member of the family who is devoting his life to the union labor movement. At the right is the Industrial mine, where he works alongside a couple of Mexicans, an Irishman, two Frenchmen, among others.[53]

Even without the story, Hapgood was impossible to miss. He spoke frequently to local civic organizations and student groups at the University of Colorado in Boulder and became a veritable regular on the podium at Heist's Grace Church.[54] Clearly, the Hapgoods enjoyed the limelight, and their backgrounds made it difficult to adopt a low profile, even if they tried, which they clearly did not.

In March, the UMW executive board sent Hapgood a lengthy, vicious reply to his UMW reinstatement request. It expounded upon the many reasons for denying Hapgood's request: He had been involved with almost every serious insurgent and dual movement against the UMW, his protestations of being a loyal UMW member rang hollow, and last but not least, Hapgood was "a man of means," and there were plenty of real, unemployed, and loyal UMW coalminers who needed to work more than he did.[55] Hapgood again asked Brophy how to respond, and this was his advice: "All Lewis understands is power," and all the "non-essential personal matters" that had been dragged into the letter were only meant to appeal "to the prejudice and suspicion of the average run of miners. I would advise that you reduce your reply to these personal matters to a minimum and that you devote your main work to a statement of the progressive program and policy, which of course includes a devastating criticism of the Lewis policy."[56] Hapgood again ignored Brophy's sage advice, and instead wrote a seven-page, single-spaced letter, refuting in excruciating detail each of the charges against him.[57]

As would be the case throughout most of his life, in March of 1929, Hapgood was deeply conflicted. He was distraught that the UMW had refused to reinstate him, yet he and Mary were happy in Lafayette and about to be happier, because Mary was pregnant and due in October.[58] Upon hearing the Hapgoods' good news, Roche suggested the doctor and hospital Mary should use, and Mary obediently followed her advice.[59] The couple thoroughly enjoyed Mary's pregnancy, because when the mine was not working,

FIGURE 7.2. *Byron Kitto had financial resources available to pay for his stay at this California sanitarium, but the thirty-one-year-old died in 1931 from tuberculosis, probably contracted during the 1927–1928 Colorado Coal Strike.*

which was often, Powers and Mary enjoyed staying home, reading to each other, and discussing their future plans.[60]

They also filled their time with their faithful correspondence. On March 23, the very day Mary Donovan Hapgood discovered she was pregnant, Mary Gallagher wrote, asking Mary to "tell the good people of Lafayette that their old friend Byron Kitto [one of the key IWW organizers during the 1927–1928 strike] is still a bed patient in the Sanitarium in Duarte, California and is not progressing as well as we would like to see."[61] Much later, as an old woman reminiscing about her life, Gallagher remembered back in 1931, sitting at Kitto's bedside when he died of tuberculosis, contracted while imprisoned during the Colorado strike. He was only thirty-one years old.[62] Gallagher sent some of Kitto's ashes to Lafayette, where Wobblies sprinkled them over the unmarked graves of four of the five victims of the Columbine Massacre buried in the Lafayette cemetery.[63] The fifth victim, Ray Jacques, had been buried separately in a family plot nearby in the Louisville cemetery, and in a very different kind of memorial, locals say his mother kept her son's bloody, bullet-ridden overalls hanging on her laundry porch the rest of her life.[64]

Although the Hapgoods enjoyed being homebodies, they also socialized often, frequently driving to Denver for cultural events and dinners at Roche's apartment, which they called "family parties." Occasionally, they reciprocated with their own dinner parties for the Roche "family" in Lafayette.[65] They enjoyed visiting with local miners and their families, and Mary baked pies for neighborhood children, especially two Mexican-American girls down the street whose widowed father left them alone while he worked in the mines.[66] They even welcomed the Baptist preacher who dropped by occasionally, who unsuccessfully tried persuading the atheistic Hapgoods to attend church.[67] So, in spite of Powers's failure to win reinstatement into the UMW, the Hapgoods' correspondence strongly suggests that living in Lafayette was probably the happiest time in their entire married lives.

After the UMW refused to reinstate Hapgood, in March, Vincent asked Hapgood to quietly resign at the RMFC-owned coalmine where he worked.[68] Ignoring Brophy's advice not to quit, Hapgood complied with Vincent's request. However, within the week, he found another coalmining job at a nearby, non-RMFC coalmine,[69] and his new status actually benefitted Roche, since it provided Hapgood legal standing to bring a petition before the CIC on behalf of the non-union northern coalminers.[70]

Roche understood she could not compete with other coal companies if she remained the only unionized operator in the state. Therefore, guided by the advice and cooperation from the new UMW officers in Colorado, the State Federation of Labor, and two out of three sympathetic CIC commissioners, a CIC hearing was scheduled for April. It would consider a petition presented by the non-unionized coalminers in the northern field, requesting their working conditions be equalized with those at the RMFC. Everybody knew the RMFC was orchestrating the entire process, that Hapgood was leading the "spontaneous" petition drive, and that he would be the star witness at the hearing.[71] After the mines closed for the season, Hapgood spent much of his time preparing his testimony, since "a good deal is expected of me by my friends," Lawson, Vincent, and Roche.[72] His subsequent actions also show that Hapgood hoped his testimony might win him reinstatement into the UMW.

The hearings began on April 23, 1929. Hapgood, Vincent, and Percy Tetlow—a UMW official and Lewis insider who had handled the initial negotiations for the UMW-RMFC contract—provided most of the testimony.[73] Hapgood testified that the RMFC offered superior pay and working conditions to non-union coalmines, and he should know, since he had worked in both. Furthermore, if the RMFC could afford to pay its workers a union wage and still run a profitable business, so could its competitors. Afterward, Hapgood privately conversed with Tetlow, and Mary reassured her anxious husband that she thought he had made a "good impression" with him.[74]

The hearing proved futile. As anticipated, two of the three commissioners agreed with the petitioners. Their award stated that the operators of the northern field coalmines "shall allow the right of collective bargaining, pay the same wage scale, and grant the working conditions now in force in the mines of the Rocky Mountain Fuel Company."[75] However, the award was worthless, because the CIC had no enforcement powers. As Roche wrote to Edward Keating, "None of the operators have granted their miners our wage scale nor have they shown the slightest interest in the commission's award," which demonstrated a decision in the operators' favor got "vigorously enforced against striking miners" but was "ignored" by the operators when it "favored the miners."[76] It is worth pointing out Roche's extreme lack of self-reflection and intellectual inconsistency here, because when that same industrial commission had denied the legitimacy of the IWW committee's strike petition in 1927, Roche supported their decision and invoked it as a legal basis to aggressively fight the strike.

After Powers testified, the Hapgoods drove east to visit their families.[77] They stayed in Massachusetts for two months, providing Mary's sister a well-deserved break from caring for their housebound father. Perhaps this family photo was taken during this visit.[78] They planted a garden, played with the many dogs on the farm (Hapgood loved dogs), visited with family and friends, and continued writing letters, many of them solicitations to help Roche. For example, Norman Thomas, head of the Socialist Party as well as an activist in the League for Industrial Democracy, wrote Hapgood, "I failed to get any money for Miss Roche out of the American [the Garland] Fund, much to my sorrow, but I think she was pretty successful elsewhere."[79] From North Brookfield, they drove to Indianapolis to visit Hapgood's parents (who paid for the couple's extensive dental work), and while there, Hapgood paid a visit

FIGURE 7.3. *This family photo was probably taken in the summer of 1929. Standing left to right, Dan Donovan, Powers, Eva Donovan (who was married to Dan Donovan). Seated left to right Mary Donovan Hapgood, Denis Donovan, Eliza Donovan (Dan and Mary's parents). Kids: sitting, Ronald Donovan (child of Dan); standing, Betty Donovan (child of Dan).*

to the UMW headquarters, where he asked to speak to Lewis. The reception-ist said Lewis was not in, but she would hand deliver Hapgood's letter to him, which might have been the lengthy response he wrote after his reinstatement rejection.[80] By the time the Hapgoods returned to Lafayette in the fall of 1929, Lewis's reply awaited them. Unlike his earlier denial, this response was short, direct, and signed by Lewis. Yet, in spite of Hapgood's pro-UMW CIC testimony and his personal appeals to Tetlow to intervene on his behalf to Lewis, the UMW executive board stood by its original decision. The answer was still no. Hapgood would not be reinstated.[81]

With Powers's UMW hopes dashed, in the fall of 1929, the Hapgoods set-tled into a new pattern of life, which included a changed relationship between Hapgood and Brophy. Hapgood stopped asking his mentor for advice, and instead, Brophy now needed Hapgood's help. After trying to earn a living by writing and running a labor college, Brophy was broke and needed a job in order to feed his family. Brophy reluctantly accepted Hapgood's standing offer to work at the CCC, and even accepted Hapgood's offer to pay his way to Indianapolis. When that check arrived, Brophy thanked Hapgood profusely, since he was down to his last dime. He added, "I'll consider it a loan, unless I find I can't pay it back."[82]

Perhaps because there was no longer any benefit to Hapgood working in a non-union coalmine, the RMFC rehired Hapgood, not as a coalminer, but as a surveyor and engineer. Even in his new, professional role, Hapgood wanted to stay active in the labor movement, so he sought information on how to start a local union of the engineers, architects, and draftsmen in Colorado.[83] By February of 1930, he was back in the labor union movement again, as president of the new local he had just formed.[84] Hapgood began taking a correspondence course, which he passed in March of 1930, that officially certified him to do the work he was already performing.[85] Hapgood thoroughly enjoyed his work, but most of all, he loved being a new father. In October, Mary had given birth to a daughter the couple named Mary Barta (after Bartolomeo Vanzetti) Hapgood. Although Powers's mother hated the name Barta, Roche, who sent both mother and baby a dozen roses each, told the couple she thought it was a delightful name.[86] Hapgood was so uncharacteristically giddy, on the day Barta was born, he wrote his mother a silly, lighthearted letter as if it were written by the baby.[87]

Personal happiness, however, was not enough to keep Powers Hapgood in Colorado. By the summer of 1930, he left Colorado forever, to pursue his dream of reinstatement into the UMW, a plan that did not work out. That same summer, Roche's plan to keep the RMFC afloat through private loans did not work out for her, either.

Like any good progressive, Roche believed in the principles of scientific management and efficiency, which at the RMFC meant increasing mechanization. Mechanization took money, and by April of 1929, Roche finally had a plan to get some. Soon after she began to exercise increasing control over the RMFC, Roche sought loans from local banks, but they turned her down. Roche explained to potential donors that a Colorado conspiracy was afoot to deprive her and her company of operating capital, because everybody in the state cowered before John D. Rockefeller Jr. and his company, the CF&I, and he did not want her to get any loans. More likely, local banks refused her financing because the RMFC was unprofitable and showed no signs of recovery.

In January of 1929, Roche set up a series of meetings with Sidney Hillman, the founder and president of the Amalgamated Clothing Workers of America (ACWA), which had founded the Amalgamated Bank in 1922. After Roche's meetings with Hillman, an Amalgamated loan officer made Roche an offer she could not refuse: It would establish a $125,000 line of credit that Roche could draw against for the RMFC, but only if she could raise $125,000 in matching personal collateral first.[88] With this lifeline, Roche feverishly set about asking for, and even receiving some, personal loans. Most of that money arrived from rich, powerful, liberal New Yorkers Roche must have networked among when she lived and worked in the city during her Columbia graduate school days. Her biggest lenders included Agnes Goddard Leach, Pauline Goldmark, Evelyn Preston, Mary Dreier, Caroline O' Day, Herbert Lehman, and Oswald Garrison Villard. Leach, a wealthy philanthropist, donated most of her money to pacifist organizations and helped underwrite Paul Kellogg's social science publication, *The Survey*. Goldmark, Louis Brandeis's sister-in-law, along with other maternalists (perhaps including Roche) compiled most of the information for the groundbreaking Brandeis Brief used in the 1908 Supreme Court case *Muller v. Oregon*. Often described as two pages of law and one hundred pages of statistics about women's health, education, and earnings, the brief was the first to rely upon social science rather than legal precedents as evidence. Philanthropist Evelyn Preston bankrolled many liberal causes, including, after marrying Roger Baldwin, the ACLU. Mary Dreier's 1909 arrest during New York City's Uprising of 20,000 surely changed the course of the walkout, because Dreier was an influential society woman who presided over the Women's Trade Union League. She led a cross-class alliance between the strikers and other women like herself (and Roche) that publicized and legitimized the strike.[89] Caroline O' Day, New York state's only female representative in its House of Representatives throughout the 1930s, also was a distinguished historian and a close friend whom Frances Perkins and her daughter could depend upon for solace and a place to live during the frequent mental breakdowns of Perkins's husband.[90] Lehman, of the Lehman Brothers family, entered politics instead of joining the family banking and investment business. In 1932, he succeeded Franklin D. Roosevelt as the governor of New York.

Roche kept few letters from the donors listed above, but she did keep some correspondence with Villard, and Villard saved even more. Villard's maternal grandfather was William Lloyd Garrison, the radical abolitionist and publisher of *The Liberator*. His father was Henry Villard, who made a fortune from railroad and General Electric investments. With his unimpeachable social justice pedigree and daddy's money, OGV (as he signed his letters) was equipped to pursue his passions, many of which could be found in the pages of *The Nation*, which he owned and edited from 1927 through the early 1930s. Villard supported organized labor, so it is hardly surprising that the magazine published two Frank Palmer articles about the 1927–1928 Colorado Coal Strike. Yet it is also not surprising that since Roche knew Villard well enough to get personal loans from him, she surely knew him well enough to convince him to stop printing any further stories about the strike. Obviously, the only way Villard's loan to Roche would be repaid was if the RMFC flourished, so after 1929, *The Nation*'s pages publicly praised Roche, Costigan, and the RMFC. Privately, however, over the next decade, Villard would harangue Roche for repayment of his 1929 loan.

Villard's letters to Roche demonstrate how the October 1929 stock market crash also crashed Roche's plan to keep the RMFC afloat with private loans from rich friends and social justice philanthropists. In the spring of 1929, Villard had responded so enthusiastically to Roche's "elevator pitch," he not only loaned her $35,000 but he urged others to do the same.[91] By February of 1930, Roche repaid $5,000 toward the principal she owed Villard, and she predicted she would be able to pay him another $12,000 in March. However, when the coal season ended that year, Roche missed that March payment, and by July, Villard was really, really worried. He had lost at least 60 percent of his personal wealth in the crash,[92] and not only had Roche stopped paying him, most worrisome of all, she ignored all his inquiries about her business.[93] By the summer of 1930, Roche had to face reality: She could not repay Villard or any of her lenders. That financial desperation would soon push Roche even more deeply into the orbit of John L. Lewis and the UMW.

8

Traces of the 1927–1928 Colorado Coal Strike

1931–1948

From the earliest years of the Great Depression through the earliest years of the Cold War, the 1927–1928 Colorado Strike continued shaping the careers of Josephine Roche, Powers Hapgood, and A. S. Embree as they helped transform organized labor from a floundering movement into a national institution. Although all three modified their earlier visions of industrial democracy, core elements of their previous beliefs continued to guide their actions. Furthermore, just as the presence of John L. Lewis and the UMW had loomed large over the 1927–1928 Colorado walkout, even though it had been an IWW-led strike, both Lewis and his union continued dominating this critical period for the nation's labor movement, as well as the personal fortunes of Roche, Hapgood, and Embree.

When the 1930 fall coal season began, both John D. Rockefeller Jr. and Roche turned to marketing efforts to save their beleaguered companies. Rockefeller's CF&I created the brand name Diavolo, hoping it might increase name recognition and increase sales for its superior southern Colorado coal.

https://doi.org/10.5876/9781646423026.c008

It did not.[1] Roche ran advertisements in local newspapers touting RMFC's unionized workers, although it is impossible to gauge what impact, if any, those ads made.[2] As profits continued plummeting, CF&I accelerated coalmine closures and dropped wages, even before going through the motions of petitioning the state industrial commission to do so. Roche placed four of six RMFC coalmines on "alternate work" (part-time) schedules and sent RMFC coalminers door-to-door, cold-calling for coal orders. Roche continued trying to blame Rockefeller Jr., not the Great Depression or the "sick" coal industry, for her problems, but in 1930, as seen below, Edward Keating suggested that Roche set Jr. up as a *public* foil:

> Why not strike at John D. Jr.? He doesn't like unfavorable publicity. Senator Costigan [who had been elected to the United States Senate in November of 1930] might wire President Hoover calling attention to the fact that the Rockefellers, probably the wealthiest group in the world, are slashing wages in Colorado and endeavoring to destroy competitors who maintain decent standards.
>
> He should point out that this is a revival of the tactics which made the elder Rockefeller infamous . . . and a deadly parallel might be drawn to demonstrate that the son is following in the footsteps of the father. Of course the protest should be given the widest publicity . . . I believe the stage could be set for quite a show. Think it over. The time is ripe.
>
> We will run a good story in next week's issue of LABOR [which Keating edited] and will endeavor to pin all the blame on the Rockefellers . . . I realize you are fighting under many handicaps, but on the other hand, you have many advantages. Public sentiment is against wage cuts, especially by multi-millionaires like Rockefeller. In addition to that, you are a woman, and the spectacle of a young woman risking her fortune to maintain wage standards and working conditions, while a Rockefeller is endeavoring to tear them down, will appeal to the imagination of the American people.[3]

Keating's idea was to claim that Jr.'s latest cost-cutting efforts were a conspiracy aimed specifically at Roche, to run her out of business. However, those attacks proved ineffective as the name Rockefeller began to lose its bogeyman quality. After the 1927–1928 Colorado Coal Strike and stock market crash, Jr. lost interest in the CF&I, and increasingly, he redirected his interests toward projects that captured his and the public's imagination more, which included the Rockefeller Foundation, Rockefeller Center, and historical preservation at Williamsburg, Virginia.

In 1931, Roche instituted mandatory part-time work at all the RMFC properties and halved wages for the first three months of the coal season. Although her actions absolutely violated the RMFC's UMW contract, that fall, a spate of national news articles appeared, all praising Roche for her "job sharing program." Journalists claimed RMFC coalminers implored Roche to make these changes, but those claims have never passed the smell test. Legally, employers or employees needed approval from the CIC to alter labor agreements. Roche's papers include a petition submitted to the CIC signed by fifty coalminers (out of over six hundred) from one (of six) RMFC coalmines. The petition asked permission for a "postponement" of "one-half the wages due us in August, September, and October, 1931" and permission to "enlist as coal salesmen to market the coal we mine."[4] Although that partial petition might be a reflection of sloppy record keeping, more likely it provides evidence that Roche had *not* been bombarded by coalminer requests to cut their wages and put them to work as outside salesmen. A 1976 oral history interview with retired coalminer Walt Celinski and an article from *Industrial Solidarity* also undercut Roche's claim. Celinski joined the Junior Wobblies during the 1927–1928 Colorado Coal Strike, but by 1931, he was old enough to mine coal at the RMFC. He remembered refusing to sign the petition and getting badly harassed for not doing so.[5] A lengthy, retrospective article published on April 4, 1933, in the IWW's *Industrial Worker* declared that many coalminers had refused to sign the petitions that Roche, not coalminers, had circulated. In retaliation, the RMFC fired non-signers when the coal season ended in the spring of 1932 and only rehired them the following fall after they threatened to go public with the reasons for their layoffs, unflattering revelations that would have damaged Roche's reformer reputation. The article also claims the RMFC never repaid those "deferred" wages.[6]

None of that negative information ever appeared in any mainstream national publications because Roche so thoroughly controlled her own press. Even more than today, a nation suffering through the Great Depression hungered for feel-good, inspirational stories and Roche, master of the press release, provided them. This is obvious to anyone who compares the uncannily identical wording of articles about Roche published in the fall of 1931.[7] Furthermore, Roche apparently demanded, and received, final editorial control. For example, *The New Republic*'s Bruce Blivens sent Roche an article draft, and after some testy back-and-forth, Blivens relented and adopted Roche's "corrections."[8] The same process unfolded with Mary Van Kleek's report, "Miners and Management: A Study of the Collective Agreement Between the United Mine Workers of America and the Rocky Mountain Fuel Company, and an Analysis of the Problem of Coal in the United States." Roche indignantly objected when Van Kleek compared the RMFC's industrial experiment to the Rockefeller Plan. That led Roche to edit Van Kleek's draft with her own facts, figures, and strikethroughs, which Van Kleek incorporated into her final document. Unsurprisingly, Roche's revisions always portrayed her and the RMFC in a favorable light.[9]

As Roche's narrative evolved, perhaps because it grew increasingly irrelevant and ineffective to portray Jr. as her primary narrative foil, Roche began to cast her own father in that role. This shows just how much she had changed since 1925, when she abandoned her promising career at the Children's Bureau to care for her ailing parents in Denver. Even after inheriting their half of the RMFC in 1927, she showed little interest in running the company until after the Columbine Massacre. A letter to Keating in June of 1928 helps explain her initial disinterest in the RMFC: "Until my father's death left me a totally new and strange responsibility in the form of coal company holdings, I had never known anything about the company except what the [1915 United States Industrial Commission] coal strike investigations had disclosed. It had no more personal significance or relation to me than any other company had. Father had been remarkable in recognizing my right to independent work and views, and we had remained the most devoted companions, with little or no reference to business between us."[10]

By 1931, Roche, who now presided over the RMFC, had transformed herself into a coal policy expert. In her evolving narrative, she presented herself as an efficient reformer who practiced principles of scientific management, which included her contract with the UMW. Roche was not lying when she portrayed her father as adamantly anti-union. What was new was her willingness to include that stance in her press releases. For example, although the first paragraph of *Time*'s September 7, 1931, article, "Rocky Mountain Gesture," begins with Rockefeller, it quickly pivots, and concludes with her father:

Unique among Colorado coal diggers is Rocky Mountain Fuel Co., second in production only to Rockefeller-owned Colorado Fuel and Iron Corp. Rocky Mountain is the only Colorado colliery to employ union labor. Last week Rocky Mountain became unique in another respect: 600 of its Union miners voted to go without half their wages for three months. Miss Josephine Roche, the company's 40-year-old, black-haired, thoroughly feminine president, gladly accepted their offer. . . . To most Colorado coal operators President [Josephine] Roche . . . is a dangerous industrial radical who brought the United Mine Workers of America back into Colorado. Her father founded Rocky Mountain Fuel. . . . For her liberal views her father had scant sympathy. He used to mock her efforts to reform Industry and Labor.[11]

Regardless of its narrative construction, the main point of the article is to celebrate Roche's job-sharing program, which suggests that Roche had begun cooperating with Lewis, who, working alongside his publicist W. Jett Lauck, was even better at public relations than she. We know why Roche might want to polish her own halo, but what did Lewis and the UMW stand to benefit by promoting Roche's narrative? Consider this: Everything about the RMFC's 1931 "voluntary" job sharing, wage deferments, and forced outside sales program absolutely violated the UMW contract. When UMW coalminers outside Colorado caught wind of Roche's contract violations, they squawked so loudly that Lewis was forced to react. UMW historian Maier B. Fox writes that "the storm blew over when Rocky Mountain Fuel righted itself—with the help of a short-term loan from the international—and full wages were restored."[12] The IWW claimed those wages were never repaid. More significantly, that "short-term" UMW loan was the first of many the UMW would make (by buying Roche's unsecured bonds) to the RMFC throughout the 1930s. Roche promoted her narrative because she was trying the save the RMFC. Lewis promoted Roche's narrative because he was trying to save himself and the UMW.

In 1936, Lauck wrote a scholarly article that helps us understand why Lewis needed Roche's sunny stories. After UMW memberships sharply declined in 1922, Lewis began aiming his UMW appeals not at coalminers, but at coal operators and politicians,[13] and one of those politicians included Herbert Hoover. Before being elected president of the United States in 1928, Hoover served throughout the decade as the influential secretary of commerce, and in 1924, it had been Hoover who suggested to Lewis that he negotiate a long-term UMW contract. Lewis took Hoover's advice and negotiated a three-year agreement that initiated the Jacksonville scale, but after coal operators refused to renew that contract, Lewis called UMW coalminers out on strike on April 1, 1927. Fifteen months later, Lewis ended the strike, a complete loss, and everywhere except Illinois the UMW was dead.[14]

Lewis seemed to learn almost nothing from that loss, however, and he continued promoting the UMW to coal operators and politicians, not coalminers. For example, in 1931, Lewis asked Hoover to call a conference between the nation's largest coal operators and the UMW to seek solutions to the nation's coal crisis. Hoover directed his secretaries of commerce and labor to send letters to operators, including Roche, asking if they would attend such a meeting. Those queries included copies of Lewis's original telegram, worded like the press release it surely was, which encapsulated the gendered and political arguments Lewis made, and would continue making, throughout the 1930s: "The Executive Board of the United Mine Workers of America feels that the inhuman plight of the women and children, the degradation of the men employed in the coalmines, all of which are breeding communism and anarchy, are of such serious moment that the government of the United States can no longer pursue a passive policy. The history of the bituminous coal industry reveals that the joint wage agreement has been the only stabilizing force the industry has ever known."[15]

Most operators declined to attend, so the conference never took place, although Roche would have enthusiastically endorsed the UMW's arguments at such a gathering, significant support lost on neither Lewis nor Lauck.[16] In 1932, Lauck once again asked Roche to help the UMW, a request that coincided with another wave of positive Roche articles. The UMW was promoting the Davis-Kelly bill (much of which would be included in the 1933 National Recovery Administration's coal code),[17] so the UMW needed witnesses for congressional hearings. Lauck wondered if Roche were available, and he also hoped she could drum up support among "her large circle of friends." Politicians needed to hear from "enlightened" voices like hers, Lauck wrote, to understand how the reforms the UMW was sponsoring would benefit not just the coal industry, but also the nation.[18]

A week before Roche received her letter from Lauck, on February 7, a lengthy feature article appeared in the *New York Times Magazine*. It was written by Louis Stark, the nation's first reporter assigned exclusively to the organized labor beat. Stark needed leads and leaks, and Lewis freely provided both, so in their highly transactional relationship, Stark probably published the Roche story as a favor to Lewis, who needed support for the Davis-Kelly bill.[19] Although this is just one of many articles published in this second wave of Roche articles, it is, in my opinion, the most over-the-top of all, so the arguments it makes bear closer examination.

The title of Stark's article is "A Woman Unravels an Industrial Knot." He begins his Roche profile by remembering Ludlow, and while he does not completely forget the Columbine, he repeats the canard that, at the time of the massacre, Roche had been powerless to prevent it. Stark next writes a paragraph so incredible that I will cite it in full, because it has been repeated, without tongue-in-cheek, in multiple sources about Roche: "Miss Roche seems to have been moving since childhood toward the parts she was to play in the Colorado coal fields. A story is told to the effect that when she was 12 years old and her father refused her permission to go down into the mines 'because it is dangerous.' She asked, 'If it is dangerous for me, why is it not just as dangerous for the men?'"

"A story is told" might well have been the title of the article. Roche turned twelve in 1898, while her father sought his fortune in Nebraska. When John Roche entered the coal business, Josephine was a college student. Why Stark would include such an origin story, or why Roche's subsequent biographers would neglect to perform the basic arithmetic completely debunking it shows how uncritically they all have been rooting for Roche. Next, Stark name-drops Roche's graduations from Vassar and Columbia, then mentions her stint as Denver's first policewoman. Stark then claims that "what apparently turned Miss Roche definitely in the direction of assisting the miners were the incidents at Ludlow," and since then, "her interest in the miners never wavered."

Next, Stark briefly describes Roche's Belgian Relief volunteer work but omits her remarkable positions as the only woman to head a department in the Committee on Public Information and as editorial division chief at the Women's Bureau. He quickly returns Roche to the RMFC where, after gaining control of the company, her "first step was to invite the miners to unionize her properties, in a State where mines were wholly ununionized." Stark describes how Roche hired Lawson, freed from murder charges by Edward

Costigan "in the sanguinary days of 1913–1914," to help win the coalminers' trust, which made possible the 1928 UMW-RMFC contract, whose preamble "sounds like an industrial Magna Carta."

Although not referring to Rockefeller by name, Stark alludes to "conspiracies" undertaken in Colorado's coalfields to run Roche out of business, stating, "It was then that the workers decided to lend the company half of their pay for three months and to continue this arrangement so long as competition made lower coal prices necessary." Appreciative coalminers called their boss Josephine, although "in this there is no suggestion of familiarity—rather of affectionate regard. Perhaps their attitude toward her can illustrated by the reply of the worker who, upon being asked how many tons he had loaded that day, replied: 'Three for the company and three for Josephine.'"

Most beneficial for Lewis's purposes, Stark claims that "the firebrands of the old days of warfare, grateful to her for having put them back to work, are among her warmest supporters. But for her, many who had been blacklisted for union activity would have no jobs today. Former Communists, I.W.W.'s and adherents of the American Federation of Labor [UMW] work side by side and seem united in their loyalty to the principles in the agreement fostered by 'Josephine.'" Furthermore, even though Roche paid the highest wages in the field, the RMFC continued to increase its efficiency and production. Stark even praised the outside sales program, which coalminers happily engaged in, because they wanted to do whatever they could to help Roche. As the last line of the article—as well as the caption under Josephine Roche's head shot—stated, "The miners have faith in her."

Stark's profile piece did not sway Congress. The Davis-Kelly bill died after passing in the House but failing to make it out of committee in the Senate. The article did, however, elevate Roche's national reputation, and it also promoted the narrative Lewis wanted told about the UMW. If enlightened coal operators such as Roche would only use the principals of scientific management and rationalize their labor policies, which included signing contracts with the UMW, they too could run efficient coal operations, employ adoring coalminers, and quash anti-capitalistic radicals sowing discontent in the nation's coalfields. More than any other historical actors, Lewis and Roche—with their mastery of public relations and aided by complicit journalists writing their first drafts of history—help explain why we remember Ludlow but forget the Columbine.

By design and necessity, textbooks over-simplify all history, including labor history, and although contents change, glacially, to incorporate important new scholarship, periodization does not change much. Most New Deal chapters begin in 1932 with FDR's election and end in 1941, with US entry into World War II, although the nation's political shift began in 1930 and stalled by 1938. In 1930, Republicans lost fifty-two seats in the House of Representatives, flipping the House to Democratic control, and Democrats picked up eight Senate seats, resulting in party line ties broken by the Republican vice president's vote. Edward Costigan, Roche's mentor and RMFC legal counsel, part of that wave election, ran as a Democrat and won every Colorado county.[20] He left some of his papers to the University of Colorado and some appear within Oscar Chapman's papers at the Truman Library. Those records show that during Costigan's single term, the relatively small federal government still ran on the power of patronage, there was more continuity than change, and the New Deal coalition was remarkably fragile.

After FDR took office in March of 1933, Costigan was able to deliver on patronage, surely arranging appointments for Oscar Chapman, Merle Vincent, and Roche. Chapman had worked alongside Roche in Lindsey's juvenile court. After law school, he joined Costigan's Denver law firm and then ran Costigan's Senate campaign. Chapman also ran the successful 1932 Democratic Senate campaign of Alva Adams, uncle to Billy Adams who served as governor during the 1927–1928 Colorado Coal Strike. One obvious reason Roche and her allies had not attacked Adams for the Columbine debacle was because they had coordinated strike control efforts with him. Another was they harbored their own political ambitions and could ill afford to irritate the Adamses's extensive political network. Since the Colorado Adams family were not New Dealers, Chapman's work for Alva demonstrated his loyalty to the Democratic Party, not ideology, which helps explains his political longevity. He served for years in the Interior department until 1949, when President Harry Truman appointed him department secretary. During Chapman's long career, his daily calendars indicate he spent almost as much time attending to Democratic Party business as to department issues. Of course, Costigan and Chapman's records could be the consequence of careful culling, but overall, most of their papers are dominated by Coloradans asking for appointments or political favors. Those records also show that during Costigan's term, while he easily found co-sponsors for his bills (who, like him, were usually former Progressives), Hoover's and then FDR's support for those bills usually ranged from lukewarm to nonexistent.

In 1934, Vincent and Roche mysteriously and acrimoniously parted ways, and afterward, Costigan probably helped find Vincent a position within the National Recovery Administration.[21] That year, Costigan encouraged Roche to run in the Democratic primary for Colorado governor. Not only did he believe she was the best candidate, a Roche win could also reshape the state Democratic Party in their image. During her campaign, she vigorously supported the New Deal but lost the primary to anti-New Dealer Democrat Edwin Johnson, who won the general election. Johnson's victory shows that FDR's Democratic support in 1934 was not monolithic and that the former Colorado Progressive ascendancy was an anomalous spike, not a shift in state politics. When Costigan, because of ill health, declined to run for reelection in 1936, Johnson won that seat and held it through 1955.

Colorado voters were not ready for a female governor, but they also perceived Roche as a national rather than statewide political figure. Her association with Lewis and the UMW, her laudatory national press, and her participation in federal coal legislative initiatives represented national, not local, political activities that only intensified after FDR's election. For example, from July 7 to 13, 1933, sixty-five major coal operators, including Roche, met in Washington, DC, and on June 19, they released a report that became a major portion of the NRA coal code.[22] On August 12, 1933, the fourth day of the coal code hearings, Roche testified and received positive national press, but that seemed to carry little political weight back home.[23]

With her statewide political ambitions dashed, in November of 1934, FDR appointed Roche assistant secretary of the Treasury, making her, after Secretary of Labor Frances Perkins, the cabinet's most prominent woman. Costigan had surely lobbied on her behalf, but Roche also could count additional, powerful advocates, including Perkins; First Lady Eleanor Roosevelt; and the head of FDR's Democratic Party women's coalition, Molly Dewson. Furthermore, Roche was more than politically connected. She was highly educated, ambitious, an experienced and talented administrator, and, in today's terms, a workaholic. After confirmation, Perkins assigned Roche to the Social Security committee, so she helped craft the New Deal's most significant legislation. Most of Roche's duties, however, related to public health.

From 1935 through 1940, Roche chaired the Interdepartmental Committee to Coordinate Health and Welfare Activities, a committee on which Chapman, representing Interior, also served. Much of their work resembled their earlier juvenile court initiatives on behalf of women and children, although the committee did take significant steps toward addressing the nation's major health problems and inequities in medical care.[24]

As chair, Roche employed methodologies learned as a progressive reformer. She identified and classified the problems to be studied, conducted detailed surveys, analyzed and organized those results, and engaged experts and stakeholders to craft proposed legislation. In 1938, she worked with New York Senator Robert J. Wagner Jr. to create a bill that would turn the committee's proposals into law. The bill never made it out of committee, in part because the American Medical Association (AMA) for the first time behaved as a lobbying body and organized against it.[25] Also, FDR offered little more than rhetorical encouragement, which was nothing new. He had not backed the 1935 Costigan-Wagner anti-lynching bill, "did not lift a finger" on behalf of the 1935 National Labor Relations Act (the Wagner Act), and did not push Wagner's 1938 National Labor Standards Act (NLSA), the last major piece of New Deal legislation to pass, which even today remains the basis of current US labor law.[26]

By 1937, this lack of support led Senator Wagner, former Progressives such as Roche, and Lewis, among others, to grow disillusioned with FDR. Lewis and other pro-labor advocates who had worked so hard for FDR's 1936 reelection felt betrayed when the first FDR-backed bill introduced into the new Congressional session was the Judicial Procedures Reform Bill of 1937. Even many Democrats viewed Roosevelt's attempt to "pack" the Supreme Court as a blatant power grab and a foolish squandering of his (and their) political capital. Next, FDR followed the advice of Roche's boss, Treasury secretary Henry Morgenthau Jr., and other fiscal conservatives who advocated ending deficit spending and balancing the budget, actions that created the 1937 Roosevelt recession. The double-whammy of court-packing and the recession produced dramatic political consequences. In the 1938 midterms, Democrats lost seventy-two seats in the House, seven in the Senate, and a new conservative coalition of Southern Democrats and Republicans took charge of the upper house, political reversals that essentially ended most New Deal reforms.

In September of 1937, citing the sudden death of RMFC president J. Paul Peabody as the cause, Roche submitted her resignation as assistant secretary of the Treasury. Peabody's funny, newsy letters to Roche show that she absolutely trusted him to run the RMFC, yet Roche also trusted RMFC vice president John R. Lawson, so there surely were additional reasons for Roche's resignation. One included the sudden illness of her longtime friend and mentor, Edward Costigan. In 1936, he and his wife, Mabel, also one of Roche's closest friends, returned to their Denver home, where Chapman addressed his frequent letters and telegrams to Roche about interdepartmental committee business. He punctuated his communications with consistent queries about "the chief's" health and he wondered how she and Mabel were holding up. Only after Costigan died in January of 1939 did Roche move into her own Denver apartment.

According to Chapman, the primary reason for Roche's 1937 resignation was tied to the split that year between Lewis and FDR. Chapman remembered that Roche resigned "when Lewis broke with Roosevelt, because her first loyalty was to him. And that goes back to historical, personal reasons; it wasn't just happen-so." Chapman thought Roche was "one of the most brilliant people, man or woman, that I had ever worked with," and he had urged Truman to appoint Roche as secretary of labor. Truman declined. Because Frances Perkins served twelve years in that position, Truman thought it unwise for another woman to fill that spot again so soon, because it would evolve into a woman's Cabinet position. Chapman also believed Truman opposed her appointment "because of her strong loyalty to John Lewis."[27] Therefore, by the mid-1940s, not only was the influence of this remarkably accomplished, maternalist generation dying out, Roche's loyalty to Lewis apparently precluded any future federal appointments for her.

Because Roche probably resigned in 1937 as a consequence of Lewis's break with FDR, because that break was caused by the CIO's Little Steel strike, and because Powers Hapgood helped lead the rise of the CIO, this next section returns to him. We last left Hapgood in the spring of 1930, living in a miner's cottage in Lafayette, Colorado, working as an RMFC engineer and enjoying homelife with Mary and baby Barta. However, like a siren's song, his coalmining compatriots continued goading him to join their efforts to dislodge Lewis, a prospect that would have been rendered irrelevant had the UMW readmitted him as he had hoped.

Illinois insurgents had hatched a particularly creative plan: They asserted that by not calling a convention (as a consequence of the complete devastation following the 1929 stock market crash), Lewis had violated the UMW constitution. Since the Illinois rebels *were* going to hold a convention, legally they would become the new UMW. This reconstituted UMW planned to coalesce under the leadership of none other than expelled UMW Kansas leader, Alexander Howat. Because Lewis had consolidated his control over the UMW using similar letter-rather-than-spirit-of-the-law maneuvers, the Illinois plotters must have delighted in giving Lewis a taste of his own medicine.

The letters Powers and Mary Hapgood preserved suggest that their time in Colorado was the happiest period in their entire married lives, but apparently, personal happiness was not enough, because Powers's subsequent actions show he was still obsessed with reinstatement into the UMW, even a reconstituted one. In March of 1930, Hapgood attended the new miners' convention in Illinois, strictly as an observer, but once there, his reservations about joining the new group disappeared. Brophy also attended the convention but left after discovering the assemblage included former UMW Illinois leader Frank Farrington, whom he considered as slimy as Lewis. Hapgood's supporters goaded him to run for vice president, but Adolph Germer—former Colorado long strike organizer, Illinois coalminer insider, and fellow expelled UMW member—trounced him, leaving Hapgood feeling "chagrined."[28] Hapgood did, however, agree to write the union's constitution and serve as a paid organizer.[29] On March 17, 1930, Powers accepted a position with the new United Mine Workers of America headquartered in Springfield, Illinois. The following day, a certified letter emblazoned with a logo indistinguishable from the UMW's in Indianapolis officially reinstituted Hapgood into the new, perhaps improved, UMW.[30]

Howat suggested Hapgood could organize in Pennsylvania or in the northern Colorado coalfields, but he refused the Colorado assignment, not wanting to undercut Roche's experiment in industrial democracy. Howat then asked Hapgood to remain in Illinois, where he was needed most. Although most of his time involved missionary work, Hapgood tried a few novel ways to win support for the new UMW. Perhaps the most unusual method was appealing directly to the mine operators, explaining the details of the

"Roche plan," which he urged them to adopt.[31] He also bought radio time, which allowed him to deliver his message directly to the homes of potential recruits too afraid to be seen in open-air meetings. He said, to date, it was the most effective thing he had ever done as an organizer.[32]

Neither Powers nor Mary was happy with Hapgood's new career choice. Powers wrote pathetic letters home to Mary, whining that he just wanted to be home with her and Bartabug. Like Roche, self-awareness was never Hapgood's strength, and he wrote as if he had no choice, expressing sentiments such as, "I can't stand the thought of being an organizer, but it seems to be expected of me and I don't know what else to do."[33] Mary refused to placate him, though. "It would be tragic," she wrote, "if you found that you had given up everything in Colorado to try to work with a gang no better than Lewis's."[34] Reasons she did not share surely had to do with being left home alone, in Colorado, with a six-month-old baby.[35] They had been so happy together in Lafayette, and now, their future together was unsettled, again.

Hapgood hated his Illinois work, so Howat sent him to Kentucky, where a wildcat coalminers' walkout was in progress. During that strike, he brought home a baby boy, just months older than Barta. Mary was back living at the family farm in Massachusetts, where she had returned for her father's funeral. Hapgood never wrote about the desperate circumstances prompting him to take the infant, but it took several anxious years for the adoption of this second child, Donovan, to be finalized.[36] Unlike Barta's first six months, Hapgood missed most of Donovan's infancy, and indeed, most of his children's early years, because from 1930 to 1941, he worked as a traveling organizer. Although Mary knew that Powers worked hard for the causes they both believed in, she wanted to work for them, too; but with two young children and Powers gone most of the time, she felt trapped and guilt ridden. She wrote to Powers, "I want to be doing some work for the working class movement," and that "somehow or other I must do some work beside wash diapers and cook food for my beautiful baby."[37] With her own ambitions thwarted, by the mid-1930s, when Powers began a torrid affair with fellow CIO organizer Rose Pesotta, that relationship further strained their already less-than-idyllic marriage.

Hapgood next visited the Pennsylvania coalfields, and what he found near Pittston broke his heart. Coalminer organization was weak, and Sam

Bonita still languished in prison.[38] Hapgood visited Alex Campbell's widow and their six children and despaired at their destitute existence.[39] Perhaps now with children of his own, he began to understand the terrible cost of Campbell's insurgency in a way unimaginable for him in 1928.

In Pennsylvania, the Communist-led NMU slowly began to gather strength, and in Illinois, the battle between the UMW and Illinois insurgents intensified. In 1930, when Mother Jones died, it was the insurgents, not the UMW, who buried her. Thousands of her old allies, including Lawson and Doyle, attended her funeral, but Lewis did not, a visible snub that dismissed her militant UMW legacy. In 1931, the Illinois Supreme Court decided that Lewis's Indianapolis UMW held legitimate claim to the union name, but it also issued an injunction that ordered Lewis's men to stop harassing opponents.[40] The insurgents renamed themselves the Progressive Miners Union (PMU), and they still exist today, the only insurgent coalmining group that survived the battles of the 1920s and early 1930s.

Seemingly out of options, Powers Hapgood returned to Indianapolis to work for his father's company, the Columbia Conserve Canning company (CCC). His experiences there damaged his relationship with his parents, exposed his father's much-touted experiment in industrial democracy as an undemocratic sham, and by 1935, led him to join forces with his former archenemy, John L. Lewis, to lead the rise of the CIO.

At the CCC, Hapgood joined the men for whom he had already secured jobs, including Brophy; Mary's brother, Dan; both assigned to outside sales; and the newest arrival, Reverend A. A. Heist. In 1930, Grace Church fired him[41] after its richest and most influential member, the grandson of former Colorado governor John Evans, led the fight that forced the "ranting red reverend" out of Denver.[42] Heist headed the CCC's Social Service Department charged with administering worker education, although most employees exhibited little desire to participate in educational programs after their workdays ended.[43]

As the depression deepened, soup sales plummeted, which led William Hapgood to institute major changes at his company. Throughout the 1920s, the CCC had sold its soups as generics to local grocers, who put their own store brand labels on the cans. By the 1930s, supermarkets—exemplifying a new, fast-expanding, national mass culture—began replacing local grocery stores,[44] and brand-name supermarket chains began stocking their aisles

the collective bargaining clause of the National Industrial Relations Act."[56] In the following sentence, Stark uses the "weasel" word "claim" when referring to the numbers of workers recruited into labor unions: "With a gain of 300,000 claimed in the last two months by one union alone, the United Mine Workers of America, [AFL] leaders are confident that the movement now under way will beat all previous membership records." Even the headline writer knew those numbers were unsubstantiated, because the subhead reads, "Impossible to Estimate Gains." In the same article, Stark quotes a speaker who claimed that the AFL had organized rubber in Ohio, steel in Pennsylvania, and shoes in New England. Those claims were false. The CIO organized rubber in 1935 and much of steel in 1937. The New England shoe industry was never unionized, although the CIO sent Hapgood there to try. In another *Times* article on July 24, 1933, Stark reported on a coal convention held in Charleston, West Virginia, attended by "2,579 delegates said [another weasel word] to represent 160,000 freshly recruited members of the United Mine Workers of America." Van Bittner told the group, "It is not a question as to whether the men will be organized," since "They have organized. That is settled."[57]

But was it really settled? For years, until the 1959 Landrum-Griffith Act required unions to keep accurate records, UMW bookkeeping was, shall we say, less than fastidious, so it is unclear if the union ever compiled accurate statistics from its 1933 membership drive. In the 1920s, the UMW had a history of downright fraudulent accounting, not just concerning membership figures but also regarding election returns, since the two were linked. Remember that Brophy claimed he lost the UMW presidency to Lewis after "shadow" (non-active) and provisional districts (such as Colorado's) overwhelmingly voted for Lewis.[58] Furthermore, Brophy also claimed that Lewis and the UMW had little to do with the 1933 UMW membership surge. He remembered that "there was no need to campaign; an organizer had only to see that he had a good supply of application blanks and a place to file them, and the rank and file did the rest."[59]

There is also little objective evidence that the 1933 UMW coalminer "surge" jumpstarted the nation's organized labor movement. In 1932, total US union membership stood at 322,600 members; in 1933, it was 285,700; and in 1934, membership was back up to 325,900.[60] That is a recovery, not a surge. Furthermore, during the purportedly quiescent 1920s, union membership stood close to half a million.[61] Union memberships did rise substantially in 1937 following the Flint sit-down strike, but the Roosevelt recession later that year shrunk memberships again. Only WWII turned the union tide, and organized labor continued increasing membership density through the mid-1950s, when it is estimated that perhaps one out of three workers belonged to a union.

The purported UMW-inspired unionization surge did not even apply to the UMW. Even after the September 1933 NIRA coal code passed, insurgents in Illinois and Pennsylvania refused to join the UMW. That was why Lewis hired John Brophy in December to try bringing them into the UMW fold.[62] Although Lewis and Brophy never overcame their mutual animosities, in 1933, they needed each other, and once again, Brophy needed a job. Lewis also offered Brophy a benefit he could not resist—reinstatement into the UMW. Also, most Pennsylvania and Illinois factions hated Lewis but respected and trusted Brophy, which allowed him to honestly assess those situations and report his solutions back to Lewis. Although Lewis did not adopt them all, he adopted enough to at last bring unity to the coalfields.[63]

What other factors might have led the UMW to dominate the nation's coalfields by 1934? It might have been coal operators themselves. Some evidence suggests that coal operators in Pennsylvania and Illinois followed Roche's lead and signed contracts with the UMW to keep radicals at bay. Today, Gifford Pinchot is mostly remembered in history for establishing the forestry department during Teddy Roosevelt's presidency, but he also served two nonconsecutive terms as Pennsylvania governor. The former Progressive and his wife Cornelia were more philosophically aligned with their friend Roche than with Pennsylvania's coal operators,[64] and in 1931, during an NMU strike, the Pittsburgh Terminal Company asked Governor Pinchot to negotiate a settlement. He did, and it yielded a contract with the UMW, which had played no role in the strike.[65] A similar agreement was negotiated in Illinois. Although the PMU represented most of the state's coalminers, when its contract expired with the Illinois Coal Operators Association (ICOA) in the spring of 1933, the association surreptitiously negotiated a contract with the UMW instead.[66] Roche's correspondence reveals she was friendly with the Pinchots and leading members of the ICOA. I have found no smoking gun evidence that she advised either to rid themselves of their radicals as she had by signing with the UMW, although they were surely too smart to conduct such conversations in writing. Lewis, of course, had been making the same argument since 1922: Only the UMW could bring peace to the coalfields, because its vision of industrial democracy advocated contracts, not social revolution. Furthermore, companies that could afford UMW coalminers could help run smaller, less efficient, non-union companies out of business, which might end the cut-throat competition driving them all into financial ruin. Therefore, one of several possible reasons that coalminers joined the UMW was because their bosses cut deals behind their backs that mandated they do so.

Even before the Supreme Court declared the NIRA unconstitutional in 1935, it had failed to revitalize organized labor. Although the UMW belonged to the AFL, that organization's sluggish organization efforts in response to the NIRA's 7(a) clause infuriated Lewis. By 1934, the UMW was at last united enough to challenge AFL leaders directly. Tensions that had simmered beneath the surface between Lewis and other AFL leaders came to a full, rolling boil during the 1935 floor debate concerning a jurisdictional grievance filed by the International Union of Mine, Mill, and Smelter Workers (Mine Mill).

Mine Mill *had* launched a massive organizational drive in response to 7(a), inspired by militants who reinterpreted their union's past in a way that explained its present and shaped its future. In 1916, the WFM had rewritten its constitution and changed its name to Mine Mill, a WWI-era calculation aimed at divorcing the union from its radical past. That conservative rebranding did not revive the union, however, and memberships dwindled to new lows in the late 1920s. In the early 1930s, the union began showing signs of life, and in 1934, Mine Mill replaced its conservative 1916 constitution, adopting, almost word-for-word, its militant 1907 preamble that included overt references to class conflict. It also reclaimed the "old motto of both the WFM and the IWW [borrowed from the Knights of Labor] 'an injury to one is an injury to all.'"[67]

In 1934, Mine Mill led a strike wave in Montana's copper regions, and the workers' principal demand was the recognition of that union as their bargaining agent. Anaconda Copper refused to negotiate with Mine Mill, however, and the company dispatched company officials to Washington, DC, to negotiate a strike settlement, arbitrated by Labor Secretary Frances Perkins, with the more conservative Metal Trades Department union, which had played no role in the walkout.[68] Mine Mill filed a formal jurisdictional complaint to the AFL executive board, which surfaced on the floor of the 1935 AFL convention. Although Lewis vigorously championed Mine Mill's position, the majority of delegates voted against it. During these floor debates, tempers flared, and this was when Lewis delivered his famous punch to the jaw of Big Bill Hutcheson, president of the Carpenters' Union.

Much has been written about this punch. Was it a sincere expression of manly indignation or a completely staged incident calculated to win over the militants attending the convention? If the latter, it served its purpose. Len DeCaux, future publicist and editor for the CIO, wrote that "with this blow, Lewis hammered home one of the main points he had come to the convention to make—that AFL fakers were blocking a real union drive, and that he was ready to lead the workers in shoving them aside and getting down to the job. His was a calculated strategy, long thought out and much subtler than some of his bold crudities made it appear."[69] Hapgood's biographer writes that John Brophy and Dan Donovan had orchestrated some "behind-the-scenes intercession," making possible Hapgood's convention attendance, a machination suggesting Lewis's slug had been staged for the benefit of Hapgood and others like him who needed to be convinced that Lewis had changed his ways. After witnessing the blow, Hapgood was " 'completely swept up by this episode,' and became convinced of Lewis' commitment to build an industrial union movement."[70]

In both language and deed, Lewis exhibited a lifelong flair for well-timed drama. Lewis needed to convince his former enemies that he had changed, and his punch rewrote the past in a way that allowed insurgents to make sense of their present, since it proved *their* vision of industrial democracy had been right all along. When enough personal narratives coalesce around a particular set of meanings drawn from an event, the process of telling and retelling creates a collective memory that eliminates events that do not support the moral to the story.[71] All good narratives need a turning point, so events leading up to it become causes and events that follow become consequences. For Hapgood and others, the insurgent coalfield struggles of the twenties became causes that led Lewis to change his mind, Lewis's dramatic punch became the turning point, and consequently, organized labor victories followed.

Even when the punch is left out of the story, it still serves as the turning point in dominant labor histories because that tumultuous 1935 AFL convention led to the formation of the CIO. Afterward, Lewis was charged with

FIGURE 8.2. *As the photo shows, a decade after their bitter rivalry, by 1937, the older John L. Lewis and John Brophy begrudgingly set aside their differences to work together at the CIO. (From John Brophy papers, 60–148, Catholic University Special Collections, The Catholic University, Washington, DC.)*

leading a study group that would investigate and report back to the AFL executive board the prospects of organizing workers industrially instead of by skills, as most unions within the AFL did. Leaders from eight separate unions, including Mine Mill and the UMW, comprised the study group, the Committee on Industrial Organization. Instead of researching, however, they began organizing workers, and by 1937, depending on one's viewpoint, the group either withdrew from or was kicked out of the AFL. With that, the Congress of Industrial Organizations was born, a rival to the AFL. The period from 1935 to 1937, known as the rise of the CIO, also coincided with the Popular Front era, when American Communists fully cooperated with the New Deal. Former coalmining insurgents enthusiastically embraced the CIO's possibilities, as did Communists and former Wobblies, such as A. S. Embree. The early CIO transcended bread-and-butter unionism, cohering into a movement embodying its activists' visions of industrial democracy that, at last, promised to reorder all of society.

The UMW bankrolled the CIO's rise and also provided most of the CIO's earliest paid organizers. With Lewis's blessing, in 1935, Brophy's first two hires were Adolph Germer and Powers Hapgood, and that triumvirate directed the rise of the CIO. The reasons Brophy, Germer, and Hapgood agreed to work for their former archenemy Lewis make sense: They needed the money, hard experience had taught them insurgency movements against Lewis were doomed to failure, and Lewis promised to reinstate them into the UMW, an organization they all felt an almost mystical reverence toward. Finally, all had worked tirelessly to organize the unorganized, a goal Lewis now claimed as his own.

Lewis also had good reasons to set aside animosities toward his former enemies, especially Brophy. Although Lewis was strong enough to keep insurgency movements against him in disarray, those movements had been strong enough to prevent the UMW from uniting the nation's coalminers, much less a national organized labor movement. Brophy, Germer, and Hapgood were beloved, effective organizers, roles that Lewis sycophants could never fill. They also had deep ties to political militants, many of whom were excellent and experienced organizers who would also be welcomed into the CIO. When reporters confronted Lewis about putting Communists on the CIO payrolls, he "famously retorted: 'Who gets the bird? The hunter or the dog?'"[72] That much-analyzed remark, along with his subsequent actions, shows that Lewis's quick conversion from a red-baiting Hoover supporter to a class-conscious, left-leaning, FDR-promoting labor leader probably did not reflect changed values or goals as much as they demonstrated changed tactics. Contrary to dominant historical narratives claiming otherwise, as the lackluster 1933 organizational effort proved, Lewis came to understand that the UMW could not grow until the insurgents quit fighting him and until all heavy industries that relied upon coal were also unionized.

As the CIO organized workers to join industrial unions, it also organized workers to vote, and in 1936, they helped reelect FDR and increase Democrats in Congress. After the election, the CIO refocused its energies on organizing workers in the rubber, steel, and automobile industries. Since autos represented the largest industry operating on a non-union basis, and since General Motors (GM) was the largest auto manufacturer, the CIO targeted GM in a strike most historians view as the turning point for organized labor in the United States. The strike began in Flint, Michigan, on December 30, 1936, but on February 1, Powers Hapgood helped shift the strike's momentum.

He and Roy Reuther (Walter Reuther's brother) led a small group of protestors to Fisher plant #9 in a feint that allowed over three thousand strikers
to occupy their actual target, Fisher plant #4. In bitterly cold weather, GM
shut off the building's electricity, to freeze the sit-down strikers out. Before
daylight, Reuther and Hapgood broke through a fence, crawled under idled
train cars, slipped past the National Guard, and convinced a sympathizer
to turn #4's power back on, which allowed the men, with the fearless support of women outside the plant, to continue their occupation.[73] The strike
ended on February 11 in a resounding victory for the strikers and the CIO.[74]

Waves of successful sit-down strikes followed Flint. In a surprise
move, taken to avoid a drawn-out sit-down strike, the United States Steel
Corporation—Big Steel—signed a contract in March of 1937 with the CIO's
Steel Workers Organizing Committee (SWOC). CIO officials and organizers
hoped that smaller steel companies, Little Steel, would also fall in line, but
when they did not, SWOC called a strike. During that walkout, on May 30,
approximately 1,500 strikers and their families marched toward the gates of
Republic Steel on Chicago's South Side, guarded by at least 250 city police.
As the crowd drew close, police opened fire, killing ten people and wounding
perhaps one hundred more.

That violence, the Memorial Day Massacre, caused a sharp break between
FDR and Lewis. In response to it, The *New York Times* reported that Roosevelt
"turned to Shakespeare for a quotation which, he said, he believed represented
the view point from which most Americans were discussing the steel strike
situation that he believed the country as a whole was saying of the strike:
'A plague on both your houses.' To emphasize the statement Mr. Roosevelt
authorized direct quotation of it, waiving the rule that remarks made at a
White House press conferences must not be directly quoted."[75]

It is important to place FDR's comment into context to appreciate its
significance. Roosevelt changed the way presidents communicated with
the press by allowing reporters inside his home and the oval office, treat-
ing them as confidants, and freely providing them scoops and other insider
access. In return, reporters granted Roosevelt wide leeway and respected his
privacy so completely that most Americans never knew he was wheelchair-
bound, simply unimaginable in today's 24/7 news cycle. Therefore, when
FDR chose the occasion of the Memorial Day Massacre to allow reporters,
for the first time, to quote him on the record during one of these previously

off-the-record, informal sessions, it was a major event. Following so closely after the 1936 elections, which the CIO helped FDR and Democrats win, Lewis was incensed. Several months later, he delivered an angry retort aimed directly at FDR. Although it rang Shakespearian, it was pure Lewis: "It ill behooves one who has supped at labor's table and who has been sheltered in labor's house to curse with equal fervor and fine impartiality both labor and its adversaries when they become locked in deadly embrace."[76]

The rift between FDR and Lewis never fully healed. As Robert Zieger documents in *The CIO*, around this time, Lewis also began losing interest in the organization. He reverted to previous practices of trying to place loyalists, including Lewis's family members, into leadership positions and phasing out employees who dared stand up to him, including Brophy. In 1940, believing that organized labor should neither unquestioningly attach itself to the Democratic Party nor support FDR's march toward war, Lewis unexpectedly threw his support to Republican presidential candidate Wendell Wilke and advised other CIO unions and their members to do the same. Some Lewis loyalists, including Roche, did, but most did not, and Roosevelt won an unprecedented third term. Lewis had threatened to resign from the CIO presidency if FDR won, and he surprised almost everyone when he kept his word. UMW vice president and SWOC director Philip Murray took over as CIO president, and one of his first actions was to rehire Brophy. Soon, conflicts between Lewis and Murphy erupted that foreshadowed their final, bitter split two years later,[77] which led Lewis to withdraw the UMW from the CIO. By then, however, the UMW was no longer the CIO's largest union, and Lewis's prominence within the organized labor movement had begun to wane.

After Roche resigned from the Treasury, she continued chairing the interdepartmental health committee and shaping national coal policies. For example, in 1935, Roche had served as the sole government witness in a lawsuit challenging the constitutionality of the 1935 Guffey-Snyder coal bill. A friendly newspaper, repackaging Roche's RMFC narrative, explained why: "Miss Roche has one of the most successful mining enterprises in the United States because long ago she applied the liberal principles of the Guffey act to her own business."[78] Although the Supreme Court declared the act unconstitutional in 1936, Roche helped revamp the 1937 Guffey legislation and its subsequent amendments through 1939. That legislation withstood constitutional challenge, but it was so complex and ineffective, Congress allowed it to expire in 1943.[79]

Roche returned to preside over the RMFC in 1937, but in 1938, Lewis selected a new management company to run the company, something his almost decades-long secret bond-buying loans gave him the power to do. Subsequently, Roche and John Lawson resigned as officers, although Roche remained heavily involved with the company. The new management transformed the Columbine coalmine into a model of mechanization, but other RMFC properties remained unimproved, and the RMFC continued to struggle.[80] In 1939, Roche applied to the Reconstruction Finance Corporation (RFC) for an RMFC loan of $475,000, a clear conflict of interest, since she chaired the federal interdepartmental health committee.[81] The RFC awarded Roche half of what she asked for, so she still could not repay the lenders who had come to her rescue before 1930, including Oswald Garrison Villard.

Although Roche had expressed disillusionment with FDR as early as 1937, in 1940, perhaps following Lewis's lead, she completely broke with Roosevelt and the Democratic Party. She wrote a long letter to Villard in August, explaining the reasons for her decision. Although she commiserated with the lifelong pacifist regarding FDR's march toward war, she aimed her harshest criticism at Roosevelt's "betrayal" of Progressivism's goals:

> The profound ignorance and superficiality of great numbers of officials—up to the top—in handling issues of profound importance to our people have resulted in a situation which is tragic; not only have constructive achievements been too often side tracked, but the excesses, wastes and stupidities have destroyed for many people faith in the very objectives that . . . could have been realized. I therefore am heartily supporting the Republicans in this election, not because I believe they have any great passion or capacity for the things I'm basically committed to, but because I think the most important thing to be done today is to clear out the present administration. There can be no rallying of Progressives with the present administration continued, too many "liberals" are still bemused by the Roosevelt personal magic and the desire to hold their jobs. Under a Republican administration we can perhaps rally again and fight for issues.[82]

Surely Roche's disillusionment with FDR was more personal than she could admit. A month after her letter to Villard, on September 29, 1940, the

Denver Post reprinted a vicious, front-page story, originally published in the anti-FDR *Chicago Tribune*. It began with this: "The once highly touted social experiment conducted in the Colorado coal fields by Josephine Roche, new deal socializer, has run onto the rocks and she has sought government funds to help bail out United Mine Workers' money which John L. Lewis put into the enterprise." Furthermore, "the labor dictator [Lewis] has poured approximately $361,000 into Rocky Mountain Fuel, through secret loans to Miss Roche. These loans have gone to help meet fixed charges which haven't been earned in at least eight years. . . . A United Mine Worker loan of about $75,000 was made some eighteen months ago to pay off a loan from the Reconstruction Finance Corporation. The RFC loan was repaid promptly in order to establish credit." Lewis, "the C.I.O. chieftain, who usually insists upon being begged for his favors, has discreetly remained behind the scenes in this case" and "is in a vulnerable spot with the union because the collateral for the loans is worth only about one-tenth of the sum loaned."[83] In spite of the negative fallout over this article, on October 8, Chapman personally set before FDR's eyes a copy of the RMFC balance sheet and its past-due loans, apparently asking him to intervene with the RFC on her behalf. FDR declined.[84] Roche soon resigned as chair of the interdepartmental health committee, forever ending her government service.

In 1942, another even more damaging story about the UMW's secret loans to the RMFC appeared. It identified Lewmurken as the sham corporation that had been formed to dispense funds, mostly to Roche, but also to other coal operators with UMW contracts who also were in financial trouble. The corporate name Lewmurken was a portmanteau created by combining the names of LEWis and his top two UMW allies, Philp MURray, and Thomas KENnedy. Although Kennedy remained a lifelong Lewis loyalist, their timing suggests that Murray probably leaked both the earlier and later stories to damage Lewis. However, against the backdrop of tumultuous world events in both 1940 and 1942, these scandals quickly faded away and did not generate long-term damage to Roche, Lewis, or the UMW.

After 1940, Lewis re-focused his efforts entirely on the UMW, and when the US entered WWII, Lewis was determined not to repeat his WWI mistakes. He ignored AFL and CIO no-strike pledges and led the UMW out on several walkouts between 1941 and 1943. Although publicly condemned, Lewis's militant defiance helped him and the coalminers secure wartime gains and reputations as fierce class warriors. Perhaps ironically, as Lewis defied wartime no-strike mandates, A. S. Embree embraced them. Perhaps paradoxically, by 1948, such wartime cooperation would be used as evidence that Mine Mill organizers and other "left-wing unions" were Communists.

In 1937, Embree finally quit the IWW and joined Mine Mill, and for almost a year, he edited that union's newspaper. Those newspapers, preserved in the Mine Mill archives, demonstrate that Embree expected much from his readers, although it was not his refusal to dumb down content that caused him to lose that position. The newspaper's scope narrowed after Mine Mill officially joined the CIO in 1938. Another former Wobbly, Len DeCaux, took over the CIO's newspaper, and, like Embree, DeCaux was an excellent writer and editor. Eventually outed as a Communist, DeCaux never admitted his membership, even in his beautifully written, snappy, and funny 1971 memoir, *Labor Radical: From the Wobblies to CIO, a Personal History.*

In 1938, Mine Mill leaders asked Embree to return to organizing, and he next appears in the historical record in Silverton, Colorado. Thomas J. Noel writes that on August 30, 1939, "the management of the Shenandoah-Dives Mine, then the biggest gold and silver producer" in the San Juan Mountains, "inspired a mob of 200 to charge into the union hall and break up a strike meeting." Embree "and the secretary of the Silverton local were forced into an automobile and deported. The mob took possession of the miners' union hall and its hospital in the name of a company union."[85] Mine Mill brought this incident before the National Labor Relations Board (NLRB), which determined that the San Juan County commissioners colluded with mine operators when they paid "goons to escort the two union men out of town." The NLRB also ordered the mining company to pay back the union dues it had collected over the previous year, reinstate the seventy-eight blacklisted Mine Mill miners, and return the union hall and hospital to the union.[86] Although Embree still organized like a fiery militant, clearly his vision of industrial democracy had tempered over time. By the 1940s, he not only agreed to but pursued contracts. He also agreed to have his case presented before a federal labor court, unimaginable in his IWW days.

The next Embree information appears in letters between him and Mine Mill president Reid Robinson, written during World War II. On February 26, 1941, Robinson tersely instructed Embree to return to Denver—immediately—from Perth Amboy, New Jersey.[87] Unfortunately, we do not know what Embree did to get in so much trouble. Embree next organized smelter workers at Denver's

Globe facility and in Wyoming.[88] In 1942, while organizing Empire Zinc work-ers in western Colorado, Embree got in hot water again, this time because of "Nick Raskovich, an old friend of mine who had been in the Silverton fight and before that in the Bisbee fight with me in 1917."[89] Raskovich kept a gun in the glove compartment of the car he and Embree drove between local organiz-ing meetings, and when local sheriffs arrested them (for what, the letters do not say), searched the car, and found the gun, they released Embree on bond, but not Raskovich. Interestingly, the FBI, not local or state officials, insisted Raskovich be kept in jail, "as he had only first papers and they claimed he was an enemy alien." Embree, who must have finally become an American citizen by this time, argued that since "Nick has always been strong the Union, I think we should arrange bond for him through the Int'l office."[90] Although Embree wrote several impassioned letters trying to get help for his old friend, his pleas not only failed, his efforts "disturbed" them at headquarters because the union did not need to "tie ourselves too closely to this case." It might "expose us to a great deal of undesirable criticism."[91]

In the midst of this controversy, Embree stopped writing letters on Raskovich's behalf and wrote a personal letter to Robinson, patriotically suggesting that Mine Mill build a destroyer. "You'll think I'm nuts," Embree wrote, but "one day's pay donated by each member of the International will almost do it." Such a ship would have "great advertising value," and we could name it "after our pioneer Local—Butte No. 1," a reference surely meant to appeal to their shared Butte backgrounds.[92] Perhaps Embree was brown-nosing Reid before again asking for help with Raskovich, but no archival evi-dence exists indicating Mine Mill ever built the destroyer, helped Raskovich, or quit being irritated by Embree. A few weeks after that letter to Robinson, Embree wrote a breezy, apologetic cover letter for an expense report he was submitting late. Again. Embree promised his bean counter recipients, "Will try to do better as I grown up."[93] He was sixty-five-years old. Then, Embree's letters abruptly stopped. Perhaps Embree retired and drew a modest Social Security pension. If so, he had Josephine Roche—whose stance as a social reformer he had denigrated during the strike—to thank, since she helped create that program, a centerpiece of her vision of industrial democracy.

Like Embree, Hapgood was an excellent organizer. After Brophy hired Germer and him at the CIO, their first major organizing effort was in Dayton, Ohio, organizing rubber workers. Powers fell madly in love with fellow CIO organizers Rose Pesotta, and they carried on a tempestuous relationship long past the strike. Mary knew about Pesotta, but stuck with her husband anyway, accurately predicting he would choose to stay with her, Donovan, and Barta. Following Dayton, Powers helped lead the 1937 Flint sit-down strike, the high point of his labor career. Next, the CIO sent Hapgood to New England to organize shoe workers. Although he helped lead several massive strikes, the shoe industry successfully resisted organizing efforts. The CIO then sent Hapgood to California to help settle a controversial maritime jurisdictional dispute, and that assignment made him painfully aware of his increasingly bureaucratic role within the organized labor movement. He longed for the dramatic days of the sit-down strikes, not the tedium of the office or the courtroom.

In September of 1941, Hapgood was appointed CIO director of Indiana.[94] Just as only child Josephine Roche in 1925 left her promising Washington, DC, career to take care of her dying parents in Denver, Hapgood returned home to help take care of his ailing parents, yet they would outlive him. Hapgood served as a mostly faithful administrator, although he devoted at least some of his energies to fighting racism within the labor movement and offering moral support to coalminers attempting to challenge Lewis's UMW control. Clearly, Hapgood's infatuation with Lewis was over, and so was his initial enthusiasm furthering the CIO's vision of industrial democracy. In less than a decade, the CIO had become another top-down, anti-Communist bureaucracy, much like Lewis's UMW he had tried to democratize from within.

By March of 1948, Hapgood was pressured to resign from the CIO. Officials said it was because of his drinking, which *was* out of control. Arrested twice for drunk driving, he even lost his driver's license back when that was hard to do.[95] He and Mary, however, believed it was not his drinking but his former and ongoing left-wing associations that ended his CIO career. On February 4, 1949, a month shy of Hapgood turning fifty, eyewitnesses reported seeing his car slowly drifting off the road and rolling to a stop in a private yard.[96] Bussel wrote that Hapgood died of a heart attack, but Pesotta wrote that he "died of a broken heart."[97] Mary Donovan Hapgood was indignant when all the CIO officials who had forced Hapgood to resign could not say enough good things about him at his funeral. When John Brophy closed the packed service for his former protégé by reciting the UMW funeral rites, apparently there had not been a dry eye in the house.[98] Perhaps the attendees were crying as much for themselves as they were for Powers Hapgood and the idealism and militancy he symbolized—all dead.

9

The Cold War, Deindustrialization, and Competing Legacies of Industrial Democracy

Even though Powers Hapgood played a pivotal role in the rise of the CIO, by 1948, it had no use for him, and the following year, the forty-nine-year-old Hapgood died a broken man. In this chapter, A. S. Embree and Josephine Roche will also die, not broken, but honored. Yet, in honoring them, even their admirers remembered Ludlow but forgot the Columbine, the turning point in their careers. The Cold War trajectories of Mine Mill and the UMW and the ways historians have examined and contextualized both help explain some of the reasons for those historical misremembrances and silences.

As Cold War tensions escalated, the 1927–1928 Coal Strike continued to influence organized labor, as seen through the influence of A. S. Embree and the actions of Josephine Roche. Embree's militant, egalitarian vision of industrial democracy inspired Mine Mill leaders Maurice Travis and Clinton Jencks, and Roche's vision of industrial democracy guided her work in the UMW's Retirement and Pension Fund from 1945 through 1972. By the 1960s, however, anti-Communist fears and US deindustrialization made both visions equally impossible to achieve.

https://doi.org/10.5876/9781646423026.c009

Worker militancy and dedicated policy wonks produced New Deal legislation that even today forms the basis of US labor law, but not until World War II did union membership flourish. After strikes rocked the nation in 1945 and 1946, however, voters put Republicans in control of both the House and the Senate, and in 1947, Congress overrode President Harry Truman's veto and passed the Taft-Hartley Act, which aimed to roll back many New Deal labor reforms. One of Taft-Hartley's many provisions required labor leaders to swear oaths that they were not members of the Communist Party (CP). This provision wreaked havoc within the nation's labor movement, especially the CIO, which had actively recruited CP leaders and members in the 1930s. Increasingly hysterical anti-Communist fervor made employing and defending former, much less current CP leaders untenable. Consequently, by 1950, CIO leaders expelled its left-leaning unions, which represented at least 20 percent of the CIO's total membership. One of those purged unions included Mine Mill. Embree retired before the CIO purge, but his militant, egalitarian vision of industrial democracy lived on through the careers of Mine Mill organizers Travis and Jencks. Although both swore Taft-Hartley oaths, the federal government decided both lied when doing so, so prosecutors charged them with perjury. Throughout the 1950s, as the Justice Department pursued them through the court system, Travis and Jencks's fates were closely linked. At the time, Travis was the more infamous of the pair, but beginning in the 1960s, Jencks's historical star began to rise as Travis's faded, a reordering that reflected the changing ways historians were practicing their craft as well as changing interpretations of the Cold War.

Although Embree influenced Jencks, his influence upon Travis was more direct, because Travis was his son-in-law. In fact, Travis claimed everything he knew about the history of the labor movement he learned from his wife, Una, and in-laws, Lucy and Sam (a name he started using as early as the 1920s) Embree.[1] Travis met Una when she worked as an executive secretary at the Mine Mill headquarters in Denver,[2] and in 1944, they married. Aided by Una's behind-the-scenes machinations and insider information,[3] Travis began rising through Mine Mill's ranks, serving as vice president (1946), president (1947), then secretary-treasurer (1948–1951).[4] Since he did not grow up in a union household, from the Embrees Travis learned about sacrifice and resistance, with a heavy dose of martyrdom, all on behalf of the working class. "All my life in the labor movement, I could rely upon Una to be a critic,"

Travis said, because she "would never allow me to deviate too far in the direction of compromise." He had to stay strong, since "I always had it in mind that I would have to cope with Una's resistance to any kind of weakness."[5]

As will soon become evident, Travis's travails with the CIO began after the passage of Taft-Hartley in 1947. The year before its passage, in 1946, the CIO initiated the Southern Organizing Campaign (SOC), which everybody called Operation Dixie. The campaign's ambitious goals were to "unionize low-wage southern workers, to protect northern CIO contract gains" from "runaway industries such as textiles that had simply shifted operations south to avoid paying northern union wages" and "to transform the southern political climate."[6] When planning Operation Dixie, CIO leaders had to decide the following: "What role would there be for the CIO's Communists and their allies who had built small but impressive enclaves of aggressive biracial unionism in Dixie? Relatedly, would SOC use the well-established militancy of black workers as the spearhead of the drive? Or would it marginalize blacks in hopes of attracting the white majority?"[7] Historians Robert Zieger and Barbara Griffith agree that the CIO chose *not* to build upon the biracial, often Communist-led unions that had made impressive gains in pockets of the South, but they disagree about which whites the CIO tried to organize. Zieger contends the CIO concentrated its efforts on organizing white, male, World War II veterans, in order to establish a respectable, patriotic presence in the region. Griffith argues the CIO funneled almost all its resources into trying to organize the southern textile industry, whose workers were mostly poor, white women.[8] Regardless of their strategies, the CIO campaign soon failed for reasons historians still examine. More recently, for example, Ken and Elizabeth Fones-Wolf argue that CIO organizers misread the crucial role religion played in the lives of the workers they tried to organize.[9] In *The Southern Key*, Michael Goldfield argues that organizers never dealt with racism. Therefore, conflicting strategies surrounding race, Communism, and religion hampered Operation Dixie, but so did competing historical memories.

In 1946, most northern CIO organizers remembered exuberant labor victories from the recent past, but southern textile workers remembered defeat and betrayal. Griffith found that, consciously or not, Operation Dixie organizers modeled their Southern strategy on what had worked during the rise of the CIO, not realizing "the extent to which their strategies were tailored to a Northern, and pre-World War II society."[10] When northern strategists moved South, they hoped to create a southern version of the 1937 Flint sit-down strike, a "transformational moment" so powerful, its impact would spread throughout the region.[11] One reason that moment never arrived was because the CIO leaders' historical memories differed so sharply from the memories of workers they tried to organize, something Jacquelyn Dowd Hall and her colleagues discovered when conducting oral histories of former southern mill town residents. They found that, through repeated tellings and retellings, individual experiences from the wave of unsuccessful strikes that swept the region from 1927 through 1934 developed into collective memories repeatedly shared and relived among those who had participated, but also among those who had not.[12]

Those textile strikes not only provide additional evidence that 1920s and early 1930s workers were far from quiescent, they also demonstrate the gendered, regional, and racial limits of New Deal labor reforms that grew even more constricted during the Cold War. Massive strikes arose and were crushed throughout the textile region, and one of the most well documented includes the Communist-led 1929 Gastonia strike at the Loray Mills near Charlotte, North Carolina, during which both the local police chief and strike leader Ella May Wiggins were killed.[13] In 1934, hoping that the promises in the newly created NIRA textile code might be true, workers tried organizing again. Although the general textile strike was "the largest industrywide strike in American history," it failed.[14] Operation Dixie strategists apparently underestimated the long-lasting consequences and memories of those losses.

Although the 1934 textile strike failed, that same year, Mine Mill began making impressive gains organizing workers in the steel mills surrounding Birmingham, Alabama, the industrial capitol of the South. Communist organizers revitalized Mine Mill in the state, "almost exclusively with black support. More blacks were elected to leadership positions within Mine Mill than any other CIO union, and its policy of racial egalitarianism remained unmatched."[15] Although union density continued increasing, in 1949, a Mine Mill contract was set to expire at a key steel facility in Bessemer, Alabama, near Birmingham, and a rival union vying for that contract appeared on the scene.

This Bessemer battle sparked a CIO crisis. Travis asserted that Philip Murray, who had presided over SWOC in the late 1930s and who then presided over the CIO, Operation Dixie, and the steelworkers' union, did far more than sidestep working with biracial unions; Travis charged Murray and the CIO of actively colluding with racist whites. When the Bessemer Industrial Union (BIU) had mounted its contract challenge, Mine Mill sent Travis to Alabama, where he discovered that angry white men who formerly belonged to the company union Mine Mill had supplanted comprised the BIU's leadership.[16] Although Mine Mill belonged to the CIO and the BIU did not, CIO organizers openly worked with the BIU. For obvious reasons, Travis believed that Philip Murray was behind this strategy, a judgement supported by the local presence of a team of tough-guy steelworker organizers, led by Nick Zonarich, who was a well-known "trouble-shooter for Mr. [Philip] Murray."[17] Furthermore, Travis recognized a group of Operation Dixie organizers within Zonarich's gang, and they all joined forces with the local Ku Klux Klan.[18] At first, these Mine Mill opponents menacingly cruised around Bessemer in their cars and loitered in front of the Mine Mill office, but as the election grew closer, they began verbally harassing white Mine Mill supporters, calling them "nigger lovers." Then, KKK members brazenly donned garb in broad daylight and burned crosses in the front yards of black Mine Mill members, actions convincing Travis it was racism, not anti-Communism, motivating secessionists angry that "Mine Mill had succeeded in eliminating dual toilet facilities, dual drinking fountains, and succeeded in upgrading Negro workers," policies that led to "some whites" being "deprived of key jobs because we were able to promote Negroes on the basis on seniority."[19]

Two days before the election, on April 20, 1949 (the thirty-fifth anniversary of Ludlow, an event none of the unionists mentioned at the time), both unions booked time at a local radio station for their final appeals to voters. The BIU organizers recalled that when the two groups crossed paths, they traded insults, which led to a fight. One organizer admitted throwing the first punch at Travis, but it was such a minor scuffle, Mine Mill officials neither fought back nor called the police. Travis remembered the encounter far differently, however. While Mine Mill president Reid Robinson was on air, Travis recalled that a "goon squad" of at least eight steelworkers, led by Zonarich, rushed into the studio. They singled out Travis, attacking him with "everything handy, including office furniture,"[20] knocking out his front teeth and pummeling his face, especially his eyes. Travis did not report the beating because he knew the police were Klansmen who would do nothing about the attack. He believed his beating was meant to send a message to white Mine Mill supporters to let them know what they could expect.[21] When the election was held, BIU received 2,696 votes over Mine Mill's 2,233. Since almost half of the voters were black, we are left to imagine the role race played in the final vote tally.[22] Mine Mill contested the election, but the results stood, and soon afterward, BIU joined the steelworkers and the CIO.

After Travis's beating, Mine Mill flew Una, who was pregnant, to Alabama to be with Travis, and she faithfully remained by his side in the Bessemer, then Birmingham hospitals. Fears that Travis's assailants would return led a rotating crew of one hundred black Mine Mill members to serve as round-the-clock armed guards outside the whites-only facilities. When Birmingham doctors determined that Travis needed to see an eye specialist, he relocated to Chicago, where doctors removed one of his eyes and barely saved the other.[23]

After Bessemer, Travis and other Mine Mill officers attacked CIO president Murray and other CIO officials with every verbal weapon at their disposal. Travis accused CIO leaders of "raiding [when one union steals members from another union], hoodlum-violence, the promotion of race hatred and discrimination and Company Unionism as part of its drive against our union," and that made the CIO "ten time worse than the giant corporation we have to fight."[24] The CIO not only "stabbed us in the back," it betrayed the very principles upon which "our labor movement" and "our democratic government itself is founded."[25] As Travis saw it, nothing less than the CIO's vision of industrial democracy was on the line.

Mine Mill leaders rallied other left-leaning unions to join the fray, which led the CIO executive board to convene a closed session meeting on May 17. Afterward, it released a public statement drawing a line in the sand: The left-wing unions could either support board policy or withdraw from the CIO.[26] The day after the ultimatum, the "Bessemer incident," as CIO officers euphemistically called it, was the topic before a House of Representatives Fair Employment Practices Committee (FEPC) hearing, and publicity from the hearings led to an even greater escalation of hostilities between the right- and left-wing CIO factions.[27] The Mine Mill newsletter expressed this growing tension when it asked, "What is happening to the CIO? This just can't be true! . . . How could it be that the CIO, the militant new federation of the thirties, the fighting union of the great sitdown strikes, the enemy of race discrimination, the bulwark against fascism, had been turned inside out?"[28]

After a month-long hospital stay in Chicago, with Una by his side, Travis continued recuperating and contemplating his next steps at a leftist-operated New Mexico ranch.[29] Reemerging on August 15, 1949, Travis called a press conference. In his first public appearance after Bessemer, resolute, defiant, and sporting a new, pirate-style, black eye patch, Travis declared that he would file his Taft-Hartley affidavit. First, though, he had a statement to make. Although he had resigned from the Communist Party, he did so with "a great sense of indignation," since "an American has as much right to be a Communist as he has to be a Republican, a Democrat, a Jew or a Catholic, or an Elk or a Mason." He believed being a Communist had made him a better trade unionist, just as it had for former WFM president and IWW founder Big Bill Haywood, who had also taken "the road to Communism." After that fiery statement, Travis filed his Taft-Hartley non-Communist affidavit.[30]

Travis held another press conference on August 31, and this time, he was joined by other left-leaning CIO leaders who had just emerged after a meeting with 1,550 union members. They had convened to discuss how Bessemer symbolized everything that had gone wrong with the postwar CIO. Travis again denounced the "aggressive and dictatorial" leadership of the CIO executive board that had directed "racism, intimidation, fear and violence" against Mine Mill in Bessemer. Although rumors ran rampant that leftists had called the press conference to announce the formation of their own labor organization, instead, they voiced their resolve to "remain in the CIO and fight all efforts to dislodge them." They were prepared to fight, to return the CIO to its founding principles.[31]

The leftists lost, however, and CIO leaders purged its "left leaning" unions in 1950.[32] Since leaders had stated their problems were with leftist union leaders, not the rank-and-file, they promised to form new unions to represent the newly disaffiliated members, but that never happened. Over the next few years, most of the expelled unions either retained or, in the case of Mine Mill, increased their memberships while the remaining CIO unions maintained the status quo.[33]

By expelling its left-wing leaders, the CIO blunted some of the most intense red-baiting against it, although in hindsight, we know the purge probably signaled the long-term decline of the US labor movement. Eric Arneson writes that the purge led to raids on red-baited, expelled unions and that the expulsions guaranteed that the South [and the West, I would argue] would remain mostly non-unionized. The purge also created a "missed opportunity" to "champion civil rights issues," and instead, "put the United States labor movement firmly behind Cold War foreign policy, including support of the Korean and Vietnam wars."[34] Beyond foreign policy concerns, playing it safe in 1950 meant that CIO leaders failed to expand what kinds of people and workers would be unionized. In deciding to conserve, not expand, its gains, the CIO consolidated its efforts among white males who worked heavy industries located in the Northeast and upper Midwest.

Unbeknownst to most, however, deindustrialization was already underway, which would begin chipping away at northern industries and their unions. As Judith Stein argues in *Running Steel, Running America: Race, Economic Policy, and the Decline of Liberalism*, there was nothing natural or inevitable about this industrial decline. She convincingly argues that deindustrialization was a consequence, perhaps unintended, of Cold War policy choices. Soon after the deaths of the old guard (AFL president William Green and CIO president Philip Murray) and tired of fighting zero-sum jurisdictional battles with each other, in 1955, the AFL and CIO united as the AFL-CIO, since there were not sufficient personal or philosophical barriers between the former bitter rivals to stand in the way.

Clinton Jencks joined Mine Mill during the union's tumultuous postwar conflicts. He grew up in Colorado Springs, attended the University of Colorado in Boulder, and after graduation, joined the Air Force and served as a navigator in the Pacific Theater during WWII. After the war, he moved to Denver, but, unable to find work as a navigator or even a mechanic, he took a job at the Globe smelter in Denver, where he joined Mine Mill and was soon elected shop steward. Mine Mill's Denver officers identified potential in the college-educated, "energetic young steward who was intimately familiar with the radical Rocky Mountain labor tradition going back to the bitter struggles of the Western Federation of Miners, the Industrial Workers of the World, and the early IUMMSW [Mine Mill],"[35] so they began grooming him for leadership.

For his first major assignment, Mine Mill sent Jencks to southwestern New Mexico, and on October 17, 1950, Jencks helped lead a walkout against

Empire Zinc near Silver City. Most of the workers there identified as Mexican American. Like Alabama's black steel workers, Mexican Americans joined Mine Mill because the union unequivocally supported equal pay and expanded civil rights for minorities. Conditions had barely budged since Embree had fought to end the Mexican wage during the 1917 Bisbee strike and the 1927–1928 Colorado Coal Strike. Paid half of what Anglos earned, Mexican Americans were also relegated to the worst, lowest-skilled, dirtiest, most dangerous jobs in the mines, regardless of their experience or seniority. Discrimination extended to their lives in the mining towns, as families lived in small, uninsulated shacks, often without electricity or running water, and most miners' children attended segregated, poorly resourced schools.[36]

In June of 1951, a local judge issued an injunction that forbade striking miners from picketing. In response, union members took an unusual vote that expanded the ballot to their wives. Since the injunction only applied to striking miners, it was decided that women and children would take over the picket line.[37] In spite of increasing hostility toward the picketers, jail terms, and disruptions to family life, this picketing led to a mostly favorable settlement for the miners in January of 1952.

During the strike, Virginia and Clinton Jencks took a vacation to the same "dude ranch for radicals" where Una and Maurice Travis stayed during his recuperation, and there, they met Sylvia and Paul Jarrico.[38] Paul belonged to the Hollywood Ten, so named because on November 25, 1947, he and nine others in the film industry refused to testify before the House Un-American Activities Committee (HUAC). Afterward, all ten were blacklisted by the Hollywood filmmaking community.[39] Jarrico understood that if he wanted to work, it would have to be outside the studio system, and the stories the Jencks told about the New Mexico strike so fascinated the Jarricos, they returned after the strike ended to make a movie about the event.

In 1954, the film they helped make, *Salt of the Earth*, co-produced by Mine Mill, opened to good reviews, but because of its Communist connections, it only showed in a few theaters and quickly disappeared, a casualty of explicit blacklisting documented well by several historians, including James Lorence. Unfortunately for Clinton Jencks, the film brought him to the attention of the federal government, which prompted prosecutors to add Jencks to the list of Mine Mill officers, including Maurice Travis, they were pursuing Taft-Hartley perjury convictions against. Although Travis and Jencks were not the only Mine Mill leaders that federal prosecutors pursued, they soon became their primary targets. By January of 1956, Mine Mill officials pressured both to resign, "for the good of the union," because the union could no longer afford to defend them. Both reluctantly resigned.[40] Union officials had hoped the resignations would end their legal troubles, but they did not, and the federal government continued to harass Travis, Jencks, and Mine Mill.

In 1957, Jencks's case landed before the Supreme Court, and it set a legal precedent that ended most federal prosecutions against Communists. In *Jencks v. The United States*, the court held that Jencks's lawyers had been entitled to *all* the evidence the federal government had used against him, which included secret testimony procured from "professional," anti-Communist informants paid for their stories. Since the federal government did not want to reveal its information, the government dropped most of its anti-Communist cases, although, for reasons too complicated to go into here, it continued pursuing Travis. His cases also landed before the Supreme Court, three times, but set no precedents, and although repeatedly found guilty, Travis never served any jail time or paid any fines. The government finally stop pursuing Travis in 1967, the year Mine Mill ceased to exist as a union. As Ellen Schrecker writes, "Though the anti-communist crusade was by then only a dim, bad dream, Mine-Mill's belated demise may well have been McCarthyism's last victory."[41]

I have found only one book, Vernon H. Jensen's *Nonferrous Metals Industry Unionism, 1932–1954*, in which Travis is a leading historical actor. Jensen wrote that the purpose of his book was to explain the following paradox: How did Mine Mill's Communist leadership infiltrate and gain control of "a union with such a strong tradition of democracy"?[42] His research focused heavily on Travis and Reid Robinson, but made no mention of Jencks, which makes sense, because his book was published the year *Salt of the Earth* was released. That same year, Senator Joseph McCarthy's attacks came crashing to an end, although the term *McCarthyism* extended beyond his four-year reign of terror. Historians have followed Ellen Schrecker's lead in defining McCarthyism more broadly, as an anti-Communist crusade waged during the late 1940s and 1950s that "used all the power of the state to turn dissent into disloyalty and, in the process, drastically narrowed the spectrum of acceptable political debate."[43]

Jensen's book falls squarely within the John R. Commons school of historiography, which focused on institutions and depended heavily upon records generated by governments, businesses, and unions. Commons was a historian, but also an economist, the founder of the field of industrial and labor relations (IRL), and a policymaker. From the progressive era through the New Deal, Commons and fellow Wisconsinite Robert LaFollette promoted the Wisconsin Idea, which shaped governmental policies far beyond their state's borders. The following is how one historian summarizes their impressive contributions:

> The Wisconsin School economists and the AALL [American Association for Labor Legislation] were the focal point for a three-decade effort to expand government regulation of employment standards, improve the operation of labor markets, and protect workers' security through social insurance programs. Examples include minimum wages, maximum hours, a ban on child labor, elimination of peonage (servitude to a creditor), minimum safety and health conditions, public employment offices, counter-cyclical public works programs, accident insurance (workmen's compensation), unemployment insurance, and old age and health insurance. All of these programs are now foundational elements of the modern welfare state.[44]

The year Commons died, 1945, a new era in postsecondary education and historiography was just beginning. Thanks in large part to the GI Bill, higher education began a rapid process of democratization, and a new generation of historians, including Ellen Schrecker, expanded the range of topics deemed worthy of study as well as the sources they used. In 1988, Schrecker's book, *Many are the Crimes*, was published, and her penultimate chapter was about Clinton Jencks. In 1954, Jensen had regarded Mine Mill's Communist and left-leaning leadership as undemocratic, but Schrecker flipped that perspective, asserting that the federal government's persecution of leftists, such as Jencks, was undemocratic. Less interested in institutional history of Mine Mill or even organized labor, Schrecker examined how Jencks's story exemplified McCarthyism's toll. She writes that when looking for case studies of the "political repression of the McCarthy era," although "no single story can encompass every element of that repression, that of Clinton Jencks comes close."[45] Subsequently, several excellent historians expanded upon Schrecker's analysis of Jencks and *Salt of the Earth*, both the strike and the film.[46]

The volume and the contrasting historiographical approaches historians took toward Travis and Jencks illustrates the wide generational and cultural historiographical shifts that evolved over the very long Cold War. Yet whether writing within or about the throes of McCarthyism, historians uniformly downplayed the vision of industrial democracy that had inspired both Travis and Jencks. In that process, they short shrifted the militant legacies of Mine Mill and its leaders, including Embree.

What probably piqued these postwar historians' interests were the film *Salt of the Earth* and the creation of the Mine Mill archives. In 1965, the film *Salt of the Earth* was rereleased in New York City, and it quickly became a cult classic.[47] In the film, Clinton and Virginia Jencks essentially play themselves in a reenactment of the 1951–1952 Empire Zinc strike won, to a large extent, by Mexican American women. As the war in Vietnam escalated, the film resonated with a new generation of viewers who were beginning to reject the Cold War fears that had buried the film's release a decade earlier. When the film's revival began, however, Jencks's no longer resembled his 1954 self. Even after winning at the Supreme Court in 1957, unable to get a job in the labor movement because of the federal government's dogged pursuit of him, in 1959, Jencks was accepted into the graduate school of economics at University of California at Berkeley. As he morphed from an activist into an academic, he and Virginia divorced, he continued his studies, and in 1964, he earned his PhD. San Diego State University took a chance hiring him, he proved its gamble had not been misplaced, and in 1986, he retired a full professor.

While teaching, "through correspondence and field works," Jencks amassed sources on the history of the WFM and Mine Mill, and during a sabbatical, he organized those materials at the University of Colorado in Boulder. At over one thousand linear feet, the archival collection includes "852 boxes of files, correspondence, publications, and cancelled checks; 500 bound volumes of minutes, ledgers, magazines, and court proceedings; and the Research Department Library consisting of individually cataloged books, pamphlets, and periodicals."[48] Understandably, because Jencks collected those materials, many relate to him, which includes records of his many legal battles and Schrecker's research materials.

With their curiosities sparked by *Salt of the Earth* and the Mine Mill archives, historians wanted to know about Jencks, the strike, the film, his Supreme Court case, the Cold War's excesses, and its consequences. While accurately depicting Jencks as a victim of federal government persecution, they less

accurately portray him as a harbinger of 1960s, identity-based political movements that promoted minority and women's rights, analysis that surely had
more to do with their own historical moment than with Jencks, who told his
biographer that his vision of industrial democracy was rooted in the past. In
his personal origin story, Jencks remembered that as a boy, his "first personal
encounter with the class struggle, one that left an indelible impression on his
mind," happened during the 1927–1928 Colorado Coal Strike. In December
of 1927, soon after the Columbine Massacre, the ten-year-old Jencks went
door-to-door, distributing Christmas food baskets. He noticed that eviction
notices posted on striking coalminers' houses were signed by a local bank
president who also served as the Sunday School superintendent where his
very religious family attended church. Jencks confronted the supervisor
whose self-defense was that he was only doing his job. That encounter led
Jencks to a personal epiphany: "There was something wrong if 'love of your
fellow man' [was] something that you only practice on Sunday, and then you
go around screwing him all the rest of the week."[49] In Jencks's memory, it
was the hypocrisy and injustice he witnessed during the 1927–1928 Colorado
Coal Strike that turned him into a lifelong, class-conscious reformer. Jencks
also credits that strike with sparking his interest in learning more about the
histories of the Western Federation of Miners and the IWW.

Instead of looking to the past for historical precedents to understand
Jencks and the *Salt of the Earth* strike and film, however, historians treated
both as forerunners of 1960s political activism. That decade's protests have
been interpreted, correctly, as emanating from identity politics, not collective labor struggles, but what strikes me as most interesting in their interpretations is how quickly the non-militant, white, male, American perception of
1950s labor unions was perceived as the norm. Long before *Salt of the Earth*,
the participation of women, children, and minorities was a well-established
practice. Apparently, historians had forgotten that Mother Jones's 1892 mop
and bucket brigades of militant women helped win the UMW's first major
contract in the Central Competitive Fields. Most of the textile strikers in the
uprising of twenty thousand between 1909 and 1915 in New York City were
young, Jewish women, recent émigrés from Russia. Over thirty different
nationalities and ethnicities comprised the majority of strikers during the
1910–1914 long strike in Colorado. Although John L. Lewis quickly memo-
rialized the women and children of Ludlow as helpless victims, UMW

organizers had located the Ludlow tent colony near a train track so women and children could harass potential scabs, to prevent them from disembarking and breaking the strike. During the 1927–1928 Colorado Coal Strike, "Amazons" often led the pickets, and women, including Flaming Milka and the Rebel Girls, symbolized the strike. Embree and other IWW leaders even created the Junior Wobblies, so children could offer additional support to the walkout. Workers with Hispanic last names comprised half or more of the striking workers, and entire families of Mexican beet workers joined the walkout, too. Women and children constituted most of the strikers during the 1927–1934 textile walkouts and played key roles in the organized labor upheavals of the 1930s. Without women's auxiliaries, the Flint sit-down strike's success would have been impossible. Families marched upon the gates of Republic Steel in Chicago, which led to the 1937 Memorial Day Massacre. In the strikes Powers Hapgood organized at New England shoe factories, most of the workers who walked off their jobs were women. Therefore, militancy among minorities, women, and children was neither unique nor unusual, but in the 1940s and 1950s, this militant, egalitarian vision of industrial democracy had been so silenced that historians studying Jencks did not understand that his style of unionism was a callback to the past, not a rehearsal for the future.

In the 1970s, graduate students working in the Oral History Center at the University of California in Berkeley discovered that Maurice Travis lived in nearby Fremont, so they sent a student out to interview him. After a few sessions, Travis decided that the student knew so little about him and the labor movement, he could never do a good job,[50] so Travis began recording his own history, sixteen cassette tapes' worth.[51] He could not afford to have them transcribed, however, so through a mutual, trustworthy contact, he sent the tapes to Mike Solski and John Smaller, former Mine Mill officers, in Sudbury, Ontario. They paid for Travis's tape transcriptions, and they also interviewed Travis—and, very briefly, Una.[52]

The transcribed Travis interview included in the Mine Mill collection is a big mess. It is often unclear who is talking or when and where the interviews took place. Even so, it is a great source of personal and professional information about Travis, and it includes some of the only background information I could find on Embree. Travis was smart, funny, and well read, but he was also an egomaniac and an insensitive, inattentive husband and father. During one session, for example, as Travis waxed poetic about what a huge influence Una and her family had been upon him, he told Solski, the interviewer, that Una had not gone to public school because her clothes were so ragged, she was refused admittance. That was why she went to secretarial school, where she learned the skills necessary to get her position at Mine Mill headquarters.[53] When Una entered the room, Solski started asking her questions about what it was like growing up having Embree as a father. That was how I found out about Embree's probation period in Idaho, the family's extreme poverty in the 1920s, and that her father, who started going by the name of Sam, joined Mine Mill in 1937. When Solski asked her about going to secretarial school, she told him that she had gone to public school her entire life and graduated from high school in Denver, which back then (in the 1930s), was quite an accomplishment. That was where she had learned her secretarial skills.[54] Solski commented that he would love to do a separate interview with Una, and she agreed, although I do not think that ever happened, because in Solski and Smaller's 1984 Mine Mill history book, much of the information they include about Embree is repeated from their interview of Travis.

In his oral history, Travis remembered that Taft-Hartley served as the division point in his life and in the labor movement,[55] and although Schrecker argues that Jencks may have been the Cold War's ultimate victim, his life seemed to have turned out better than Travis's. After all, Jencks got to enjoy his adulation as a cultural warrior after the 1960s revival of *Salt of the Earth*, he had several excellent histories written about him, and he had a long, successful career as an academic, too. On the other hand, Travis's legal fights bankrupted him, although he did manage to work long enough for the Maritime union to draw a small pension and do enough restaurant work to qualify for Social Security.[56] Una rose to head Jacuzzi's swimming pool division, so she earned a good salary for a woman, but ill health plagued both her and Travis in their old age. With their combined retirements, the couple spent their old age in a modest apartment a few doors down from their daughter, who attended to their daily needs, since they were both "enfeebled."[57] What really came through in Travis's interview was how thankful he was to be telling his story. He was glad somebody wanted to hear it, because he had a lot to say about himself, the labor movement, and Mine Mill. He hated Jensen's book and the dissertations he had read pertaining to Mine Mill, because none of them captured the significance of the union and its "irrevocable impact on the history of the nations of the modern world in the period from World War I up through the Korean and Viet Nam war."[58] He was eager for Mine Mill's story to be told, and he had kept all the copies of Mine Mill records from his time in the union, but he could not afford to mail them. Apparently, even if he had the money, he did not know at the time of his interview who to mail them to, which might indicate he did not know about Jencks's Mine Mill archival work. I do not know if Travis's records ever made it into the Mine Mill archives, or even how Travis's interview transcript landed there. I do not know where his cassette tapes are or if Una was ever interviewed. I have also seen fleeting references to a biography that Embree wrote, but I never found that, either.

What I did find was the book that Mike Solski and John Smaller were researching when they interviewed Maurice and Una Travis, *Mine Mill: The History of the International Union of Mine, Mill and Smelter Workers in Canada Since 1895*, published in 1984. Throughout their history, short profiles of important Mine Mill leaders appear, and the very first labor leader they feature is A. S. Embree. It begins when Embree joined the WFM in 1893, and later, the IWW in 1905. It claims that Embree participated in the Ludlow long strike, but the only place I have seen that information was in their interview with Travis, who was not always a reliable source. Then, the essay praises Embree's role as a Mine Mill organizer during World War II. Even though the authors trace Mine Mill's origins to the WFM and the IWW, their profile completely omits the 1927–1928 Colorado Coal Strike. Therefore, even when honoring this militant labor organizer, the authors remember Ludlow but forget the Columbine.[59] Accompanying the Embree article is a photograph, and later in the book, another photograph appears. Let us compare those side-by-side and see what we can make of them.[60]

Notice the mural in the background of the two photos and the commemorative ribbons the men are wearing. These suggest the photos were taken on the same occasion, a convention held from February 27 to 29, 1956, in Sudbury, Ontario. Note the symbol dominating the mural. The date at the bottom of the Mine Mill emblem is 1893, the year the WFM was founded. As the introduction to Solski and Small's book explains, Mine Mill's symbol was an amalgamation that combined the WFM and IWW emblems, which makes sense, because the revived Mine Mill traced its institutional memory

FIGURE 9.1. *The photo of Embree accompanied the first profile of Mine Mill labor leaders in Solski and Smaller's history.*

to those two unions. In the group photo, Solski is on the far left. Standing next to him is Paul Robeson.

Who was Robeson and why was he there? Son of a slave, outstanding athlete, Columbia law school graduate, film actor, and Broadway icon, Paul Robeson got caught in the red scare's web for controversial comments he made in April of 1949, the same month Travis was savagely beaten in Alabama, at a peace conference in Paris. Newspapers quoted Robeson saying that since slaves helped create the United States' wealth, their descendants deserved a share of it. Even more controversially, he compared US foreign policy to Hitler's, saying it was folly to imagine "American negroes would go to war on behalf of those who have oppressed us for generations against a country [the Soviet Union] which in one generation has raised our people to the full dignity of mankind."[61] Outrage quickly followed, and in an unprecedented move, the State Department withdrew Robeson's passport until 1958. Until his passport was reinstated, Robeson only left the United States twice, in 1952 and 1956, both times at the behest of Mine Mill. During the latter visit, the photograph above was taken. Therefore, in the brief interlude after

FIGURE 9.2. *Later in the same book appears this photo. Solski is on the far left and next to him stands Paul Robeson.*

the film *Salt of the Earth* was released but before Travis and Jencks resigned from Mine Mill, one of the most militant Mine Mill locals hosted a union convention where its officials honored two of their heroes: Paul Robeson and A. S. Embree.

In entertainment and academic circles, Robeson remains a legendary figure, but Embree's legacy is mostly limited to a subset of labor historians who have studied the Bisbee deportation or the IWW.[62] In spite of his anonymity follow-ing the 1927–1928 Colorado Coal Strike, however, Embree lived long enough to see his remarkably consistent vision for industrial democracy emulated, celebrated, and documented. He served as an aspirational role model for Clinton Jencks, but even more directly for his son-in-law, Maurice Travis. Both endeavored to continue Embree's militant, egalitarian goals that contrasted with the bread-and-butter unionism that came to dominate the postwar organized labor movement. In 1953, University of California doctoral student Donald J. McClurg interviewed Embree about the 1927–1928 Colorado Coal Strike, a conversation that signaled a renewed historical interest in him and the IWW. In 1958, at the age of eighty-seven, A. S. Embree died, a year after being honored by militant Mine Mill unionists. Melvyn Dubofsky's history of the IWW, *We Shall Be All*, was published in 1969. He argued that although the IWW as a labor organization died out after WWI, its fighting spirit lived on. He even chose Embree to deliver the last line of his book: "Yet no better epitaph could be written for the American Wobbly than A. S. Embree's comment from his prison cell in 1917: 'The end in view is well worth striving for, but in the struggle itself lies the happiness of the fighter.'"[63]

When Dubofsky researched and wrote about the IWW, at least part of his interest was sparked by trying to imagine a counterfactual, even countercultural vision of industrial democracy unionism that stood in stark contrast to the "sleepy monopoly" organized labor had evolved into by the 1960s.[64] Some postwar historians viewed industrial union leaders as opportunists who had joined the "establishment," and their Cold War conformity included support for the increasingly unpopular war in Vietnam. More critical assessments viewed most unions as bloated, bureaucratic cesspools of racism, sexism, militarism, and outright corruption.

By 1969, one union that definitely fit the cesspool description was the UMW, and since Roche played a central role in shaping that union's postwar trajectory, it is time to return to her. After resigning from the Treasury in 1937 and from the interdepartmental health committee in 1940, Roche never again served in government. In spite of a decade of secret loans and a new management company, the UMW could not save the RMFC, and by the early 1940s, it fell to Roche to oversee bankruptcy proceedings.[65] Although the RMFC had never succeeded as an experiment in industrial democracy, Roche still believed that capitalism could be civilized, which might have led her to return to her maternalist, Progressive roots. From 1940 through 1944, she served as president of the National Consumers' League (NCL). Although women had always run the NCL since Florence Kelley's Progressive-era leadership, Roche served as its first female president.

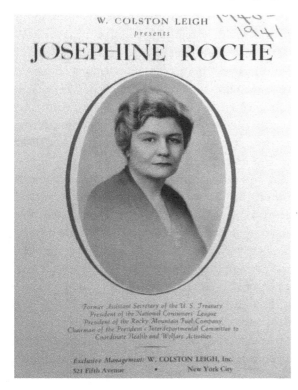

FIGURE 9.3. *This is the cover of a four-page brochure the W. Colston Leigh speaking agency would have sent to prospective customers who might want to book Roche.*

While administering RMFC's bankruptcy and presiding over the NCL, perhaps to remain in the public eye, to earn some money, or both, Roche signed a contract with the W. Colston Leigh speakers' agency. Audiences could hear Roche deliver lectures entitled "Industrial Democracy," "Our Stake in Industrial Democracy," "Industrial Democracy, the Safeguard of Political Democracy," or "New Concepts of Industrial Democracy."[66] Perhaps from lack of interest in Roche's topic, in Roche, or both, on March 19, 1947, the agency gently released her from her contract, since her speaking career "just happens to be one of those things that didn't click as we had hoped it would."[67]

In 1945, Roche took a research trip sponsored by the Russel Sage Foundation to study coalmine conditions in Great Britain and France, and her observations convinced her that public ownership of the coalmines was a mistake. That trip, combined with her own and Lewis's political experiences, reinforced their beliefs that linking their interests to the federal government, or even to the Democratic Party, was a mistake. Therefore, they set about creating a privatized pension and health insurance program for the UMW, and between 1946 through 1949, UMW coalminers waged official and wildcat strikes to achieve that goal. Since Robyn Muncy's *Relentless Reformer* but especially Richard P. Mulcahy's *A Social Contract for the Coal Fields: The Rise and Fall of the United Mine Workers of America Welfare and Retirement Fund* already provide detailed information about Roche's role in creating and administering the fund, there is no need for me to do so here, so I will provide only a short summary of how that process unfolded.[68]

The fund was created in 1946, and it had been one of the central demands of a strike so bitterly contested that President Truman invoked his still-intact war power authorities trying to stop it. As the fund's structure developed—much of it designed by Roche and other former federal government employees with experience in public health—the 1947 Taft-Hartley Act required that any retirement funds administered by unions be overseen by a board of trustees to prevent corruption or racketeering. That was why the UMW Fund would consist of three trustees: one representing the UMW, one representing the coal operators, and one, a neutral trustee, representing the rights of the public. Clearly, that structure was a callback to the many commissions formed during the progressive era and afterward, including the CIC, formed in response to the Ludlow Massacre. In 1948, Lewis named Roche the fund's administrator. After another long, bitter, and mostly successful 1949–1950 UMW strike, waged primarily to award the UMW the authority to determine who served as trustees, in 1950, Lewis appointed Roche the neutral trustee. Of course, Roche was never neutral. In fact, for the next nineteen years, she voted with Lewis 100 percent of the time.[69] Because Roche and Lewis controlled two of the three trustee votes, they controlled the fund.

As soon as Roche was named neutral trustee, UMW strikes stopped, just like that, and that sudden pacification of one of the nation's most militant unions was a consequence of the fund's structure. Coal operators paid royalties (fees) per ton of coal mined to finance the fund, so if coalminers went on strike, there would be no royalties. Beginning in 1950, both coal operators and the UMW seemed to get what they wanted. Big coal operators were freed from strikes, they exercised a near monopoly over the coal industry, and the structure of the fund encouraged them to mechanize as much as they wanted. In return, Lewis and Roche got relatively well-paid coalminers who seemingly worked in safer conditions and drew steady paychecks. Without having to rely upon fickle politicians, coalminers also received a pension and health care benefits, and even better, coal operators footed the bill.

Lewis hoped the fund would be his greatest UMW legacy.[70] At last, he and Roche were free to enact their vision of industrial democracy that—except for a decade-long, class warrior phase in the 1930s—had remained remarkably consistent. That vision had never included the democratic half of the term, however, and soon, the industrial half began to slip away. Between 1950 and 1960, the coal industry lost over half its workers, job losses that continue today.[71] Although changing energy sources contributed to coal's decline, most coalmining jobs disappeared because operators adopted the principles of scientific management that Lewis had been promoting since the 1920s. As both Mulcahy and Muncy make clear, although the UMW Welfare and Pension Fund was a bold experiment that challenged and influenced the ways health care might be delivered, fewer, but much larger and thoroughly mechanized, coal companies employed fewer coalminers.

That coal workforce shrinkage doomed the UMW Welfare and Pension Fund's long-term survival, and the fund's governance structure hid that fundamental truth for decades. Although Taft-Hartley required the UMW and the fund to be legally separate entities, Roche and Lewis treated the fund as an extension of the UMW, since the health of the latter determined the solvency of the former. The fund required coal operators to deposit their royalties into a Washington, DC, bank, owned and operated by the UMW. Just as Lewmurken had propped up the RMFC and other struggling UMW coal operations during the 1930s, the UMW bank extended unsecured loans to coal operators under contract with the UMW to make expensive mechanization upgrades. Because the fund's funding relied upon royalties, "Lewis had to drive out of business all marginal properties regardless of their union standing,"[72] which meant Lewis favored coal operators over coalminers. Dubofsky and Van Tine contend that stance signaled a sharp shift in Lewis's thinking, but as previously documented, he had done the same thing throughout the 1930s. Beginning in 1950, Lewis put into practice the vision of industrial democracy he had been advocating since the 1920s. A smaller, well-paid, thoroughly unionized coalmining workforce worked in safer, mechanized workplaces. Small, nonunion coal operations that, through cut-throat competition, had driven down wages and risked coalminers' lives were disappearing. Finally, the UMW had created mutually beneficial relationships with major coal operators and, when necessary, the federal government.

Although Lewis sincerely believed mechanization would produce safer coalmines, as machines began removing most coal, they dispersed a finely ground dust byproduct, silica, that invaded coalminers' lungs. That led to a painful, irreversible, and increasingly prevalent respiratory disease coalminers called black lung. Furthermore, as mechanization reduced the active coalminer workforce, the percentage of retirees—many in poor health—increased, which stressed the fund's finances. Further stressing the fund's finances, when coal operators deposited royalties into the UMW-owned bank, instead of investing those funds, Roche and Lewis deposited them into a low-interest savings account. Consequently, as early as the mid-1950s, the fund's benefits had to be adjusted cyclically, usually downward, and Roche did this in an imperious manner, without consulting anyone, including fund recipients.[73] To add insult to injury—literally—in a decision made perhaps for financial reasons or from a sincerely held but incorrect conviction that it did not exist, the fund refused to pay for any costs associated with black lung. That denial of benefits helped fuel a nascent coalminer rebellion.

Amid this context, in 1960, after four decades at the helm, Lewis at last stepped down as UMW president. However, he retained his position as the UMW Fund trustee. His longtime, but very old loyalist, ally Thomas Kennedy (the "ken" in LewMurKen, its official corporate capitalization), served a few years as UMW president before he died. Tony Boyle succeeded Kennedy, a man many UMW members believed, correctly or not, Lewis had tapped for the UMW presidency. Boyle exhibited all of Lewis's undemocratic tendencies, but none of Lewis's rhetorical talent, charm, charisma, or passion for the working class, which led, in 1969, to a crime so shocking that coalminers finally took meaningful steps to begin democratizing their union from within. That year, reform candidate Jock Yablonski mounted a spirited campaign against Boyle, but during the first truly competitive UMW election since 1922, Lewis was invisible. His declining health had turned him into a recluse inside his Alexandria, Virginia, home, where he allowed only his paid caretakers and Roche to attend to his needs. After one such visit, the increasingly frail, eighty-three-year-old Roche fell and broke her hip.[74] A week later, on June 11, 1969, Lewis died, and Boyle immediately assumed

Lewis's trustee position on the fund. As Roche recuperated in the hospital, Boyle told the coal operator trustee that Roche had delegated her proxy vote to him. Using it, Boyle increased the retirees' pensions from $115 to $150 per month. Consequently, appreciative retirees almost certainly swung the UMW presidential contest to Boyle.[75]

Throughout the campaign, Yablonski had complained of widespread violations, but his charges could not be dismissed after what happened on December 31, 1968. That night, invaders broke into Yablonski's Pennsylvania house, where they shot and killed him, his wife, and their adult daughter. The two adult Yablonski sons discovered their family's bodies six days later. At the first press conference they called after their horrifying discovery, the brothers directly blamed UMW corruption for the murders, and they also announced the formation of a new group, Miners for Democracy, to fight it. Joining this unlikely coalition of UMW reformers were law school students and professors, especially from the University of West Virginia, and Ralph Nader and his Nader's Raiders. Together, they attacked Boyle's corrupt practices and the UMW's weak safety record, especially focusing on problems surrounding black lung. Piling on, coalminers and dependents whose benefits had been cut brought a class action lawsuit against the fund, charging that it had been governed badly and capriciously.

In 1971, their case, *Blankenship v. Boyle*, appeared before a federal judge, and the fund lost.[76] The judge ruled that, at the very least, the fund consistently demonstrated a lack of financial transparency. At its worst, the fund operated as a "conspiracy by Lewis, Roche and the [UMW] bank" that led to its gross mismanagement. In his blistering decision, the judge demanded both Boyle and Roche be removed as trustees.[77] However, historians disagree to what extent Roche and Lewis had mishandled the fund, and evidence supports both points of view. The most forgiving interpretation comes from Mulcahy, who concludes the judge overreacted. Since both Lewis and Roche had lived through the Great Depression, he argues, they distrusted the stock market and other investments. They also distrusted banks, which was why the UMW had started its own. They viewed keeping the Fund's royalties in a savings account as safe, not irresponsible. So, although the end result was the same—financial mismanagement of the fund—Roche and Lewis's shortcomings should be attributed to extreme financial conservatism, not criminal malfeasance. Joseph E. Finley vehemently disagrees. He argues that

Lewis and Roche's financial sins were far more extensive than requiring coal operators to deposit royalties into accounts that earned absurdly low interest, since they repeatedly used the UMW bank assets as a private slush fund that promoted a wide variety of unwise union policies of dubious legality that helped coal operators and hurt coalminers. Finley paints an especially pathetic portrait of the elderly Roche, Lewis's *only* defender during the trial, but he saves his greatest outrage for Lewis, whose dictatorial "despotism," he argues, caused "the great undoing of the Fund."[78]

The Yablonski murders and the Blankenship case ignobly signify the end of the Lewis era at the UMW. In 1972, Boyle lost his reelection bid for the UMW presidency. Furthermore, prosecutors traced the Yablonski murders back to Boyle, who in 1975 was sentenced to life in prison for contracting those assassinations. In 1976, Roche died in a Maryland nursing home just outside Washington, DC, but not before she had worked hard, and successfully, to salvage her historical legacy. A few years before her death, Roche received an honorary doctorate from the University of Colorado in Boulder, probably in appreciation for her carefully culled, forty-one feet of archival materials she donated to the university. Whoever wrote the introduction to those papers cited no materials from Roche's collection, but instead relied upon secondary sources, including Louis Stark's *New York Times* article, "A Woman Unravels an Industrial Knot," to summarize Roche's life and historical significance. That essay omitted Roche's dismissal from the fund and praised her life as a reformer. The rewriting of Roche's legacy had begun.

Josephine Roche's subsequent sanctification was a by-product of early women's history, a field that emerged in the 1960s and evolved into today's gender studies. As historians first began researching and writing about women and other underserved historical actors in history—which included almost everybody except dead, white, males—the search intensified for heroic historical actors such as Roche, who had lived remarkable lives but whose significant accomplishments went mostly undocumented. In this process of democratizing history, a new generation of talented historians, including Robyn Muncy, rediscovered the maternalists. In Muncy's 1994 *Creating a Female Dominion of Reform, 1890–1935*, Roche appears as a bit player, although she must have captured Muncy's imagination, which led her to write her 2014 biography, *Relentless Reformer: Josephine Roche and Progressivism in Twentieth-Century America*.

Before Muncy, historians rarely dug deeply into sources about Roche, so she was portrayed as a rather one-dimensional historical actor. Even Finley portrayed Roche as a pathetic, old woman who slavishly followed Lewis's lead at the UMW. His negative Roche assessment was followed by a short burst of articles—women's history hagiographies, really—that, for sources, relied upon the wildly favorable articles about Roche published in the 1930s, articles based upon Roche's own self-generated press releases.[79] Historians writing about the 1927–1928 Colorado Coal Strike did not examine Roche's actions surrounding the walkout, either.[80] They, like the women's historians, repeated what by then had become the standard Roche narrative: Roche could not have prevented the Columbine Massacre, because when it occurred, she did not control the Rocky Mountain Fuel Company. Only after she gained control of the RMFC could she defy convention and sign an agreement with the UMW in 1928, which initiated her noble career as a labor reformer.

Although Muncy's Roche biography is no hagiography, she does repeat Roche's elevator pitch regarding her role in the 1927–1928 Colorado Coal Strike.[81] Since it was that strike, and specifically the Columbine Massacre, that turned Roche into a public figure and led to her alliance with Lewis and the UMW, understanding Roche's actions surrounding that walkout is critical to understanding Roche. Muncy approached Roche through her expertise in women's history and the progressive movement, but as Muncy well knows, progressives (the movement) and Progressives (the party) exhibited twin, inseparable impulses—social reform and social control. Understanding that duality makes it especially puzzling why Muncy would argue that Roche's frequent, unethical, often dictatorial behaviors were aberrations, or "temporary reversals."

My research shows that, like Lewis, Roche demonstrated remarkable consistency throughout her lifetime. From her Columbia master's thesis on white slavery through her stint as Denver's first policewoman, from her departmental administration at the Committee on Public Information through her public relations' machinations before and after the Columbine Massacre, from her earliest collaborations with Lewis to the ignoble end of her career at the UMW Welfare and Retirement Fund, Roche was consistent. She cared passionately about social inequality and wanted to fix it, but she also viewed herself as intellectually and morally superior to just about everyone around her. For Roche, like Lewis, the ends justified the means. Furthermore, Roche's own sense of self-righteousness and her apparent lack of introspection seemed to blind her to her own inconsistencies. She gave lip service to democracy, industrial and otherwise, but her actions often contradicted her own press releases, rhetoric, and actions. Her views did shift over time, but Roche remained a proud product of the progressive era in which her values were formed, with all its positive and negative attributes, which included both social reform and social control.

Muncy ponders why history has mostly forgotten Roche, and she blames sexism. As evidence, she cites the federal judge's statements about Roche in the *Blankenship* case. During the trial, he "belittled her intelligence, questioned her independence, and disparaged her business experience. He attributed her investment decisions, not to corruption, but to 'naiveté,' claiming that she 'idolized John L. Lewis and felt entirely confident to follow his leadership in financial matters, apparently without independent inquiry.'"[82] Subsequent historians, Muncy argues, then followed the judge's lead and dismissively regarded Roche as nothing more than Lewis's subservient stooge.[83] Of course, there is no denying that Roche and Lewis voted together 100 percent of the time on the fund, but Muncy provides evidence that Lewis often followed Roche's lead, not the other way around. In a strange twist cited to prove Roche's agency, Muncy provides evidence demonstrating that Roche not only knew but encouraged small coal operators to *appear* to contribute royalties into the fund, when in reality, the UMW bank illegally made those payments.[84] Therefore, because Roche connived as corruptly as Lewis and convinced him to follow her lead in doing so, Roche was not subservient to Lewis. In spite of that, and other damning evidence, Muncy cannot be shaken from her thesis: Except for a few "temporary reversals"—which sometimes lasted for decades—because her unethical means were always intended, in Roche's mind at least, to achieve an ethical end, Roche was a lifelong "relentless reformer."

As she wraps up her Roche biography, Muncy returns to one of her opening arguments, that Roche lived her life to right the wrongs of Ludlow. Again, however, she offers compelling evidence contradicting that assertion. In 1972, after her removal from the fund, Roche appeared to change her ways. She opposed Boyle's reelection and supported Arnold Miller's candidacy for UMW president as he ran on the Miners for Democracy platform. When campaigning for Miller, "Roche routinely tied 1972 to 1914," and "when rehearsing her own biography for reporters, she invariably began with the Ludlow Massacre." Muncy clearly recognizes the self-serving nature of Roche's Ludlow remembrances, since "what Roche did not openly admit was labor relations had changed so substantially since Ludlow that though workers continued to be exploited by their employers, they were also sometimes exploited by their own institutions."[85] Immediately following this wise analysis, Muncy then sunnily surmised that in campaigning for Miller, "Roche had resumed her commitment to democracy."[86] What Muncy did not fully appreciate was this: As Roche remembered Ludlow, to save her historical reputation, she just as consistently forgot the Columbine Massacre and over four decades' worth of consequences that flowed from that willful amnesia: Beginning in 1927, Roche aided Lewis in promoting the false narratives and undemocratic institutional structures within the UMW that made the Yablonski murders possible.

Without Roche's work with Lewis, it is doubtful New Deal labor reforms, as outdated as they are, would have ever passed. As a fellow labor historian once expressed to me about Lewis, "he was a dictator, but he was our dictator." Yet given the state of organized labor today, it is not clear that his dictatorial ways and undemocratic practices built a sustainable, democratic, socially just labor movement that could survive when giants such as Lewis threw off their mortal coils, a florid assessment with which even he might agree. Perhaps Roche, Lewis, Embree, Travis, and Jencks all did the best they could, but the intense anti-Communist pressures of the Cold War, coupled with deindustrialization, meant that, in the United States at least, all of their visions of industrial democracy proved inadequate when it came to building a long-term, sustainable path forward for organized labor.

10

Trying to Remember the Columbine
but Still Remembering Ludlow

The generation of historians who came of age after World War II did not witness the militant struggles in the 1930s and 1940s that transformed organized labor into an established American institution by 1955, when the AFL and CIO merged. What they saw instead were industrial unions comprised of mostly white, male members, whose leaders focused on negotiating favorable adjustments to their long-term contracts, improving their pay and benefits packages—but just for them, not the rest of society. Occasionally, such status quo conservatism was punctuated by some excitement, even outright corruption, such as the UMW's 1969 Yablonski murders.

Such negative views of unions, along with growing cultural and political divides, which accelerated in the 1960s with mounting opposition to the Vietnam War, inspired postwar historians' rediscovery of the IWW, a union that in every way seemed the antithesis of what organized labor had become. Wobblies had loathed labor bureaucrats and rejected labor contracts, and their perceived advocacy of racial, class, and, occasionally even gendered equality appealed to historians eager to learn about a more egalitarian path

https://doi.org/10.5876/9781646423026.c010

the labor movement might have taken. In spite of their best intentions, however, historians often produced overly romanticized IWW narratives as incomplete as the institutional histories they sought to supplant, and in their periodization of the union, declaring it mostly dead after World War I, they almost all failed to recognize the significance of the 1927–1928 Colorado Coal Strike. To an overwhelming extent, the historical silencing surrounding that strike can be attributed to their overreliance upon unofficial IWW historian Fred Thompson, who, as we shall see, was not always a reliable narrator.

Many of the same cultural and political impulses that inspired a resurgent interest in the IWW also rekindled historic interest in Ludlow, which resonated more with New Left activists—mostly young, mostly educated, and unaffiliated, like the 1930s Old Left had been, with organized labor—than with labor leaders and union members. Republican President Richard Nixon, first elected in 1968, understood and accentuated this cultural shift to his own, and his party's, benefit, effectively peeling away most of organized labor from the New Deal coalition a full decade before the official rise of the New Right in 1980.

The Watergate scandal and the souring toward career politicians led voters to elect political outsider Jimmy Carter to the presidency in 1976. Although generally described as the United States' first neoliberal president, he did harken back to FDR's cultural roots when he increased the National Endowment for the Humanities (NEH) budget, and big chunks of that increased funding were earmarked for community oral history projects, which included the Colorado Coal Project (CCP). Fifty years after the 1927–1928 Colorado Coal Strike, participants were finally asked to tell their sides of the story, but they struggled to remember much. For a variety of reasons, including the overwhelming influence of Barron Beshoar's 1942 book *Out of the Depths*, even when interviewers and their informants tried their hardest to remember the Columbine, they still remembered Ludlow.

More than any other person, Fred Thompson shaped the IWW historical narrative that we know today. From 1955 until his 1987 death, awestruck historians treated Thompson's voice as IWW gospel, but their faith was misplaced, at least regarding the 1927–1928 Colorado Coal Strike and A. S. Embree. On those subjects, for very personal reasons, Thompson was a most unreliable narrator. Although Thompson did not expend much effort remembering Ludlow, he definitely contributed to the historical forgetting of the Columbine.

Thompson's influence as an IWW historian began in 1955, when his book, *The I.W.W.: Its First Fifty Years*, was published. He wrote it because IWW old-timers were dying off fast and the remaining Wobblies, all one hundred or so of them, wanted something to preserve their legacy.[1] Thompson's history might have played a role in sparking a renewed historical interest in the IWW. When searching history databases for scholarly IWW articles, their proliferation in the early 1960s is stunning. Two of those articles, by Donald J. McClurg and Charles Bayard, even focus on the 1927–1928 Colorado Coal Strike.[2] In 1964, Joyce Kornbluh introduced the IWW to a broader reading public with *Rebel Voices: An IWW Anthology*, which is filled with short essays and reproductions of a wide range of ephemera—song lyrics, songbooks, stickers, posters, etc.—that she had collected to memorialize the Wobblies.

Kornbluh worried those IWW materials might not be preserved for future historians, a concern Thompson shared, so they began working with the archivists at Wayne State University in Detroit to assemble the IWW collection housed in the Walter P. Reuther Library.[3] When I did my research there a decade ago, 116 of 181 IWW folders contained materials relating to Thompson, and his personal collection runs an additional 17½ linear feet. Those materials help explain why Thompson had such a tremendous influence over IWW historiography. Perhaps even more importantly, Thompson readily availed himself to just about anybody doing research on the IWW. From New Left activists to New Labor historians, from budding high school journalists to seasoned professionals (including Studs Terkel, who included an oral history with Fred Thompson in his book, *Hard Times: An Oral History of the Great Depression*), from the late 1950s until his death in 1987, it seems that just about anybody who wanted to know what it had been like to be an authentic Wobbly interviewed Thompson.[4] Articulate, irreverent, funny, and passionate, but most important, *alive*, having called himself a Wobbly for over half a century, Thompson long outlasted his rivals, so when the IWW historical revival began, which he probably helped kickstart, he was more than eager to expound upon its history as he saw it. Although Thompson kept excellent records, it is really his faithful correspondence, especially with historians, that dominates his personal collection. Historians wrote to him because he was the closest thing to an official historian the Wobblies had ever produced, and they hungered for his authentic voice to legitimize their work.

One of the many historians who interviewed Thompson was Melvyn Dubofsky, whose 1969 book, *We Shall Be All: A History of the I.W.W.*, remains the most authoritative source on the IWW. Born in 1934, Dubofsky belongs to a cohort of college students who benefitted from the post–GI Bill world that helped democratize higher education. As mentioned in the previous chapter, before the war, most labor historians belonged to the John R. Commons school of historiography, which relied heavily upon union, government, and industrial records as sources. The postwar generation of historians expanded their subjects, methodologies, and sources. They often applied the quantitative methods of social history and used ephemeral cultural artifacts and oral histories for evidence, and the topics they researched reflected their non-elitist upbringings. In 1963, the publication of E. P. Thompson's seminal book, *The Making of the English Working Class*, changed labor history even more dramatically. Instead of analyzing politics or strikes, Thompson instead focused on the shared culture among workers. His book kickstarted the field of New Labor history, and Dubofsky is among the field's founding fathers. Others include David Brody, David Montgomery, Herbert Gutman, and, occasionally, founding mother Alice Kessler-Harris.

The New Labor categorization played upon the term *New Left*, a movement comprised of a loose coalition of rebels, often young, often college students, who emerged in the 1960s and early 1970s to protest "the establishment" that had institutionalized a wide variety of social injustices, including the military-industrial complex that perpetuated the increasingly unpopular war in Vietnam. Unlike the Old Left of the 1930s—a coalition of leftists often led by organized labor—the New Left for the most part eschewed organized labor, which it believed had *become* the establishment, led by white males more concerned with promoting their own self-serving agendas than with social justice. In turn, many critics charged that New Left protestors—who pushed the expansion of civil rights to a widening array of previously underrepresented segments of society, including Chicanos, Native Americans, and women—had no clear agenda beyond advocating identity politics.

Both New Leftists and New Labor historians generally saw themselves as inheritors of rebellious Wobbly traditions that had also challenged the establishment, and Dubofsky's *We Shall Be All* was at least partly inspired by this sentiment. In a 2007 interview with his former student, Bryan Palmer,

Dubofsky remembered that his book had begun as a history of metal miners in the West but evolved into a book about the IWW, because the "echoes between what could be called the New Left and the Yippies and the generation of the IWW seemed so comparable that it may have just been a natural transition."[5] Dubofsky was in his thirties as he researched the IWW, and I was half his age in 1969, the year his IWW history was published. That year, proving that the IWW revival was not just an academic movement, Joan Baez sang "The Ballad of Joe Hill" at Woodstock, a musical performance included in the *Woodstock* documentary released the following year. Six months pregnant as she sang, Baez dedicated the song to her husband, who was serving time in jail as a Vietnam War draft dodger and leading a hunger strike of fellow political prisoners. When Utah executed Joe Hill for murder in 1915, Wobblies declared that he, too, had been a political prisoner, killed not for any crimes he had committed, but because he was a Wobbly, fighting for the working class. The IWW turned Joe Hill into a political martyr, and his purported final words—"Don't mourn, organize!"—became a slogan so often repeated and reproduced in print that in today's world it would be considered a meme, although its earlier repetition had been far less transitory.

As already mentioned, like most IWW historians, Dubofsky interviewed Fred Thompson, although Thompson did not influence Dubofsky as heavily as he did most. Dubofsky did, however, adopt Thompson's periodization of the IWW when he claimed that the IWW ceased to be a significant movement after World War I. Although Dubofsky includes the 1927–1928 Colorado Coal Strike in his book, it appears in his epilogue as a deathbed rattle. Probably since Dubofsky's book is the gold standard for subsequent IWW histories, I have never read an account published after it that challenges Dubofsky's or Thompson's historiographical periodization of the IWW.

One of the first accounts I ever read on the 1927–1928 Colorado Coal Strike was in Thompson's IWW history, so I was eager to explore the IWW archives for additional strike materials, but what I found there explained less about the strike than about the foibles of memory. Despite Thompson's reputation as a stickler for facts and accuracy—possessing a memory like an elephant—between 1928 and 1981, he remembered at least three different versions of the 1927–1928 Colorado Coal Strike, Embree's actions during that walkout, and his own reactions to both.

Contemporaneous, institutional records from the Chicago IWW head-quarters provide a fourth version of events, so I will start there. In 1922, soon after joining the IWW, like many other Wobblies at the time, Thompson was jailed. Soon after his release in March of 1928, the IWW General Executive Board (GEB) sent him to Colorado a month after the 1927–1928 Colorado Coal Strike ended. Almost immediately, Thompson joined Tom Connors in attacking Embree. Remember that Connors had arrived in Colorado in early November, 1927, after Embree and other original strike leaders were jailed. In their absence, Connors seemed to usurp strike control away from Embree and other IWW organizers. After the Columbine Massacre, the CIC finally began public hearings on the strike, but Embree disagreed with Connors's insistence on linking the walkout to those hearings. Embree also accused Connors of behaving like a dictator and not allowing the strikers themselves to determine strike decisions. After Thompson's March arrival, Connors appears to have begun employing Thompson as his attack dog.[6] Thompson first accused Embree of working as a spy for the UMW, a charge so ludicrous that it quickly disappeared.[7] Thompson next accused Embree of misappropriating strike funds, and on this, the IWW constitution was clear: Embree's IWW membership had to be suspended while those charges were investigated.[8] The GEB hired a professional accounting firm that soon cleared Embree of all charges, doubtlessly because, in spite of his extreme mobility, which included several stints in jail, Embree kept remarkably good financial records.[9]

Let us examine the timing of Connors's and Thompson's attacks in the spring and summer of 1928. The coalmines were closed, and after staying out on strike for most of the previous season, coalminers were broker than usual. Although Roche was desperately urging UMW officials to send organizers and negotiators to Colorado, few, if any, were on the ground, which meant the IWW still was the only union with any real presence in the state. In July, the UMW lost its own 1927–1928 strike, a disaster all the coalminers would have known about. It was in this critical time period, knowing full well their accusations would remove him from the field, that Thompson and Connors chose to attack Embree. Understandably, this enraged Embree.[10]

By 1929, Embree no longer served on the IWW's GEB, but Connors and Thompson did. So did Kristen Svanum, who had co-led the Colorado strike with Embree. Although Svanum was often absent and rarely spoke even when present, when he did, his comments were hilarious and pithy. For example, as the IWW's finances continued cratering, the GEB discussed whether they should close IWW offices and quit publishing *Industrial Solidarity*, not only to save money, but also because of its messaging. Svanum agreed with a fellow board member that the newspaper was harmfully "spreading the defense psychosis and the martyr complex through our press," but "I can't see how we can censor the editor for it." Even while defending the editor's freedom to publish what he wanted, he believed that GEB members were "killing themselves with democracy. . . . The eternal voting and discussion is a sacrifice of the substance of democracy to its forms."[11] Svanum charged that Connors's General Defense Committee had "degenerated into a radical ladies' Aid Society collecting Xmas presents for the prisoners," and he also criticized its "autocratic, centralized structure."[12] On July 28, 1929, the GEB discussed whether or not to reinstate Embree as the IWW organizer in Colorado's northern coalfields, but as the GEB dithered on this topic, Roche's contract with the UMW approached its one-year anniversary, a reality the board ignored.[13] In the midst of this endless debating, Svanum officially resigned from the IWW on January 1, 1930,[14] and afterward, there is no further mention ever again of either Svanum or Embree.

After the disappearance of the 1927–1928 Colorado Coal Strike leaders from the IWW's GEB, Connors and Thompson continued driving what was left of the IWW into the ground. The GEB sent Thompson back to Colorado to reorganize what was left of the Wobblies, but his effectiveness was thwarted for several reasons. The most obvious was Roche's contract with the UMW. Also, because Colorado coalminers loved Embree, they resented his shabby treatment from the IWW. Furthermore, unlike Embree, Thompson knew nothing about mining, which further alienated him from those he was supposed to be organizing.[15] Although Thompson lived long enough in the coalmining town of Superior to marry a coalminer's daughter, the first of three marriages for Thompson, he left the state in 1931 and never returned.[16] At the same time, Connors continued pursuing the same strategy that had driven him and Embree apart during the Colorado strike, which focused on pursuing costly public relations–oriented legal battles instead of organizing workers.[17] For example, in 1931, the IWW General Defense Fund spent $28,000 in legal fees associated with the 1931 coal strike in Harlan County, Kentucky, although it appears that little IWW membership resulted from those efforts.[18] The Harlan strike so depleted the IWW's defense fund that when IWW members working on the Boulder (later Hoover) Dam were arrested for striking and perhaps committing sabotage, the GEB flatly declared that when it came to legal help, they were on their own.[19]

By the time Thompson rose through the IWW ranks to chair the GEB in 1934, the union really was irrelevant, and it would become even more so after the creation of the CIO the following year. Although Thompson remained a lifelong Wobbly, when he published his 1955 IWW history, the union functioned mostly as a geriatric society whose members reminisced about their glory days. With that context in mind, the excerpt below concludes Thompson's two-page entry on the 1927–1928 Colorado Coal Strike:

> Following the strike came elections of pit committees and checkweighmen and procedure for grievances. White cards of the striking miners had been issued during the dispute with IWW cards only to a minority. It was a significant victory and all considered it an IWW strike, for UMWA did not participate, but little unionism came out of it though efforts continued into the early thirties and a number of locals were maintained which assured election of checkweighmen and pit committees. This situation seems to have grown out of the strike arrangements with little actual union recruiting. It was later found that some officers of the union were planning during the strike to form a new miners body out of the Colorado miners, the Kansas followers of Howat and dissatisfied miners elsewhere as those who followed the communist line in Pennsylvania and those were to step over the traces in Illinois a few years later.[20]

This brief critique offers no hint of the heated conflicts that transpired between Embree and Thompson. Although Thompson does not mention Embree by name, he claims that strike leaders had not actively recruited IWW members because they were attempting to form a new, non-IWW union, which the white cards proved. Remember that Embree and Svanum had issued those white cards for several reasons. One of the most important was to provide the IWW a "front" so it could interact with the CIC. Without that front committee and its white cards, the IWW would have had no institutional presence in Colorado at all. Furthermore, Embree contended that most coalminers *did* belong to the IWW, although it was difficult to collect dues from striking coalminers going without paychecks. Although Howat's followers did send some strike relief funds[21] and Embree did work with James Cannon and the ILD, there is no evidence that Embree wanted to form a new union with the dissatisfied coalminers in Kansas and Pennsylvania. He did, however, envision rebuilding the IWW by forming coalitions among non-AFL workers.

Thompson and Connors ridiculed these coalition-building efforts, sarcastically labeling them as the "Embree policy."[22] While counterfactual history is always a dangerous exercise, it is fascinating to ponder what might have happened if the IWW really had adopted the Embree policy. During the strike, the ACLU and the ILD worked alongside the IWW's General Defense Fund. Embree hoped to increase IWW membership by uniting old-timer Wobblies like himself, newly recruited Wobblies (such as Colorado coalminers), coalminer insurgents (such as those in Illinois, Pennsylvania, and elsewhere) and other non-UMW coalminers, and even Communists, almost a decade before such a coalition emerged to lead the rise of the CIO. In 1928, there were about 650,000 coalminers in the United States who far outnumbered the 80,000 UMW members that Lewis represented. As demonstrated not just in Colorado but elsewhere, militant coalminers were willing to strike, although whether their hatred of Lewis was strong enough to unite them will always remain a matter of speculation. Maybe the time was not yet ripe, but it was in 1937, when Embree enthusiastically joined Mine Mill and the CIO, doubtlessly because it looked so much like the Embree policy he had tried to implement a decade earlier. On the other hand, Fred Thompson, ever the purist, continued to eschew collaborations with other organizations, and he continued to cast his organizational lot with the increasingly moribund and irrelevant IWW.

In 1955, the AFL and CIO merged, and Fred Thompson published his IWW history. As the CIO came to be viewed as part of the establishment, especially in the 1960s, suddenly, Fred Thompson was newly relevant. Historians eagerly sought him out, including David Roediger, who compiled a series of Thompson's interviews and personal musings in his book, *Fellow Worker: The Life of Fred Thompson*. In the introduction, Roediger writes that "Fred tended to open up most when he thought his past held lessons,"[23] and he astutely observed that "Thompson often told the same thing, in nearly the same words, to different interviewers and correspondents, sometimes even when they posed rather different questions."[24] This kind of well-rehearsed storytelling evolves over time, and while such narratives may not be an accounting of literal truth, they are an accounting of what lessons the speaker believes have been learned from the past. As Alessandro Portelli reminds us, "Oral sources tell us not just what people did, but what they wanted to do, what they believed they were doing and what they now think they did."[25]

What lessons from the past did Thompson's well-rehearsed stories need to prove? One lesson was this: Embree, not Thompson, destroyed the 1927–1928 Colorado Coal Strike's gains. As psychologist Daniel Schacter contends, "The self's preeminent role in encoding and retrieval, combined with a powerful tendency for people to view themselves positively, creates fertile ground for memory biases that allow people to remember past experiences in a self-enhancing light."[26] In other words, we construct and reconstruct our memories to make ourselves look good.

To preserve his high opinion of himself, Thompson consistently shifted blame from himself onto Embree, but the ways he did so changed over time. By the 1960s, Thompson recalled that in 1928 he had discovered letters written among four correspondents: Embree, Svanum, Alexander Howat, and William Z. Foster.[27] Remember that Lewis expelled Howat from the UMW in the early 1920s and that by March of 1930, Howat presided over the reconstituted UMW formed by Illinois insurgents. Foster led the American Communist Party in the late 1920s and early 1930s, fell from favor, then reemerged to lead what was left of the party after 1945. During the Colorado strike, Embree closely collaborated with James Cannon, perhaps because Cannon had been a Wobbly in its early days, and they were friends. Cannon quit the IWW, joined the Communist Party (CP), and in 1925, visited Big Bill Haywood in Moscow, where they "kicked around" the idea that developed into the ILD.[28] In 1928, Haywood died. Later that year, Joseph Stalin outmaneuvered Leon Trotsky and took control of the Soviet Communists. Consequently, Cannon was expelled from the party because he was a Trotskyite. Foster was not, and he took over the American CP. Stalin ended the "boring from within" policy, and Communists were instructed to form their own unions. Consequently, this was when coalminers formed the National Miners Union (NMU).

Therefore, since Embree allied with Cannon in 1927 and early 1928, it is highly unlikely he would have been corresponding with Foster. Before November of 1928, was Embree secretly a Communist, and were he and

Cannon "boring from within" in the IWW? Although I have found no evidence, it is possible. However, if true, Thompson would have found letters from Cannon, not Foster. Furthermore, Howat was no fan of Communists, and anyway, the Illinois coalminers insurgents formed in March of 1930, two years after the Colorado strike ended. The clearest evidence that Thompson imagined all this byzantine intrigue is this: There is no documentation of any of these letters in the IWW archives, even in the GEB minutes, which are highly detailed and descriptive.

I am suggesting that by the 1960s, Thompson, as do we all, had shifted the chronologies of his memories so they would make sense. Psychologists know that all humans do this, because we construct and reconstruct our memories in narrative formats—with beginnings, middles, turning points, ends, and lessons learned—in order to remember them. Over time, our narrative structures harden as we tell and retell those memories as stories, as Roediger remarked that Thompson did. Over time, in the stories we tell and retell to ourselves and each other, we omit details that do not support strong narrative structures. Obviously, such constructions and reconstructions lead to shifting chronologies and anachronistic thinking.

Alessandro Portelli has shown how chronological shifts occur, not just in individual memory, but in collective memories, too. In Portelli's historical exploration surrounding the death of Luigi Trastulli, newspaper records and other primary sources clearly showed that Trastulli, "a 21-year-old steel worker from Tern" and an active member of the Communist Party, "died in a clash with the police on 17 March 1949 as workers walked out of the factory to attend a rally against the signing of the North Atlantic Treaty by the Italian government."[29] However, within a few years, Communists no longer actively opposed Italy's membership in NATO, and by the early 1950s, other issues had taken center stage, including the closure of the steel plant where Trastulli had been shot. When the plant closed, the city erupted in riots, and the plant closure became the single most important event in the town's history. Over time, individual and collective memories of Trastulli's death shifted chronologically, until eventually, oral histories uniformly placed Trastulli's death within the context of the 1952 steel plant riots, not the 1949 NATO protest. Within the context of the NATO protest, Trastulli's death had no continuing meaning, but in the context of the 1952 riots, it did.

Sometimes, personal memories turn into collective memories, and in so doing, they support a larger political agenda. Roediger provides yet another example of Thompson's chronological reordering of past events regarding Embree and the strike that does just that. Thompson recalled that he and "other Wobs had been questioning this white card policy, but Embree insisted on the importance of keeping all the miners united whether they were for IWW aims or not." Although that remembrance consistently repeats Thompson's 1955 claims, a few sentences later, Thomson recalled that Embree "was employed by Mine, Mill & Smelter workers when it was, according to most, under CP control. Nonetheless we should not in retrospect have any illusion that CP antics were what kept the IWW from becoming a successful organization."[30] Therefore, Thompson's memory conflated Embree, the 1927–1928 strike, and Mine Mill's Communist persecution from 1948 through 1967, all in the same narrative.

By 1981, Thompson's memories about the 1927–1928 strike shifted yet again. That year, labor activist Bob Rossi wrote Thompson, asking him to enclose an informational query into the upcoming *Industrial Worker* about the 1927–1928 Colorado Coal Strike, since "nothing had been written about the strike or its meaning to the labor movement."[31] Thompson declined, since the strike had already been "thoroughly chronicled."[32] As proof, Thompson referred Rossi to four published sources about the strike: the McClurg and Bayaud journal articles, his own IWW history, and a chapter by Ronald McMahan in Joseph Conlin's just-published 1981 IWW anthology, *At the Point of Production*, to which I will soon return. For now, I turn to Conlin.

In the introduction to his book, a chronological anthology of IWW strike articles, Conlin explicitly affirms Thompson's role in shaping IWW history. He writes that Thompson had "donated his assistance to every effort in the writing of Wobbly history since he did his own account in 1955. Fred Thompson is well known to every historian interested in the I.W.W., whether in his voluble and hospitable person or through his voluminous letters in response to, no doubt often stupid questions."[33] After Conlin describes Thompson's instrumental role in constructing the IWW archives, he adds that "the files in his [Thompson's] head, however, remain the single greatest repository of Wobbly lore and interpretation from which he graciously draws for the benefit of every investigator who approaches him. He is not so gentle a critic as he is generous an advisor." Not only did Conlin ask for,

FIGURE 10.1. *This high school senior portrait of Fred Thompson was taken in 1921. (Courtesy of Fred Thompson collection, Walter P. Reuther Library, Wayne State University.)*

and receive, Thompson's advice during every stage of his book, he also adopted Thompson's (and Dubofsky's) IWW chronology, which explains why McMahan's essay on the Colorado strike is grouped in the last section, "The I.W.W. After the Fall."

After Thompson listed those 1927–1928 strike sources, he shared his own memories with Rossi. He remembered finding correspondence proving "in black and white" that Embree and Svanum were "planning to build a communist party coal miners union based on miners under CP influence" that would unite coalminers in Kansas, Pennsylvania, and Colorado. He remembered sending that correspondence to the Chicago leadership, but then admitted, "I don't know where that is now."[34] Apparently Thompson's inability to locate that smoking gun correspondence troubled him, because later that day, he wrote a letter wondering in whose possession that incriminating evidence might be, since he did not have it.[35]

Between 1928 and 1981, Thompson remembered at least three different versions of the strike, Embree's role in it, and his own reactions, and none of them aligns with contemporaneous IWW records. But Roediger called Thompson "perhaps the most avid fact-checker on the American left." When reviewing academic books, Thompson "regularly identified dozens of factual errors large and small. In editing other people's memoirs, he was loathe to accept their memories on the smallest points." However, Roediger admits that he himself never "interrogated Thompson's memory," even though he suspected Thompson "claimed greater precision of memory than he in fact had."[36]

Roediger's over-deference to Thompson was hardly unique. Thompson joined the IWW in 1922, the year after graduating from high school, when many Wobblies, including Embree, languished in prisons. Therefore, Thompson was not an IWW member, much less a leader during most of the 1905–1923 heyday period he so frequently described. Yet historians eager to speak and correspond with a real, live Wobbly did not challenge him on that impossibility. Since most of the IWW's records were destroyed during the World War I-era red scare, it is unclear how Thompson got most of his historical information about the IWW's purported golden age, unless it came from the old-timers' stories he had heard so often that he incorporated them into his own memories. So, while Thomson was an interesting, engaging, romantic, and extremely responsive correspondent and oral interview subject, he was not a reliable narrator. More than any other factor, Thompson's self-serving and shifting memories of Embree and the 1927–1928 Colorado Coal Strike changed the way historians researched and wrote about the history if the IWW, and these historical assessments have been incorporated into the dominant United States historical narrative. They declare that the IWW died as a consequence of its WWI-era persecution and that the 1920s and early 1930s was a quiescent era for labor. Somehow, spontaneously and out of nowhere, in 1933, those beaten-down workers arose, inspired by the fearless leadership of great men, including President Franklin D. Roosevelt and UMW President John L. Lewis, doing great deeds. But this narrative is a political distortion that puts the cart before the horse. The proximate cause of New Deal labor reforms was widespread worker militancy that scared the daylights out of policymakers.

In their search for authentic, non-elite voices from the past, New Left historians over-eagerly elevated the voices of former Wobblies, especially Thompson, to the status of noble class warriors who, like themselves, had rebelled against the establishment. Such a narrative downplayed the IWW's petty infighting that the Thompson-Embree split exemplifies so well, divisive drama made possible by the IWW's overabundance of democracy embedded within its egalitarian vision of industrial democracy. Along with the vicious, relentless, reckless, undemocratic, and well-documented WWI-era persecution orchestrated by local, state, and federal government authorities and their allies, the IWW's self-created problems also doomed the union's survival as a sustainable labor institution. Fully documenting that interpretation, however, might have meant that perhaps the New Left did not have as much to learn or as much to admire from the Wobblies as it hoped.

In January of 1977, Jimmy Carter was inaugurated as president of the United States and television's second ever "mini-series," *Roots*, became the highest-rated show in viewing history. For eight consecutive nights, 85 percent of American television owners were glued to their sets, watching a drama based upon Alex Haley's 1976 Pulitzer Prize-winning book of the same name.[37] Haley said he had based much of this personal origin story upon his own family's oral histories, and the success of *Roots* helped spawn the oral history boom of the 1970s. For four brief years, with the explicit support of the National Endowment for the Humanities (NEH), the federal government helped fund that explosion.[38]

In 1965, President Lyndon B. Johnson signed the NEH into law, "to support post-doctoral fellowships, research, programs designed to improve education at all levels, and projects fostering a wider public awareness of the humanities."[39] Under his direction, during Carter's administration, from 1977 to 1981, the NEH substantially increased its budget and staff.[40] Furthermore, Carter made clear, "'I want to be sure that any elitist attitude is ended' in the management of Federal dollars for culture. And his concerns were further underlined in the budget message he sent to Congress," because Carter "wanted emphasis placed on reaching 'underserved populations.'"[41]

Growing up poverty-stricken in Georgia during the Great Depression, Roosevelt's cultural New Deal deeply influenced Carter, and in interviews, he cited *Let Us Now Praise Famous Men*, published in 1940, by James Agee and

Walker Evans, as his favorite book, which had been funded by federal dollars. That book, like the film *Salt of the Earth*, proved far more influential in the 1960s than when released. Agee's self-conscious analysis on the impoverished lives of his subjects—desperately poor Southern sharecroppers and tenant farmers—combined with Evans's stark, modernist, unsentimental photographs, impressed Carter and an entire generation.[42] Another factor was this: In 1976, one-third of newly minted PhDs in history were unable to find jobs.[43] The newly expanded NEH could serve the same dual purposes the New Deal arts programs had in the 1930s—creating jobs while also creating democratic history and art.

The House Select Education Subcommittee, in charge of the NEH budget, held hearings in several major cities across the country where representatives heard a "growing enthusiasm among Americans to discover their own roots."[44] When NEH funding followed, conducting history "from the bottom up" became more than the purview of New Labor historians; it became official governmental policy. For the first time since the 1930s, the federal government enthusiastically funded historical research projects whose aim was to collect oral histories from previously unheard voices.

It was during this burst of NEH funding that, for the first time, survivors of the 1927–1928 Colorado Coal Strike were asked about their experiences from fifty years earlier. Their memories, however, no longer conveyed literal truths, and tapes and transcripts show that the interviewers rarely appreciated that discrepancy. In northern Colorado, four local oral history projects began, two by local historians Joanna Sampson and Phyllis Smith, who often concentrated their interviews on the roles women and families had played within coalmining communities, and two funded by NEH grants. One of those NEH projects was conducted by Lafayette librarians Effie Amicarella and Donna Carbone, and the other by two University of Colorado Boulder sociology graduate students, Ronald McMahan and Eric Margolis, who eventually named their work the Colorado Coal Project (CCP).

Sampson's books and the Lafayette oral histories are mostly for local consumption, but Smith's book, *Once a Coal Miner: The Story of Colorado's Northern Coal Fields*, reached a national audience, as did the CCP. Furthermore, Ronald McMahan wrote the aforementioned essay about the 1927–1928 Colorado Coal Strike that Joseph Conlin included in his IWW anthology. Almost anything written about Colorado coalmining since 1980 has cited the CCP, but after delving into the collection, I came to realize that most researchers had cherry-picked the materials in order to provide picaresque "local color" and occasional direct quotes to their works.

The order in which I encountered these sources reveals some of the underlying structures of this local coalfield memory. From first to last, I read McMahan, Smith, Sampson, the Lafayette library transcripts, and the CCP. In 2020, during the coronavirus lockdown, a Lafayette librarian showed me a personal memoir written by a strike participant that I had missed during my initial research, probably because it was not included within the oral history collection, a memoir to which I will soon return. In 2005, Denver Wobblies published *Slaughter in Serene: The Columbine Coal Strike Reader*, and it includes essays by Sampson, Margolis, and others, including one by Richard Myers, a self-taught historian and IWW activist who, more than any other, deeply researched the 1927–1928 strike.[45] None of these sources, however, place the strike within a larger national context.

A Boulder company published Smith's book in 1989, perhaps to help commemorate Lafayette's centennial celebration. Because her account of the 1927–1928 Colorado Coal Strike especially focuses on women, she celebrates Roche and emphasizes Elizabeth Beranek's role in the strike and at the Columbine Massacre. Likewise, Sampson emphasized Beranek, and both she and Smith interviewed one of the Beraneks' daughters.[46] Since Sampson's husband was a retired coalminer, she had almost unlimited access to many old-timers, especially around her hometown of Marshall. Unsurprisingly, coalminers and their families are always the heroes in her books. Amicarella and Carbone conducted interviews with their friends and family members, and since Smith and Sampson also spoke with many of the same people during this same time period, there is definitely a self-referential loop at play in these interviews.

The Lafayette Public Library currently houses the oral cassette tapes (some of which have been digitized) and interview transcriptions, but a major limitation is that the interviewers only spoke with informants in the 1970s and 1980s who still resided around Lafayette and who spoke English. At least half of the strikers had spoken Spanish as their first language, and furthermore, my evidence suggests that most strikers moved soon after the 1927–1928 strike ended or after the remaining coalmines closed in the 1940s and early 1950s.

Therefore, although oral histories help democratize history by telling a more "bottom up" rather than "top down" story, the "bottom" often lived more mobile, insecure lives than those who stayed behind. Furthermore, many had good reasons to leave after the strike. For example, records show that by 1930, black Louisville coalminer, William Lofton, who was such an important IWW strike leader, had moved to Denver. Although Lofton left no records explaining what happened to him after the strike, Duffy Allander Parker did, and his is the undated memoir I recently read. It was donated to the Lafayette Public Library sometime after Effie Amicarella found it "while cleaning out some drawers in my desk." Significantly, Parker's is the *only* first-person source I have read that conforms with and adds to contemporaneous records. In his lucid, well-written account, he proudly and unapologetically documents his role as an IWW strike leader. Afterward, working at the RMFC, he got in a tiff with John Lawson, quit, and moved to Denver. In Roche's records, I found evidence that the Allander family opened a bookstore, and enthusiastically switched their allegiances to the Communist Party. Clearly, Parker no longer felt welcome in the community, and Lofton probably did not either, so they left and were not included in the 1970s and early 1980s oral history projects.

Another instance of strike supporters who moved away has taken on increased meaning in Lafayette, especially within the town's Latino community. It also illustrates how historical silences can fester, but also literally whitewash history. In 1933, the town decided to build a swimming pool. Most of the money came from the federal government's Civil Works Administration (CWA), a precursor to the Works Progress Administration (WPA).[47] The CWA required communities to contribute financially to their projects, so in Lafayette, locals were asked to donate bags of cement. The Lueras family contributed ten bags, one of the biggest donations in town, yet when Rose Lueras took her daughter Annabelle to swim in the new pool, they were turned away. The local fire department, which had taken over running the pool, had posted a large sign that read, White Trade Only. By 1933, that sign provided painful evidence that Latinos were no longer considered white. Mrs. Lueras, joined by many other Latino community members, filed a lawsuit. I know from newspaper accounts but especially the post-Columbine CIC transcript that most of those plaintiffs, including the Lueras family, had been active participants and supporters of the 1927–1928 strike. Just five years later, so much had happened in the community—Roche's contract between the RMFC and the UMW, the stock market crash, the worsening of the Great Depression, the scapegoating of Latinos as unemployment continued rising—neighbors turned against neighbors. In reaction to the pool lawsuit, the Ku Klux Klan, which seemingly died out elsewhere by the late 1920s, held a parade in Lafayette. Rose Lueras felt so threatened that she and her daughter moved to southern California, where, tragically, a driver struck and killed her with his car. Thirteen-year-old Annabelle moved back to Lafayette and, incredibly, became the lead plaintiff in the case. In 1934, because of the bad feelings generated by lawsuit, the city council decided to fill in the pool with dirt. Still, the plaintiffs continued their appeals. Eventually, they lost on a legal technicality, not constitutional grounds. There would not be another municipal swimming pool until 1989.[48] How many Latinos left Lafayette after the strike? How many stayed, and if they did, how many were not included in the oral history project because they did not speak English or were never asked to participate? What stories could they have told that were never incorporated into local, much less national, historical narratives?

If we pay close attention, the spate of local oral histories that were collected reveal other historical silences, too. For example, Effie Amicarella's husband and his brother, who were teenagers in 1927, became two of the most interviewed, and cited, informants surrounding the Columbine Massacre. They remembered coming home in the wee morning hours as their father readied for work on the morning of November 21, 1927. When the shooting started, they dove for cover as bullets riddled their house. Their memories reveal at least two facts they were neither asked about nor volunteered: If they were just getting home as their father readied for work, they had probably been out partying with the other teenagers who continued drinking after the big Sunday afternoon IWW rally in Boulder. Also, if their father was getting ready for work, he was a strikebreaker. Their remembrances reinforce the evidence that most of those who stayed in the community after the 1927–1928 walkout might not have been strikers or strike supporters.

Other Lafayette library interviews include informants Mary Borstnick, Dorothy Fleming, Andy Borrego, Frank Deborski, and Walt Celinski. Borstnick and her husband lived in dozens of coal camps in both the southern and northern Colorado coalfields, but after the long strike ended, she and her husband moved north. Her memories illustrate the mobility between

Colorado's coal fields and Ku Klux Klan activism, since she remembered Klan members burning crosses in front of the local Catholic church. In 1927, they lived next door to the Amicarellas in Serene, so her husband was also a strikebreaker. Like many informants, her memories focused on "the old lady Beranek," who came "screaming and running back of my house" that morning of the massacre.[49] Even though her husband was a scab, community relationships between the scabs and strikers seemed amicable enough, because, like the Amicarella brothers, she attended many IWW rallies, probably because they were a great source for entertainment.

Dorothy Fleming was the daughter of John Eastenes, and she was six years old when her father was killed during the Columbine Massacre. Fleming remembered her father's back so completely blown off, "they had to put some sort of cotton or padding or something," to prop him up, but even with that, he appeared "abnormally low in the coffin."[50] She had grown up hearing that a sheriff named "Sheratt" had "pulled a handgun" and "shot my father once in each side of the chest,"[51] a story I never heard or read anyplace else. Three additional informants also identified Sheratt as the leader of the militia at the Columbine, but it was Louis Scherf who commanded the state police that day. That misremembered, yet widely repeated misinformation was my personal turning point in this project. Sheratt, you see, had been a much-hated community figure during the 1910–1914 long strike, not the 1927–1928 strike.[52] Why were informants confusing the two strikes, especially since most of them were far too young to have participated in the earlier one? Why were informants remembering Ludlow, which most had been too young to have participated in, but forgetting the Columbine, which they had lived through?

In none of the oral histories did informants openly admit to being strikebreakers. Neither did they remember joining the Wobblies, although Andy Borrego came the closest.[53] Borrego would have been twenty-three years old in 1927. In one breath, he remembered being at the Columbine the morning of the massacre, but in the next, he remembered arriving right after the shooting stopped. A few sentences later, he places himself back at the Columbine: "They opened a machine gun on them. And Beranek, she didn't get shot, I don't think, but they beat her up. I seen her when she put the flag over Adam Bell; they beat him up and then she threw the flag over him."[54] Both Sampson and Smith relate the same story, exactly, although contemporaneous evidence shows that Adam Bell had been pulled over the fence by the strike police and beaten. He had not carried the flag, although the flag was central in every single account. Borrego also claimed he was the second striker hired back at the Columbine when it reopened. Since that was during the strike, therefore, he also became a strikebreaker. Here is how he described his rehiring: "There was only 13 of us—only 13 union men working there when the United Mine Workers took over. They told us we either join the United Mine Workers or get out of the camp. We didn't know what the heck to do and Charlie Metz [a local Wobbly and the same man Vincent later fired] said that we were lost and we'd better join the United Mine Workers or we were going to be out all together. And so we did."[55]

Although Borrego's version of events is slightly off chronologically, it has the ring of truth and is also corroborated by other sources.[56] IWW newspapers identified Metz as a leader, and after the strike, many coalminers held dual IWW and UMW memberships. However, after Roche's 1928 contract with the UMW made the RMFC a closed shop, there was no reason for coalminers to pay dues to two organizations when only one would get them a job, surely one of the reasons IWW memberships dwindled. Although Borrego as an old man spouted the official story that praised Roche and the UMW, accounts that even praise their handling of the black lung crisis, genuine flashes of anger surface in his oral history, and these emotions contradict the narrative that workers were completely happy with Roche and their UMW contract. For example, Borrego was upset that the men who had scabbed during the strike got to keep their jobs at the Columbine while the RMFC blacklisted most of the IWW strikers except for him and a few others who also agreed to join the UMW. Borrego also angrily remembered when he and others were pressured to sign the petition presented to the CIC to cut their wages. He contends he did not sign it but the majority did, because if they refused, they would have been fired.[57] I did not see Borrego's name on the petition presented to the CIC in Roche's papers, which supports his claim. However, Borrego remembered that petition circulated *before* the UMW came in, but it circulated in 1931, three years *after* the union arrived. So, while Borrego's chronology is off in a way that reinforces his later allegiance to Roche and the UMW, his resistance and anger ring true. Oral histories may not be accurate snapshots of the past, but they do communicate important truths.

Although no coalminer openly admitted joining the IWW, Deborski and Celinski fondly remembered joining the Junior Wobblies. Deborski recalled joining other children in acting out plays throughout the Denver area to raise strike funds.[58] Celinski also loved the Junior Wobblies, and he freely admitted that his father organized for the IWW. After the strike, however, people in the community always referred to him and his dad as no-good radicals, but "that's what you get from people. That's how they reward you."[59] Celinski's oral history helps explain why so many of the 1927–1928 strikers probably moved away, never to be interviewed.

As I read these fascinating interviews, I grew increasingly confused, especially when informants freely transposed names (such as Sheratt and Scherf) and events between the 1910–1914 and 1927–1928 strikes. They left out key pieces of information about themselves, including whether or not they had been Wobblies or scabs. They also contradicted themselves and confused their chronologies. Some memories, such as Dorothy Eastenes Fleming's, were unique, but inconsistent, while other stories were repeated, almost verbatim, such as the stories about Mrs. Beranek during the Columbine Massacre, as if the informants had rehearsed telling those stories. Of course, like Fred Thompson, they had. Significantly, almost none of their memories aligned with contemporaneously generated evidence.

Only after reading *Doña María's Story* by Daniel James did I understand why these oral histories made little factual sense. For almost a decade, James interviewed Doña María, an Argentine labor leader who had been active in the mass protests that brought Juan Perón to power in 1945. She remained a *peronista* long after Perón's policies hurt the working class that had propelled him to power. Therefore, Perón's mixed legacy created conflicting memories for Doña María. She could not bring herself to acknowledge her feelings openly, ambiguities that surfaced in her oral interviews. James explores the inconsistencies, silences, and literary conventions she employed when reconstructing her own life's narrative, while he also explores the ways his role as an American scholar shaped their conversations.

Reading James led me to Alessandro Portelli, generally considered the most influential historian in the field of oral history analysis.[60] He teaches American literature in Rome, illustrating well how scholarly interest in oral histories has helped blur disciplinary boundaries, since it draws liberally from psychology, literature, linguistics, anthropology, folklore, and other fields, including criminology. Portelli's quote, which became my mantra for analyzing the oral histories I was reading, bears repeating: "Oral sources tell us not what people did, but what they wanted to do, what they believed they were doing and what they now think they did."[61]

During the NEH-funded oral history boom, oral histories tended to be accepted as relatively accurate snapshots of the past. After that boom, postmodern linguistic methods emerged, suggesting new ways to evaluate oral histories. Led by academics including James and Portelli, who usually had the luxury of asking their own questions of their informants, they self-consciously knew that they, as interviewers, actively participated in the interview process. Trying to unravel the stories that community members told about the 1927–1928 Colorado Coal Strike in general and about the Columbine Massacre specifically thus became doubly difficult, because I did not conduct those interviews and there was no re-interviewing to be done because the participants are dead. Moreover, Smith, Sampson, and other local interviewers did not seem to take their own roles as interviewers into account. From their writings, it became clear that both women had been looking for—as I once had—and therefore found heroic struggles of brave women, like Roche and Beranek, and working-class coalminers who had stood up for themselves against all odds.

These same problems persist within the Colorado Coal Project (CCP). Although Margolis and McMahan professed extreme self-awareness as interviewers, this was not the case, because both also found what they went looking for. When they started their work in 1974, the graduate students began interviewing retired Colorado coalminers, and they preserved these interviews on cassette tapes, since that was all they could afford. The Colorado Endowment for the Humanities funded these initial interviews with a small grant, but in 1977, the research partners won a $352,000 award, direct from the NEH. Flush with cash, they bought video equipment, hired a small crew, and began re-interviewing people, this time on videotape. This was when they renamed their research the Colorado Coal Project. It contains over two hundred hours of videotape, twelve hundred photographs, and seventy-five tape-recorded interviews (about half of which are transcribed), all housed at the University of Colorado archives in Boulder.[62]

In their grant application, the deliverables that Margolis and McMahan promised to create were a series of documentaries for Colorado public television.[63] In a 1994 essay describing how materials were organized for those videos, Margolis wrote, "Historical categories were not imposed by the editor [Margolis] but were nominated by coal people out of their own experience," because "ethnographic editing techniques allowed the raw materials to inspire both form and content."[64] Their transcribed interviews, however, contradict Margolis's assertion. Even though it did not begin that way, by the time Margolis and McMahan finished, memories of Ludlow overwhelmed their entire project. Margolis wrote that the Ludlow Massacre was "mentioned by every miner interviewed; it was the most important event in the community's history," yet it is hardly a mystery why every coalminer or community member mentioned it.[65] Margolis and McMahan *asked* every person they interviewed about Ludlow.

Margolis and McMahan began their interviews just two years after the publication of George McGovern and Leonard Guttridge's book on the Ludlow strike, *The Great Coalfield War.* Guttridge reworked McGovern's 1954 Northwestern dissertation into a trade book published in 1972, the year McGovern challenged Nixon for the presidency of the United States. The book focused on the 1913–1914 extraordinarily violent phase of Colorado's long strike, with the Ludlow Massacre serving as the narrative turning point. I long for the days when a politician thought a well-researched history book would boost his chances at getting into the White House, but the book did not achieve what had surely been one of its intended effects, rallying organized labor to vote for McGovern. Most union members instead voted for Nixon, who had figured out a way to effectively peel organized labor away from the New Deal coalition: He appealed to culture war divisions rather than economic self-interest.[66]

Organized laborers no longer identified with the workers and their supporters in the long strike, but New Leftists, including Margolis and McMahan, did. Even though McGovern warned his readers that Barron Beshoar's 1942 book *Out of the Depths: The Story of John R. Lawson, A Labor Leader,* was deeply biased, he still cited it liberally, and his basic narrative structure paralleled Beshoar's, as have most subsequent Ludlow histories. Like McGovern, the views of Margolis and McMahan, but especially their informants, had been irrevocably shaped by Beshoar's book. Ostensibly a biography of John R. Lawson, it really spun an engaging, entertaining, dramatic, dialogue-filled narrative of the 1913–1914 violent phase of Colorado's long strike.

Beshoar is to Ludlow history what Thompson is to IWW history. Both men function as the center of self-referential, narrative historical source loops that, so far, have proven difficult to break. Not just his book, but Beshoar himself directly shaped the CCP narrative. After spending over five years collecting interviews, including hours with Beshoar, the graduate students' grant money was running out. As I learned in my interview with McMahan, he and Margolis faced increasing pressures to make their videos, graduate, and get on with their lives. Although McMahan had a scholarly article published, which helped fulfill the sociology department's graduation requirements, the pair was still obligated, under the terms of their NEH grant, to make ten one-hour documentaries for Colorado Public Broadcasting. They were able to negotiate their deliverables down to three films that seasoned television journalist Bill Moyers saw potential in.[67] His crew edited that footage down into a one-hour documentary broadcast in 1984, the eighteenth out of nineteen episodes in his Emmy-award winning series for the Public Broadcasting Service (PBS), *A Walk Through the Twentieth Century*. The episode, "Out of the Depths" aired on Labor Day weekend, and it focused exclusively on the Ludlow Massacre.

Moyers's Ludlow documentary was a far cry from what Margolis and McMahan originally had in mind when they had begun their research,[68] but as McMahan had admitted to Beshoar, "We've got so much stuff Barron and if you can't save it for us, I don't know what we're going to do."[69] What began as help soon turned into control. As ethnographers, Margolis and McMahan had allowed, even encouraged, their informants, these "little cameos of people," to go on tangents, because those stories transported their interview subjects "to another place," which sometimes yielded "the most fascinating story you ever heard."[70] Beshoar, however, advised them to cut such tangents out of their films,[71] because "it's got to be dramatic."[72] The informants could not construct a coherent narrative because, "you see, there isn't any one of these people you interviewed that can do that whole thing for you. Cause all any of them saw was little pieces that interested them. Practically none of them saw the broad picture." Furthermore, "did any one really know who Rockefeller was? A lot of them didn't speak English. They didn't know what was going on; they didn't know how these things developed; they can't tell you."[73] The miners were "too busy working. And they were not trained to observe and to tell."[74]

Beshoar asked Margolis and McMahan critical questions they seemed not to have considered before, such as, "Who's going to watch this?"[75] The researchers thought their viewers would consist of "your basic liberal audience," every coalminer in the nation, and women.[76] Since liberals and women would be watching, Beshoar told them their story had to take place not underground, but "on the surface."[77] Beshoar, a retired journalist, also advised the pair to cover the five Ws of journalism: who, what, where, when, and why. Furthermore, their script needed to be dramatic, narrative, and linear.[78]

Margolis and McMahan got so swept up by Beshoar, just as labor historians got swept up by Fred Thompson, they decided he should be their narrator. Like historians inspired by Thompson's authenticity, Margolis and McMahan loved that Beshoar was not an academic—their delivery was too "uppity"— yet he was articulate and passionate.[79] We can watch the film and see for ourselves that, as Beshoar narrates the film, he carries he own copy of *Out of the Depths*. He consults it often, although he understood the filming could not cover the whole book, only "the high spots."[80] Unsurprisingly, the narrative structure Beshoar imposed upon the overwhelmed graduate students followed the exact same narrative structure of his 1942 book.[81]

Although Ludlow histories written since 1942—even the newest and best ones—acknowledge Beshoar's bias, like McGovern, they still cite Beshoar's book and mostly follow Beshoar's narrative structure. They also cite the CCP, usually for quotes. They begin, briefly, with the strike in the northern Colorado coalfields, but only for background. The action really begins in 1913, when the strike, and violence, move south. The Ludlow Massacre serves as the turning point, then the strike sputters to an end in December of 1914. Some of the biggest changes in the newest Ludlow histories are that coalminers and their families are no longer portrayed as complete victims. In Beshoar's telling, coalminers were always the good guys, but in *Blood Passion*, for example, Scott Martelle makes clear that when it came to committing violent acts, coalminers gave better than they got. In *Killing for Coal*, Thomas Andrews focuses on the environmental causes and consequences of the long strike. In spite of such updates, however, most long strike narratives conclude at the Ludlow memorial, where authors try to assess the long-term significance of the strike and its violence. Most, but not all, accounts follow Beshoar's lead, claiming that the Ludlow deaths led to New Deal labor reforms, an interpretation that Roche and Lewis would have endorsed.

Beshoar's narrative has proven so powerful because it not only determined the questions that Margolis and McMahan asked and the narrative structure of Moyers's documentary, it shaped the informants' responses before they were ever interviewed. Incredibly, Margolis and McMahan told Beshoar they found a copy of his book in *every* miner's house they were invited into.[82] Although Beshoar was flattered to hear this, he said most of the miners interviewed for the CCP had been too young during the 1913–1914 strike to remember it, and he thought most of their memories came from his book.[83] Most discordant of all, the CCP informants had a hard time remembering much about the 1927–1928 Colorado Coal Strike, an event most of them had actually participated in or at least lived through.

Clearly, Beshoar's book had already played a critical role in organizing informants' memories long before Margolis and McMahan ever arrived. This intermingling of personal and published memory was often directly captured on videotape. Mike Livoda—probably the most interviewed person ever surrounding the Ludlow Massacre, who was so identified with the strike that he is the only person buried at the Ludlow monument site—can be seen thumbing through the book when his own words escaped him.[84] Beshoar even questioned Livoda's memories of the strike, saying, "Now he [Livoda] was nothing but a kid himself when the strike started here. Just among ourselves his role was pretty minor," which was not quite true, since Livoda had been in his early twenties during the long strike. Yet when Beshoar said, "You know one time my father told me . . . some of these old time stories . . . I've told them over and over and to tell you the truth I can't remember whether they happened to my father or to me," he could just as easily have been referring to the stories Livoda or any of the other CCP informants were telling, too.[85]

Beshoar's own memories of the Ludlow strike were as problematic as those of the other CCP's informants. Although Beshoar was a child during the 1913–1914 phase of the strike in southern Colorado, his childhood memories were more vivid to him than those from the 1927–1928 strike, which occurred when he attended the University of Colorado in Boulder, just ten miles from where the Columbine Massacre took place. Almost three decades after Ludlow, Beshoar began conducting research for his 1942 book, and since the strike occurred "when I was a boy of six; most of these characters I did not know."[86] Therefore, he remembered that his biggest advantage was that

I had John Lawson at elbow [they were then working together on the WWII War Manpower Commission], I had Horace Hawkins the noted attorney for

Denver labor organizers led by a contingent of contemporary Wobblies who later published *Slaughter in Serene: The Columbine Coal Strike Reader*, began organizing efforts to memorialize the Columbine Massacre, seventy years after it happened.

That time lag is just one of the many stark differences between the memorializations of the Columbine and Ludlow massacres. In 1915, the UMW had leased the property on which the Ludlow tent colony was built and then bought it after the long strike ended. Just three years later, in 1918, John L. Lewis helped orchestrate the quick construction and dedication of the Ludlow memorial, as I have argued, to begin appropriating the memories and meaning of the massacre and to erase the roles played by the strike's revered leaders, John Lawson, Ed Doyle, and Mother Jones. The UMW continues to hold annual memorial services there. Attendance ebbs and flows over the years, and ceremonies generally celebrate all organized labor. In 2003, probably as a consequence of a nearby labor dispute, vandals decapitated the man and woman figures (but not the child). Two years later, the UMW paid to fix the monument and organized a ceremony celebrating the monument's restoration. In 2009, activists celebrated the site's designation as a National Historic Landmark, and in 2014, historians, labor activists, community members, and strike descendants convened for the centennial memorial. Many attendees wore red bandanas around their necks in honor of the strike's original rednecks.

In contrast to the quickly constructed memorial near the actual massacre site, the geographic location where the Columbine Massacre took place is, literally, buried under a solid waste trash dump, the Front Range Landfill. Erie residents jokingly refer to that landfill as "Mt. Erie." Vista Ridge, a high-end golf course community, encircles the dump, and it is doubtful that the residents who walk their dogs at Columbine Mine Park or who reside on Lawson Avenue, Serene Drive, or Columbine Court know much about the origins of those names. Directly south of the dump stands a recently built strip mall, anchored by a King Soopers grocery store.

South across Baseline Road—a thirty-eight-mile, east-west stretch of highway constructed along the 40th parallel, designated in the 1854 Kansas-Nebraska Act as the boundary separating slave and free territories and later as the primary baseline for surveying the newly acquired western land—is a sign commemorating the Columbine Massacre, erected in 2002 by the

FIGURE 10.2. *The front of the headstone lists the victims' names on the front. Photo by the author.*

FIGURE 10.3. *The back of the headstone lists two very generalized donors on the back. Photo by the author.*

FIGURE 10.4. *This sign greets visitors and residents who live at Josephine Commons. Photo by the author.*

Colorado Historical Society, the Colorado Department of Transportation, and the Federal Highway Administration. In 2006, another high-end residential development broke ground, and city planners required developers to include green spaces, parks, and trails, which led to the construction of a small pocket park built around the 2002 sign. Developers wanted the big wooden sign gone, however, so it was moved to the backyard of the Lafayette History Museum. When both Columbine signs were erected, Baseline was a two-lane road surrounded by open land. When developers built the pocket park, drivers could easily see the sign from the road, and they might pull over to read it and maybe enjoy a pleasant lunch at the nearby picnic table. Today, however, with five lanes of 55-mile-per-hour traffic whizzing by, even if sharp-eyed drivers see the sign, they would be foolish to risk pulling over to view it.

Unless biking or walking on the adjoining trail, the Columbine sign on Baseline, three miles south of the original massacre site, is too dangerous to view. The Columbine sign in the back yard of the Lafayette History Museum is easy to see, but one must know where to look, since the museum is tucked away in a residential neighborhood. One must *really* know where to look for the 1989 memorial, which is one of hundreds of gravestones in the Lafayette public cemetery. Remember that as Lafayette's 1989 centennial drew near, locals and Denver Labor Forum activists began collaborating on ways to memorialize the Columbine Massacre, and they decided to focus their efforts on installing a headstone at the still-unmarked gravesite where five of the six strikers killed are buried.[102] Marshaling enough resources to construct the monument took meticulous organization, widespread community effort, and good-natured, respectful cooperation among unlikely partners, which included contemporary Wobblies and old-timer Lafayette and Erie residents. Since Jim and Beth Hutchison were doing most of the work for the Lafayette centennial book, Jim agreed to serve as secretary for the committee raising money for the Columbine memorial. The committee got a bargain price for an unclaimed headstone, and a mason ground off the old inscription and engraved a new, more elaborate one that commemorated the Columbine dead. As Hutchison's detailed bookkeeping shows, although some donations arrived from the local Erie and Lafayette historical societies and the San Francisco and Michigan Wobblies, individual donations—including one from Joyce Kornbluh—made up well over half of the $2,300 needed for the monument.[103]

As seen in the photographs, the headstone is simple, relatively cheap, and blends in well as part of Lafayette's public cemetery, located south of the town's skatepark and west of the recreation center, which was also constructed in 1989 and includes a huge indoor swimming pool. When construction workers began digging the recreation center's foundation, they hit the concrete remains of the swimming pool that prompted Rose Lueras's 1934 lawsuit. Several miles east of the Columbine Massacre headstone, abutting the Josephine Roche Open Space, is Josephine Commons, a subsidized apartment complex completed in 2012 that houses some of Boulder County's burgeoning senior citizen population.

Gary Cox and other members of the Denver Labor Forum organized the Columbine headstone dedication ceremony, held on June 10, 1989.[104] For posterity, the Lafayette Historical Society videotaped the event.[105] Cox spoke first, followed by a folksinger who earnestly strummed her guitar and sang several songs. Last, the talented visual artist Carlos Cortez, at that time the best-known living Wobbly, produced a big surprise. In 1915, after the state of Utah executed IWW songwriter Joe Hill, Wobblies paid for his body to be sent to Chicago, where a massive public funeral took place. Afterward, Hill's body was cremated and envelopes filled with his ashes were sent to IWW offices across the country. During the 1917 IWW raids, most of the contents of those offices had been destroyed, including the envelopes filled with Hill's ashes. However, one letter that included Hill's remains got lost and found its way into the National Archives. In the mid-1980s, the IWW got wind of the letter and demanded its return. Although the archives insisted on keeping the letter, in 1988 it returned a vial of Hill's ashes to the chair of the IWW's GEB.[106] In a gesture freighted with historical significance for Cortez and the other Wobblies, for the grand finale of the Columbine Memorial ceremony, Cortez stepped forward and scattered a portion of the last remaining ashes of Joe Hill over the graves of five of the Columbine Massacre's victims.[107]

Although those ashes carried great symbolic meaning for the Wobblies, most of those who attended the ceremony, including those old enough to remember the 1927–1928 Colorado Coal Strike, probably had no idea who Joe Hill had been or understood his significance to the IWW.

Also unclear is how much the contemporaneous Wobblies knew about the history or significance of the strike. During the ceremony, none of the speakers mentioned Adam Bell, Mrs. Beranek, Kristin Svanum, A. S. Embree, or Flaming Milka. None of them mentioned the Junior Wobblies (though surely a few were in attendance) or the Mexican sugar beet workers who also had also joined the strike. There was no mention of the Latino strikers and their families who, empowered by the IWW's egalitarian message, had brought a lawsuit against the city that tried to segregate them, as physical evidence recently unearthed just steps away from the newly erected Columbine monument proved. Nobody even mentioned Josephine Roche, who, within the decade, would get both open space and a senior housing complex named after her. Even as he sprinkled Joe Hill's ashes, Carlos Cortez made no mention of Byron Kitto, the handsome, young, charismatic IWW strike leader whose ashes, more than fifty years earlier, had been scattered over the exact same spot.

Unlike the annual ceremonies at the Ludlow monument, the ceremony commemorating the Columbine Massacre victims was a local, one-time commemoration that had more to do with Lafayette's centennial celebration and romantic remnants of the IWW than with the strike, its victims, or its historical legacies. By the time of the commemoration, IWW narratives, shaped by Fred Thompson, had erased the significance of the 1927–1928 Colorado Coal Strike in Wobbly histories. The strike had never been incorporated into the national labor narrative, because the 1920s and early 1930s has been falsely portrayed as a quiescent era for labor. Invoking Ludlow from two decades earlier, not the more temporally immediate Columbine, Josephine Roche, John L. Lewis, New Deal officials, and sympathetic journalists helped spread the narrative that portrayed Roche and the RMFC as models of industrial democracy that, if emulated, could fix the Great Depression, a story that was never true. Subsequent historical narratives perpetuated those great men, great deeds versions of history that downplayed to near extinction the proximate cause of New Deal labor reforms: militant workers. Barron Beshoar and subsequent Ludlow narratives he influenced assured that the violent, 1913–1914 phase of Colorado's long strike would remain the most written about event in Colorado coalmining history, even though the 1927–1928 strike and the Columbine Massacre exercised a far greater, longer lasting, but more ambiguous impact on United States labor. When historians wrote about Embree, they froze him in time at Bisbee. When historians examined Mine Mill, they ignored the militant, egalitarian legacies originating from Embree's vision of industrial democracy, instead analyzing Mine Mill's historical significance through the lens of Cold War persecution and 1960s identity politics. Roche's biographers did not dig deeply into her role surrounding the 1927–1928 Colorado Coal Strike and chose to celebrate her as a do-gooder icon of women's history. Even during the oral history boom, when researchers at last tried getting workers' voices back into the story of the 1927–1928 Colorado Coal Strike, memories of Ludlow drowned them out. When the 1989 Wobblies invoked memories of Joe Hill during the Columbine Massacre memorial ceremony, their memories were only slightly less anachronistic than their red bandanas. Even for those most passionate about reviving the significance and memories of the Columbine, like those who preceded them, they remembered Ludlow instead.

Epilogue and Acknowledgments

The most infamous Columbine Massacre took place on April 20, 1999, at Columbine High School in Littleton, Colorado. Two high-school seniors shot and killed twelve other students and a teacher, wounded twenty-one more students, including some who will never walk again or construct a coherent sentence, and then killed themselves. Using a thirty-minute delay, networks broadcast the entire day on television. By nightfall, a powerful narrative was already in place: two bullied outsiders who belonged to a "Trench Coat Mafia" invaded their school and methodically targeted their tormentors, especially Christians and jocks.[1]

Although this narrative was false—the shooters were relatively popular, the "trench coat mafia" was more rumor than real, and their victims were random—responses to it drove reforms aimed at preventing future school shootings.[2] For example, by "setting a perimeter"—a barrier with no entry, even by police, only exits—around the school, officers behaved exactly as trained. After Columbine, protocols changed. In an active shooter situation, police are now trained to immediately enter buildings and directly confront,

https://doi.org/10.5876/9781646423026.co11

and perhaps kill, anyone with a gun (which is one of many reasons why arming teachers is such a bad idea). Many school districts responded to Columbine by instituting anti-bullying programs. Some undertook costly remodels, building new, windowed ante-rooms in front of older school entrances. Visitors now present themselves and their identification to cameras, and only if they pass muster will the front staff buzz them into the building, where they show their drivers' licenses, sign in, and get numbered badges. All school doors are also supposed to stay locked to prevent any unauthorized entry.

Obviously, these reforms have not worked. Students, friends, relatives, families, and parents have lost their children, spouses, kin, and neighbors in many school shootings since Columbine, including those in 2012 at Sandy Hook Elementary in Newtown, Connecticut (twenty first-graders and six adults dead), in 2018 at Marjory Stoneman Douglas High School in Parkland, Florida (fifteen students and two adults dead with seventeen wounded), and in 2022 at Robb Elementary School in Uvalde, Texas (nineteen children and two teachers dead with seventeen wounded). In Uvalde, inexplicably, at least 350 officers from the school and city police departments, alongside the United States Border Patrol, reverted to pre-Columbine protocols. Even as dying children inside their classrooms frantically texted for help, police "set the perimeter" instead of confronting the shooter.[3]

The 1999 Columbine Massacre also produced horrific unintended consequences. Rightwing provocateur, conspiracy peddler, and health supplement huckster Alex Jones asserted that the Sandy Hook parents were actors in a "false flag" operation enacted to justify gun confiscation. After some of Jones's fervent listeners threatened Sandy Hook parents, the parents organized and brought lawsuits against Jones. A decade after their children's deaths, a judge awarded those parents almost one billion dollars for their torment, and more lawsuits are still underway.[4] Jones's crazy conspiracy mongering is not just aimed at grieving parents, however. He has proven himself a financial and operational model for promoting equally crazy conspiracies that undermine our national system of government. As a featured organizer and speaker, he encouraged his followers to converge on Washington, DC, on January 6, 2021, and then he helped rile the mobs who attacked the Capitol.

Another unintended consequence of the 1999 Columbine Massacre is the "Columbine effect." Perhaps because its initial 24/7 news coverage yielded mountains of publications, soul-searching, and blame, Columbine is still considered a historical marker that has inspired numerous copycat killings, not just in the United States but internationally. For example, on September 26, 2022, in Izhevsk, Russia, a gunman killed eleven children and six adults before killing himself. "When police finally reached the body of the gunman, they encountered another recognizable trope of school shootings everywhere: a direct reference to the massacre 23 years ago at Columbine High School in Littleton, Colo. This time, they found braided cords labeled 'Dylan' and 'Eric' [the Columbine killers] attached to two of the Izhevsk attacker's pistols."[5]

We humans seem hardwired to construct narratives that help us create meaning in our lives. Often, however, these narratives, whether individual or collective, are false, and sometimes they produce unintended consequences. Certain narratives, like those surrounding the 1999 Columbine Massacre, form quickly. Josephine Roche's narrative about herself, her company, and the 1927–1928 Colorado Coal Strike took a few years to solidify, and it helped form the basic labor narrative that appears in most textbooks today, which portray New Deal labor laws as organized labor's crowning achievement. Today, however, those laws more often hinder rather than help workers, so that narrative needs reframing. Factual interpretations inside the pages of our US textbooks, our national creation myths, take years to form, and I hope this book helps nudge that narrative. Although my original research goals were to examine the causes, course, and consequences of the lesser-known Columbine Massacre and the 1927–1928 Colorado Coal Strike, what I found led me to expand my scope, to understand why we knew so little about the strike and why it, and others like it, have not been included in the bigger picture of labor or United States history. New Deal labor laws are important, but they were political compromises enacted in reaction to militant workers, not gifts from enlightened great men doing great deeds. Textbooks that cite militant workers as the cause, not the consequence, of those laws not only would be more accurate, they would also certainly be more inspiring and empowering.

Currently, I teach at the University of Colorado in Denver. My PhD in history helped me get that position, but I have spent most of my life teaching US history in public schools. To get a bump on my union-negotiated salary scale, I desperately needed to get more degrees, and when my husband and

I were finally financially able, I returned to school, where the history department at the University of Colorado Boulder enthusiastically supported me as I got my master's degree in 2005 and my PhD in 2013. For that long journey, I have many people to thank. Scott Miller, the graduate school administrative assistant, guided me though every step of applying to, getting accepted into, and navigating graduate school. He also let me complain in his office behind closed doors without too much eye rolling. University of Colorado Boulder archivist David Hays guided me through Josephine Roche's and the WFM/Mine Mill records. He continued encouraging me as I discovered that Roche, while remarkable, needed her halo tarnished a bit. Only because Julie Greene agreed to take me on as a graduate student was I admitted into the graduate history program. Although she moved on to the University of Maryland in College Park, we have kept in touch, and she even helped me fine-tune my prospectus, so, thank you, Julie for getting me started in the field of labor history. No graduate student ever had a better advisor than I did with Phoebe Young. Although she is a cultural and environmental historian, her fresh perspective, analytical skills, and incisive advice helped me shape my dissertation into something we were both happy with. Thomas Andrews helped me with my dissertation, too. If you have not read his book, *Killing for Coal*, which provides the best and most beautifully written account of the 1913–1914 long strike in Colorado, please do. Since I took many of his historical actors fifteen years into their future, he knew enough about Colorado coalmining history to keep me from making many dumb mistakes. So did the other advisors on my dissertation committee: CU Boulder law professor Ahmed White and Mark Pittenger, who both read every word, closely. Therefore, any mistakes in this book are strictly my own.

Professor Pittenger taught the second class I ever took in the graduate department, and his excellent scholarship, teaching, but more importantly, his welcoming attitude, made me believe I could actually finish my degrees, even though I was twice the age of most of the other students, I was teaching high school full time, and two of our three boys still lived at home and needed to see their mother once in a while. I would also like to thank professors Fred and Virginia Anderson. Both are brilliant historians, excellent teachers, and wonderful people. They encouraged me more than they will ever know.

Like many books published by academic presses, this book is a shortened, sharpened, better argued adaptation of my dissertation. Thanks to the University of Colorado Press and my peer reviewers. You have all been prompt, professional, and your insightful suggestions have made this book better. Thanks also to the many archivists who helped me wrangle the images for this book, especially Victoria Miller at the Steelworks archive in Pueblo, Elizabeth Clemens at the Walter P. Reuther library at Wayne State University in Detroit, Brandi Marulli at Catholic University in Washington, DC, and Bridgit Bacon at the Louisville, Colorado, Historical Museum. I had absolutely no idea how to turn my images into formats that could be printed, so my friend Gerry Morrell, who started Morrel Printing in Lafayette, Colorado, came to my rescue. When I wanted to find a photograph of Powers and Mary Donovan Hapgood, the Lilly Library at Indiana University archives was closed for renovation. After some Internet sleuthing, I tracked down a woman I suspected might be granddaughter of the Hapgoods. It turns out she is, and she sent me a family photograph from her personal collection. Thank you, Katherine Hapgood Nading, for sharing your family photo of your remarkable ancestors with me.

My mother, Johnye Faye Shelton, and father, Jerry Gene Campbell, are both dead, and I miss them a lot. They would have been very pleased to see their daughter get a book published. Their intellectual curiosity, hard work, and sacrifices made my middle-class upbringing and education possible. In 1949, the year my sister, Cindy Earnest (my best friend and sounding board), was born, my dad was out on the UMW strike that the coalminers won, and one of their demands made Josephine Roche the "neutral" UMW trustee. My dad worked so few days in 1949, he decided to quit coalmining altogether, and his life was better for it. Within a few years, General Motors hired him. Contrasted to coalmining, work conditions at GM were clean and relatively safe, at least physically. He no longer worried about cave-ins but instead heart attacks, which led to his early retirement at the young age of forty-eight. Back then, however, his GM job came with a good pension—back in the days when that sort of thing was possible—and GM financially supported him and my mom for the rest of their lives.

Those days are gone, because even though my dad was a white-collar guy, the blue-collar guys with great union contracts made our comfortable lives possible. GM took a chance hiring my high-school-graduate dad, but they would not have taken a chance on hiring someone with a similar background who was black or female, something I did not realize until I reached adulthood. My sister is a retired nurse, and I am a retired public school teacher. We both trained for some of the best jobs available for women, something that has also changed dramatically in my lifetime. We have also both benefitted from excellent union representation that planted us firmly in the middle class. Every person deserves the same.

At several critical junctures, the graduate school at the University of Colorado directly provided or steered me toward grants that made my research possible. Boulder Valley School District and my union, the Boulder Valley Education Association, negotiated a contract that reimbursed me for much of my tuition over the years, and I simply could not have finished my degrees without that financial support. My graduate education made me a better teacher, and I am a firm believer that school districts and unions should reimburse their teachers for subject-area content, not pedagogy, at the graduate level, but that is a topic for another day.

My wonderful and interesting children, Benjamin, James, and John, have grown into wonderful and interesting adults. I appreciate their love and support throughout the years. The person most responsible for everything good in my life over the past forty-two years, however, is my husband, Charley Peters Hale. His unqualified support and love have been, and continue to be, my lifeline.

Notes

Introduction

1. Elinor McGinn, *A Wide-Awake Woman: Josephine Roche in the Era of Reform* (Denver: Colorado Historical Society, 2002).

2. Robyn Muncy, *Relentless Reformer: Josephine Roche and Progressivism in Twentieth-Century America* (Princeton, NJ: Princeton University Press, 2014).

3. George H. Douglas, *The Golden Age of the Newspaper* (Westport, CT: Greenwood Press, 1999), 129.

4. For example, I know that my grandfathers, who mined coal in Arkansas, were out on strike in the late 1920s and early 1930s, but the *Times* did not cover those strikes at all.

5. The following (in chronological order) are some of the books written about the 1913–1914 Colorado Coal Strike and the Ludlow Massacre: Barron B. Beshoar, *Out of the Depths: The Story of John R. Lawson, A Labor Leader* (Denver: The Colorado Labor Historical Committee of the Denver Trades and Labor Assembly, 1942); Zeese Papanikolas, *Buried Unsung: Louis Tikas and the Ludlow Massacre* (Lincoln: University of Nebraska Press, 1982); Leon Stein and Philip Taft, *Massacre at Ludlow: Four Reports*, republished as *American Labor: From Conspiracy to Collective Bargaining* (New York:

Arno Press, 1972); George S. McGovern and Leonard F. Guttridge, *The Great Coalfield War* (Boulder: University of Colorado Press, 1972); Howard Gitelman, *Legacy of the Ludlow Massacre* (Philadelphia: University of Pennsylvania Press, 1988); Priscilla Long, *Where the Sun Never Shines: A History of America's Bloody Coal Industry* (New York: Paragon House, 1989); Joanna Sampson, *"Remember Ludlow!": Ludlow Massacre, April 20, 1914* (self-published, 1999); Howard Zinn, *Three Strikes: Miners, Musicians, Salesgirls, and the Fighting Spirit of Labor's Last Century* (Boston: Beacon Press, 2001); Scott Martelle, *Blood Passion: The Ludlow Massacre and Class War in the American West* (Piscataway, NJ: Rutgers University Press, 2007); Thomas G. Andrews, *Killing for Coal: America's Deadliest Labor War* (Cambridge, MA: Harvard University Press, 2008).

6. James A. McCartin, *Labor's Great War: The Struggle for Industrial Democracy and the Origins of Modern American Labor Relations, 1912–1921* (Chapel Hill: The University of North Carolina Press, 1997), 50–51.

7. Muncy, *Relentless Reformer*, 2, 76, 78, 110, 111, 132.

8. In 1935, the CIO stood for Committee for Industrial Relations. By 1937, the CIO stood for the Congress of Industrial Relations. For simplicity, I will just use the acronym CIO.

Chapter 1: Josephine Roche: Becoming a Maternalist Reformer, 1886–1927

1. Muncy, *Relentless Reformer*, 9.

2. Muncy, *Relentless Reformer*, 2, 76, 78, 110, 111, 132.

3. Molly Ladd-Taylor created this clever term in her book *Mother-Work: Women, Child Welfare, and the State, 1890–1930* (Urbana: University of Illinois Press, 1995). It has been used by many historians since.

4. "Fuel Company Head Dies at Home," *Rocky Mountain News* (Denver, CO), January 14, 1927, 9.

5. McGinn, *A Wide-Awake Woman*, 7.

6. *Vassar Encyclopedia, Alumnae/i of Distinction*, "Josephine Roche," accessed July 20, 2011, http://vcencyclopedia.vassar.edu/alumni/josephine-roche.html.

7. Frances Perkins wrote her own account of her New Deal days in *The Roosevelt I Knew*, and there are also hours of oral interviews with Perkins archived and now available online at "Frances Perkins," Columbia University Libraries, Oral History Research Office, accessed November 21, 2011, http://www.columbia.edu/cu/lweb/digital/collections/nny/perkinsf/audio_transcript.html.

8. "Welfarer," *Time*, November 26, 1934, accessed 28 February 2007, www.time.com/time/printout/0,8816,882299,00html; Letter from Josephine Roche to Frances Perkins, July 22, 1959, Josephine Roche to Frances Perkins, April 14, 1960, Frances Perkins to Josephine Roche March 25, 1959, 5–14, Josephine Roche Papers, Special

Collections & Archives, University of Colorado Boulder Libraries, (hereafter referred to as Roche papers).

9. Christine Stansell, *American Moderns: Bohemian New York and the Creation of a New Century* (New York: Metropolitan Books, 2000), 117.

10. George Martin, *Madam Secretary: Frances Perkins* (Boston: Houghton Mifflin Company, 1976), 72–75; Kirsten Downey, *The Woman behind the New Deal* (Norwell, MA: Anchor Press, 2010), chapter 3.

11. Downey, *The Woman behind the New Deal*, 45.

12. McGinn, *A Wide-Awake Woman*, 44; "Biography of Edward Hale Bierstadt," *Jacket Quest*, accessed June 30, 2013, http://www.jacketquest.com/authors-j/366 -biographies/5856-biography-of-edward-hale-bierstadt.html.

13. The following are some books about maternalist reformers: Robyn Muncy, *The Female Dominion of Reform*, Peggy Pascoe, *Relations of Rescue: The Search for Female Moral Authority in the American West, 1874–1939* (New York: Oxford University Press, 1990), Linda Gordon, *Pitied But Not Entitled: Single Mothers and the History of Welfare* (Cambridge, MA: Harvard University Press, 1994), Molly Ladd-Taylor, *Raising a Baby the Government Way: Letters to the Children's Bureau, 1915–1932* (New Brunswick, NJ: Rutgers University Press, 1986).

14. Pascoe, *Relations of Rescue*, xv.

15. Downey, *The Woman behind the New Deal*, 318; McGinn, *A Wide-Awake Woman*, 92.

16. Downey, *The Woman behind the New Deal*, 12–13; McGinn, *A Wide-Awake Woman*, 103.

17. Landon R. Y. Storrs has documented well the links between ethical consumption and progressive activism in *Civilizing Capitalism: The National Consumers' League, Women's Activism, and Labor Standards in the New Deal* (Chapel Hill: The University of North Carolina Press, 2000), 1, 15.

18. Storrs, *Civilizing Capitalism*, Lizabeth Cohen, *A Consumers' Republic: The Politics of Mass Consumption in Postwar America* (New York: Alfred A. Knopf, 2003); Dana Frank, *Purchasing Power: Consumer Organizing, Gender and the Seattle Labor Movement, 1919–1929* (New York: Cambridge University Press, 1994).

19. Storrs, *Civilizing Capitalism*, 15.

20. C. C. Quale, *Thrilling Stories of White Slavery* (Chicago: Hamming Publishing Co., 1912), Google eBook, reprinted by the Sallie Bingham Center for Women's History and Culture.

21. Brian Donovan, *White Slave Crusades: Race, Gender, and Anti-Vice Activism, 1887–1917* (Urbana: University of Illinois Press, 2006), 2.

22. Ken Burns, *Unforgiveable Blackness: The Rise and Fall of Jack Johnson*, PBS (Public Broadcasting Service) Paramount, 2005, DVD, 214 min.

23. Frederick K. Grittner, *White Slavery: Myth, Ideology, and American Law* (New York: Garland Publishing, Inc., 1990), 95.

24. Grittner, *White Slavery*, 87.

25. Jane Addams, *A New Conscience and an Ancient Evil* (New York: The Macmillan Company, 1912), vii. (This book first appeared in serialized form in 1911 by the S. S. McClure Company and the McClure Publications, Inc., publisher of *McClure's* magazine.)

26. Charles Larsen, *The Good Fight: The Remarkable Life and Times of Judge Ben Lindsey* (Chicago: Quadrangle Books, 1972), 37–41.

27. "Fuel Company Head Dies at Home," *Rocky Mountain News*, 9.

28. Gail M. Beaton, "The Widening Sphere of Women's Lives: The Literary Study and Philanthropic Work of Six Women's Clubs in Denver, 1881–1945," in *Women's Clubs of Denver*, Essays in Colorado History, No. 13, 1992 (Denver: Colorado Historical Society, 1993), 27.

29. George Creel, *Rebel at Large: Recollections of Fifty Crowded Years* (New York: G. P. Putnam's Sons, 1947), 96–119.

30. Pat Pascoe, *Helen Ring Robinson: Colorado Senator and Suffragist* (Boulder: University of Colorado Press, 2011), 44.

31. Creel, *Rebel at Large*, 104.

32. Kathy Peiss, *Cheap Amusements: Working Women and Leisure in Turn-of-the-Century New York* (Philadelphia, PA: Temple University Press, 1986), 5.

33. Creel, *Rebel at Large*, 105–106.

34. Janis Appier, *Policing Women: The Sexual Politics of Law Enforcement and the LAPD* (Philadelphia, PA: Temple University Press, 1998), 41–42.

35. Alice Rohe, "Denver's Petticoated Copper," *Sunday News* [Rocky Mountain News?], December 1, 1912, 10-5, Josephine Roche papers. I took the photo.

36. Rohe, "Denver's Petticoated Copper"; There are at least thirty articles describing the hiring, firing, reinstating, and working without pay in Roche's 10-5 archival file.

37. Josephine Roche, "Economic Conditions in Relation to the Delinquency of Girls" (unpublished master's thesis in political science), Columbia University, 1910, 10-4, 1, Roche papers.

38. Roche, "Economic Conditions," 28–29.

39. Roche, "Economic Conditions."

40. For example, Adam Cohen, *Imbeciles: The Supreme Court, American Eugenics, and the Sterilization of Carrie Buck* and Paul A. Lombardo, *Three Generations, No Imbeciles: Eugenics, the Supreme Court, and Buck v. Bell.*

41. Creel, *Rebel at Large*, 105.

42. Creel, *Rebel at Large*, 105.

43. I took this photo from Roche's clippings file. It appeared in the *Denver Times*, January 31, 1913, clipping file, 10-5, Josephine Roche papers. This was definitely not what Roche wore on the job. She wore street clothes, but also donned a large badge, which she included in her personal papers.

44. "Creel After War of Words Becomes Minority Worker," *Denver Republican*, January 31, 1913, clipping file, 10-5, Roche papers.

45. "Seeks Habeas Corpus Writ for Girl Held Without Court Trial," *Denver Republican*, January 31, 1913, clipping file, 10-5, Roche papers.

46. "George Creel Tells of Work to Wipe Out Vice in Denver and Warns of 'Redlight' Menace," *Daily News*, February 5, 1913, 10-5, Roche papers.

47. "Woman 'Cop' Dares Jesse James Gang in 'Movies' Lair," *Denver Republican*, January 8, 1913, 10-5, Roche papers.

48. "Woman 'Cop,'" 10-5, Roche papers.

49. "22 Women of Redlight District Sent to Jail," *Rocky Mountain News*, January 23, 1913, 10-5, Roche papers.

50. "City Hall Busy Uplifting Moral Tone of Denver," *Rocky Mountain News*, January 19, 1913, 10-5, Roche papers.

51. "Women Brand Ousting of Josephine Roche as Infamous Outrage," *Denver Express*, April 26, 1913; "Mass Meeting to Urge Reinstatement of Josephine Roche," *Denver Times*, April 29, 1913; Roche papers, 10-5.

52. "Josephine Roche Gets Her Old Job Back," *Denver Post*, July 9, 1913; "Resignation of Miss Roche is Loss to Denver, letter to the editor by Edward Costigan," *Denver Express*, August 5, 1913, 10-5, Roche papers.

53. Letter from Josephine Roche to Dr. Caroline Spencer, Secretary of the Colorado Women's Party, October 23, 1916, 6-7, Roche papers.

54. Commission for Relief in Belgium, 1915–1916, Roche papers, 10–11.

55. I took this photo of Roche's approved State Department travel authorization, 10–11, Roche papers.

56. "Miss Roche Tells of Work of Feeding the Belgians," Rutland, Vermont, newspaper clipping, March 27, 1915, 10–11, Roche papers.

57. Josephine Roche, *Wage Earning Women and Girls in Baltimore: A Study of the Cost of Living in 1918* (New York: National Consumers' League, 1918), 11, 10–12, Roche papers.

58. David M. Kennedy, *Over Here: The First World War and American Society* (New York: Oxford University Press, 1980), 59–66.

59. George Creel, *How We Advertised America* (New York: Arno Press, 1972), 191; This reprint was originally published in New York by Harper & Brothers, 1920.

60. "A Study of the Needs and Problems of the Foreign Born and of What is Being Done to Meet Them, With Suggestions for Further Work Which the

Situation Calls For" (submitted to the Commonwealth Fund seeking contributions, [1919–1920]), Box 11, Roche papers.

61. Robyn Muncy, *Creating a Female Dominion of Reform, 1890–1935* (New York: Oxford University Press, 1991), 38.

62. Muncy, *Creating a Female Dominion*, 38.

63. "Lindsey is Ousted as Denver Judge," *New York Times*, January 24, 1927, www .nytimes.com.

64. In 1927, the magazine was called *Red Book*. It eventually became *Redbook*, and did not cease print publication until 2018, although it is still available online.

65. Beth Baily, *Sex in the Heartland* (Cambridge, MA: Harvard University Press, 1999), 46.

66. Ben Lindsey and Wainright Evans, *The Revolt of Modern Youth* (New York, NY: Boni and Liveright, 1925).

67. Judge Ben Lindsey and Wainwright Evans, *The Companionate Marriage* (Garden City, NY: Garden City Publishing Co., Inc., 1929), viii; Ben Lindsey, "The Moral Revolt," *Red Book*, February 1927, 155.

68. Lindsey and Evans, *The Companionate Marriage*, 155.

69. Larsen, *The Good Fight*, 200, 227.

70. "Whitford, Tyrant, In Whom Is Not Drop of Warm Blood," *Denver Post*, April 11, 1911, 1.

71. *Report of Commission on Industrial Relations*, page 6934, bound copy containing Doyle's testimony only, housed at the Miners Museum in Lafayette, Colorado.

72. "Press release," July 11, 1927, Benjamin Barr Lindsey Papers, Box 74, Library of Congress, Washington, DC.

73. Rupert Hughes, "Ben Lindsey's Holocaust," *Denver Post*, October 16, 1927, 8.

74. Beshoar, *Out of the Depths*, 187.

75. Letter from William Chenery to Josephine Roche, July 15, 1927, 2-9, Roche papers.

76. Oscar L. Chapman, "Oral Interview with Oscar L. Chapman," interview by Jerry N. Hess, August 18, 1972, Harry S. Truman Library & Museum, http://www .trumanlibrary.org/oralhist/chapman7.htm#368.

77. "Mary Pickford Obtains Divorce in Surprise 3-Minute Hearing," *New York Times*, January 11, 1935, www.nytimes.com; Elaine Tyler May, *Great Expectations: Marriage and Divorce in Post-Victorian America* (Chicago: The University of Chicago Press, 1980), 75–76. May wrote an entire chapter about the celebrity, idealized marriage of Pickford-Fairbanks and their subsequent divorce.

78. "No-fault Divorce: 10 Years Later, Some Virtues, Some Flaws," *New York Times*, March 30, 1979, www.nytimes.com.

79. Rocky Mountain Fuel Company Annual Report and Statement for Stockholders: 1928, 13-4, Roche papers.

80. In the Supreme Court of the State of Colorado, *The Rocky Mountain Fuel Company, a Corporation v. Walter Belk*, No. 12621, July 1, 1930, 13-3, Roche papers. Most standard Ludlow histories cite the first murder during the 1913–1914 phase as Belk gunning down Gerald Lippiatt in the streets of Trinidad. Lippiatt worked closely with John Lawson and Ed Doyle and arrived just days before his death, moving from the northern to the southern fields to organize.

81. "Merle D. Vincent for Operators Says Operators Will Obey Law and Strikers are Violating It," *Daily Camera* (Boulder, CO), October 19, 1927, 3.

Chapter 2: Powers Hapgood: Becoming a Working-Class Hero, 1899–1928

1. Robert Bussel, *From Harvard to the Ranks of Labor: Powers Hapgood and the American Working Class* (University Park: The Pennsylvania State University Press, 1999).

2. Bussel, *From Harvard to the Ranks*, 108–110.

3. Bussel, *From Harvard to the Ranks*, 8.

4. Bussel, *From Harvard to the Ranks*, 4–5.

5. Bussel, *From Harvard to the Ranks*, 10.

6. Powers Hapgood's 1919–30 March 1920 diary, 111, Powers Hapgood papers, The Lilly Library, Indiana University, Bloomington, Indiana, (Hereafter, Powers Hapgood papers). Since Powers Hapgood's papers are arranged chronologically, hereafter, I will only cite the letters by dates, not folder and box numbers.

7. Mary Donovan Hapgood, 1912–1948, The Lilly Library, Indiana University, Bloomington, Indiana (Hereafter, Mary Donovan Hapgood papers). Powers Hapgood's early journals are in her papers, and he made this reference on October 5, 1920.

8. Bussel, *From Harvard to the Ranks*, 27.

9. Bussel, *From Harvard to the Ranks*, 24.

10. Robert Bussel writes that Hapgood graduated from Harvard in 1920, but according to the answer on 9 October 2012 from an email query I sent to the Harvard Research Staff, he graduated in 1921. Their source is the *Quinquennial Catalog of Harvard University, 1636–1930*. That means his six-month hobo experience occurred between his junior and senior years, not after he graduated, which changes Hapgood's career trajectory a bit.

11. Bussel, *From Harvard to the Ranks*, 19.

12. W. Jett Lauck, *Political and Industrial Democracy, 1776–1926* (New York: Funk and Wagnalls, 1926), 286.

13. Lauck, *Political and Industrial Democracy*, 216.

14. Melvyn Dubofsky and Warren Van Tine, *John L. Lewis, A Biography*, abridged edition (Urbana: University of Illinois Press, 1986), 103.

15. John L. Lewis, *The Miners' Fight for American Standards* (Indianapolis, IN: The Bell Publishing Company, 1925), 128.

16. Lewis, *The Miners' Fight*, 48.

17. "Lewis Calls Strike 100% Effective," *New York Times*, April 6, 1922, www .nytimes.com; "Strikers Centre Fire on Non-Union Fields," *New York Times*, April 6, 1922, www.nytimes.com.

18. John Brophy, *A Miner's Life* (Madison: The University of Wisconsin Press, 1964), 245.

19. Brophy, *A Miner's Life*, 186.

20. Mildred Allen Beik, *The Miners of Windber: The Struggles of New Immigrants for Unionization, 1890s–1930s* (University Park: The Pennsylvania State University Press, 1996, 1998).

21. Beik, *The Miners of Windber*, 113.

22. "Howat Pleas Fail in Supreme Court," *New York Times*, March 14, 1922, www .nytimes.com.

23. "Lewis Ousts Howat for Outlaw Strike," *New York Times*, October 14, 1921, www.nytimes.com.

24. "Miners Stand by Howat," *New York Times*, November 16, 1921, www.nytimes .com.

25. "Miners Stand by Howat."

26. Letter from Powers Hapgood to Mary Donovan Hapgood, June 12, 1930, Powers Hapgood papers, Box 5, June 1930 folder, Powers Hapgood papers.

27. Elliot Gorn, *Mother Jones: The Most Dangerous Woman in America* (New York: Hill and Wang, 2002), 67–68, 237.

28. Jarod Roll, "White, American, Non-Union: Making Sense of Missouri's Notorious Strikebreaking Miners," presented at the Labor and Working-Class History Association Conference, New York, June 6, 2013. Since I first heard him deliver this paper, he expanded upon the topic in *Poor Man's Fortune: White Working-Class Conservatism in American Metal Mining, 1850–1950* (Chapel Hill: The University of North Carolina Press, 2020).

29. Ann Schofield, "An 'Army of Amazons': The Language of Protest in a Kansas Mining Community, 1921–1922," *American Quarterly* 37, no. 5 (Winter, 1985), 686, www.jstor.org.

30. Schofield, "An Army of Amazons'," 686.

31. Dubofsky and Van Tine, *John L. Lewis*, 117.

32. Dubofsky and Van Tine, *John L. Lewis*, 117.

58. Dean A. Strang, *Keep the Wretches in Order: America's Biggest Mass Trial, the Rise of the Justice Department, and the Fall of the IWW* (Madison: The University of Wisconsin Press, 2019). Strang agrees with the dominant narrative declaring that the federal persecution killed the IWW.

59. William Preston Jr., *Aliens and Dissenters: Federal Suppression of Radicals, 1903–1933*, 2nd ed. (Urbana: University of Illinois Press, 1994), 110.

60. Dave Walter, "Who Killed Tom Manning?" in *More Montana Campfire Tales: Fifteen Historical Narratives* (Helena, MT: Farcountry Press, 2002), 213.

61. Quote from Harold Lloyd Varney, "X-Raying the Red Philosophy," *McClure's,* August 1920, 28, in Phipps, "A. S. Embree," 38.

62. Walter, "Who Killed Tom Manning?," 214.

63. Phipps, "A. S. Embree," 38.

64. Report from Agent J. L. Webb in Butte, Montana, on April 21, 1920, M1086, available through www.footnote.com/1351626, accessed June 7, 2010.

65. Walter, "Who Killed Tom Manning?," 216.

66. "H. H. Mock report from Tucson, Arizona, submitted 10 December 1917," M1085, available through www.footnote.com/image/1352900, accessed June 7, 2010.

67. "H. H. Mock report," M1085.

68. Letter from Department of Justice Agent E. B. Sisk to W. E. Allen, Acting Chair [Justice] on April 15, 1919, M1085, available through www.fold.com/image/1353190, accessed June 17, 2012.

69. Report from Agent E. W. Byrn Jr., in Butte, Montana, December 16, 1919, Mo185, available through www.fotnote.com/1351605, accessed June 7, 2010.

70. "Adolphus Stewart Embree," Report on 10 November 1919, available through www.footnote.com/1349941, accessed June 7, 2010.

71. Bisbee deportation list, Arizona Memory Collection.

72. Letter from Department of Justice employee E. B. Sisk to W. E. Allen on May 19, 1919, available through www.fold3.com/1353789, accessed June 17, 2012.

73. Memo from H. B. Mock in Tuscon, Arizona, to Chicago Bureau of Investigation Office, December 10, 1917, 2-3, 5, www.footnote.com/image/1352900; Letter from E. F. Kinknead, Major, US Army to Mr. A. Bruce Bielaski, Chief, Bureau of Investigation, Department of Justice, Washington, DC, September 12, 1918, www.footnote.com/image/1352986; both accessed June 7, 2011; Letter from W. W. Laurar, Office of the Solicitor, Post Office Department, to Mr. A. B. Bielaski, Chief, Bureau of Investigation, September 13, 1918, www.fold3.com/image/1354220, accessed June 17, 2012.

74. Report from Agent J. L. Webb from San Antonio on June 16, 1920, M1086, available through www.footnote.com/1351207, accessed June 7, 2010.

75. *"Whitney v. California*—The California Criminal Syndicalism Act," *Law Library, American Law and Legal Information*, http://law.jrank.org/pages/22799 /Whitney-v-California-California-Criminal-Syndicalism-Act.html, accessed August 15, 2013; Byrkit, *Forging the Copper Collar*, 280; Preston, *Aliens and Dissenters*, 123–25.

76. Photostat of letter from Mr. H. J. Hull to Agent F. M. Kelly, May 29, 1920, Justice Report of June 4, 1920, M1086, available through www.footnote.com/1351068, accessed June 7, 2010.

77. Photostat of letter from Mr. H. J. Hull to Agent F. M. Kelly, May 29, 1920.

78. Report from Special Agent D. H. Dickason in Butte, Montana, June 1, 1920, available through www.footnote.com/1350963, accessed June 7, 2010.

79. Report from Special Agent D. H. Dickason in Butte, Montana, May 29, 1920, M1086, available through www.footnote.com/1350990, accessed June 7, 2010.

80. Report from Special Agent D. H. Dickason in Butte, Montana, May 29, 1920.

81. Phipps quoting Justice Department records, "A. S. Embree: Labor Leader and Prisoner of Conscience," 40.

82. Phipps quoting Justice Department records, 40.

83. From two letters part of Agent F. M. Kelly's June 4, 1920, report; Letter from Agent Charles K. Andrews to Agent F. W. Kelley on June 1, 1920, www.footnote .com/1351068; Letter from agent F. W. Kelley to H. J. Hull on June 4, 1920, M1086, www.footnote.com/1351001, accessed June 7, 2010.

84. Phipps quoting Department of Justice records, 39.

85. Phipps quoting Department of Justice records, 39.

86. Solski and Smaller, *Mine Mill*, 10.

Chapter 4: The 1927–1928 Colorado Coal Strike: March 1926-October 18, 1927

1. Report from A. S. Embree to the Metal Mine IWW meeting, March 3–4, 1926, 51–16, IWW archives.

2. Report from A. S. Embree to the Metal Mine IWW meeting, March 3–4, 1926, 51–16, IWW archives.

3. Stephen Brier, Bruce C. Levine, and Joshua Freeman, eds., *Who Built America? Working People and the Nation's Economy, Politics, Culture and Society*, vol. 2, *From the Gilded Age to the Present*, American Social History Project (New York: Pantheon Books, 1992), 293.

4. Letter from Frank Hefferly to John L. Lewis, December 19, 1924, Hefferly Collection, 15-2, Special Collections & Archives, University of Colorado Boulder Libraries.

5. "Statement of the General Executive Board of the I.W.W.," September 21, 1926, General Executive Board, 7–11, IWW archives.

6. John S. Gambs, *The Decline of the I.W.W.* (New York: Columbia University Press, 1932); Paul Frederick Brissenden, *The I.W.W.: A Study in American Syndicalism* (New York: Columbia University, 1920).

7. Gambs, *The Decline of the I.W.W.*, 6, 125.

8. Gambs, *The Decline of the I.W.W.*, 145.

9. In a footnote in his article, "The Colorado Coal Strike of 1927," Donald McClurg said he interviewed Embree on August 17, 1953, in Denver, and that Embree firmly denied Gambs's assessment. Yet, McClurg also wrote that Embree had been imprisoned in Montana (as Melvyn Dubofsky wrote in *We Shall Be All*), when he had been jailed in Idaho, so I wonder how in-depth the interview was, and to what extent Embree's memories of the strike had changed over twenty-five years. McClurg also interviewed Merle D. Vincent, but his memories were even more self-serving. Unfortunately, McClurg left no transcripts of either interview.

10. Bobbalee Shuler, "Scab Labor in the Colorado Coal Fields: A Statistical Study of Replacement Workers during the Columbine Strike of 1927–1928," in *Essays and Monographs in Colorado History*, edited by David N. Wetzel (Denver: Colorado Historical Society, 1988), 66–67.

11. "Walsenburg and Trinidad, Canon City and Western Slope Coal Fields," published by Colorado Fuel & Iron (CF&I), [early 1930s], Steelworks Archives, courtesy of Steelworks Center of the West, Pueblo, CO.

12. Letter from A. S. Embree to John T. Turner, December 6, 1926, 17–15, IWW archives.

13. Letter from A. S. Embree to John T. Turner, December 6, 1926, 17–15, IWW archives.

14. Letter from A. S. Embree to John T. Turner, December 6, 1926, 17–15, IWW archives.

15. Memo from R. L. Hair, General Superintendent, CF&I, to all Superintendents, July 25, 1972; Minutes of CF&I Superintendents' Meeting, Trinidad District, September 7, 1927; Unidentified meeting, September 13, 1927, INR 1300-9, CF&I archives.

16. Strike poster, INR 1300-7, courtesy of Steelworks Museum.

17. General Executive Board (GEB) Minutes, July 8, 1927, 51–18, IWW archives.

18. General Executive Board (GEB) Minutes, July 8, 1927, 51–18, IWW archives.

19. "Minutes, Walsenburg District Conference, July 10, 1927," 51–18, IWW archives.

20. "Minutes, Walsenburg District Conference, July 10, 1927," 51–18, IWW archives.

21. David Montgomery, *The Fall of the House of Labor* (New York: Cambridge University Press, 1987), 463.

22. Donald McClurg, "The Colorado Coal Strike of 1927—Tactical Leadership of the IWW," *Labor History* 4, no. 1 (1963): 68–92.

23. "Mass protest meeting flyer," INR1300-7, Steelworks Archives, courtesy of Steelworks Center of the West (henceforth referred to simply as Steelworks).

24. Letter to H. L. Hair from GBP, September 24, 1927, INR 1299-9, Steelworks.

25. Donald McClurg, "Labor Organization in the Coal Mines of Colorado, 1878–1933," unpublished dissertation, University of California, 1959, available at the Carnegie Branch Library, Boulder, CO.

26. "Leaders Claim Protest Walkout not Under Law Exacting 30-Day Notice," *Pueblo Chieftan*, August 7, 1927, 2.

27. "Leaders Claim Protest Walkout," 2.

28. "A General Review of the Strike," *Lafayette Leader*, December 8, 1911, Colorado Historic Newspapers Collection, https://www.coloradohistoricnewspapers.org/?a=d&d=LFL19111208-01.2.4&srpos=20&e=01-01-1911-31-12-1911--en-20--1-byDA-img-txIN%7ctxCO%7ctxTA-United+Mine+Workers-------0-Boulder-Lafayette---.

29. Daniel Yergin, *The Prize: The Epic Quest for Oil, Money, and Power* (New York: Free Press, 1991, 2009), 90–92.

30. "International Organization Takes Over Dependent Districts," *United Mine Workers Journal* XXVII, no. 42 (February 15, 1917), 11, accessed through Google Books, https://books.google.com/books?id=uLJELF8k3DIC&pg=RA9-PA3&lpg=RA9-PA3&dq=United+Mine+Journal,+Vol.+XXVII,+No.+42&source=bl&ots=gLSglT-VmDi&sig=ACfU3U2dyHLP8_tKWgNVD785VXKqBuFNaQ&hl=en&sa=X&ved=2ahUKEwifwLDziYXtAhVIHM0KHXm-BQEQ6AEwB3oECAoQAg#v=onepage&q=United%20Mine%20Journal%2C%20Vol.%20XXVII%2C%20No.%2042&f=false.

31. "The Seed of Freedom," *United Mine Workers Journal* XXVII, no. 51 (April 19, 1917), 4, https://www.google.com/books/edition/United_Mine_Workers_Journal/uLJELF8k3DIC?hl=en&gbpv=1&dq=The+United+Mine+Workers+Journal+1917&pg=RA19-PA7&printsec=frontcover.

32. Jesse Paul, "A 1917 Coal Mine Explosion in Southern Colorado Killed 121. But it's Just a Faint Memory in the State's History," *Denver Post*, April 27, 2017, https://www.denverpost.com/2017/04/27/hastings-mine-explosion-1917-colorado-history/.

33. As quoted in Gorn, *Mother Jones*, 249.

34. Oliver E. Aultman, "Ludlow Monument," scan from negative 93.322.1828, Stephen H. Hart Research Center, History Colorado Center, Denver, CO, accessed June 27, 2021.

35. Colin B. Goodykoontz, ed., "Platform of Progressive Party in Colorado, 1914," in *Papers of Edward P. Costigan Relating to the Progressive Movement in Colorado, 1902–1917* (Boulder: University of Colorado, 1941), 294; Progressive Party papers, 10-7, Josephine Roche Papers, Archives, University of Colorado Boulder Libraries.

36. Edward T. Devine, John Augustine Ryan, John A. Lapp, Denver Commission of Religious Forces, Federal Council of the Churches of Christ in America, Commission of the Church and Social Service, and National Catholic Welfare Council (US) Department of Social Action, *The Denver Tramway Strike of 1920: Report of an Investigation Made Under the Auspices of the Denver Commission of Religious Forces, the Commission on the Church and Social Service of the Federal Council of the Churches of Christ in America*, the Department of Social Action of the National Catholic Welfare Council, 1921, 47, 56, 60, original book from the collections of the University of Michigan, https://archive.org/details/denvertramwaystooactigoog.

37. John P. Lewis, "On Ranger System 'Smokes Out' Shoup," *Rocky Mountain News* (Denver, CO), October 13, 1926, 1; "Labor and Farmers Indorse Adams for Office of Governor," October 21, 1926, *Rocky Mountain News* (Denver, CO), 1; "Shoup Caught in Dilemma as He Attempts to Dodge Boomerang of Ranger Law," October 17, 1926, *Rocky Mountain News* (Denver, CO), 1; "State Ranger Law to be Chief Issue in Governor's Race," *Rocky Mountain News*, October 12, 1926, 3.

38. Robert Alan Goldberg, *Hooded Empire: The Ku Klux Klan in Colorado* (Urbana: University of Illinois Press, 1981), 87.

39. "Parade in Denver Preceding a Convention of Klansmen," May 31, 1926, Denver Public Library Special Collections, X-21543, accessed June 11, 2021, 93.

40. "Parade in Denver Preceding a Convention," 93.

41. "Parade in Denver Preceding a Convention," 94.

42. "The Demands of the I.W.W. in the Coal Fields of Colorado," INR 1300–13, CF&I archives.

43. McClurg, "The Colorado Coal Strike," 73.

44. Lewis, "On Ranger System Smokes Out Shoup," 1.

45. "I.W.W. Ignored by the State at Pueblo Meet," *Daily Camera* (Boulder, CO), October 15, 1927, 1.

46. McClurg, "The Colorado Coal Strike," 75–76.

47. "Mexican Workers in Beet Fields Being Organized," *Daily Camera* (Boulder, CO), October 11, 1927, 1.

48. "I.W.W. Ignored by the State," 1.

49. "Mrs. McCready of Lafayette Kidnaped [*sic*] for a Short Ride," *Daily Camera* (Boulder, CO), October 14, 1927, 1.

50. Transcribed oral interview of Mary Borstnick by Donna Carbone, 1983, Tape #1044, Lafayette Public Library.

51. "Mayor and Citizens of Walsenburg Broke Up Headquarters of I.W.W. and Notified the Members of Organization to Stay Out of Town," *Daily Camera* (Boulder, CO), October 17, 1927, 1.

52. "Thousands of Colorado Coal Miners Strike Under Orders of I.W.W.," *Daily Camera* (Boulder, CO), October 18, 1927, 1.

Chapter 5: The 1927–1928 Colorado Coal Strike: October 18, 1927–November 4, 1927

1. "Hoage Says Federation Won't Play with I.W.W.," *Daily Camera* (Boulder, CO), October 18, 1927, 1.

2. "Thomas Annear Leaves for Boulder County to Compel Obedience to Law—He says Strike Illegal," *Daily Camera* (Boulder, CO), October 19, 1927, 1.

3. "Merle D. Vincent for Operators Says Operators Will Obey Law and Strikers Are Violating It," *Daily Camera* (Boulder, CO), October 19, 1927, 3.

4. In Josephine Roche's papers is a copy of the original proposed plan for the industrial commission that was included in the 1914 Colorado Progressive Party platform. The edits and authorship are credited to Merle Vincent.

5. The inspirations for both Kali N. Gross, *Colored Amazons: Crime, Violence, and Black Women in the City of Brotherly Love, 1880–1910* (Durham, NC: Duke University Press, 2006) and Tera W. Hunter, *To Joy My Freedom: Southern Black Women's Lives and Labors after the Civil War* (Cambridge, MA: Harvard University Press, 1997) came from post–Civil War newspaper articles describing black women as criminals and strikers, respectively, but both were referred to as Amazons. Laurel Thatcher Ulrich's chapter, "Amazons," in *Well-Behaved Women Seldom Make History* (New York: Vintage, 2008), beautifully explores the mixed-messaging concepts that the term *Amazons* has been used for in history.

6. "Walsenburg Jail Holds 60 Picketers, Twenty of Them Chattering Women," *Daily Camera* (Boulder, CO), October 21, 1927, 1.

7. "Amazons Jailed for Hurling Rocks," *Daily Camera* (Boulder, CO), October 22, 1927, 1.

8. "Amazon Leader and Other I.W.W. Jailed Today," *Daily Camera* (Boulder, CO), October 24, 1927, 1.

9. "Two Strike Leaders," *Denver Post*, October 29, 1929, 1.

10. Written transcription of tape "Memory of Mary Gallagher about Byron Kitto" made for part of the oral history collection for University of California, 1955, 23–26, IWW papers.

11. Martelle, *Blood Passion*, 197–202.

12. Richard Myers, "The Women of the Twenties Coal Strikes," in *Slaughter in Serene: The Columbine Strike Reader*, edited by Lowell May and Richard Myers (Denver, CO: Bread and Roses Workers' Cultural Center & the Industrial Workers of the World), 161–162.

13. Myers, "The Women of the 'Twenties Coal Strikes," 161–162.

14. *The Military Occupation, Coal Strike Zone of Colorado, Colorado National Guard, 1913–1914: Report of Commanding General to the Governor for the Use of the Congressional Committee* (Denver, CO: Press of the Smith Brooks Printing Company, 1914), 27–28.

15. The photo in figure 5.1, taken some time in 1927 or 1928 in Lafayette, Colorado, is from the private collection of Paula Enrietto, who donated the image to the Louisville Historical Museum, Louisville, Colorado. Ms. Enrietto gave her permission for me to use it in this book. I have tried to enhance this image to read the sign at the head of this women's parade, and what I can read is this: "Women's Educational Society of (illegible) of the I.W.W."

16. "I.W.W. Amazons Lead Fray in Colorado Strike; Stone and Dare Guards, Men Staying Behind," *New York Times*, October 23, 1927, https://www.nytimes.com/1927/10/23/archives/iww-amazons-lead-fray-in-colorado-strike-stone-and-dare-guards-men.html?searchResultPosition=1.

17. Frances Whayne, "Strikers Hear Rival Calls of Two Women," *Denver Post*, October 28, 1927, 1.

18. Whayne, "Strikers Hear Rival Calls," 1.

19. Whayne, "Strikers Hear Rival Calls," 1.

20. "Colorado Governor Denounces the I.W.W.," *New York Times*, October 27, 1927.

21. Beshoar, *Out of the Depths*, 152–153, 164; McGovern and Guttridge, *The Great Coalfield War*, 156–157, 172, 186, 192, 205–207; Howard Zinn, "The Colorado Strike, 1913–1914," 35, in Howard Zinn, Dana Frank, and Robin D.G. Kelley, Three Strikes: Miners, Musicians, Salesgirls, and the Fighting Spirit of Labor's Last Century (Boston: Beacon Press), 2001; Long, *Where the Sun Never Shines*, 290; Martelle, *Blood Passion*, 158–159; Andrews, *Killing for Coal*, 270.

22. "Longmont Sugar Factory Allowed a Tax Reduction," *Daily Camera* (Boulder, CO), October 19, 1927, 3.

23. "Gov. Adams Expected to Send Units of Troops to Mines," *Daily Camera* (Boulder, CO), November 16, 1927, 1.

24. "Pickets Stationed by the Strikers at the Columbine," *Daily Camera* (Boulder, CO), October 19, 1927, 1.

25. Meeting of Employees with Mr. Hair and Mr. Matteson, November 3, 1927, INR 1300-9, CF&I archives; During the Weld County coroner's inquest, several witnesses indicated they had been hired as strikebreaking coalminers, but as the time of the Columbine, had been reassigned to guard duty.

26. Meeting of Employees with Mr. Hair and Mr. Matteson.

27. "Picketing in County Reported Here Today," *Daily Camera* (Boulder, CO), November 4, 1927, 1.

28. *"Thornhill v. Alabama,"* *Oyez*, https://www.oyez.org/cases/1940-1955/310us88, accessed May 30, 2019.

29. "Joe Bear" Beranek and Betty Shapowal Beranek gave me a copy of this photo from their private collection when I interviewed them in their Lafayette, Colorado, home in December of 2004. Since it is a copy of a copy of a copy, my friend Gerry Morrell, who founded Lafayette's Morrell Printing in Lafayette turned the photo into a high-enough resolution image that I could include it here.

30. This repetition can be understood by reading the testimonies of the strikers before coroners' juries after the November 21, 1927, Columbine Massacre and the January 12, 1928, shootings in Walsenburg. At both inquests, IWW members and their supporters volunteered to testify, and it is remarkable how many people use the exact words when describing events such as having the right to march where there was a post office, or insisting that none of them was armed, since they had been instructed never to carry weapons of any kind, "not even a pocket knife." Some examples include the testimonies of Bill Allander (202) at the *Weld County Inquest* (202) and the testimonies of Pete Verbich (29), Mrs. Fluena Pappas (36), and Nemesio Edilla (43) at the Huerfano County Coroner's Inquest, CF&I papers, INR, 1300–21.

31. "Incorporation Doctrine," Legal Information Institute, https://www.law.cornell.edu/wex/incorporation_doctrine, accessed May 30, 2019.

32. *The Methodist Federation for Social Service, News Letter No. 3,* February 20, 1923, 1910–1964, Reverend Aaron Allen Heist Papers, Southern California Library for Social Studies, Los Angeles, California.

33. "Colorado Students Back Up Strikers," *Industrial Worker*, No. 49—Whole No. 477, December 14, 1927, 3, Josephine Roche Papers, 5–1; Letter from Heist to Win (no last name), December 13, 1927; "Industrial Relations in the Coal Industry of Colorado," *Information Service*, published by the Department of Research and Education, Federal Council of Churches, Vol. X, No. 11, March 14, 1931, 9, Heist Papers. I have never found these interviews, although I have read many references to them.

34. Ted Morgan, *A Covert Life: Jay Lovestone, Communist, Anti-Communist, and Spymaster* (New York: Random House, 1999), 57–60.

35. Diary entry September 6, 1928, labor delegation trip to USSR, John Brophy Papers, Series 3, Box 29, Subseries 3.2, 30-4, The American Catholic History Research Center and University Archives, The Catholic University of America, Washington, DC.

36. Upon their return, their findings were published in American Trade Union Delegation to the Soviet Union, *Russia After Ten Years: Report of the American Trade Union Delegation to the Soviet Union* (New York: International Publishers, 1927). The full delegation consisted of Palmer, L. E. Sheppard, James H. Maurer, John Brophy,

James William Fitzpatrick, and Albert Coyle. Some of the technical and advisory staff included Stuart Chase, Jerome Davis, Paul Douglas, and Rex Tugwell.

37. Frank L. Palmer, "National Leaders Honor Denver Minister," undated editorial, no publication listed, Heist Papers. Even though this is undated, I know from other sources I have seen that this probably coincides with a big dinner Roche organized to honor Heist that was held in August of 1928. As I show later, this was the time Heist split with the IWW.

38. Hazel Glenny, "A History of Labor Disputes in the Northern Colorado Coal Mining Fields with Emphasis on the 1927–1928 Strike," master's thesis, University of Colorado, Boulder, 1938, 81. Ms. Glenny taught school in Lafayette during the strike, and she cited as evidence an editorial from *The Pueblo Star Journal*, 221 October 21, 1927, 4, as evidence, but she also reported that Big Bill Haywood himself had arrived in August of 1927 to help lead the strike!

39. Letter from IWW Secretary-Treasurer Lee Tullin to organizer A. K. Payne, September 20, 1927; Letter from A. K. Payne to Kristen Svanum, September 28, 1927, INR 1300–13, CF&I archives.

40. Letter from A. S. Embree to Joseph Wagner (Chairman of the IWW General Executive Board), July 6, 1928, 96–10, IWW papers.

41. A. S. Embree, "Great Strike Scheduled for October 18," *Industrial Solidarity* X, no. 38: 1, INR 1299-4, CF&I archives.

42. *Songs to Fan the Flames of Discontent* (Chicago: IWW, 1927), INR 1299-8, CF&I archives.

43. Leo Michaels, "Lafayette Branch Report," *Industrial Worker* X, no. 2 (January 14, 1928): 3, INR 1300-6, CF&I archives.

44. "Whee! Here's the Spirit of the I.W.W.: Trinidad Hall Re-opened, Picketing Resumed!" *Industrial Worker* X, no. 2, (January 14, 1928): 2, INR 1300-6, CF&I archives.

45. A. A. Swain, "I.W.W. to Tell Gov. Adams How Good They Are," *Daily Camera* (Boulder, CO), October 25, 1927, 1.

46. "States Immigration Officer at Port of Arrival," Ellis Island Records, http://ellisislandrecords.org/cgi-bin/tip2gif.exe?T=h:\t715–1927\t715–19271025.tif& . . . , accessed December 10, 2004.

47. Emily Kemme, "A Look at Windsor Colo.'s Sugar Beet Heritage," *The Fence Post* (Windsor, CO), September 4, 2018, https://www.thefencepost.com/news/a-look-at-windsor-colo-s-sugar-beet-heritage/.

48. Bernadette Peters, "Elusive Justice in the Colorado Beet Fields," presentation at the Labor and Working Class History Association Conference, Durham, NC, June 1, 2019.

49. I interviewed "Joe Bear" Beranek and his wife, Betty Shapowal Beranek, at their house in Lafayette, Colorado, in 2004.

50. "One Thousand Led by the I.W.W. Held Meeting Here Sunday," *Daily Camera* (Boulder, CO), November 21, 1927, 1.

51. "Preacher Turns to Wobblies in Colorado Strike of Mine Workers," *Industrial Worker* IX no. 47 (November 26, 1927), INR 1300-6, CF&I.

52. A. K. Orr, "Wm. H. Lofton," *Industrial Solidarity*, December 14, 1927, 2.

53. "Columbine Mine Program," Tape #1086 (transcribed), November 19, 1988, Lafayette Public Library.

54. A. V. Azuara, "The One Big Union of Coal Mine Workers," INR 1299-8, CF&I archives.

55. "Howdy! Said Governor Adams," *Denver Post*, October 28, 1927, 1.

56. "Gov. Adams Tells Camera That Clemens Statement Issued Today is Absurd," *Daily Camera* (Boulder, CO), November 3, 1927, 1.

57. "From Karl Clemens to all Branches of the Colo. Miners Effected in Strike," November 3, 1927; Receipt from Balaban Brothers, Printers and Publishers, Denver, made out to Kristen Svanum, November 5, 1927 for 20,000 printed petitions costing $81.69, INR 1299-3, CF&I archives.

58. J. F. Myhan note, November 12, 1927, INR 1300-9CF&I archives.

59. "50 Cars Took Lafayette Strikers to Fremont County," *Daily Camera* (Boulder, CO), October 26, 1927, 1.

60. Undated copy of Colorado Attorney General's analysis of the strike, undertaken by a request from Edward Costigan and Merle Vincent, 15-1, Roche papers.

61. "Adams Details Armed Guards to Strike Zone," *Rocky Mountain News* (Denver, CO), November 5, 1927, 1.

62. "Order to Close C.F.& I. 14-Inch Mill Revoked," *Rocky Mountain News* (Denver, CO), November 3, 1927, 2.

Chapter 6: The 1927–1928 Colorado Coal Strike: November 4, 1927-February 19, 1928

1. "Adams Orders Armed Guards to Enforce Anti-Picketing Edict in Southern Colorado," *Rocky Mountain News* (Denver, CO), November 6, 1927, 1.

2. "Gov. Adams Revives The State Law Enforcement Department," *Daily Camera* (Boulder, CO), November 4, 1927, 1.

3. Phyllis Smith, *Once a Coal Miner: The Story of Colorado's Northern Coal Field* (Boulder, CO: Pruett Publishing Company, 1989), 172.

4. "Most of Arrested Pickets in Southern Colorado 'Lost'," *Rocky Mountain News* (Denver, CO), November 9, 1927, 2.

5. "Strikers Plan New Moves in Picketing 'War' with Guards," *Rocky Mountain News* (Denver, CO), November 6, 1927, 2.

6. Telegram from Juan Noriega, Walsenburg, November 7, Box 5, Folder 20, IWW Archives.

7. "Picketers Terrorized Miners at the Columbine and Not One of the 175 Working Miners is Working in the Weld County Property," *Daily Camera* (Boulder, CO), November 7, 1927, 1.

8. "Columbine Miners Were Threatened by Large Meeting of the Strikers," *Daily Camera* (Boulder, CO), November 8, 1927, 1.

9. Staughton Lynd, ed., *"We are All Leaders": The Alternative Unionism of the Early 1930s* (Urbana: University of Illinois Press, 1996), 7; "Solidarity Forever" lyrics, *Industrial Workers of the World*, https://archive.iww.org/history/icons/solidarity_forever/, accessed February 4, 2021.

10. "16 Persons injured as Strikers and State Guards Stage Wild Battle at I.W.W. Headquarters," *Rocky Mountain News* (Denver, CO), November 9, 1927, 1.

11. Ivy Lee, *Facts Concerning the Struggle in Colorado for Industrial Freedom*, issued by the Coal Mine Managers, [1914–1915?], 10, INR 1300, CF&I archives. Lee is not attributed as the author on the book's cover, but he is attributed in the CF&I archives file folder title.

12. R. W. Roskelley, *Population Trends in Colorado* (Fort Collins, CO: Cooperative Plan of Rural Research, Division of Research, WPA, 1940), 56.

13. "Member lists of IWWs to Mine Superintendents," January 27, 1928, INR-1300, F11, CF&I Archives.

14. Letter of introduction for Ramon Gonzalez by Kristen Svanum (confiscated during an arrest of another IWW organizer), INR 1300–11, CF&I archives.

15. Vicki L. Ruiz, *Cannery Women, Cannery Lives: Mexican Women, Unionization, and the California Food Processing Industry, 1930–1950* (Albuquerque: University of New Mexico Press, 1987), dedication.

16. Email from Vicki Ruiz to me on August 22, 2013.

17. Sarah Deutsch, *No Separate Refuge: Culture, Class, and Gender on an Anglo-Hispanic Frontier in the American Southwest, 1880–1940* (New York: Oxford University Press, 1987), 34–35.

18. "Sugar Factory Men and Beet Field Workers Urged to Strike," *Daily Camera*, November 11, 1927, 1.

19. Deutsch, *No Separate Refuge*, 158.

20. Zaragosa Vargas, *Proletarians of the North: A History of Mexican Industrial Workers in Detroit and the Midwest, 1917–1933* (Berkeley: University of California Press, 1993), 156.

21. "Strikers Ignore State Police and Parade Inside Enclosure Columbine Mine early Today," *Daily Camera* (Boulder, CO), November 12, 1927, 1.

22. "Mass Protest Meeting" flyer, INR1300-7, Steelworks Museum, accessed June 2021.

23. "Meetings of Strikers at Denver on Sunday When Speakers Denounced Gov. Adams for Using Guardsmen and Jailing I.W.W.," *Daily Camera* (Boulder, CO), November 14, 1927, 1.

24. "Columbine Mine Closed: Attack on Deputies of Weld County by Picketers Wins," *Daily Camera* (Boulder, CO), November 14, 1927, 1; During the Weld County Coroner's Inquest, the first group to testify was the state police. They mostly told the same story. Following them, the local Weld County sheriffs testified. They felt their authority had been usurped and that no violence had or would have taken place under their watch.

25. "Strikers Warned Shooting May Commence at Columbine," *Daily Camera* (Boulder, CO), November 15, 1927, 1.

26. "Machine Gun and a Few Troopers Stood Off Picket at Columbine," *Daily Camera* (Boulder, CO), November 16, 1927, 1.

27. "Gov. Adams Expected to Send Units of Troops to Mines," *Daily Camera* (Boulder, CO), November 16, 1927, 1.

28. "Troops Will be Ordered Out by Adams Thinks Mr. Swain," *Daily Camera* (Boulder, CO), November 17, 1927, 1.

29. "Tho Machine Guns Were Aimed at Men I.W.W. Led Strikers into the Columbine," *Daily Camera* (Boulder, CO), November 18, 1927, 1.

30. "One Thousand Led by the I.W.W. Held Meeting Here Sunday," *Daily Camera* (Boulder, CO), November 21, 1927, 1.

31. Joe (Cotton) Fletcher, Tape #1083 (no date)—transcribed, 8, Lafayette oral histories, Lafayette Public Library, Lafayette, Colorado.

32. Archie Green, "Remembering Jack Fitch," in *Torching the Fink Books and Other Essays on Vernacular Culture* (Chapel Hill: The University of North Carolina Press, 2001), 174.

33. "Jacques Fined $100 and Pays up for Selling Booze," *Daily Camera* (Boulder, CO), October 24, 1927, 1.

34. Undated statement of John R. Lawson to Rev. A. A. Heist [September of 1928?], 11, JR Papers, 15–1; Testimony of Joe Beranek (the inquest mistakenly identifies him as Joe Veranek) at the Colorado Industrial Commission hearings, December 19–22, 1927, 41, JR Papers, 14-1.

35. "Coroner's Inquest into the Deaths of John Eastenes and Nick Spanudakhis, November 22–23, 1927," Columbine Mine Massacre Collection (1927), 1-1, Special

Collections, Archives and Preservation, University of Colorado Boulder Libraries Special Collection.

36. Undated John R. Lawson notes on events preceding the strike, written to Rev. A. A. Heist, Box 11, Roche Papers.

37. At the Weld County inquest, the state police, county sheriffs, and volunteer witnesses from the crowd all agree on this. See pages 38, 79, 158, and 198.

38. Scherf's Weld County inquest testimony, 41.

39. This exact quote repeatedly appears in coalminers' testimonies in both the Weld County and Huerfano County inquests. For example, when IWW leader Nemesio Edilla was interviewed during the inquest over the two men killed on January 12, 1928, in Walsenburg, he was asked if any Wobblies were armed. He replied, "Before the parade I told the men not to carry nothing, not even a pocket knife," quoted in "Notes Taken at Coroner's Inquest Held January 16th, 1927 [*sic*, meant 1928]," INR 1300–21, 43, CF&I archives.

40. Testimony of Mrs. George Kubic, *Weld County Coroner's Inquest into the Deaths of John Eastenes and Nick Spanudakhis, November 23–24*, 175, Columbine Mine Massacre Collection, Archives, University of Colorado at Boulder Libraries 175.

41. Testimony of Dr. Bixler, *Weld County Coroner's Inquest*, 9.

42. "Union Service Offering for Mrs. Eastenes," *Daily Camera* (Boulder, CO), November 23, 1927, 2; "Mullen Offers to Provide for Eastenes Orphans," *Daily Camera* (Boulder, CO), November 28, 1927, 3.

43. "Burial of Columbine Dead Began at Lafayette Today," *Daily Camera* (Boulder, CO), November 23, 1927, 1.

44. Mike Vidovich, Boulder County death certificate, November 29, 1927, copy from the private collection of Beth and Jim Hutchison, Lafayette, Colorado.

45. "Burial of Columbine Dead Began at Lafayette Today," *Daily Camera* (Boulder, CO), November 23, 1927, 1; "Another Miner at the Columbine Died From Shot by the Guard," *Daily Camera* (Boulder, CO), November 28, 1927, 1.

46. Strike Bulletin no. 5, December 2, 1927, INR 1300-9, CF&I archives.

47. "Troops Patrol Strike Zone After Battle," *Rocky Mountain News* (Denver, CO), November 22, 1927, 1.

48. Smith, *Once a Coal Miner*, 187; "F. R. Palmer Held for Attack Made on State Officers and Militia," *Daily Times* (Longmont, CO), December 16, 1927, Colorado Historic Newspapers.

49. Letter from Frank Palmer to Josephine Roche, December 13, 1927, 15-3, Roche Papers; "Miners Will Reject Peace Offer," *Rocky Mountain News* (Denver, CO), January 2, 1928, 1.

50. McClurg, "The Colorado Coal Strike," 86.

51. Frank L. Palmer, "Solidarity in Colorado," *The Nation*, February 1, 1928.

52. "Trinidad I.W.W. Wins Court Fight on Meetings," *Rocky Mountain News* (Denver, CO), January 6, 1928, 7.

53. "Mexico May be Asked to Take Action," *Rocky Mountain News* (Denver, CO), January 5, 1928, 5.

54. Palmer, "Solidarity in Colorado."

55. These victims' names were spelled differently and crazily almost every time they appeared in print. In most accounts, Chavez's first name is spelled Klemente, and maybe that really was how he spelled his name, but I doubt it, which is why I have written it here as Clemente.

56. A. V. Gullette, "Eye-Witnesses Tell Story of Rioting in Walsenburg," *Rocky Mountain News* (Denver, CO), January 13, 1928, 1.

57. "Trouble Zone Well Policed," *Rocky Mountain News* (Denver, CO), January 13, 1928, 1.

58. Huerfano County Coroner's Inquest, INR, 1300–21, CF&I archives.

59. The *Industrial Solidarity* headline "Police Blamed for Murder" can be seen in a photo propped up next to about thirty ax handles and clubs. This are several variations of this photo; one has the IWW newspaper and the two do not. One of those two includes the following written on the back of the photo: "Last Bunch of Clubs taken from 'Hobbly' Hall." It is doubtful the clubs really were taken from the hall, because the IWW was repeatedly instructed to remain unarmed. Also, why would there be an IWW newspaper with its damning headline be next to the clubs? These photos are from the Industrial Relations/Medical Safety/Strike rescue Box 01, Folder I.W.W. Strike 1927–1928, SCM-3954.

60. McClurg, "The Colorado Coal Strike," 86.

61. *Rocky Mountain News* (Denver, CO), February 20, 1928, quoted in Donald McClurg's "The Colorado Coal Strike of 1927—Tactical Leadership of the IWW."

Chapter 7: The Aftermath of the 1927–1928 Colorado Coal Strike: 1927–1930

1. "Eyewitness Describes Battle," *New York Times*, November 22, 1927, https://www.nytimes.com/1927/11/22/archives/eyewitness-describes-battle.html?searchResultPosition=1.

2. "Reds Again Blame the Rockefellers," *New York Times*, November 25, 1927, https://www.nytimes.com/1927/11/25/archives/reds-again-blame-the-rockefellers-communists-here-see-attempt-to.html?searchResultPosition=1.

3. "Coal Company to Co-operate," *Rocky Mountain News* (Denver, CO), November 26, 1927, 1.

4. Letter from Heist to Merle Vincent, November 28, 1927, 15-2, Roche papers.

5. Frank L. Palmer, "War in Colorado," *Nation* cxxv, no. 3257, December 7, 1927, 623–624.

6. Peart's testimony, Weld County Coroner's Inquest, 115.

7. Alessandro Portelli, *The Order Has Been Carried Out: History, Memory, and Meaning of a Nazi Massacre in Rome* (New York: Palgrave McMillan, 2003), 1.

8. Portelli, *The Order Has Been*, 5, 3, 12, 236.

9. Robyn Muncy provided great detail on this, but she has more faith in Roche's financial records and personal truthfulness than I do. Furthermore, there is a quirky lawsuit in Roche's archival records suggesting how Roche gained voting, but not financial control, over the RMFC in 1928. Roche's attorney, Edward Costigan, argued that in 1922 Roche's partner signed over majority control of the RMFC to John Roche, but, because both were now dead, that evidence hinged on the new "scientific" evidence of handwriting analysis. The judge decided in Roche's favor in March of 1928, and in his decision, he noted that it awarded Roche voting, but not financial control over the RMFC.

10. Letter from Merle Vincent to Frank Palmer, undated [probably December of 1927], 5–4; Letter from Frank Palmer to Josephine Roche, December 13, 1927, 15-3, Roche papers.

11. "Rocky Mt. Fuel Co. Announces Liberal Policy," *Rocky Mountain News* (Denver, CO), March 19, 1928, 1.

12. Untitled petition presented by IWW Attorney Fred Caldwell to the Colorado Industrial Commission on behalf of the State Executive Committee of the Colorado Striking Coal Miners, Roche papers, 15-1.

13. "Nailing a Lie!" IWW flyer circulated in the strike fields, 15-2, Roche papers.

14. Letter from Percy Tetlow to Merle Vincent, July 30, 1928, 16-1, Roche papers.

15. Undated letter [in the month of August of 1928] from Rev. A. A. Heist to editor of *Industrial Worker* referring to "John Lawson, Proletarian" article published in the *Rocky Mountain News* on August 28, 1928, 15-2, Roche papers.

16. "21 New Strike Death Suits Being Drawn," *Rocky Mountain News* (Denver, CO), November 1, 1928, 15-2, Roche papers.

17. "A Summary of the Cash Receipts and Expenses of the General Defense Committee for the Fiscal Year—October 1, 1933, to October 1, 1934," IWW archives, General Executive Board, 7–15.

18. *Eastenes v. RMFC* (No. 12735), 73-4, Roche papers.

19. Letter from Baldwin to Roche, October 20, 1928; Telegram from Roche to Baldwin, October 29, 1928; Telegram from Roche to Baldwin, October 29, 1928; Telegram from Roche to Baldwin, November 2, 1928; Letter from Baldwin to Roche, October 30, 1928; Telegram from Baldwin to Roche, November 7, 1928;

Letter from Baldwin to Fred Caldwell (IWW/ACLU attorney), November 14, 1928, 15-9, Roche papers.

20. Letter from Powers Hapgood to his parents, September 4, 1927, Powers Hapgood papers.

21. Letter from Powers Hapgood to Mary Donovan, December 23, 1927, Powers Hapgood papers.

22. Letter from Powers Hapgood to Mary Donovan, December 23, 1927, Powers Hapgood papers.

23. "Two More Killed in Mine Union Feud," *New York Times*, February 29, 1928, https://www.nytimes.com/1928/02/29/archives/two-more-killed-in-mine-union-feud-insurgent-leaders-are-slain-by.html?searchResultPosition=1.

24. "Loud Threats Made at Dead Miner's Grave," *New York Times*, March 3, 1928, https://www.nytimes.com/1928/03/03/archives/loud-threats-made-at-dead-miners-grave-detectives-induce-friend-of.html?searchResultPosition=1.

25. "Powers Hapgood Jailed in Mine Row," *New York Times*, March 5, 1928, https://www.nytimes.com/1928/03/05/archives/powers-hapgood-jailed-in-mine-row-held-with-bride-former-sacco.html?searchResultPosition=1.

26. Telegram from William Hapgood to Powers Hapgood, March 5, 1928, Powers Hapgood papers.

27. Telegram from Roger Baldwin to Powers Hapgood, March 5, 1928, Powers Hapgood papers.

28. "Hapgoods Acquitted of Inciting Coal Riot," *New York Times*, April 13, 1928, https://www.nytimes.com/1928/04/13/archives/hapgoods-acquitted-of-inciting-coal-riot-judge-directs-verdict-when.html?searchResultPosition=1.

29. "Mine Union Leader Guilty of Killing," *New York Times*, April 15, 1928, https://www.nytimes.com/1928/04/15/archives/mine-union-leader-guilty-of-killing-jury-convicts-bonita-of.html?searchResultPosition=1.

30. Letter from Anthony Minerich to Powers Hapgood, June 19, 1928, Powers Hapgood papers.

31. Letter from John Brophy to Powers Hapgood, June 20, 1928, Powers Hapgood papers.

32. Letter from Frank Palmer to Powers Hapgood, September 5, 1928, Powers Hapgood papers.

33. Letter from Powers to Mary Donovan Hapgood, September 8, 1928, Powers Hapgood papers.

34. Letter from Powers Hapgood to Mary Hapgood Donovan, September 9, 1928, Powers Hapgood papers.

35. "Six Miners Injured in Riot over Lewis," *New York Times*, September 10, 1928, https://www.nytimes.com/1928/09/10/archives/six-miners-injured-in-riot-over-lewis-one-is-believed-dying-in.html?searchResultPosition=1.

36. "Six Miners Injured in Riot over Lewis," *New York Times*, September 10, 1928, https://www.nytimes.com/1928/09/10/archives/six-miners-injured-in-riot-over-lewis-one-is-believed-dying-in.html?searchResultPosition=1.

37. Letter from Powers Hapgood to Mary Donovan Hapgood, October 5, 1929, Powers Hapgood papers.

38. Letter from Powers Hapgood to his father, January 9, 1929, Powers Hapgood papers.

39. Letter from Powers Hapgood to his father, January 9, 1929, Powers Hapgood papers.

40. Check receipts for Powers and Mary Donovan Hapgood for the month of February of 1928 show they paid $9.25 for half the house and garage rent, Powers Hapgood papers.

41. Letter from Powers Hapgood to parents, January 16, 1929, Powers Hapgood papers.

42. Letter from Powers Hapgood to parents, January 16, 1929, Powers Hapgood papers.

43. Letter from Powers Hapgood to parents, January 16, 1929, Powers Hapgood papers.

44. Letter from Powers Hapgood to his parents, January 16, 1928, Powers Hapgood papers.

45. Letter from Powers Hapgood to his parents, January 16, 1928, Powers Hapgood papers.

46. In footnote 21 in chapter 6, Bussel writes the following: "Columbia Conserve not only provided Rocky Mountain Fuel with moral support but even granted Josephine Roche a $20,000 interest-free loan in 1929 to assist the company through a lean period. See Minutes, Special Business Council Meeting, October 25, 1929, CCC Papers."

47. Letter from John Brophy to the American Fund for Public Service, Inc., April 30, 1928, John Brophy papers, 1–3; Letters from Powers Hapgood to his parents, July 10, 1927 and July 17, 1927, Powers Hapgood papers.

48. Fox, *United We Stand*, 309.

49. "Warning to Colorado Miners," *Industrial Worker*, September 1, 1928: 1, Josephine Roche papers.

50. Letter from Powers Hapgood to his parents, January 16, 1928, Powers Hapgood papers.

51. Letter from Gerry Allard to Powers Hapgood, February 19, 1929, Powers Hapgood papers.

52. Letter from John Brophy to Powers Hapgood, February 3, 1929, Hapgood papers.

53. L. A. Chapin, "Hapgood, Son of Rich Canner, Works in Mine," *Denver Post*, February 13, 1929, Powers Hapgood papers.

54. Powers Hapgood wrote his parents at least twice a week, and in almost every letter he mentions that he has been a speaker somewhere, usually at Grace Church, but also at the University of Denver, the University of Colorado, or at local meetings.

55. Letter from Thos. Kennedy, Sec-Treas., UMWA, to Powers Hapgood, March 9, 1929, Powers Hapgood papers.

56. Letter from John Brophy to Powers Hapgood, March 18, 1929, Powers Hapgood papers.

57. Letter from Powers Hapgood to the Members of the International Executive Board, United Mine Workers of America, March 30, 1929, Powers Hapgood papers.

58. Letter from Powers Hapgood to William Hapgood, March 23, 1929, Powers Hapgood papers.

59. Letter from Powers Hapgood to his parents, July 30, 1928, Powers Hapgood papers.

60. Letter from Powers Hapgood to his mother, March 19, 1929, Powers Hapgood papers.

61. Letter from Mary E. Gallagher to Mary Donovan Hapgood, March 23, 1929, Powers Hapgood papers; photo labeled "Byron Kitto, Sanitarium, California, 1920s-1930s," Walter P. Reuther Library, https://reuther.wayne.edu/11565.

62. (4961) "Byron Kitton, Sanitarium, California, 1920s–1930s," Walter P. Reuther Library, Wayne State University, http://reuther.wayne.edu/node/11565, accessed November 15, 2020. The descriptor read, "Snapshot of IWW organizers and publicist, Byron Kitto." Photograph was probably taken at the California sanitarium where he was being rerated for tuberculosis that he contracted during the Colorado Coal Strike. He died of the disease March 14, 1931, at age 30.

63. Byron Kitto folder contained obituary (no newspaper title) from April 11, 1931, listed his cremation of March 17, 1931 in Los Angeles, 23-6, IWW papers.

64. Author's interview with James and Beth Hutchinson, Lafayette, Colorado, March 30, 2010.

65. Letter from Powers Hapgood to Eleanor Hapgood, March 23, 1928, Powers Hapgood papers.

66. Letter from Powers Hapgood to Eleanor Hapgood, no date [April 1929?]; Letter from Mary Donovan Hapgood to Eleanor Hapgood, February 16, 1928, Powers Hapgood papers.

67. Letter from Powers Hapgood to Eleanor Hapgood, no date [April 1929?]; Letter from Mary Donovan Hapgood to Eleanor Hapgood, February 16, 1928, Powers Hapgood papers.

68. Letter from Powers Hapgood to Eleanor Hapgood, March 13, 1928, Powers Hapgood papers.

69. Letter from John Brophy to Powers Hapgood, February 3, 1929, Powers Hapgood papers.

70. Letter from Powers Hapgood to William Hapgood, March 23, 1929, Powers Hapgood papers.

71. Letter from Powers Hapgood to William Hapgood, March 23, 1929, Powers Hapgood papers.

72. Letter from Powers Hapgood to William Hapgood, March 23, 1929, Powers Hapgood papers.

73. Letter from Mary Donovan Hapgood to Eleanor Hapgood, April 25, 1929, Powers Hapgood papers.

74. Letter from Mary Donovan Hapgood to Eleanor Hapgood, April 25, 1929, Powers Hapgood papers.

75. *In the Matter of the Employes* (1929 spelling) *of the Centennial Mine, Employes, vs. the Operators of the Centennial Mine*, State of Colorado, s.s., Before the Industrial commission of Colorado, File No. 1406, Findings and Award, 5, Powers Hapgood papers.

76. Telegram from Josephine Roche to Edward Keating, August 3, 1929, 4-1, Roche papers.

77. Telegram from Josephine Roche to Edward Keating, August 3, 1929, 4-1, Roche papers.

78. In response to my request, Powers and Mary Donovan Hapgood's granddaughter, Katherine Hapgood Nading, sent me a copy of this photo, with permission to reprint it, in a personal email on July 30, 2021. Pictured standing are Donovan Hapgood, Mary's brother, and Powers Hapgood. Sitting are Mary, her parents, and Donovan's wife. The photo includes their children. Since Mary got pregnant in 1930 and her father died later that year, the photo was probably taken in 1929.

79. Letter from Norman Thomas to Powers Hapgood, June 3, 1929, Powers Hapgood papers.

80. Letter from John L. Lewis to Powers Hapgood, June 29, 1929, Powers Hapgood papers.

81. Letter from John L. Lewis to Powers Hapgood, September 20, 1929, Powers Hapgood papers.

82. Letter from John Brophy to Powers Hapgood, October 29, 1929, Powers Hapgood papers.

83. Letter from C. L. Rosemund to Powers Hapgood, November 25, 1929, Powers Hapgood papers.

84. Letter from Oscar Ameringer to Powers Hapgood, February 21, 1930, Powers Hapgood papers.

85. Letter from Mary Donovan Hapgood to Powers Hapgood, March 10, 1930, Powers Hapgood papers.

86. Letter from Powers Hapgood to Eleanor Hapgood July 30, 1929; Telegram from Powers Hapgood to Elizabeth Donovan, October 22, 1929, Powers Hapgood papers.

87. Telegram from Powers Hapgood to Elizabeth Donovan, October 22, 1929; Letter from Powers Hapgood to Eleanor Hapgood, October 23, 1929, Powers Hapgood papers.

88. The series of letters between Josephine Roche and Amalgamated vice president, Jacob Potofsky, run from 1928 to 1931, 1-5, Josephine Roche papers.

89. Ann Schofield, "Mary Dreier, 1876–1963," in *To Do and to Be* (Boston: Northeastern University Press, 1997), 50; Richard A. Greenwald, *The Triangle Fire, the Protocols of Peace, and Industrial Democracy in Progressive Era New York* (Philadelphia, PA: Temple University Press, 2005), 37–38.

90. Downey, *The Woman Behind the New Deal*, 286, 301–302, 358.

91. Letter from Oswald Garrison Villard to Amos Pinchot, March 13, 1929; letter from Oswald Garrison Villard to Roger Baldwin, April 12, 1929, MS Am 1323–3282, Oswald Garrison Villard Papers, Houghton Library, Harvard University (hereafter referred to as Villard papers).

92. Letter from Oswald Garrison Villard to Josephine Roche July 5, 1932, Villard papers.

93. Letter from Josephine Roche to Oswald Garrison Villard, July 7, 1930; Letter from Oswald Garrison Villard to Roger Baldwin, April 18, 1929; Letter from Oswald Garrison Villard to Amos Pinchot, March 13, 1929; Letter from Oswald Garrison Villard to Josephine Roche letting her know he had contacted Morris Ernst of the Garland Fund and Civil Liberties Union and set up an appointment between Roche and Ernst, March 14, 1929; Villard papers.

Chapter 8: Traces of the 1927–1928 Colorado Coal Strike: 1931–1948

1. In 1920, CF&I had twenty-six coal mines, produced 4,161,450 tons of coal, and employed 4,942 coalminers. In 1928, it had twenty-six coal mines, produced 2,690,997 tons of coal, and employed 3,207 coalminers. By 1930, it had eleven coal

59. Brophy, *A Miner's Life*, 236.

60. Bureau of Labor Statistics, "Table E-I: Membership of Labor Unions, 1897–1950," in *Handbook of Labor Statistics*, Bureau of Labor Statistics, 1950, US Department of Labor (Washington, DC: US Government Printing Office), https:// www.google.com/books/edition/Bulletin_of_the_United_States_Bureau_of/ eR4JWlnkB28C?hl=en&gbpv=1&dq=Bureau+of+Labor+Statistics,+Table+E-1: +Membership+of+labor+unions,+1897-1950&pg=PA139&printsec=frontcover.

61. "Labor Unions During the Great Depression and New Deal," Library of Congress, n.d., https://www.loc.gov/classroom-materials/united-states-history -primary-source-timeline/great-depression-and-world-war-ii-1929-1945/labor-unions -during-great-depression-and-new-deal/, accessed February 24, 2021.

62. Letter from John Brophy to John L. Lewis, December 31, 1933, 7-2, Brophy papers.

63. Brophy, *A Miner's Life*, 241–242.

64. Roche surely knew Pinchot, because Pinchot and Costigan were close, as evidenced by the correspondence exchanged between the two in Goodykoontz, *Papers of Edward P. Costigan*; Also, Roche's papers include personal correspondence between her and Cornelia Pinchot, Gifford Pinchot's wife, regarding her failed campaign for a House seat in 1932.

65. James Gray Pope, "The Western Pennsylvania Coal Strike of 1933, Part II: Lawmaking from Above and the Demise of Democracy in the United Mine Workers," *Labor History* 44, no. 2 (n.d.), 255.

66. Pope, "The Western Pennsylvania Coal Strike," 257.

67. Vernon H. Jensen, *Nonferrous Metals Industry Unionism, 1932–1954: A Story of Leadership Controversy* (Ithaca, NY: Cornell University, 1954), 12.

68. Jensen, *Nonferrous Metals Industry Unionism*, 14–15.

69. Len DeCaux, *Labor Radical: From the Wobblies to the CIO* (Boston: Beacon Press, 1970), 216–217.

70. Bussel, *From Harvard to the Ranks*, 140.

71. Dan P. McAdams, *The Stories We Live By: Personal Myths and the Making of Self* (New York: The Guilford Press, 1993) and *The Redemptive Self: Stories Americans Live By* (New York: Oxford University Press, 2006); with Ruthellen Josselson and Amia Lieblich, *Up Close and Personal: The Teaching and Learning of Narrative Research* (Washington, DC: American Psychological Association, 2003).

72. Joe Richard, "Hunters and Dogs," *Jacobin*, 28 October 2016, https://www .jacobinmag.com/2016/10/cio-unions-communist-party-socialist-party-afl/.

73. Bussel, *From Harvard to the Ranks*, 154; Nelson Lichtenstein, *Walter Reuther: The Most Dangerous Man in Detroit* (Urbana: University of Illinois Press, 1995), 78–79.

74. Women played key roles throughout the strike, as documented in the film, *With Babies and Banners: Story of the Women's Emergency Brigade*, directed by Loraine Gray, produced by the Woman's Labor History Film Project, 1978, now available on YouTube. This documentary, first shown on Public Broadcasting Service (PBS), was nominated in 1979 for an Academy Award for best documentary.

75. "President Quotes: He Calls Labor Strife 'A Plague on both Their Houses,'" *New York Times* June 30, 1937, www.nytimes.com.

76. Brophy, *A Miner's Life*, 278.

77. Louis Stark, "John L. Lewis to Control C.I.O. Convention by Appointing Left Wing to its Committees," *New York Times*, November 12, 1940, www.nytimes.com.

78. *Press-Atlantic City*, November 17, 1935, 19-4, Roche papers.

79. Roche kept newspaper articles describing her testimony before the National Bituminous Coal Commission in Washington, DC, February 9, 1938; Letter from John Carson from the Consumers' Counsel to Josephine Roche, February 21, 1938; Copy of the 1939 National Bituminous Coal Act; Letter from Josephine Roche to John A. Howe, Chairman, Committee for Amendment of the Coal Act, February 27, 1939, 20-3, Roche papers. Percy Tetlow was the UMW official sent to Colorado to negotiate the 1928 UMW-RMFC contract. By 1939, he served as one of the commissioners on the National Bituminous Coal Commission.

80. "Miss Roche Out as Colorado Coal Firm Head," *New York Herald Tribune Financial News*, June 25, 1939, 17-4, Roche papers.

81. "Josephine Roche Seeks U.S. Loan to Pay off Lewis," *The Denver Post*, September 29, 1939, 17-4, Roche papers.

82. Letter from Josephine Roche to Oswald Garrison Villard, August 31 (although the letter does not specify, because of the context, the year has to be 1940), Villard papers.

83. "Josephine Roche Seeks U.S. Loan to Pay Off Lewis," *The Denver Post*, September 29, 1940, 1, 17-4, Roche papers.

84. Copy of Josephine Roche's RMFC records, with handwritten note at the top by Oscar Chapman, indicating that he communicated with Roche that he had shown them to FDR, asking for his intervention, October 8, 1940, Box 29, Chapman papers.

85. Thomas J. Noel, "William D. Haywood: 'The Most Hated and Feared Figure in America,'" in *Western Voices: 125 Years of Colorado Writing*, edited by Steve Grinstead and Ben Fogelberg (Golden, CO: Fulcrum Publishing, 2004), 178–179. It is worth noting is that Mine Mill operated its own hospital, a practice the UMW, under Roche's management, began emulating on a larger scale in the 1950s.

86. Noel, "William D. Haywood," 179.

87. Letter from Reid Robinson to A. S. Embree, February 26, 1941, 37-5, Western Federation of Miners/International Union of Mine, Mill and Smelter Workers archives, Special Collections, Archives and Preservation, University of Colorado Boulder Libraries (Hereafter, WFM/IUMMSW).

88. Letters from A. S. Embree to Howard Goddard, July 30, 1941; August 1, 1941; August 4, 1941; October 6, 1941; October 10, 1941; October 18, 1941; 37-5, WFM/IUMMSW.

89. Letter to Bill (no last name) from A. S. Embree, March 9, 1942, 37-5, WFM/IUMMSW.

90. Letter to Bill (no last name) from A. S. Embree, March 9, 1942, 37-5, WFM/IUMMSW.

91. Letter from Allan D. McNeil to A. S. Embree, March 17, 1942, 37-5, WFM/IUMMSW.

92. Letter from A. S. Embree to Reid Robinson, March 12, 1942, 37-5, WFM/IUMMSW.

93. Letter from A. S. Embree to Mac (no last name), March 27, 1942, 37-5, WFM/IUMMSW.

94. Bussel, *From Harvard to the Ranks*, 181.

95. Elaine Leeder, *The Gentle General: Rose Pesotta, Anarchist and Labor Organizer* (Albany: State University of New York Press, 1993), 135; Bussel, *From Harvard to the Ranks*, 192.

96. "Powers Hapgood, CIO Leader Dead," *New York Times*, February 5, 1949, www.nytimes.com.

97. Leeder, *The Gentle General*, 136.

98. Letter from Mary Donovan Hapgood to Liza and Eva (no last names), February 10, 1949, Mary Donovan Hapgood Papers, 1949–1983, The Lilly Library, Indiana University, Bloomington, Indiana.

Chapter 9: The Cold War, Deindustrialization, and Competing Legacies of Industrial Democracy

1. Maurice Travis interview, 188, Box 951, WFM/IUMMSW.

2. City directories show that Constance Doyle, Ed Doyle's daughter, also worked as a secretary at Mine Mill (information including in the Denver city directory). Constance donated her father's papers and many photographs to the Denver Public Library.

3. Travis interview, 188.

4. Appendix A, Officers and Board Members, Jensen, *Nonferrous Metals Industry Unionism*, 308.

5. Travis interview, 198.

6. Robert Zieger, *The CIO, 1935–1955* (Chapel Hill: The University of North Carolina Press, 1995), 227; Barbara S. Griffith, *The Crisis of American Labor: Operation Dixie and the Defeat of the CIO* (Philadelphia, PA: Temple University Press 1988), xiii, 46.

7. Zieger, *The CIO*, 232–233.

8. Griffith, *The Crisis of American Labor*, 25.

9. Ken Fones-Wolf and Elizabeth Fones-Wolf, *Struggle for the Soul of the Postwar South: White Evangelical Protestants and Operation Dixie* (Urbana: University of Illinois Press, 2015).

10. Griffith, *The Crisis of American Labor*, 16.

11. Griffith, *The Crisis of American Labor*, 8, 169.

12. Jacquelyn Dowd Hall, James Leloudis, Robert Korstad, Mary Murphy, Lu Ann Jones, and Christopher B. Daly, *Like a Family: The Making of a Southern Cotton Mill World* (Chapel Hill: The University of North Carolina Press, 1987), 212.

13. John A. Salmond, *Gastonia, 1929: The Story of the Loray Mill Strike* (Chapel Hill: The University of North Carolina Press, 1995); John A. Salmond, *The General Textile Strike of 1934: From Maine to Alabama* (Columbia, MO: University of Missouri Press, 2002).

14. Salmond, *Gastonia, 1929*, 59; Janet Irons, *Testing the New Deal: The General Textile Strike of 1934 in the American South* (Urbana: University of Illinois Press, 2000).

15. Robin D. G. Kelley, *Hammer and Hoe: Alabama Communists During the Great Depression* (Chapel Hill: The University of North Carolina Press, 1990), 144–145.

16. Jensen, *Nonferrous Metals Industry Unionism*, 235.

17. Joseph A. Loftus, "Clashes Expected at CIO Conference," *New York Times*, May 12, 1949, www.nytimes.com.

18. Jensen, *Nonferrous Metals Industry Unionism*, 237.

19. Maurice Travis interview by Mike Hardwick August 3, 1978, Box 951, 130, WFM/IUMMSW.

20. Travis interview, 132; Jensen, *Nonferrous Metals Industry Unionism*, 238.

21. Travis interview, 131–132.

22. Jensen, *Nonferrous Metals Industry Unionism*, 238.

23. Jensen, *Nonferrous Metals Industry Unionism*, 132–134.

24. Jensen, *Nonferrous Metals Industry Unionism*, 237.

25. Jensen, *Nonferrous Metals Industry Unionism*, 237.

26. Jensen, *Nonferrous Metals Industry Unionism*, 240–241.

27. Jensen, *Nonferrous Metals Industry Unionism*, 242–243.

28. Jensen, *Nonferrous Metals Industry Unionism*, 242.

29. Travis interview, 202–203.

30. "Quits Communist Party, but Officer of Mine Mill Union Will 'Fight' for its Goals," *New York Times*, August 16, 1949, www.nytimes.com.

31. "Left-Wing Faction Will Not Quit CIO," *New York Times*, August 31, 1949, www.nytimes.com.

32. Zieger, *The CIO*, 253; Bureau of Labor Statistics, "Table E-1: Membership of Labor Unions, 1897–1950," *Handbook of Labor Statistics: 1950*, 1939, Google Books, accessed August 5, 2013.

33. Jensen, *Nonferrous Metals Industry Unionism*, 270–271, 274–279.

34. Eric Arneson, ed., *Encyclopedia of U.S. and Working Class History, vol. 1* (New York: Routledge, 2007), 1246.

35. Arneson, *Encyclopedia of U.S.*, 41.

36. James J. Lorence, *The Suppression of Salt of the Earth* (Albuquerque: University of New Mexico Press, 1999), 45–46.

37. Ellen R. Baker, *On Strike and On Film: Mexican American Families and Blacklisted Filmmakers in Cold War America* (Chapel Hill: The University of North Carolina Press, 2007), 1.

38. Baker, *On Strike and On Film*, 178.

39. James J. Lorence, "Mexican American Workers, Clinton Jencks, and Mine-Mill Social Activism in the Southwest, 1945–1952," in *Labor's Cold War: Local Politics in a Global Context*, edited by Shelton Stromquist (Urbana: University of Illinois Press, 2008), 218.

40. "Clinton Jencks Biographical Sketch," 6, Clinton E. Jencks Collection, within the WFM/IUMMSW archives.

41. Ellen Schrecker, *Many are the Crimes: McCarthyism in America* (Princeton, NJ: Princeton University Press, 1998), 358.

42. Jensen, *Nonferrous Metals Industry Unionism*.

43. Schrecker, *Many are the Crimes*, xii.

44. Bruce E. Kaufman, "John R. Commons and the Wisconsin School on Industrial Relations Strategy and Policy." *Industrial and Labor Relations Review* 57, no. 1 (2003): 8, https://www.jstor.org/stable/3590979.

45. Schrecker, *Many are the Crimes*, 310.

46. In 1999, Lorence's *The Suppression of Salt of the Earth* examined the process that led to the film's blacklisting. A biography Lorence wrote with Jencks's full cooperation, *Palomino: Clinton Jencks and Mexican-American Unionism in the American Southwest* (Urbana: University of Illinois Press, 2013). Baker's 2007 *On Strike and On Film* included a history of Jencks, the *Salt of the Earth* strike and film, as well as information gathered from her own interviews with the some of the strike's participants, which shifted her focus toward the key roles women played in the strike, including Virginia Jencks. In 2019, Raymond Caballero's *McCarthyism vs. Clinton*

Jencks (Norman: University of Oklahoma Press, 2019) examined the historical context surrounding the 1957 Supreme Court decision in *Jencks v. the United States*.

47. Bosley Crowther, "'Salt of the Earth' Opens at the Grand: Filming Marked by Violence," *New York Times*, March 15, 1954; "'Salt of the Earth' Back," *New York Times*, November 1, 1965, www.nytimes.com.

48. "Scope and Contents," Western Federation of Miners/International Union of Mine, Mill & Smelter Workers collection, https://archives.colorado.edu/repositories/2/resources/225, accessed February 7, 2020.

49. Lorence, *Palomino*, 8–9.

50. Memo from M. E. Travis to Mike Solski, June 12, 1983, Box 951, 2, WFM/IUMMSWU.

51. Memo from M. E. Travis, 3.

52. Letter from M. E. Travis to Mike Solski, August 1, 1983, Box 951, 1 and 2, WFM/IUMMSWU.

53. Travis interview, Box 951, 192, WFM/IUMMSWU.

54. Travis interview, 194–195.

55. Travis interview, 209.

56. Letters to Mike Solski from Maurice Travis, June 12, 1983 and August 1, 1983, Box 941, WFM/IUMMSW.

57. Letters to Mike Solski.

58. Letter from Travis to Solski, August 1, 1983, 2-3, WFM/IUMMSWU.

59. Solski and Smaller, *Mine Mill*, 9–10.

60. Solski and Smaller, *Mine Mill*, 9, 118.

61. Matin Vauml Duberman, *Paul Robeson* (New York: Alfred A. Knopf, 1988), 342.

62. For anyone unfamiliar with Robeson, I recommend Googling "Paul Robeson Old Man River;" the first hit will probably be him singing that song from the 1936 film *Show Boat*. If there has ever been a more glorious bass captured forever on film, I do not know who that would be.

63. Dubofsky, *We Shall Be All*, 484.

64. Melvyn Dubofsky and Foster Rhea Dulles, *Labor in America: A History*, 7th ed. (Wheeling, IL: Harland Davidson, Inc., 1999), 352–353.

65. The company is still undergoing liquidation. The current RMFC president, who self identifies as a gadfly contrarian, has been running the company since the early 1970s, and he revels in that permanent liquidation company status.

66. I took this photo of a publicity flyer the W. Colston Leigh, Inc., Agency must have sent out to publicize Roche as a speaker, 8-2, Roche papers.

67. Letter to Roche from the W. Colston Leigh, Inc., Agency, March 19, 1947, 8-2, Roche papers.

68. Richard P. Mulcahy, *A Social Contract for the Coal Fields: The Rise and Fall of the United Mine Workers of America Welfare and Retirement Fund* (Knoxville: The University of Tennessee Press, 2000).

69. Joseph E. Finley, *The Corrupt Kingdom: The Rise and Fall of the United Mine Workers* (New York: Simon and Schuster, 1972), 162.

70. Dubofsky and Van Tine, *John L. Lewis*, 511.

71. Mulcahy, *A Social Contract*, 40–41.

72. Dubofsky and Van Tine, *John L. Lewis*, 510.

73. Mulcahy, *A Social Contract*, 43, 130.

74. Robert H. Zieger, *John L. Lewis: Labor Leader* (Boston: Twayee Publishers, 1988), 181.

75. Mulcahy, *A Social Contract*, 150–151.

76. Finley, *The Corrupt Kingdom*, 234–235, 256–259.

77. Finley, *The Corrupt Kingdom*, 201.

78. Finley, *The Corrupt Kingdom*, 200–201, 204.

79. Here are some of those sources: Tillie Fong, "Capitalist and Humanitarian: Coal Mine Owner Fought for Workers' Rights," *Rocky Mountain News* (Denver, CO), July 13, 1999; Marjorie Hornbein, "Josephine Roche: Social Worker and Coal Operator," *The Colorado Magazine*, 53 (summer 1976): 243–260; Jeanette G. Carrol, "Josephine Aspinwall Roche: Industrialist—Crusader—Humanitarian," 3, http://color adowomeninhistory.org/contents/roche.html, accessed September 8, 2004; McGinn, *A Wide-Awake Woman*; I know Ms. McGinn, and she also in the early 2000s would perform a one-woman performance as Roche. She made a video about Roche that was posted on YouTube to celebrate the opening of the Josephine Roche affordable senior housing complex in Lafayette entitled "Boulder County Department of Housing and Human Service: The Story of Josephine Roche," October 19, 2012, http://www.youtube.comwatch?v=S4h8eXF4deU, accessed June 30, 2013; Vassar also has a brief biography of Roche, and it has been altered somewhat over the years as I have done my research. The first time I checked it, the entry said the United Mine Workers had waged the 1927–1928 Colorado Coal strike, a mistake that has been fixed. The most recent example of an article praising Roche that I have found is this one: Ellen Terrell, "Josephine Aspinwall Roche: A Changemaker You've Likely Never Heard of!" *Inside Adams: Science Technology & Business* (blog), Library of Congress, March 22, 2019, https://blogs.loc.gov/inside _adams/2019/03/josephine-aspinwall-roche-a-changemaker-youve-likely-never -heard-of/, accessed November 16, 2020.

80. Smith, *Once a Coal Miner*; Lowell May and Richard Myers, eds., *Slaughter in Serene: The Columbine Coal Strike Reader* (Denver, CO: Bread and Roses Workers' Cultural Center, 2005); Glenny, "A History of Labor Disputes"; Harry O. Lawson,

"The Colorado Coal Strike of 1927–1928," master's thesis, University of Colorado, 1950 (both of these masters' theses are in the University of Colorado at Boulder archives); McClurg, "The Colorado Coal Strike"; McClurg, "Labor Organization in the Coal Mines"; Ronald McMahan, " 'Rang-U-Tang': The I.W.W. and the 1927 Colorado Coal Strike," in *At the Point of Production: A Local History of the I.W.W*, edited by Joseph R. Conlin.

81. For example, Muncy only briefly examines one, conflicting rationale that challenged Roche's glowing, self-promoting story regarding her 1931 "job sharing" program.

82. Muncy, *Relentless Reformer*, 291.

83. Muncy, *Relentless Reformer*, 292.

84. Muncy, *Relentless Reformer*, 285.

85. Muncy, *Relentless Reformer*, 287.

86. Muncy, *Relentless Reformer*, 288.

Chapter 10: Trying to Remember the Columbine but Still Remembering Ludlow

1. Fred W. Thompson and Patrick Murfin, *The I.W.W.: Its First Seventy Years, 1905–1975* (Chicago: Industrial Workers of the World, 1976), 201. This book is an updated reprint of the 1955 version; Letter from C. E. Setzer to W. H. Westman, February 7, 1956; Letter from C. E. Setzer to R. L. Kurland February 20, 1956, Box 20, 21-3, IWW archives.

2. McClurg, "The Colorado Coal Strike," 68–92; Charles J. Bayard, "The 1927–1928 Colorado Coal Strike," *Pacific Historical Review* XXXII, no. 3 (August 1963): 235–250.

3. Undated letter from Joyce Kornbluh to Carey McWilliams. At the time, McWilliam edited *The Nation*, and Kornbluh was describing to him that she had just secured a contract for her book, so maybe this was 1962 or 1963, 23-7, IWW archives; Joseph R. Conlin, ed., *At the Point of Production: The Local History of the I.W.W.* (Westport, CT: Greenwood Press, 1981), vii–viii.

4. Melvyn Dubofsky interviewed Thompson for *We Shall be All*; Kornbluh's research record and correspondence for her book are included in the IWW archives; and David Roediger interviewed Thompson for his book *Fellow Worker: The Life of Fred Thompson* (Chicago: Charles H. Kerr Publishing Company, 1993).

5. Bryan D. Palmer, "A City Kid's View of Working-Class History: An Interview with Melvyn Dubofsky," *Labor: Studies in Working-Class History of the Americas* 7, no. 2 (Summer 2010), 76.

6. Letter from A. S. Embree to Joseph Wagner, Chairman of the General Executive Board, July 6, 1928, 96–10, IWW archives.

7. Letter from A. S. Embree to F. W. [Fred] Thompson, July 12, 1928, 96–11, IWW archives.

8. GEB Minutes, 96–10, 96–11, IWW archives.

9. "Report of Audit, July 17, 1925, to March 31, 1928," by Rowland, Thomas & Company, "Certified Public Accountants, Butte & Billings, Montana," 51–21, IWW archives.

10. 96–15, 96–16, IWW archives.

11. General Executive Board #28 Newsletter, July 15, 1929, communication from Kristen Svanum to W. H. Westman, the GEB Chairman, Box 8, Series II, IWW archives.

12. Circular letter from Kristen Svanum to W. H. Westman about A. S. Embree (who, once again, was suspended from the IWW), July 18, 1929, Box 8, Series II, IWW archives.

13. GEB Bulletin #29, August 1, 1929, Box 8, Series II, IWW archives.

14. Letter from Lee Tulin to GEB, December 15, 1929, Box 8, Series II, IWW archives.

15. Letter from A. S. Embree to F. W. [Fred] Thompson, July 12, 1928, 96–11, IWW archives.

16. Roediger, *Fellow Worker*, 62.

17. Letter from Tom Connors to Herbert Mahler, July 15, 1931, IWW archives, 129–11; also, *Workers' Defense* 1, no. 1, the "Official Organ of the General Defense Committee," a newsletter, was published in October of 1931, 129–21, IWW archives.

18. GEB Minutes, 1933, 7–14, IWW archives.

19. Andrew J. Dunar and Dennis McBride, *Building Hoover Dam: An Oral History of the Great Depression* (Reno: University of Nevada Press, 1993), 47–56, 113–114, 264, 307; GEB Minutes, 1933, 7–14, IWW archives.

20. Thompson and Murfin, *The I.W.W.*, 153.

21. Personal memoir from Duffy Allander Parker, Lafayette (Colorado) Public Library.

22. Letter from A. S. Embree to Joseph Wagner, Chairman of the General Executive Board, July 6, 1928, 96–10, IWW archives.

23. Roediger, *Fellow Worker*, 7.

24. Roediger, *Fellow Worker*, 7.

25. Alessandro Portelli, *The Death of Luigi Trastulli and Other Stories: Form and Meaning in Oral History* (Albany: State University of New York Press, 1991), 50.

26. Daniel L. Schacter, *The Seven Sins of Memory: How the Mind Forgets and Remembers* (Boston: Houghton Mifflin Company, 2001), 151.

27. Roediger, *Fellow Worker*, 62.

28. Bryan D. Palmer, *James P. Cannon and the Origins of the American Revolutionary Left, 1890–1928* (Urbana: University of Illinois Press, 2007), 262.

29. Portelli, *The Death of Luigi Trastulli*.

30. Roediger, *Fellow Worker*, 62.

31. Letter from Fred W. Thompson to Bob Rossi, December 10, 1981, Box 9–12, Frederick W. Thompson Collection.

32. Letter from Fred W. Thompson to Bob Rossi, December 10, 1981, Box 9–12, Frederick W. Thompson Collection.

33. Conlin, *At the Point of Production*, vii–viii.

34. Conlin, *At the Point of Production*, vii–viii.

35. Letter from Thompson to Rochelle (no last name, but from the context, she appears to be the editor of the IWW newspaper), December 10, 1981, 9–12, Thompson papers.

36. Roediger, *Fellow Worker*, 8.

37. *Roots*, aired January 23–30, 1977, on ABC, "*Roots*: The Most Important TV Show Ever?" British Broadcasting Network (BBC), June 1, 2016, https://www.bbc.com/culture/article/20160602-roots-the-most-important-tv-show-ever.

38. Testimony Regarding Staffing before Hearings before the Subcommittee on Education, Arts and Humanities of the Committee on Labor and Human Resources, 96th Congress, 1st Session, June 27, 1979, 262, accessed June 22, 2022, from the Hathi Trust Library, https://catalog.hathitrust.org/Record/011342669. In his prepared statement, National Endowment for the Humanities chair Joseph D. Duffey stated that funding requests had increased as a consequence of "the reawakened interest Americans have in their 'roots,'" an interest reaching "beyond narrow genealogical concerns to a new and changed perception of the whole society and how various groups shape and contribute to this process." Jeffrey K. Olick, Vered Vinitzky-Seroussi, and Daniel Levy, eds., *The Collective Memory Reader* (New York: Oxford University Press, 2011), 3.

39. National Endowment for the Humanities, *Second Annual Report, Fiscal Year 1967* (Washington, DC: US Government Printing Office, 1968).

40. Susan Boren, *Arts, Humanities, and Museum Services: Background, Funding, and Issues*, November 15, 2006, CRS Report for Congress, received through the CRS Web, RL33725 (Washington, DC: Congressional Research Office), 4–8, accessed June 22, 2022 from Every CRS Report, https://www.everycrsreport.com/files/2006 1115_RL33725_fec2398ee2d63c1f448d02f71ad6edada8708e32.pdf.

41. National Endowment for the Humanities, "The Cultural Explosion: The Hunger for Humanities," *Thirteenth Annual Report of the National Endowment for the Humanities* (Washington, DC: Government Printing Office, 1978), 5.

42. "Jimmy Carter: A President of Peace," Academy of Achievement, A Museum of Living History, updated March 26, 2011, 2, http://www.achievement.org/autodoc/page/caroint-2; "Things You Never Asked," *Time*, November 27, 1978, http://www.time.com/time/magazine/article/0,9171,9164467,00.html.

43. Frank Freidel, "Backlogging," *New York Times*, June 2, 1976, https://www.nytimes.com/1976/06/02/archives/backlogging.html?searchResultPosition=1.

44. National Endowment for the Humanities, "The Cultural Explosion," 6.

45. Lowell May and Richard Myers, eds., *Slaughter in Serene: The Columbine Coal Strike Reader* (Denver, CO: Bread and Roses Workers Cultural Center and the Industrial Workers of the World, 2005).

46. Sampson interviewed Mrs. Peter Ross, the Beranek's daughter, on January 15, 1970. That means she would have been twenty years old in 1927 and seventy years old when interviewed.

47. Forrest A. Walker, *The Civil Works Administration: An Experiment in Federal Work Relief, 1933–1934* (New York: Garland Publishing, Inc, 1979), ii.

48. Lafayette resident Frank Archuleta worked with Rachel Hansen, who works for the City of Lafayette (Colorado) and others to help bring attention to this silenced event in Lafayette's history. This is a link to the exhibit at The Collective: https://www.lafayetteco.gov/DocumentCenter/View/29221/1934-Pool-Exhibit-Complete-compressed, accessed November 7, 2020.

49. "Mary Borstnick, interviewed by Donna Carbone," Tape #1044, transcription, 1983, Lafayette (Colorado) Public Library.

50. "Dorothy Estaneous [*sic*] Fleming, interviewed by Effie Amicarella," Tape #1046 (transcribed), May 7, 1980, Lafayette Public Library.

51. "Dorothy Estaneous [*sic*] Fleming, interviewed by Effie Amicarella," Tape #1046 (transcribed), May 7, 1980, Lafayette Public Library.

52. "Denies Jury Trial to Miners," *Lafayette Leader* (Colorado) VII, no. 23, July 7, 1911, Colorado Historic Newspapers Collection, https://www.coloradohistoricnewspapers.org/?a=d&d=LFL19110707-01.2.3&srpos=13&e=01-01-1911-31-12-1911--en-20--1-byDA-img-txIN%7ctxCO%7ctxTA-United+Mine+Workers-------0-Boulder-Lafayette---.

53. Bill Boas, "Borrego Has Seen History Evolve," (no newspaper title) December 18, 1985, 27, Andy Borrego file, Lafayette (Colorado) Public Library.

54. "Andy Borrego, interviewed by Donna Carbone," Tape #1044 (transcribed), 1983, 2, Lafayette Public Library.

55. "Andy Borrego, interviewed by Donna Carbone," 5.

56. Letter from A. S. Embree to F. W. [Fred] Thompson, July 12, 1928, 96–11, IWW archives.

57. Letter from A. S. Embree to F. W. [Fred] Thompson, 4.

58. "Columbine Mine Program," Tape #1086 (transcribed), November 19, 1988, Lafayette (Colorado) Public Library.

59. "Transcribed Interview with Walt Celinski," May 1976, Lafayette (Colorado) Public Library.

60. Alexander Stille, "Prospecting for Truth in the Ore of Memory," *New York Times*, March 10, 2001, www.nytimes.com.

61. Alessandro Portelli, *The Death of Luigi Trastulli*, 50.

62. Guide to the Eric Margolis Coal Project (1974–1984), 2, Special Collections, Archives and Preservation, University of Colorado Boulder. In some places, the collection is called the Eric Margolis Coal Project, and in their research, it is called the Colorado Coal Project. I have chosen to cite it as the latter, to acknowledge the work also done by Ronald McMahan. There is a bit of a sordid story here, so here goes. When I first viewed the collection, it was very clearly named the Eric Margolis Colorado Coal Project, and to use it required written permission from Margolis. I emailed him, got permission, and Margolis very generously sent me some additional links to articles he had written about that work. However, the more interview transcripts I read, the more I realized Margolis had a partner, and I figured out his name was Ronald McMahan. Through some Google-stalking, I figured out that McMahan lived in Boulder, and he very graciously met with me. We had a very interesting talk. Among many of the topics we discussed, McMahan said that after he and Margolis graduated, Margolis pursued the life of an academic and McMahan went into business, so he did not care that Margolis took all the credit for the project, because Margolis needed it for tenure, and McMahan did not. I could see him bristling, however, so I must have sparked a long-suppressed resentment. Afterward, I forwarded McMahan's personal information to David Hays, the University of Colorado Boulder archivist, who contacted McMahan. Subsequently, McMahan paid to have much of this collection digitized. He also reshot Bill Moyers' *Out of the Depths* television documentary and literally reinserted himself into the footage. (He had been cut out.) Here is a link to those digitized resources, which include the recut documentary: https://cudl.colorado.edu/luna/servlet. I think it is interesting that McMahan was the interviewer asking about the 1927–1927 Colorado Coal Strike, because he grew up in Lafayette. His grandfather was a Greek immigrant who had arrived in Colorado during the long strike and died in a grisly coalmining accident in the 1940s. Surely his grandfather participated in the 1927–1928 strike, but even when McMahan re-edited *Out of the Depths*, perhaps not wanting to do additional research, he kept the focus on Ludlow.

63. The Colorado Coal Project, Ronald McMahan interview with the Amicarella brothers, 7-3, 16–17, Special Collections, Archives and Preservation, University of Colorado Boulder.

64. Eric Margolis, "Video Ethnography: Toward a Reflexive Paradigm for Documentary," 12. Margolis sent me this article as an email attachment as a response to an email query I sent him about this project. It is accessible via his website at Arizona State University where he is a professor in the education department, but the article was originally published in the journal *Jump Cut* as "Video Ethnography" in 1994, 122–131, https://visualethnography.me/articles/video-ethnography-toward -a-reflexive-paradigm-for-documentary/.

65. Margolis, "Video Ethnography," 13.

66. A great source on Nixon's pointed strategies aimed at appealing to organized labor can be found in Jefferson Cowie, *Stayin' Alive: The 1970s and the Last Days of the Working Class* (New York: The New Press, 2012).

67. These films recorded on video cassettes can be checked out at the Lafayette Historical Society in Lafayette, Colorado. There is no additional information on the films to cite.

68. Transcribed interview with Beshoar, 06208-2, The Colorado Coal Project, 18–19.

69. Transcribed interview with Beshoar, 06208-2, The Colorado Coal Project, 14.

70. Transcribed interview with Beshoar, 06208-2, The Colorado Coal Project, 1, 29.

71. Transcribed interview with Beshoar, 06208-2, The Colorado Coal Project, 1, 29.

72. Transcribed interview with Beshoar, 06208-2, The Colorado Coal Project, 15.

73. Transcribed interview with Beshoar, 06208-2, The Colorado Coal Project, 16.

74. Transcribed interview with Beshoar, 06208-2, The Colorado Coal Project, 17.

75. Transcribed interview with Beshoar, 06208-2, The Colorado Coal Project, 9.

76. Transcribed interview with Beshoar, 06208-2, The Colorado Coal Project, 9.

77. Transcribed interview with Beshoar, 06208-2, The Colorado Coal Project, 10.

78. Transcribed interview with Beshoar, 06208-2, The Colorado Coal Project, 14.

79. Transcribed interview with Beshoar, 06208-2, The Colorado Coal Project, 12.

80. Transcribed interview with Beshoar, 06208-3, 17, 33, 8-2, The Colorado Coal Project.

81. See the entire transcripts of "Barron Beshoar #1, Wild Sound, 06238-1," The Colorado Coal Project, 7–8. As Margolis, McMahan, Beshoar, and their crew film, their conversations between and during takes are recorded and transcribed. Included in the transcription are highlighted, photocopied pages of *Out of the Depths* with time cues next to specific portions of the book that Beshoar read for the narrative documentary voice over.

82. Interview with Barron Beshoar, 3, 8–2 Interview with Barron Beshoar, #06228-1, The Colorado Coal Project.

83. Interview with Barron Beshoar, 25, 8-1, The Colorado Coal Project.

84. Interview with Mike Livoda, 23, The Colorado Coal Collection 10–7; Harold Black interview with Mike Livoda November 15, 1968, 8, 14, 18, 10-6, The Colorado Coal Collection.

85. "Barron Beshoar, Interview 132, Cassette #2, C," 1976, 10–11, The Colorado Coal Project.

86. Beshoar interview, #132-A, 35, The Colorado Coal Collection.

87. Beshoar, 06228-1, 2, 8-2, The Colorado Coal Collection.

88. One of many examples sprinkled throughout all the Beshoar interviews can be found in the following, "Barron Beshoar," Interview 132-A, 1976, 3, The Colorado Coal Project.

89. Beshoar, 06228-1, 38, 8-2, The Colorado Coal Collection.

90. Beshoar interview #132-A, The Colorado Coal Project, 35.

91. Beshoar interview #132-A, The Colorado Coal Project., 35–36.

92. "One Thousand Led by the I.W.W. Held Meeting Here Sunday," *Daily Camera* (Boulder, CO), November 21, 1927, 1.

93. Hilton Kramer, "Reagan Aides Discuss U.S. Role in Helping Arts and Humanities," *New York Times*, November 26, 1980, https://www.nytimes.com/1980/11/26/archives/reagan-aides-discuss-us-role-in-helping-arts-and-humanities.html?searchResultPosition=1; James Traub, "Aiding the Humanities: Arguing Ends and Means," *New York Times*, February 22, 1981, https://www.nytimes.com/1981/02/22/weekinreview/aiding-the-humanities-arguing-ends-and-the-means.html?searchResultPosition=1.

94. Kramer, "Reagan Aids Discuss U.S. Role"; Traub, "Aiding the Humanities."

95. Kramer, "Reagan Aids Discuss U.S. Role"; Traub, "Aiding the Humanities."

96. Kramer, "Reagan Aids Discuss U.S. Role"; Traub, "Aiding the Humanities."

97. Irvin Molotsky, "Head of Humanities Fund Assails 'Obscure' Studies," *New York Times*, November 21, 1982, www.nytimes.com.

98. Elaine Sciolino, "The 2000 Campaign: The Spouse; The Real Conservative in the Family," *New York Times*, July 26, 2000, www.nytimes.com.

99. For more on this debacle, read Gary B. Nash, Charlotte Crabtree, and Ross E. Dunn, *History on Trial: Culture Wars and the Teaching of the Past* (New York: Vintage Books, 1997).

100. On how this law and Cheney's role in the history debates has not only reduced the amount of time students spend on history in public schools but also influenced *"whose* history should be taught," see Diane Ravitch, *The Death and Life of the Great American School System: How Testing and Choice are Undermining Education* (New York: Basis Books, A Member of the Perseus Books Group, 2010), 17.

101. Lafayette Historical Society, *Lafayette, Colorado History: Treeless Plain to Thriving City, 1889–1989* (Dallas, TX: Curtis Media Corporation, 1990).

102. May and Myers, *Slaughter in Serene*.

103. "Columbine Memorial Fund," copy of fund record from the private files of Beth and James Hutchinson in Lafayette, Colorado.

104. James D. Hutchison, director, Lafayette, Colorado: Treeless Plain to Thriving City, Centennial History, 1889–1989 (Dallas, TX: Curtis Media Corporation, 1989), 26.

105. Video, Lafayette Historical Society in Lafayette, Colorado.

106. "IWW's Joe Hill Executed as Murderer 73 Years Ago: Ashes of Legendary Union Organizer, Martyr Turned Over to 'Wobblies,'" *Los Angeles Times*, November 20, 1988, www.articles.latimes.com/print/1988-11-20/news/mn-590_1_joe-hill-s -ashes.

107. Columbine memorial video, Lafayette (Colorado) Miners Museum.

Epilogue and Acknowledgments

1. Dave Cullen, *Columbine* (New York: Twelve, Hachette Book Group, 2009), 64, 151.

2. Cullen, *Columbine*, chapter 2: "Rebels," 150, 226–229, 277; chapter 52: "Quiet."

3. Robin Stein and Alexander Cardia, "Visual Investigations: State Investigation Fueled Flawed Understanding of Delays during Police Response in Uvalde," *New York Times*, October 12, 2022, https://www.nytimes.com/2022/10/12/us/uvalde -shooting-police-response-investigation.html.

4. Joanna Slater, "Alex Jones Ordered to Pay Nearly $1 Billion to Sandy Hook Families," *Washington Post*, October 12, 2022, https://www.washingtonpost.com /nation/2022/10/12/alex-jones-sandy-hook-verdict/.

5. Nicholas Goldberg, "The Long Reach of the Columbine Killers' Influence," *Los Angeles Times*, October 6, 2022, https://www.latimes.com/opinion/story/2022 -10-06/columbine-eric-harris-dylan-klebold-russia-school-shooting.

Bibliography

Archives

Arizona Memory Collection, Arizona State Library, Archives and Public
Records, History and Archives Division, Phoenix, Arizona

"Marriage Records," British Columbia Archives, Canada

John Brophy Collection, Catholic University, Washington, DC

Oscar Chapman Papers, within the Harry S. Truman Library and Museum,
Independence, Missouri

Denver Public Library, Denver, Colorado

Mary Donovan Hapgood Papers, Lilly Library, Indiana University, Bloomington,
Indiana

Powers Hapgood Papers, Lilly Library, Indiana University, Bloomington, Indiana

Allen Heist Papers, Southern California Library for Social Studies, Los Angeles,
California

Hefferly Collection, Special Collections & Archives, University of Colorado
Boulder Libraries

Beth and James Hutchinson private collection, Lafayette, Colorado

IWW Archives, Walter P. Reuther Library, Wayne State University, Detroit, Michigan

Clinton Jencks Collection, Special Collections & Archives, University of Colorado Boulder Libraries

Lafayette Historical Society, formerly Miners Museum, Lafayette, Colorado

Louisville Historical Museum, Louisville, Colorado

Benjamin Lindsey Papers, Library of Congress, Washington, DC

Mt. Allison University Libraries and Archives, Sackville, New Brunswick, Canada

National Archives Records Administration, College Park, Maryland

Josephine Roche Papers, Special Collections & Archives, University of Colorado Boulder Libraries

Steelworks Museum, Pueblo, Colorado

The Colorado Coal Project, Special Collections & Archives, University of Colorado Boulder Libraries

The University of Arizona, Tempe, Arizona

Fred Thompson Papers, Walter P. Reuther Library, Wayne State University, Detroit, Michigan

Oswald Garrison Villard Papers, Houghton Library, Harvard University

Western Federation of Miners/International Union of Mine, Mill and Smelter Workers, Special Collections & Archives, University of Colorado Boulder Libraries

"16 Persons injured as Strikers and State Guards Stage Wild Battle at I.W.W. Headquarters." *Rocky Mountain News* (Denver, CO), November 9, 1927.

"50 Cars Took Lafayette Strikers to Fremont County." *Daily Camera* (Boulder, CO), October 26, 1927.

"Adams Details Armed Guards to Strike Zone." *Rocky Mountain News* (Denver, CO), November 5, 1927.

"Adams Orders Armed Guards to Enforce Anti-Picketing Edict in Southern Colorado." *Rocky Mountain News* (Denver, CO), November 6, 1927.

Addams, Jane. *A New Conscience and an Ancient Evil.* New York: The Macmillan Company, 1912.

Albro, Ward S. *Always a Rebel: Ricardo Flores Magón and the Mexican Revolution.* Fort Worth: Texas Christian University, 1992.

"Amazon Leader and Other I.W.W. Jailed Today." *Daily Camera* (Boulder, CO), October 24, 1927.

"Amazons Jailed for Hurling Rocks." *Daily Camera* (Boulder, CO), October 22, 1927.

American Trade Union Delegation to the Soviet Union. *Russia After Ten Years: Report of the American Trade Union Delegation to the Soviet Union.* New York: International Publishers, 1927.

Andrews, Thomas G. *Killing for Coal: America's Deadliest Labor War.* Cambridge, MA: Harvard University Press, 2008.

"Another Miner at the Columbine Died From Shot by the Guard." *Daily Camera* (Boulder, CO), November 28, 1927.

Appier, Janis. *Policing Women: The Sexual Politics of Law Enforcements and the LAPD.* Philadelphia, PA: Temple University Press, 1998.

Arneson, Eric, ed. *Encyclopedia of U.S. and Working Class History*, Vol. 1. New York: Routledge, 2007. Accessed through Google Books, https://www.google.com/books/edition/Encyclopedia_of_U_S_Labor_and_Working_cl/zEWsZ81Bd3Y C?hl=en&gbpv=1&bsq=CIO%20purge.

Baily, Beth. *Sex in the Heartland.* Cambridge, MA: Harvard University Press, 1999.

Baker, Ellen R. *On Strike and On Film: Mexican American Families and Blacklisted Filmmakers in Cold War America.* Chapel Hill: The University of North Carolina Press, 2007.

Bayard, Charles J. "The 1927–1928 Colorado Coal Strike," *Pacific Historical Review* XXXII, no. 3 (August 1963): 235–250.

Beaton, Gail M. "The Widening Sphere of Women's Lives: The Literary Study and Philanthropic Work of Six Women's Clubs in Denver, 1881–1945." In *Women's Clubs of Denver.* Essays in Colorado History. Denver: Colorado Historical Society, 1993.

Beik, Mildred Allen. *The Miners of Windber: The Struggle of New Immigrants for Unionization, 1890s–1930s.* University Park: The Pennsylvania State University Press, 1998.

Benton-Cohen, Katherine. *Borderline Americans: Racial Division and Labor Sar in the Arizona Borderlands.* Cambridge, MA: Harvard University Press, 2009.

Beshoar, Barron B. *Out of the Depths: The Story of John R. Lawson, A Labor Leader.* Denver: The Colorado Labor Historical Committee of the Denver Trades and Labor Assembly, 1942.

"Blackhead Methodist Parish Birth Records (1842–1900)." NL GenWeb, Parish Records, Conception Bay North—Northern District. https://sites.rootsweb.com/~cannf/cbnorth_norbhuc2801, accessed July 21, 2022.

Blaisdell, Lowell L. *The Desert Revolution: Baja California, 1911.* Madison: The University of Wisconsin Press, 1962.

Boal, William M. "New Estimates of Paid-up Membership in the United Mine Workers, 1902–1929, by State and Province." *Labor History* 47, no. 4 (November 2006): 537–546.

Boren, Susan. *Arts, Humanities, and Museum Services: Background, Funding, and Issues.* November 15, 2006. CRS Report for Congress, received through the CRS Web, RL33725. Washington, DC: Congressional Research Office, 48. Accessed June 22,

2022, https://www.everycrsreport.com/files/20061115_RL33725_fec2398ee2d63c
1f448d02f71ad6edada8708e32.pdf.

"Boulder County Department of Housing and Human Service: The Story of
Josephine Roche." Narrated by Elinor McGinn. October 19, 2012, https://www
.youtube.com/watch?v=S4h8eXF4deU&t=986s.

Brier, Stephen, Bruce C. Levine, and Joshua Freeman, eds. *Who Built America?
Working People and the Nation's Economy, Politics, Culture and Society.* Vol. 2, *From
the Gilded Age to the Present.* American Social History Project. New York: Pantheon Books, 1992.

Brissenden, Paul Frederick. *The I.W.W.: A Study in American Syndicalism.* New York:
Columbia University, 1920.

Brophy, John. *A Miners' Life.* Madison: The University of Wisconsin Press, 1964.

Bureau of Labor Statistics. "Table E-I: Membership of Labor unions, 1897–1950." In
Handbook of Labor Statistics. Bureau of Labor Statistics, 1950, US Department of
Labor. Washington, DC: US Government Printing Office. https://www.google
.com/books/edition/Bulletin_of_the_United_States_Bureau_of/eR4JWlnkB28
C?hl=en&gbpv=1&dq=Bureau+of+Labor+Statistics,+Table+E-I:+Member
ship+of+labor+unions,+1897-1950&pg=PA139&printsec=frontcover.

"Burial of Columbine Dead Began at Lafayette Today." *Daily Camera* (Boulder, CO),
November 23, 1927.

Burns, Ken. *Unforgiveable Blackness: The Rise and Fall of Jack Johnson.* Public Broadcasting Service (PBS). Paramount, 2005, DVD, 214 min.

Bussel, Robert. *From Harvard to the Ranks of Labor: Powers Hapgood and the American
Working Class.* University Park: The Pennsylvania State University Press, 1999.

Byrkit, James W. *Forging the Copper Collar: Arizona's Labor-Management War, 1901–1921.*
Tucson: The University of Arizona Press, 1982.

Caballero, Raymond. *McCarthyism vs. Clinton Jencks.* Norman: University of Oklahoma Press, 2019.

Cameron, Ardis. *Radicals of the Worst Sort: Laboring Women in Lawrence, Massachusetts, 1860–1912.* Urbana: University of Illinois Press, 1993.

Carrol, Jeannette G. "Josephine Aspinwall Roche: Industrialist—Crusader
—Humanitarian." Colorado Women in History, accessed September 8, 2004.
http://coloradowomensinhistory.org/contents/roche.html (site discontinued).

Cohen, Lizabeth. *Making a New Deal: Industrial Workers in Chicago, 1919–1939.* Cambridge, MA: Harvard University Press, 1990.

Cohen, Lizabeth. *A Consumers' Republic: The Politics of Mass Consumption in Postwar
America.* New York: Alfred A. Knopf, 2008.

Columbine Memorial. Lafayette (Colorado) Historical Society, VCR tape, June 10,
1989.

"Columbine Mine Closed: Attack on Deputies of Weld County by Picketers Wins."
Daily Camera (Boulder, CO), November 14, 1927.

"Columbine Miners Were Threatened by Large Meeting of the Strikers." *Daily Camera* (Boulder, CO), November 8, 1927.

Conlin, Joseph R., ed. *At the Point of Production: A Local History.* Westport, CT: Greenwood Press, 1981.

Cowie, Jefferson. *Stayin' Alive: The 1970s and the Last Days of the Working Class.* New York: The New Press, 2012.

Creel, George. *How We Advertised America.* New York: Arno Press, 1972. Reprint, New York: Harper & Brothers, 1920.

Creel, George. *Rebel at Large: Recollections of Fifty Crowded Years.* New York: G. P. Putnam's Sons, 1947.

"Coroner's Inquest into the Deaths of John Eastenes and Nick Spanudakhis, November 22–23, 1927," Columbine Mine Massacre Collection (1927), 1-1, Special Collections & Archives, University of Colorado Boulder Libraries.

Cullen, Dave. *Columbine.* New York: Twelve, Hachette Book Group, 2009.

DeCaux, Len. *Labor Radical: From the Wobblies to the CIO.* Boston: Beacon Press, 1970.

"Denies Jury Trial to Miners." *Lafayette Leader* (Colorado) VII, no. 23, July 7, 1911.

Deutsch, Sarah. *No Separate Refuge: Culture, Class, and Gender on an Anglo-Hispanic Frontier in the American Southwest, 1880–1949.* New York: Oxford University Press, 1987.

Devine, Edward T., John Augustine Ryan, John A. Lapp, Denver Commission of Religious Forces, Federal Council of the Churches of Christ in America, Commission of the Church and Social Service, and National Catholic Welfare Council (US) Department of Social Action. *The Denver Tramway Strike of 1920: Report of an Investigation Made under the Auspices of the Denver Commission of Religious Forces, the Commission on the Church and Social Service of the Federal Council of the Churches of Christ in America, the Department of Social Action of the National Catholic Welfare Council.* Denver, CO: The Denver Commission of Religious Forces, 1921. Original book from the collection of the University of Michigan. https://archive.org/details/denvertramwaystooactigoog.

Donovan, Brian. *White Slave Crusades: Race, Gender, and Anti-Vice Activism, 1887–1917.* Urbana: University of Illinois Press, 2006.

Douglas, George H. *The Golden Age of the Newspaper.* Westport, CT: Greenwood Press, 1999.

Downey, Kirsten. *The Woman behind the New Deal.* Norwell, MA: Anchor Press, 2010.

Duberman, Matin Fauml. *Paul Robeson.* New York: Alfred A. Knopf, 1988.

Dubofsky, Melvyn. *We Shall Be All: A History of the Industrial Workers of the World.* Chicago: Quadrangle Books, 1969.

Dubofsky, Melvyn. *"Big Bill" Haywood.* New York: St. Martin's Press, 1987.

Dubofsky, Melvyn, and Foster Rhea Dulles. *Labor in America: A History.* 7th ed. Wheeling, IL: Harland Davidson, Inc., 1999.

Dubofsky, Melvyn, and Warren Van Tine. *John L. Lewis: A Biography*. Urbana: University of Illinois Press, 1986.

Dunar, Andrew J., and Dennis McBride. *Building Hoover Dam: An Oral History of the Great Depression*. Reno: University of Nevada Press, 1993.

Dunne, William F. "The Thirtieth Convention of the United Mine Workers of America." Originally published in *The Communist* 1, no. 1 (March 1927). Transcription markup by Brian Reed, Marxists Internet Archive, 2009. https://www.marxists.org/archive/dunne/1927/03/x01.htm.

Emmons, David M. *The Butte Irish: Class and Ethnicity in an American Mining Town, 1875–1925*. Urbana: University of Illinois Press, 1990.

"F. R. Palmer Held for Attack Made on State Officers and Militia." *Daily Times* (Longmont, CO), December 16, 1927.

Finley, Joseph E. *The Corrupt Kingdom: The Rise and Fall of the United Mine Workers*. New York: Simon and Schuster, 1972.

Fogelson, Robert M., and Richard E. Robenstein, eds. *Mass Violence in America*. New York: Arno Press & The New York Times, 1969. Reprint of Harrison George. *The I.W.W. Trial: Story of the Greatest Trial in Labors' History by One of the Defendants*, probably published by the IWW Press in Chicago in 1918.

Foner, Philip S. *Fellow Workers and Friends: I.W.W. Free-Speech Fights as Told by Participants*. Westport, CT: Greenwood Press, 1981.

Fones-Wolf, Ken, and Elizabeth Fones-Wolf. *Struggle for the Soul of the Postwar South: White Evangelical Protestants and Operation Dixie*. Urbana: University of Illinois Press, 2015.

Fong, Tillie. "Capitalist and Humanitarian: Coal Mine Owner Fought for Workers' Rights." *Rocky Mountain News* (Denver, CO), July 13, 1999.

Fox, Maier B. *United We Stand: The United Mine Workers of America, 1890–1990*. N.p.: United Mine Workers of America, 1990.

Frank, Dana. *Purchasing Power: Consumer Organizing, Gender and the Seattle Labor Movement, 1919–1929*. New York: Cambridge University Press, 1994.

Freidel, Frank. "Backlogging." *New York Times*, June 2, 1976, https://www.nytimes.com/1976/06/02/archives/backlogging.html?searchResultPosition=1.

"Fuel Company Head Dies at Home." *Rocky Mountain News* (Denver, CO), January 14, 1927.

Gambs, John S. *The Decline of the I.W.W.* New York: Columbia University Press, 1932.

Gitelman, Howard. *Legacy of the Ludlow Massacre*. Philadelphia: University of Pennsylvania Press, 1988.

Glenny, Hazel. "A History of Labor Disputes in the Northern Colorado Coal Mining Fields with Emphasis on the 1927–1928 Strike." Master's thesis, University of Colorado, 1938.

Goldberg, Nicholas. "The Long Reach of the Columbine Killers' Influence." *Los Angeles Times*, October 6, 2022, https://www.latimes.com/opinion/story/2022-10-06/columbine-eric-harris-dylan-klebold-russia-school-shooting.

Goldberg, Robert Alan. *Hooded Empire: The Ku Klux Klan in Colorado*. Urbana: University of Illinois Press, 1981.

Goldfield, Michael. "The Myth of Section 7(a): How the Coal Miners Organized," Presentation at the Labor and Working Class History Association Conference, New York, June, 2013.

Goldfield, Michael. *The Southern Key: Class, Race, and Radicalism in the 1930s and 1940s*. New York: Oxford University Press, 2020.

Goldfield, Michael, and Cody R. Melcher. "The Myth of Section 7(a): Workers Militancy, Progressive Labor Legislation, and the Coal Miners." *Labor: Studies in Working-Class History of the Americas* 16, no. 4 (2019): 49–65.

Goodykoontz, Colin B., ed. *Papers of Edward P. Costigan Relating to the Progressive Movement in Colorado, 1902–1927*. Boulder: University of Colorado, 1941.

Gorn, Elliott. *Mother Jones: The Most Dangerous Woman in America*. New York: Hill and Wang, 2002.

"Gov. Adams Expected to Send Units of Troops to Mines." *Daily Camera* (Boulder, CO), November 16, 1927.

"Gov. Adams Revives The State Law Enforcement Department." *Daily Camera* (Boulder, CO), November 4, 1927.

"Gov. Adams Tells Camera That Clemens Statement Issued Today is Absurd." *Daily Camera* (Boulder, CO), November 3, 1927.

Gray, Loraine, dir. *With Babies and Banners: Story of the Women's Emergency Brigade*. Produced by the Woman's Labor History Film Project. Aired 1978, on PBS. Now available on YouTube. https://www.youtube.com/watch?v=pa75V-tdBko.

Green, Archie. "Remembering Jack Fitch." In *Torching the Fink Books and Other Essays on Vernacular Culture*. Chapel Hill, The University of North Carolina Press, 2001.

Greenwald, Richard A. *The Triangle Fire, the Protocols of Peace, and Industrial Democracy in Progressive Era*. Philadelphia, PA: Temple University Press, 2005.

Griffith, Barbara S. *The Crisis of American Labor: Operation Dixie and the Defeat of the CIO*. Philadelphia, PA: Temple University Press, 1988.

Grittner, Frederick K. *White Slavery: Myth, Ideology, and American Law*. New York: Garland Publishing, Inc., 1990.

Gross, Kali N. *Colored Amazons: Crime, Violence, and Black Women in the City of Brotherly Love, 1880–1910*. Durham, NC: Duke University Press, 2006.

Gullette, A. V. "Eye-Witnesses Tell Story of Rioting in Walsenburg." *Rocky Mountain News* (Denver, CO), January 13, 1928.

Hall, Jacquelyn Dowd, James Leloudis, Robert Korstad, Mary Murphy, Lu Ann Jones, and Christopher B. Daly. *Like a Family: The Making of a Southern Cotton Mill World*. Chapel Hill: The University of North Carolina Press, 1987.

Hapgood, William P. *An Experiment in Industrial Democracy: The Results of Fourteen Years of Self-Government*. Self-published, Indianapolis, IN, 1930.

Hapgood, William Powers. *The Columbia Conserve Company: An Experiment in Workers' Management and Ownership*. The American Utopian Adventure. Philadelphia, PA: Porcupine Press, 1975.

"Hapgoods Acquitted of Inciting Coal Riot." *New York Times*, April 13, 1938, https://www.nytimes.com/1928/04/13/archives/hapgoods-acquitted-of-inciting-coal-riot-judge-directs-verdict-when.html?searchResultPosition=1.

Hart, John M. *Anarchism and the Mexican Working Class, 1860–1931*. Austin: University of Texas Press, 1987.

Hearings Before the Subcommittee on Education, Arts and Humanities of the committee on Labor and Human Resources. 96th Congress. 1st Session (June 26, 27 and 28, 1979). In Congressional Research Service (CRS), Report for Congress (RL33725), "Arts, Humanities, and Museum Services: Background, Funding, and Issues," November 15, 2006. Accessed through CRS web, CRS-19.

Higgins, Jenny. "19th Century Migration." Newfoundland and Labrador Heritage, 2008. www.heritage.nf.ca/society/19th_migration.html.

Higgins, Jenny, and Luke Callanan. "19th Century Communications and Transportation." Newfoundland and Labrador Heritage, 2008. www.heritage.nf.ca/society/19th_comm.html.

"Hoage Says Federation Won't Play with I.W.W." *Daily Camera* (Boulder, CO), October 18, 1927.

Hornbein, Marjorie. "Josephine Roche: Social Workers and Coal Operator." *The Colorado Magazine*, 53 (summer 1976): 243–260.

"Howat Pleas Fail in Supreme Court." *New York Times*, March 14, 1922, https://www.nytimes.com/1922/03/14/archives/howat-pleas-fail-in-supreme-court-appeals-against-sentences-for.html?searchResultPosition=1.

"Howdy! Said Governor Adams." *Denver Post*, October 28, 1927.

Hughes, Rupert. "Ben Lindsey's Holocaust." *Denver Post*, October 16, 1927, 8.

Hunter, Tera W. *To Joy My Freedom: Southern Black Women's Lives and Labors after the Civil War*. Cambridge, MA: Harvard University Press, 1997.

Hutchison, James D., dir. *Lafayette, Colorado: Treeless Plain to Thriving City, Centennial History, 1889–1989*. Dallas, TX: Curtis Media Corporation, 1989.

Huthmacher, J. Joseph. *Senator Robert F. Wagner and the Rise of Urban Liberalism*. New York: Atheneum, 1968.

"International Organization Takes Over Dependent Districts." *United Mine Workers Journal* XXVII, no. 42 February 15, 1917, 11.

Irons, Janet. *Testing the New Deal: The General Textile Strike of 1934 in the American South*. Urbana: University of Illinois Press, 2000.

"I.W.W. Amazons Lead Fray in Colorado Strike; Stone and Dare Guards, Men Staying Behind." *New York Times*, October 23, 1927, https://www.nytimes.com/1927/10/23/archives/iww-amazons-lead-fray-in-colorado-strike-stone-and-dare-guards-men.html?searchResultPosition=1.

"I.W.W. Ignored by the State at Pueblo Meet." *Daily Camera* (Boulder, CO), October 15, 1927.

"IWW's Joe Hill Executed as Murderer 73 Years Ago: Ashes of Legendary Union Organizer, Martyr Turned Over to 'Wobblies.'" *Los Angeles Times*, November 20, 1988. www.articles.latimes.com/print/1988-11-20/news/mn-590_1_joe-hill-s-ashes.

"Jacques Fined $100 and Pays up for Selling Booze." *Daily Camera* (Boulder, CO), October 24, 1927.

Jensen, Vernon H. *Nonferrous Metals Industry Unionism, 1934–1954: A Story of Leadership Controversy.* Ithaca, NY: Cornell University, 1954.

"Jimmy Carter: A President of Peace." Academy of Achievement, A Museum of Living History. Updated March 26, 2001. http://www.achievement.org/autodoc/page/caroint.

Kaufman, Bruce E. "John Commons and the Wisconsin School on Industrial Relations Strategy and Policy." *Industrial and Labor Relations Review* 57, no. 1 (October 2003): 3–30. https://www.jstor.org/stable/3590979.

Kelley, Robin D. G. *Hammer and Hoe: Alabama Communists During the Great Depression.* Chapel Hill: The University of North Carolina Press, 1990.

Kemme, Emily. "A Look at Windsor Colo.'s Sugar Beet Heritage." *The Fence Post* (Windsor, CO), September 4, 2018. https://thefencepost.com/news/a-look-at-windsor-colo-s-sugar-beet-heritage.

Kennedy, David M. *Over Here: The First World War and American Society.* New York: Oxford University Press, 1980, 59–66.

Kornbluh, Joyce L., ed. *Rebel Voices: An I.W.W. Anthology.* Ann Arbor: University of Michigan Press, 1964.

Kramer, Hilton. "Reagan Aides Discuss U.S. Role in Helping Arts and Humanities." *New York Times*, November 26, 1980, https://www.nytimes.com/1980/11/26/archives/reagan-aides-discuss-us-role-in-helping-arts-and-humanities.html?searchResultPosition=1.

"Labor and Farmers Indorse Adams for Office of Governor." October 21, 1926, *Rocky Mountain News* (Denver, CO).

"Labor Unions During the Great Depression and New Deal." Library of Congress, n.d. Accessed February 24, 2021. https://www.loc.gov/classroom-materials/united-states-history-primary-source-timeline/great-depression-and-world-war-ii-1929-1945/labor-unions-during-great-depression-and-new-deal.

Ladd-Taylor, Molly. *Mother-Work: Women, Child Welfare, and the State, 1890–1930.* Urbana: University of Illinois Press, 1995.

Lafayette Historical Society. *Lafayette, Colorado History: Treeless Plain to Thriving City: Centennial History, 1889–1989.* Vol. 1. Dallas, TX: Curtis Media Corporation, 1990.

Larsen, Charles. *The Good Fight: The Remarkable Life and Times of Judge Ben Lindsey.* Chicago: Quadrangle Books, 1972.

Lauck, W. Jett. *Political and Industrial Democracy, 1776–1926*. New York: Funk and Wagnalls, 1926.

Lauck, W. Jett. "Coal Labor Legislation: A Case." *The Annals of the American Academy of Political Science* 184, no. 1 (March 1936): 130–137. https://doi.org/10.1177/000271623618400119.

Lawson, Harry O. "The Colorado Coal Strike of 1927–1928." Master's thesis, University of Colorado, 1950.

"Leaders Claim Protest Walkout not Under Law Exacting 30-Day Notice." *Pueblo Chieftan*, August 7, 1927, 2.

Leeder, Elaine. *The Gentle General: Rose Pesotta, Anarchist and Labor Organizer*. Albany: State University of New York Press, 1993.

"Lewis Calls Strike 100% Effective." *New York Times*, April 6, 1922, https://www.nytimes.com/1922/04/06/archives/lewis-calls-strike-100-effective-miners-president-arrives-to-take.html?searchResultPosition=1.

Lewis, John L. *The Miners' Fight for American Standards*. Indianapolis, IN: The Bell Publishing Company, 1925.

Lewis, John P. "On Ranger System 'Smokes Out' Shoup." *Rocky Mountain News* (Denver, CO), October 13, 1926, 1.

"Lewis Ousts Howat for Outlaw Strike." *New York Times*, October 14, 1921, https://www.nytimes.com/1921/10/14/archives/lewis-ousts-howat-for-outlaw-strike-union-chief-suspends-kansas.html?searchResultPosition=1.

Lichtenstein, Nelson. *Walter Reuther: The Most Dangerous Man in Detroit*. Urbana: University of Illinois Press, 1995.

Lindsey, Ben B. "The Moral Revolt." *Red Book*, February 1927.

Lindsey, Ben B., and Wainwright Evans. *The Companionate Marriage*. Garden City, NY: Garden City Publishing Co., Inc., 1929.

"Lindsey Is Ousted as Denver Judge." *New York Times*, January 24, 1927, https://www.nytimes.com/1927/01/25/archives/lindsey-is-ousted-as-denver-judge-colorado-supreme-court-rules-he.html?searchResultPosition=2.

Long, Priscilla. *Where the Sun Never Shines: A History of America's Bloody Coal Industry*. New York: Paragon House, 1989.

"Longmont Sugar Factory Allowed a Tax Reduction." *Daily Camera* (Boulder, CO), October 19, 1927.

Lorence, James J. *The Suppression of Salt of the Earth*. Albuquerque: University of New Mexico Press, 1999.

Lorence, James J. "Mexican American Workers, Clinton Jencks, and Mine-Mill Social Activism in the Southwest, 1945–1954." In *Labor's Cold War: Local Politics in a Global Context*. Urbana: University of Illinois Press, 2008.

Lorence, James J. *Palomino: Clinton Jencks and Mexican-American Unionism in the American Southwest*. Urbana: University of Illinois Press, 2013.

"Loud Threats Made at Dead Miner's Grave." *New York Times*, March 3, 1928, https://www.nytimes.com/1928/03/03/archives/loud-threats-made-at-dead-miners-grave-detectives-induce-friend-of.html?searchResultPosition=1.

Lukas, J. Anthony. *Big Trouble: A Murder in a Small Western Town Sets off a Struggle for the Soul of America*. New York: Simon and Schuster, 1997.

Lynd, Staughton, ed. *"We are All Leaders": The Alternative Unionism of the Early 1930s*. Urbana: University of Illinois Press, 1996.

"Machine Gun and a Few Troopers Stood Off Picket at Columbine." *Daily Camera* (Boulder, CO), November 16, 1927.

Malone, Michael P. *The Battle for Butte: Mining and Politics on the Northern Frontier, 1867–1906*. Helena: Montana Historical Society Press, 1981.

Margolis, Eric. "Video Ethnography: Toward a Reflexive Paradigm for Documentary." Visual Ethnography. https://visualethnography.me/articles/video-ethnography-toward-a-reflexive-paradigm-for-documentary/. First published in *Jump Cut* 39, 1994: 122–131.

Martelle, Scott. *Blood Passion: The Ludlow Massacre and Class War in the American West*. Piscataway, NJ: Rutgers University Press, 2007.

Martin, George. *Madam Secretary: Frances Perkins*. Boston: Houghton Mifflin Company, 1976.

May, Elaine Tyler. *Great Expectations: Marriage and Divorce in Post-Victorian America*. Chicago: The University of Chicago Press, 1980.

May, Lowell, and Richard Myers, eds. *Slaughter in Serenen: The Columbine Coal Strike Reader*. Denver, CO: Bread and Roses Workers Cultural Center and the Industrial Workers of the World, 2005.

"Mayor and Citizens of Walsenburg Broke Up Headquarters of I.W.W. and Notified the Members of Organization to Stay Out of Town." *Daily Camera* (Boulder, CO), October 17, 1927.

McAdams, Dan P. *The Stories We Live By: Personal Myths and the Making of the Self*. New York: The Guilford Press, 1993.

McAdams, Dan P. *The Redemptive Self: Stories Americans Live By*. New York: Oxford University Press, 2006.

McAdams, Dan P., Ruthellen Josselson, and Amia Lieblich. *Up Close and Personal: The Teaching and Learning of Narrative Research*. Washington, DC: American Psychological Association, 2003.

McCartin, James A. *Labor's Great War: The Struggle for Industrial Democracy and the Origins of Modern American Labor Relations, 1912–1921*. Chapel Hill: The University of North Carolina Press, 1997.

McClurg, Donald. "Labor Organization in the Coal Mines of Colorado, 1878–1933." Dissertation, University of California, 1959. Available at the Carnegie Branch Library, Boulder, Colorado.

McClurg, Donald J. "The Colorado Coal Strike of 1927—Tactical Leadership of the IWW," *Labor History* 1, no. 1 (1963): 68–92.

McGinn, Elinor. *A Wide-Awake Woman: Josephine Roche in the Era of Reform*. Denver: Colorado Historical Society, 2002.

McGovern, George S., and Leonard F. Guttridge. *The Great Coalfield War*. Boulder: University Press of Colorado, 1972.

McMahan, Ronald. "'Rang-U-Tang': The I.W.W. and the 1927 Colorado Coal Strike." In *At the Point of Production: A Local History*. Westport, CT: Greenwood Press, 1981.

"Meetings of Strikers at Denver on Sunday When Speakers Denounced Gov. Adams for Using Guardsmen and Jailing I.W.W." *Daily Camera* (Boulder, CO), November 14, 1927.

"Merle D. Vincent for Operators Says Operators Will Obey Law and Strikers Are Violating It." *Daily Camera* (Boulder, CO), October 19, 1927, 3.

"Mexican Workers in Beet Fields Being Organized." *Daily Camera* (Boulder, CO), October 11, 1927.

"Mexico May be Asked to Take Action." *Rocky Mountain News* (Denver, CO), January 5, 1928.

"Mine Union Leader Guilty of Killing." *New York Times*, April 15, 1928, https://www.nytimes.com/1928/04/15/archives/mine-union-leader-guilty-of-killing-jury-convicts-bonita-of.html?searchResultPosition=2.

"Miners Will Reject Peace Offer." *Rocky Mountain News* (Denver, CO), January 2, 1928.

"Miners to Stand by Howat." *New York Times*, November 16, 1921, https://www.nytimes.com/1921/11/16/archives/miners-to-stand-by-howat-will-refuse-to-return-to-work-in-kansas.html?searchResultPosition=1.

Molotsky, Irvin. "Head of Humanities Fund Assails 'Obscure' Studies." *New York Times*, November 21, 1982, https://www.nytimes.com/1982/11/21/us/head-of-humanities-fund-assails-obscure-studies.html?searchResultPosition=1.

Montgomery, David. *The Fall of the House of Labor*. New York: Cambridge University Press, 1987.

Morgan, Ted. *A Covert Life: Jay Lovestone, Communist, Anti-Communist, and Spymaster*. New York: Random House, 1999.

"Most of Arrested Pickets in Southern Colorado 'Lost'." *Rocky Mountain News* (Denver, CO), November 9, 1927.

"Mrs. McCready of Lafayette Kidnaped [*sic*] for a Short Ride." *Daily Camera* (Boulder, CO), October 14, 1927.

Mulcahy, Richard P. *A Social Contract for the Coal Fields: The Rise and Fall of the United Mine Workers of America Welfare and Retirement Fund*. Knoxville: The University of Tennessee Press, 2000.

"Mullen Offers to Provide for Eastenes Orphans." *Daily Camera* (Boulder, CO), November 28, 1927.

Muncy, Robyn. *Creating a Female Dominion in American Reform, 1890–1935*. New York: Oxford University Press, 1991.

Muncy, Robyn. *Relentless Reformer: Josephine Roche and Progressivism in Twentieth-Century America*. Princeton, NJ: Princeton University Press, 2014.

Myers, Richard. "The Women of the Twenties Coal Strikes," In *Slaughter in Serene: The Columbine Strike Reader*, edited by Lowell May and Richard Myers. Denver, CO: Bread and Roses Workers' Cultural Center & the Industrial Workers of the World, 2005.

National Endowment for the Humanities. *Second Annual Report, Fiscal Year 1967*. Washington, DC: US Government Printing Office, 1968.

National Endowment for the Humanities. "The Cultural Explosion: The Hunger for Humanities." *Thirteenth Annual Report of the National Endowment for the Humanities*. Washington, DC: Government Printing Office, 1978.

Noel, Thomas J. "William D. Haywood: 'The Most Hated Man in America.'" In *Western Voices: 125 Years of Colorado Writing*, edited by Steve Grinstead and Ben Fogelberg. Golden, CO: Fulcrum Publishing, 2004.

Olick, Jeffrey K., Vered Vinizky-Seroussi, and Daniel Levy, eds. *The Collective Memory Reader*. New York: Oxford University Press, 2011.

"One Thousand Led by the I.W.W. Held Meeting Here Sunday." *Daily Camera* (Boulder, CO), November 21, 1927.

"Order to Close C.F.& I. 14-Inch Mill Revoked." *Rocky Mountain News* (Denver, CO), November 3, 1927.

Orr, A. K. "Wm. H. Lofton." *Industrial Solidarity*, December 14, 1927.

Palmer, Bryan D. *James P. Cannon and the Origins of the American Revolutionary Left, 1890–1928*. Urbana: University of Illinois Press, 2007.

Palmer, Bryan D. "A City Kid's View of Working-Class History: An Interview with Melvyn Dubofsky." *Studies in Working-Class History of the Americas* 7, no. 2 (Summer 2010): 53–81.

Palmer, Frank L. "Solidarity in Colorado." *The Nation*, February 1, 1928.

Palmer, Frank L. "War in Colorado." *Nation* cxxv, no. 3257, December 7, 1927.

Papanikolas, Zeese. *Buried Unsung: Louis Tikas and the Ludlow Massacre*. Lincoln: University of Nebraska Press, 1982.

Pascoe, Pat. *Helen Ring Robinson: Colorado Senator and Suffragist*. Boulder: University Press of Colorado, 2011.

Pascoe, Peggy. *Relations of Rescue: The Search for Female Moral Authority in the American West, 1874–1939*. New York: Oxford University Press, 1990.

Paul, Jesse. "A 1917 Coal Mine Explosion in Southern Colorado Killed 121. But it's Just a Faint Memory in the State's History." *Denver Post*, April 27, 2017. https://www.denverpost.com/2017/04/27/hastings-mine-explosion-1917-colorado-history/.

Peiss, Kathy. *Cheap Amusements: Working Women and Leisure in Turn-of-the-Century New York*. Philadelphia, PA: Temple University Press, 1986.

Peters, Bernadette. "Elusive Justice in the Colorado Beet Fields." Presentation at the Labor and Working Class History Association Conference, Durham, NC, June 2019.

Phipps, Stanley. "A. S. Embree: Labor Leader and Prisoner of Conscience." *The Speculator: A Journal of Butte and Southwest Montana History* 2, no. 2 (summer 1985): 35–41.

"Picketers Terrorized Miners at the Columbine and Not One of the 175 Working Miners is Working in the Weld County Property." *Daily Camera* (Boulder, CO), November 7, 1927.

"Pickets Stationed by the Strikers at the Columbine." *Daily Camera* (Boulder, CO), October 19, 1927.

Piper, Liza. "Newfoundland Methodism." Newfoundland and Labrador Heritage, 2000. www.heritage.nf.ca/society/methodist.html.

Pope, James Gray. "The Western Pennsylvania Coal Strike of 1933, Part II: Lawmaking from Above and the Demise of Democracy in the United Mine Workers." *Labor History* 44, no. 2 (n.d.): 235–264.

Portelli, Alessandro. *The Death of Luigi Trastulli and Other Stories: Form and Meaning in Oral History.* Albany: State University of New York Press, 1991.

Portelli, Alessandro. *The Order Has Been Carried Out: History, Memory, and Meaning of a Nazi Massacre in Rome.* New York: Palgrave McMillan, 2003.

"Powers Hapgood Jailed in Mine Row." *New York Times*, March 5, 1928, https://www.nytimes.com/1928/03/05/archives/powers-hapgood-jailed-in-mine-row-held-with-bride-former-sacco.html?searchResultPosition=1.

Preston, William Jr. *Aliens and Dissenters: Federal Suppression of Radicals, 1903–1933.* 2nd ed. Urbana: University of Illinois Press, 1994.

Quale, C. C. *Thrilling Stories of White Slavery.* Chicago: Hamming Publishing Co., 1912. Google eBook, reprinted by the Sallie Bingham Center for Women's History and Culture.

"Red Plot on Labor Moves Federation to Spurn Soviet." *New York Times*, October 13, 1926, www.nytimes.com.

Report of Commission on Industrial Relations, 1915. Excerpt in bound copy housed at the Lafayette Historical Society, Lafayette, Colorado.

Richard, Joe. "Hunters and Dogs." *Jacobin*, October 28, 2016. https://jacobinmag.com/2016/10/cio-unions-communist-party-socialist-party-afl.

"Rocky Mt. Fuel Co. Announces Liberal Policy." *Rocky Mountain News* (Denver, CO), March 19, 1928.

Roediger, David. *Fellow Worker: The Life of Fred Thompson.* Chicago: Charles H. Kerr Publishing Company, 1993.

Roll, Jarod. "White, American, Non-Union: Making Sense of Missouri's Notorious Strikebreaking Miners." Presented at the Labor and Working-Class History Association Conference, New York, June 2013.

Roll, Jarod. *Poor Man's Fortune: White Working-Class Conservatism in American Metal Mining, 1850–1950.* Chapel Hill: The University of North Carolina Press, 2020.

"Roots: The Most Important TV Show Ever?" British Broadcasting Network (BBC), June 1, 2016, https://www.bbc.com/culture/article/20160602-roots-the-most-important-tv-show-ever.

Roskelley, R. W. *Population Trends in Colorado.* Fort Collins, CO: Cooperative Plan of Rural Research, Division of Research, Works Progress Administration, 1940.

Ruiz, Vicki L. *Cannery Women, Cannery Lives: Mexican Women, Unionization, and the California Food Processing Industry, 1930–1950.* Albuquerque: University of New Mexico Press, 1987.

Salmond, John A. *Gastonia, 1929: The Story of the Loray Mill Strike.* Chapel Hill: The University of North Carolina Press, 1995.

Salmond, John A. *The General Textile Strike of 1934: From Maine to Alabama.* Columbia, MO: University of Missouri Press, 2002.

Sampson, Joanna. *"Remember Ludlow!": Ludlow Massacre, April 20, 1914.* Self-published, 1999.

Sandos, James A. *Rebellion in the Borderlands: Anarchism and the Plan of San Diego, 1904–1923.* Norman: University of Oklahoma Press, 1992.

Schacter, Daniel L. *The Seven Sins of Memory: How the Mind Forgets and Remembers.* Boston: Houghton Mifflin Company, 2001.

Schofield, Ann. "An 'Army of Amazons': The Language of Protest in a Kansas Mining Community, 1921–1922." *American Quarterly* 37, no. 5 (winter 1985), 686–701. https://www.jstor.org/stable/2712616?searchText=ann%20schofield&searchUri=%2Faction%2FdoBasicSearch%3FQuery%3Dann%2Bschofield%26so%3Drel&ab_segments=0%2FSYC-6451%2Ftest&refreqid=fastly-default%3A851bc7e8177c13ff809f953ef7f5aa80.

Schofield, Ann. "Mary Dreier, 1876–1963," in *To Do and To Be.* Boston: Northeastern University Press, 1997.

Schrecker, Ellen. *Many are the Crimes: McCarthyism in America.* Princeton, NJ: Princeton University Press, 1998.

Schuler, Bobbalee. "Scab Labor in the Colorado Coal Fields: A Statistical Study of Replacement Workers during the Columbine Strike of 1927–1928." In *Essays and Monographs in Colorado History*, edited by David N. Wetzel. Denver: Colorado Historical Society, 1988.

Sciolino, Elaine. "The 2000 Campaign: The Spouse; The Real Conservative in the Family." *New York Times*, July 26, 2000, www.nytimes.com.

"Shoup Caught in Dilemma as He Attempts to Dodge Boomerang of Ranger Law." *Rocky Mountain News* (Denver, CO), October 17, 1926.

"Six Miners Injured in Riot over Lewis." *New York Times*, September 10, 1928, www.nytimes.com.

Slater, Joanna. "Alex Jones Ordered to Pay Nearly $1 Billion to Sandy Hook Families." *Washington Post*, October 12, 2022, https://www.washingtonpost.com/nation/2022/10/12/alex-jones-sandy-hook-verdict/.

Smith, Phyllis. *Once a Coal Miner: The Story of Colorado's Northern Coal Field.* Boulder, CO: Pruett Publishing Company, 1989.

Solski, Mike, and John Smaller. *Mine Mill: The History of the International Union of Mine, Mill and Smelter Workers in Canada Since 1895.* Ottawa, ON: Steel Rail Publishing, 1984.

Stansell, Christine. *American Moderns: Bohemian New York and the Creation of a New Century.* New York: Metropolitan Books, 2000.

"State Ranger Law to be Chief Issue in Governor's Race," *Rocky Mountain News* (Denver, CO), October 12, 1926.

Stein, Leon, and Philip Taft. *Massacre at Ludlow: Four Reports.* Republished as *American Labor: From Conspiracy to Collective Bargaining.* New York: Arno Press, 1972.

Stein, Robin, and Alexander Cardia. "Visual Investigations: State Investigation Fueled Flawed Understanding of Delays during Police Response in Uvalde." *New York Times*, October 12, 2022, https://www.nytimes.com/2022/10/12/us/uvalde-shooting-police-response-investigation.html.

Stille, Alexander. "Prospecting for Truth in the Ore of Memory." *New York Times*, March 10, 2001, https://www.nytimes.com/2001/03/10/arts/prospecting-for-truth-in-the-ore-of-memory.html?searchResultPosition=1.

Storrs, Landon R. Y. *Civilizing Capitalism: The National Consumers' League, Women's Activism, and Labor Standards in the New Deal.* Chapel Hill: The University of North Carolina Press, 2000.

Strang, Dean A. *Keep the Wretches in Order: America's Biggest Mass Trial, the Rise of the Justice Department, and the Fall of the IWW.* Madison: The University of Wisconsin Press, 2019.

"Strikers Centre Fire on Non-Union Fields." *New York Times*, April 6, 1922, https://www.nytimes.com/1922/04/06/archives/strikers-centre-fire-on-nonunion-fields-fear-continuation-of-output.html?searchResultPosition=1.

"Strikers Ignore State Police and Parade Inside Enclosure Columbine Mine Early Today." *Daily Camera* (Boulder, CO), November 12, 1927.

"Strikers Plan New Moves in Picketing 'War' with Guards." *Rocky Mountain News* (Denver, CO), November 6, 1927.

"Strikers Warned Shooting May Commence at Columbine." *Daily Camera* (Boulder, CO), November 15, 1927.

"Sugar Factory Men and Beet Field Workers Urged to Strike." *Daily Camera* (Boulder, CO), November 11, 1927.

Swain, A. "I.W.W. to Tell Gov. Adams How Good They Are." *Daily Camera* (Boulder, CO), October 25, 1927.

Taylor, Lawrence D. "The Magonista Revolt in Baja California: Capitalist Conspiracy or Rebelion de los Pobres?" *The Journal of San Diego History, San Diego*

Historical Society Quarterly 45, no. 1 (winter 1999). Accessed January 13, 2012. www
.sandiegohistory.org/journal/99winter/magonista.htm.

Terrell, Ellen. "Josephine Aspinwall Roche: A Changemaker You've Likely Never
Heard of!" *Inside Adams: Science Technology & Business* (blog), *Library of Congress*,
March 22, 2019. https://blogs.loc.gov/inside_adams/2019/03/josephine-aspin-
wall-roche-a-changemaker-youve-likely-never-heard-of/.

"The Bisbee Deportation: A University of Arizona Web Exhibit." University of Arizona, Tempe, March 4, 2018. https://wayback.archive-it.org/8851/2018030403
3448/http://www.library.arizona.edu/exhibits/bisbee/index.html.

*The Military Occupation, Coal Strike Zone of Colorado by the Colorado National Guard,
1913–1914: Report of Commanding General to the Governor for the Use of the Congressional Committee.* Denver, CO: Press of the Smith Brooks Printing Company, 1914.

"The Seed of Freedom." *United Mine Workers Journal* XXVII, no. 50 (April 12, 1918), 4.

"Things You Never Asked." *Time*, November 27, 1978. http://www.time.com/time
/magazine/article/0,9171,9164467,00.html.

"Tho Machine Guns Were Aimed at Men I.W.W. Led Strikers into the Columbine."
Daily Camera (Boulder, CO), November 18, 1927.

"Thomas Annear Leaves for Boulder County to Compel Obedience to Law—He
Says Strike Illegal." *Daily Camera* (Boulder, CO), October 19, 1927.

Thomas, William H. Jr. *Unsafe for Democracy: World War I and the U.S. Justice Department's Covert Campaign to Suppress Dissent.* Madison: The University of Wisconsin
Press, 2008.

Thompson, Fred, and Patrick Murfin. *The I.W.W.: Its First Seventy Years, 1905–1975.*
Chicago: Industrial Workers of the World, 1976.

"Thousands of Colorado Coal Miners Strike Under Orders of I.W.W." *Daily Camera*
(Boulder, CO), October 18, 1927.

Traub, James. "Aiding the Humanities: Arguing Ends and Means." *New York Times*,
February 22, 1981, https://www.nytimes.com/1981/02/22/weekinreview/aiding
-the-humanities-arguing-ends-and-the-means.html?searchResultPosition=1.

"Trinidad I.W.W. Wins Court Fight on Meetings." *Rocky Mountain News* (Denver,
CO), January 6, 1928.

"Troops Patrol Strike Zone After Battle." *Rocky Mountain News* (Denver, CO),
November 22, 1927.

"Troops Will be Ordered Out by Adams Thinks Mr. Swain." *Daily Camera* (Boulder,
CO), November 17, 1927.

"Trouble Zone Well Policed." *Rocky Mountain News* (Denver, CO), January 13, 1928.

Turner, Ethel Duffy. *Revolution in Baja California: Ricardo Flores Magón's High Noon.*
Detroit, MI: Blain Ethridge Books, 1981.

"Two More Killed in Mine Union Feud." *New York Times*, February 29, 1928, https://
www.nytimes.com/1928/02/29/archives/two-more-killed-in-mine-union-feud
-insurgent-leaders-are-slain-by.html?searchResultPosition=1.

Ulrich, Laurel Thatcher. "Amazons," in *Well-Behaved Women Seldom Make History*. New York: Vintage, 2008.

"Union Service Offering for Mrs. Eastenes." *Daily Camera* (Boulder, CO), November 23, 1927.

US Congress. Senate. Testimony Regarding Staffing before Hearings before the Subcommittee on Education, Arts and Humanities of the Committee on Labor and Human Resources, 96th Congress, 1st Session, June 26, 27, and 28, 1979. Accessed June 22, 2022, Hathi Trust Digital Library, https://catalog.hathitrust.org/Record/011342669.

Vargas, Zaragosa. *Proletarians of the North: A History of Mexican Industrial Workers in Detroit and the Midwest, 1917–1933*. Berkeley: University of California Press, 1993.

Vogels, Jonathan B. "'Put to Patriotic Use': Negotiating Free Speech at Boston's Old South Meeting House, 1925–1933." *The New England Quarterly* 72, no. 1 (March 1999): 3–27.

Walker, Forrest A. *The Civil Works Administration: An Experiment in Federal Work Relief, 1933–1934*. New York: Garland Publishing, Inc., 1979.

"Walsenburg Jail Holds 60 Picketers, Twenty of Them Chattering Women." *Daily Camera* (Boulder, CO), October 21, 1927.

Walter, Dave. "Who Killed Tom Manning?" in *More Montana Campfire Tales: Fifteen Historical Narratives*. Helena, MT: Farcountry Press, 2002.

Whayne, Frances. "Strikers Hear Rival Calls of Two Women." *Denver Post*, October 28, 1927.

"Whitford, Tyrant, In Whom Is Not Drop of Warm Blood." *Denver Post*, April 11, 1911, 1.

Yergin, Daniel. *The Prize: The Epic Quest for Oil, Money, and Power*. New York: Free Press, 2009.

Zieger, Robert H. *John L. Lewis: Labor Leader*. Boston: Twayee Publishers, 1988.

Zieger, Robert. *The CIO, 1935–1955*. Chapel Hill: The University of North Carolina Press, 1995.

Zinn, Howard. *Three Strikes: Miners, Musicians, Salesgirls, and the Fighting Spirit of Labor's Last Century*. Boston: Beacon Press, 2001.

Index

Page numbers followed by *f* indicate figures. Page numbers followed by *n* indicate endnotes.